CHRISTIAN HOPE through FULFILLED PROPHECY

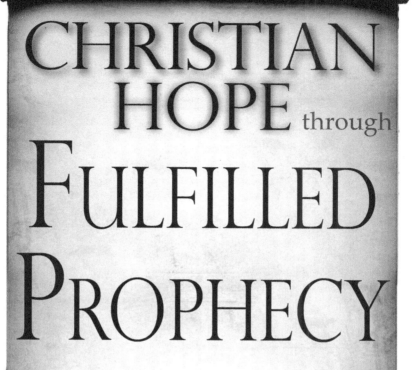

CHRISTIAN HOPE through FULFILLED PROPHECY

Is Your Church Teaching Error
about the Last Days
and Second Coming?

An Exposition of
Evangelical Preterism

CHARLES S. MEEK

Third Edition
June 2016

The journey through the Word is a journey in search of Truth. It is a journey without end as we strive to know our Father. *Christian Hope through Fulfilled Prophecy* is a marvelous book, which uncovers truths that are often missed – truths that can only be found if we shed our preconceptions and read Scriptures with a mindset as close as possible to the original audience. This book strips away the clutter that accompanies our tradition and preconceptions, and gets right down to what the Scripture actually says. This is an invaluable aid, which helps us stay on course in our journey. We need only open our eyes, our mind, and our spirit as we open His Word. Bravo!

Daniel E. Harden, author of *Gathered Into the Kingdom.*
Munroe Falls, Ohio

Charles Meek writes a thorough yet concise rendering of a fulfilled view of Bible prophecy. He lays out the scriptural basis, passage by passage, while anticipating questions and decimating objections along the way. This is a first-rate handbook for anyone seeking to understand Covenant Eschatology.

Riley O'Brien Powell, Ed. M. (Harvard), M. Div. (Princeton Theological Seminary). Minneapolis, MN

This book is fantastic! I thoroughly enjoyed reading through every page, hanging on every word. Meek has produced a product here that takes people through the title issues very methodically and intriguingly. You'll have to work very hard to ignore the arguments. Go ahead. Read this superbly written book. And then ask your pastor the very simple questions you'll find inside. Discover whether your church actually values truth over tradition. Whatever you discover, you will not regret the time spent in this book.

Alan Bondar, author of *Reading the Bible through New Covenant Eyes*, Pastor of New Covenant Eyes Church. Fort Myers, FL

Charlie, I thoroughly enjoyed your book. I have been a Christian all my life and the points you make, incredibly, were never mentioned in any church I ever attended. It has changed the way that I will look at Scripture forever! Very easy reading and very clear. This is the kind of book

I have been seeking to help me make sense of the competing views on eschatology. A real page turner! I am sending copies to many friends. Thanks for sharing this with me—I have truly been blessed!

Steve Bailey, President, Gulf Energy Exploration Corporation.
Austin, Texas

The covenant eschatology community is in debt to Mr. Meek for writing this valuable new book. Far from being written by one theology professor to another, the informed layman will feel perfectly at home in this study. If you are looking for insightful arguments and comments on nearly every relevant passage, you will find them here. What a resource for a full preterist needing help in answering objections from skeptics, inquirers or even other preterists who may not be clear in some areas. Mr. Meek likely will supply a good answer. Exhaustive research and study abounds! Take advantage of it. No regrets!

Walt Hibbard, Founder and former chairman of
Great Christian Books. Wilmington, Delaware

This book is gold! Mr. Meek's masterpiece is both simple and straightforward. Simple in that it is easy to understand, straightforward in that it takes eschatological topics head-on with the Word of God, rather than with the tiresome arguments of men. A true two-edged sword! This could be the book that breaks the stranglehold that dispensationalists presently have on the book market. Be encouraged to read it, study it, and add it to your home library. Apply 2 Timothy 2:15 and decide for yourself if it is in the spirit of Acts 17:11.

Michael Day, editor and primary author of *The Fulfilled Covenant Bible,* pastor, evangelist, and radio talk show co-host.
Anthem, Arizona

God will not hold guiltless those who purvey foolish, ill-grounded speculations about so-called end time prophecy that perplex the faithful and hold up their Lord to the ridicule of the faithless. The Christian community struggles with a number of disabling realities in its effort to speak truth and hope to a morally degraded and intellectually dissipated culture. Might there be more pressing concerns than the church's crisis in eschatology dissected so meticulously by Charles Meek in this new book? Perhaps. But Christian leaders must face honestly—and resolve with clarity—what has emerged in our day as a major embarrassment to the faith. Meek does much more than sound a needed alarm. He brings us back *ad fontes* to recover a truly biblical and apostolic understanding of *fulfilled* prophecy. Rightly divided, the word of God does not confuse; it coheres and liberates. Meek's new book adds significantly to the emergent body of study pointing to the power of a realized and covenant-grounded grasp of the immensity of Christ's victory. This is what must be recovered. Fear not to be challenged and changed.

Bruce Thevenot, former Ruling Elder, Presbyterian Church in America. Dripping Springs, Texas

The modern Christian church desperately needs to confront the perplexing issue of eschatology, and the perceived failure of Jesus and the NT writers. Skeptics abound who point to this so-called failure. Charles Meek has produced a well documented, logically persuasive book, not only for the preterist community, but for anyone interested in the important topic of eschatology. Can one find some areas of disagreement? Of course. But that is true of any book. The point is that Charles has done his homework, and has given us a calm, kind spirited, understandable, well written book that will help anyone who will spend the time carefully reading it to better understand what God accomplished in AD 70. I am glad to recommend this book.

Don K. Preston, D. Div, President, Preterist Research Institute and author of numerous books on biblical eschatology. Ardmore, Oklahoma

Chistian Hope through Fulfilled Prophecy:
Is Your Church Teaching Error about the Last Days
and Second Coming? An Exposition of Evangelical Preterism

ISBN-13: 978-0615705903

ISBN-10: 0615705901

Library of Congress Control Number: 2012918191

Faith Facts Publishing
26109 Wild River Road,
Spicewood, Texas 78669
www.FaithFacts.org

Cover Design by Lisa Hainline
www.LionsGateBookDesign.com

This book is dedicated to the many believers down through the ages who stood boldly for God's Word against opposition, often at great personal cost.

ACKNOWLEDGMENTS

T hanks are extended to my futurist friends whose skepticism about covenant eschatology made me dig that much deeper to get to the truth. Truth is a glorious thing.

Special thanks to the extraordinarily talented team who contributed to this project. Each gave many tedious hours of review and thoughtful reflection to help make this book the next step forward in the *surging preterist challenge to eschatology*:

Stephen L. Bailey

Tina Rae Collins

Samuel G. Dawson

T. Everett Denton

Jerel Kratt

Riley O'Brien Powell

Bruce D. Thevenot

and

David A. Green, editor

The editor, David Green, is a bright, thoughtful, and articulate student of God's Word. His assistance is enormously appreciated.

The contributors may not agree with everything in the book. The author's use of the "editorial we" indicates the opinions of the author, and not necessarily that of every contributor.

NOTES

    Unless otherwise noted, passages of Scripture are from the New King James Version (NKJV). We occasionally put certain words in the texts in bold for emphasis. We have also un-italicized words to make reading easier. These changes are consistent with many other translations. We have left the verse numbers in some passages when it was deemed helpful to do so.

    While we have left the pronouns that refer to God or Jesus capitalized (He, Him), we have uncapitalized the possessive form (his). This is consistent with many Bible translations. There are just too many capitalizations in Christian writing! We have made somewhat arbitrary decisions not to capitalize such words as hades (why capitalize hades when hell or heaven are not normally capitalized?), biblical ("Bible" is a proper name but "biblical" is not), tribulation, rapture, kingdom, and resurrection. An exception is Great Tribulation, which is more of a proper name form of the tribulation. We also capitalize Second Coming but generally not the Greek word parousia, except as a synonym for Jesus' Second Coming. We refer to the online Blue Letter Bible for definitions of Greek and Hebrew words, and we use their transliteration rendering for spelling. We are indebted to Bible Gateway whose website offers online versions of many different translations of the Bible. These resources are very helpful to the Bible student.

    The wonderful charts in Appendix B are from Riley O'Brien Powell. They should be extraordinarily helpful to the student.

    We have footnoted our sources liberally. Many of our sources are from articles on the Internet. Unfortunately, as the inevitable rotation of material on the Internet occurs, some of these links will be lost. Such is the nature of modern communications. Also, it is noted that the URL's in the endnotes in the printed version of the book are difficult to copy to the Internet. The reader may find an online version of the endnotes at http://

prophecyquestions.wordpress.com/2010/12/01/endnotes-chris-
tian-hope-through-fulfilled-prophecy.

✎ Caveat: The fact that a source appears in this book does not
constitute an endorsement for the source.

TABLE OF CONTENTS

FOREWORD

⌘

The last days are approaching—the last days of futurism, that is. Out of the dying and conflicting ism's of the tradition of futurism is arising the faith-confirming truth of full preterism. Its ascent has been slow, but steady and sure. The life-blood of this "resurrection" has been the enduring and zealous love of humble saints—love for God's house and love for His word.

Charles Meek is one of those saints. This book, written out of a deep love for the Lord Jesus and His church, is an exhortation to teachers and pastors to re-examine their eschatological traditions. It is an announcement of comfort to those struggling believers who have found it impossible to reconcile the things they have been taught about Bible prophecy with the Bible itself. It is the answer to the enemies of Christianity who have called Christ and the writers of the New Testament false prophets. And it is a call for Christians to open their eyes anew in the realm of eschatology, and to let the Bible actually say what it says.

For many of you who have never heard of full preterism, this book will not only be eye-opening; it will be earth-shaking. The things you will learn herein will leave you in a sort of shock. You will see the edifice of what you thought you knew and believed, begin to crumble and sink into the sand of Scripture-nullifying traditions. And that edifice will, at length, vanish. If you find yourself in that place while reading this book, cling to Christ to the end of that faith-crisis, and you will discover that you are standing on the solid rock of God's word with a footing that is more firm and sure than ever. "*So shall the knowledge of wisdom be unto thy soul: when thou hast found it, then there shall be a reward, and thy expectation shall not be cut off*" (Prov. 24:14).

May believers everywhere experience such "growth pains" in the faith. May all believers—all churches—become more and more united in doctrine and in love. May this book, and others like it, help to bring God's people closer to this ideal. May it show us how that the church's hope ("Christ in you") is fulfilled, and that as a result, we live in the Holiest of Holies here and now, and should live in the purity and grace of our Father. And may it show us that our personal Christian Hope (surpassing and eternal blessedness in heaven) is not tentative, but sure, and that it will be realized immediately when we die.

As you read this book, you will find that Charles Meek is aptly named. His gentle and mild approach makes spending time with his book like sitting at the feet of your favorite Sunday School teacher. He speaks to "every man" in a conversational way while he asks and answers a wide array of questions about full preterism. This book thus bridges a gap in the literature. While it is the product of exhaustive research, the author makes it clear that he does not pretend to have all the answers to all the questions. He is open to being taught by you, the reader. And he invites you to do just that.

— David A. Green

PREFACE

❧

The stunning photo on the previous page is one I took in 2011 of a billboard near our Texas home. Perhaps you remember this. Christian prognosticator Harold Camping predicted the soon end of the world. Indeed, the Bible guaranteed it. Camping's end-of-the-world campaign caught the attention of Americans everywhere, including the secular media. It was a great opportunity for skeptics to make fun of Christians. If you are reading this book in 2050, there will no doubt be other Christian prognosticators in the news who are just as wrong.

While some Christians would dismiss Camping as a kook, his approach to the Bible is not that far removed from much of mainstream American evangelicalism. It is the norm for Christians to read the Bible through the lens of daily news events. A 2012 survey showed that an astounding 65% of evangelical Protestants in the U.S. thought that the severity of recent natural disasters was evidence the world was coming to an end, as predicted in the Bible.[1] Indeed, many Christians have been predicting the last days, the end of the world, and the literal physical Second Coming of Christ since the second century AD! But, of course, they are always wrong.

These false predictions are an embarrassment to the Christian faith. Yet Christians keep gobbling up "end-times" books like they were gospel. And the Christian airwaves are filled with warnings of the end-times that never materialize. What's wrong with this picture?

❧

I have had a life-long interest in theology. My wife and I started our FaithFacts.org website near the beginning of the Internet revolution. It was one of the first Christian apologetics sites. Apologetics can be defined as using reason and evidence to advance and defend the Christian faith. At Faith Facts, we have articles that defend biblical Christianity against its toughest critics, including atheists, Muslims, and cultists. This book is a continuation of my effort to defend the truth of the Bible—from Genesis to Revelation.

1

Several years ago I became challenged by questions about Bible prophecy that came from visitors to our website. So I decided to examine the evidence of what the Bible really teaches on the subject. I assumed that it wouldn't take long to identify the few key passages in the Bible that would settle the issue. As I pieced it all together, I realized that there are more prophetic passages in the Bible than I first supposed—with numerous overlapping concepts—encompassing at least one-fourth of the New Testament. And much of this material draws on Old Testament imagery that is critically necessary to understand the words of Jesus and his apostles.

Though a life-long Christian, as I thought about it, I became concerned about the lack of clear teaching I had heard on eschatology (the study of so-called "end times" or "last things") in the churches we have attended. And what I heard seemed speculative and disconnected, and did not match up with what the Bible actually says. So I set out on a journey of discovery that has lasted over a decade. It is my hope that you the reader will share, through this book, the excitement I've gained in the realization that this wonderful topic helps confirm the truth of Scripture.

Let me ask you a few questions. Have you ever taken the time to examine *for yourself* what the Bible teaches on eschatology? Have you ever heard an explanation of a Bible prophecy that just did not quite make sense to you? Do you realize that there are over a hundred passages in the New Testament that anticipated the Second Coming and related events to occur *during the lifetimes of first-century Christians*? Why do the questions we ask about Bible prophecy provoke different answers depending on which denomination one is in? Why do many Christians keep reading current news events into Scripture, while other Christians do not? Why have some Christians been praying for 2,000 years for Jesus to come soon—and yet He never has? Why are there so many different opinions on eschatology?

There are several popular and competing views on eschatology. Most if not all of them have to be wrong, since they contradict each other at critical points. **Could *your church* be wrong about the last days, the end of the world, and the Second Coming?**

It is amazing what people can be convinced to believe if it comes from a human source they perceive to be reliable—whether in politics, science, religion, or most any other topic. I have reluctantly concluded that many Christians rely more on sectarian tradition than what the Bible actually teaches. They are willing to blindly follow teachers, not only regarding prophecy, but other topics as well. Worse, Christians often read into the Bible what is not there at all. There is a strong reluctance to examine our underlying assumptions and presuppositions. Believers often rely on an organization to tell them what the Bible says, rather than do the necessary study to check it out for themselves—as Scripture itself instructs us to do (1 Thessalonians 5:21; Acts 17:11).

Too many Christians place their allegiance in a faith *system* or denominational *tradition* that, for all they know, contradicts what Jesus actually taught. They accept, without much critical thinking, that because they are comfortable with most aspects of their group, everything they are being taught there is trustworthy. They *assume* that what their pastor or priest has taught them and what the Bible teaches are equivalent. They may or may not be.

Errors become reinforced as even theologians are subject to sectarian peer pressure to maintain a particular view, rather than to critically examine doctrinal teaching by God's Word itself. I will point out instances of this in the book. You will also become aware of a surprising number of Bible passages that you previously failed to consider carefully.

Christians often have a rather narrow focus. They fail to understand the Old Testament's terminology, especially Hebraic apocalyptic language and its application to the New Testament. As a result, they have unknowingly twisted Scripture into meanings that are far removed from how the original hearers would have understood it. Many have maintained eschatological doctrines by cherry-picking only a few of the many, many passages in the Bible on the subject, and ignoring those that don't fit their preconceived ideas.

And, especially, they have *ignored* numerous statements in the Bible that establish a time frame for an *imminent* first-century fulfillment of key prophecies! In other words, many teachers have "Bible passage amnesia." We have heard sermon after sermon in which the preacher conveniently skipped over these imminency passages. But we can no longer skip over them or try to explain them away. It was my frustration with these distortions of Scripture that led me to write this book.

Thankfully, Christians are taking a serious second look at these important passages, and many students of the Scriptures are concluding that their church (or their pastor) has been biased—perhaps flat wrong—about Bible prophecy. More often than not, pastors feel constrained to teach the "party line," and attempt to teach eschatology without having studied it carefully. Consequently, they are teaching error.

In our modern era of communications one can no longer hide behind sectarian traditions about important doctrines. Many Bible students are no longer satisfied to accept *carte blanche* what is being fed to them, and they are ready to re-examine church teaching. They want solid exegetical answers unfettered by questionable sectarian tradition.

In this book we will examine the fastest growing view of prophecy among Christians—*preterism*. This is the view that many, if not all, prophetic events have already been fulfilled! While yet a minority view, it is a view of prophecy that has been held by at least some Christians since the first century. Fulfilled prophecy will be a hard pill to swallow for some because of ingrained allegiances and assumptions. But this book challenges Christians to return to the Scriptures for answers. It will demonstrate that preterism is the only view of eschatology that (a) is faithful to Scripture, (b) answers the skeptic's objections about the authority of Christ, (c) unifies the Bible, and (d) truly leads to an optimistic worldview. In my studies, preterism has brought astonishing clarity to Scripture. Its message is compelling and consistent.

There are many books available on eschatology, including several from the preterist perspective. However, most of them either: (a) avoid the most controversial passages, (b) are limited in scope, covering only a specific eschatological topic, (c) approach prophecy from the point of view of the daily newspaper or other extra-biblical material rather than the Bible, (d) fail to address objections to preterism adequately, (e) fail to give the Old Testament background necessary to understand New Testament prophecy, or (f) are difficult for most Christians to follow, as they were written for theologians.

This book is written for the informed laymen, and seeks to avoid these shortcomings. So this book is unique, meeting an important unmet need for Christians. My goal has been to organize and clarify this complicated topic. I believe that the evidence presented in this book is on the cutting edge of scholarly thinking on eschatology. I offer some original insights—ideas not found anywhere else. But most of the material presented here can be found in available literature. I am primarily providing the functions of organizer, reporter, and clarifier. There are over 200 endnotes documenting sources and offering places to go for further study.

Another life-long interest of mine is the stock market, which is how I formerly made my living. The stock market and theology have some disciplines in common. For one, both require putting many pieces of diverse information together to reach a conclusion. For another, there is a strong component of *crowd psychology* in both of them! My observation is that "group think," while it can be helpful in some ways, is detrimental in other ways. I'm convinced that this is one reason why there are so many opposing doctrinal views entrenched within Christianity.

I wrote my Master's Degree thesis on stock market cycles and their component of crowd psychology. I included this research in my 1991 book *Money Matters*, published by Probus Publishing Company. In markets, there are times when the vast majority of investors, including the brightest minds on Wall Street, completely misinterpret the facts. Very intelligent people fail to understand what may appear to be completely obvious through hindsight at a later date.

The effects of crowd psychology are evident in other endeavors as well. Throughout history there have been cycles and trends not only in markets but even in theology. Amazingly, sometimes a majority of people cannot see what is right before their eyes. And as ideas begin to change, they miss the trend changes until they are far advanced. It is early, but I see an upheaval developing in theology as regards the field of eschatology.

An advantage I have in writing this book is that I owe no allegiance to any denomination or sect. While I attend church regularly, I am not on any church's payroll. Nor do I receive any remuneration from any Christian organization. So I am not subject to peer pressure or to what I call "ecclesiastical tyranny." I have only one foundational allegiance, and that is to God's Word. I am persuaded that the entire Bible is inspired by the creator God of the universe. My motivation is my love for God's Word and for the purity of Christ's church.

I am not asking you to blindly believe anything I say. Rather, I am asking that you consider seriously what *Jesus* said, and how the *inspired biblical writers understood* what Jesus said. But I must ask you to think about your mental preparedness for such a study. Are you ready to listen to what God's Word teaches?

The reader has a right to ask where I am coming from. I am conservative. I am evangelical. I hold to the essential doctrines of the Christian faith, those that one would find on the websites of most evangelical churches. We will touch on many of these doctrines in the book. The only major exception is that when Jesus said that all prophecy would be fulfilled in his generation, I take Him at his word. I don't much care for labels, so I would prefer to be called simply a Christian. But the view for which I will be arguing is called *evangelical preterism*.

Every Christian group has at least some doctrines, or combinations of doctrines, that are unique to their group. And we notice that they will often not seriously consider challenges to those doctrines no matter how much biblical evidence may be presented against them. It is almost as though their self-worth is wrapped up in accepting every aspect of their sect's peculiar teachings. And yet we notice that other groups are just as strongly *opposed* to these same doctrines. Every group is convinced that their positions are biblically correct!

Perhaps someone gave you a copy of this book. If your first reaction to fulfilled prophecy is to immediately run to your computer and do an Internet search for ways to refute it, then you are probably not ready to hear what God's Word has to say on this matter. Or if you approach this book by glossing over much of it while lasering in on the parts you think you can reject out of hand, you are likewise probably not ready for this study. However, if you can at least hold your "yes but's" until the end of the book, this should be a marvelous study for you, even if you don't concur with all of it. There are a lot of moving parts to the study of biblical eschatology. It is recommended that the reader hold off on piecemeal objections until seeing the whole picture.

This book can be used for a group Bible study. It will lead to challenging and informative discussions in which "iron will sharpen iron." It will give everyone in the group the opportunity to support their current assumptions scripturally, and to refute the arguments in this book (if they think they can)!

I have taken pains to present the material in an easy-to-understand format. In fact, while there are some challenging sections, the concepts are quite easy to grasp for the Christian who has a basic understanding of the Bible and an open mind. But you should be prepared to stop and think about what you are reading from time to time. And you are invited to cross-check to be sure that I am not trying to pull the wool over anyone's eyes!

If you have never encountered this material previously, you may find it fascinating and exciting. On the other hand, you might resist it. As carefully as I, with the help of my contributors, have presented the material, and as biblically faithful as we have endeavored to be, the words of this book may fall on rocky ground. I hope not. I love God's Word and hope you do too. At certain points, you may well feel that your toes are being stepped on. But fear not to be challenged or changed.

My suggestion is that you make notes about your thoughts as you proceed. I would be pleased if you gave me your feedback including epiphanies, questions, suggestions, or reasoned objections. Modern "Print on Demand" publishing makes updating a book easy. Suggestions or corrections can be incorporated in future editions of the book. Email me at faithfacts@msn.com. Put "book" in the subject line.

CHRISTIAN HOPE through
FULFILLED PROPHECY

Introduction and Background

Some of his disciples were remarking about how the temple was adorned with beautiful stones and with gifts dedicated to God. But Jesus said, "As for what you see here, the time will come when not one stone will be left on another; every one of them will be thrown down." "Teacher," they asked, "**when will these things happen**? And what will be the sign that they are about to take place?" He replied: "Watch out that **you** are not deceived. . . . When **you** see Jerusalem being surrounded by armies, **you** will know that its desolation is near. Then let those who are in Judea flee to the mountains, let those in the city get out, and let those in the country not enter the city. For **this is the time** of punishment [**these are the days** of vengeance, NKJV] **in fulfillment of all that has been written**. . . . At that time they will see the **Son of Man coming** in a cloud with power and great glory. . . . Truly I tell you, **this generation** will certainly not pass away until **all** these things have happened. . . . Be always on the watch, and pray that **you** may be able to escape all that is **about to happen**, and that you may be able to stand before the Son of Man." (*Luke 21:5-8a, 20-22, 27, 32, 36, New International Version*)

THE SETTING

Let's travel back in time to the first century. It is the year AD 66, just over three decades since Jesus' ascension into heaven. Christianity has mushroomed from its humble beginnings in Jerusalem. Indeed, according to the New Testament writer the apostle Paul, it has already spread into all nations of the world (Romans 1:8; 16:26; Colossians 1:6, 23).

Nero is the emperor of Rome. Due to some seemingly innocuous religious insults to the Jews by the Greeks in Judea, the Jewish high priest ceases prayers and sacrifices at the temple for the Roman Emperor. Protests over taxation, as well as the cruel and hateful abuses of the Roman procurator Gessius Florus, join the list of Jewish grievances that provoke the Roman Governor of Syria (Cestius Gallus) to surround Jerusalem with troops to quell the civil unrest. The Romans launch random attacks upon the Jews and perceived traitors in and around Jerusalem. But Cestius' army retreats and the Jewish rebels are encouraged by their victory.

In early AD 67 the Roman legions under Vespasian and his son Titus move to crush the rebellion. War grips Judea and the surrounding area, that is, the area we think of today as Israel. The war later becomes known as the Jewish-Roman War. It culminates in the destruction of Jerusalem and the demolition of the spectacular Jewish temple in AD 70.[2]

Nero, one of the most remarkably tyrannical leaders in all of history, commits suicide in AD 68. His legacy includes not only the action against the Jews in Judea, but also the persecution of Christians. Even members of his own family could not escape his murderous wrath. After his death and a series of emperors, Vespasian becomes the new emperor in AD 69. Titus assumes command of the army to finish the war in Judea.

The siege of Jerusalem, the capital city of the Jews, stalls because of its high walls. But in AD 70, the Roman army breaches the walls and ransacks and burns the city. Many of those trying to escape the city are crucified; as many as 500 crucifixions occur each day.

The most extensive eyewitness account of the war is that of Flavius Josephus, who wrote extensively about the history of the period. From his book, *The Wars of the Jews*, we know that an estimated 1,100,000 locals died in the war, some by starvation.[3] The horrors of the situation were grotesque. Josephus recounted the story of a woman named Mary, daughter of Eleazar, who slew her own infant son, roasted him, and ate the child in order to survive.[4] Josephus also reported that 97,000 survivors of the siege were sold into slavery into Egyptian mines. He described the situation in these terms:

> Neither did any other city ever suffer such miseries, nor did any age ever breed a generation more fruitful in wickedness than this was, from the beginning of the world. . . . The multitude of those that therein perished exceeded all the destructions that either men or God ever brought upon the world.[5]

After conquering Jerusalem, the Roman army moves throughout the region slaughtering the inhabitants. While the rebellion sputters on until AD 73 when the fortress of Masada is taken, the culmination of the tragedy is in AD 70. Keep these events in mind as we explore the pages of Scripture.[6]

THE IMPORTANCE OF AD 70

Why is AD 70 important? It is important for several reasons. It is important because the obliteration of the Old Testament Jewish nation and the destruction of the temple took place that year. And since many of the events of AD 70 were prophesied in the Bible, that year is also important in relation to the accuracy and authority of the Bible.

When Israel ceased to be a nation and the temple was demolished in AD 70, these events fulfilled what Jesus said would happen **in his generation**. Just as Jesus predicted (Matthew 24:2; Mark 13:2; Luke 19:44; 21:6), *not one stone of the temple was left upon another.* This was unthinkable. The stones of the temple weighed five tons each, with even some weighing many times more than that.[7]

This has to be one of the most remarkable predictions ever made by anyone. It would be like predicting that the city of Chicago will cease to exist within the lifetime of some of you reading this book. And then by some absolutely unforeseen event, Chicago is completely destroyed within forty years.

But it is more remarkable than that from the perspective of theology. One very important thing to understand is that with the destruction of the temple, the age-old Jewish system of temple sacrifices for sin—instituted by God himself—ended forever! This was the end of the Old Covenant Age. This is critically important. The system of sacrifices for sin was a central part of the ancient Jewish covenantal system. The coming of the New Covenant was an event that had been foretold in the Old Testament. For example, in Jeremiah 31 we read:

> Behold, the days are coming, says the LORD, when I will make a **new covenant** with the house of Israel and with the house of Judah. (*Jeremiah 31:31; cf. Isaiah 42:6; 59:20-21; 61:8; Ezekiel 34:25; 37:26*)

The New Testament book of Hebrews is concerned with how God was fulfilling his promise of a New Covenant. Hebrews chapter 8 quotes this verse from Jeremiah, and in chapters 8, 9, and 10 (note in particular Hebrews 8:6-13; 9:1-28; 10:16-29; also 12:12-24 and 13:20) the writer explains how the Old Covenant was, in his day, in the *process* of being replaced by the New Covenant. The consummation of the change of the covenants was to take place soon after Hebrews was penned. Hebrews was written between Jesus' time on earth and the events of AD 70. We will take a closer look at several of these passages as we progress.

While the death and resurrection of Jesus ushered *in* the New Covenant order, it was the destruction of the temple (which ended the system of sacrifices for sin nearly forty years later) that formally ushered *out* the Old Covenant order. To this day Jews no longer practice the ritual of temple sacrifices for sin.[8]

CHALLENGES TO THE AUTHORITY OF SCRIPTURE

As we will explore in this book, many important Bible prophecies point to the events surrounding the destruction of Jerusalem and its temple, and the national judgment upon Israel. These prophecies are found, among other places, in the so-called Olivet Discourse, which is a sermon given by Jesus on the Mount of Olives. It is contained in Matthew 24-25, Mark 13, and Luke 21. If you are not familiar with the content of these chapters, you might want to stop here and read them. They contain the greatest body of predictive material in the New Testament outside the book of Revelation. When people speak of the Second Coming of Christ, they primarily point to these texts. Keep your Bible by your side as we go through the various passages.

We have a friend who became convinced that the various prophetic events of the Olivet Discourse had to have been fulfilled in AD 70. He came to this conclusion by writing out the three Olivet Discourse texts in large print and putting them on his wall. For months he studied these three passages side-by-side and reluctantly concluded that what he had been taught by his church about prophecy was incorrect. Coming to a conclusion that disagrees with the views held by most of those around you is always difficult, but God calls us to embrace truth no matter what the cost.

Something we must consider up front are the challenges that are made to the authority of the Bible, and even to the credibility of Christianity itself. The Bible gives indications not only of *what* events would happen but *when* they would happen. Concerning the timing of fulfillment of key prophecies, skeptics give two lines of argumentation in an attempt to show that the Bible is not authoritative. The first is that the prophecies were written after AD 70 and *back-dated to make Jesus look good* about his prediction of the temple's destruction. The second charge is that certain of Jesus' predictions, assuming that He really did make them in advance—especially his prediction about the Second Coming—did not occur in the **time frame** He predicted. In other words, Jesus predicted that He would return within his own generation (Matthew 24:34; Mark 13:30; Luke 21:32); but He did not, making Him a false prophet. These are serious challenges to the credibility of the Bible that Christians must answer.

First, did Jesus really make the prediction about the destruction of the temple? Or did the writers of the New Testament, writing after the fact, put words in his mouth? Skeptics, including some of the liberal persuasion within the church itself, sometimes say the latter! They say that this prediction by Jesus was so prescient that it must have been written after the fact. But the primary "evidence" provided by these skeptics is simply that the prediction was too correct.

Our charge is that people who hold this view are not thinking the issue through, nor examining the text carefully. We challenge liberal Christians especially on this. Do you really think the writers of the New Testament doctored the texts? If so, how can you trust *anything* the Bible says?

Nowhere does any New Testament writer mention the destruction of the temple as a past event. *It is always mentioned as a future event!* The Bible never looks backward in time and says anything like, "Jesus predicted the destruction of the temple and all these other things that we see have now happened." Not only were his predictions given as statements that were made to his contemporaries before the events took place—but the New Testament writers themselves all looked forward to AD 70 too, not back on it. There is no evidence that the New Testament writers colluded to "predict" the fall of the temple after it happened.

So, we first note that the destruction of Jerusalem (and the temple) was always referred to as a *future* event. Second, there are *no embellishments* in the Bible *of the details* of what actually happened to the temple, Jerusalem, and the nation of Israel. If the New Testament had been written after AD 70, and the writers abstained from any description of these spectacular events, it would have been like writing a history of the destruction of the Twin Towers by terrorists in 2001 without including any details of the events surrounding it (who was involved, how many were killed, emotions of Americans at the time, etc.).

Actually, it would be more problematic than that. It would be like writing a history of a major international city during the lives of eye-witnesses who saw its *total destruction*—without mentioning dramatic details of its destruction! Remember, not only was the temple destroyed but all of Jerusalem itself. If the New Testament was written after AD 70, the writers certainly could not have resisted discussing the events of AD 70 in the past tense, and describing the horrific details of the war. The prophecies are specific enough to clearly identify them with AD 70, but not nearly as specific as they would have been if they had been written after the fact—when, for example, Josephus wrote.

Indeed, if the prophecies were recorded after the fact, the problem would be even *more* dramatic! It would be as though *several* writers, who did not have the benefit of modern communications, all writing historical accounts after the total destruction of a major city, somehow *conspired* to leave out the crucial events of the history of the city's destruction!

If it can be shown that at least the "synoptic gospels" of Matthew, Mark, and Luke were written prior to AD 70, the predictions of Jesus have tremendous weight. We have such evidence. Edward E. Stevens summarizes:

> It is easy to support a pre-70 date for the gospels of Matthew, Mark and Luke, since Luke and Acts were clearly written before Paul was released from his imprisonment in AD 63, and Luke claims that he was aware of at least two other gospel accounts (Matthew and Mark) before he wrote his gospel (Luke 1:1). Furthermore, the gospel of Luke contains some of the unique material found in either Matthew *or* Mark, but not in both. Therefore, Matthew and Mark's gospels must have been among Luke's research material, thus predating his gospel. Luke's gospel, however, does not show any awareness of the unique material in John's gospel, suggesting that it was probably written after Luke.

We can also date all fourteen of Paul's epistles (including Hebrews, which is found in all extant ancient complete collections of Pauline epistles) prior to his martyrdom under Nero in AD 64. We also know that James, the Lord's brother, wrote his epistle before he was martyred in AD 62. The epistle of Jude appears to have been written about the same time as the second epistle of Peter, since there is considerable similarity of content. Since Peter was martyred under Nero in AD 64-65, his two epistles were obviously written before AD 70. This puts a pre-70 date on all New Testament books except the writings of the Apostle John.[9]

While Stevens places Paul's death three years earlier than some other scholars, there is broad agreement that Paul died prior to AD 70. There is other evidence for a pre-AD 70 date for the synoptic gospels.[10] But many scholars—even some liberal scholars—are convinced that indeed *all 27 books of the New Testament were written prior to AD 70.*[11]

Here is another interesting consideration that will surprise many Christians. The book of Revelation, authored by the Apostle John, is often considered to be one of the last books written. But we can conclude that even Revelation (which has sometimes been dated around AD 95) was also written before AD 70. In Chapter 9, where we cover the book of Revelation, we will consider its dating in some detail.[12]

A further observation is noteworthy. There are references in every book of the New Testament (except Philemon) that express the imminence of Jesus' Second Coming and/or related prophetic events that can be tied to the Jewish-Roman War and its culmination in AD 70. This will become clear in subsequent chapters. The writers of the New Testament undoubtedly received this prophetic information from Jesus himself (either first or second hand), and specifically received it from Jesus' sermons as recorded in the Olivet Discourse. Scholars *agree* that at least some of the books of the New Testament were written *prior* to AD 70, so it is verifiable that there are references to important eschatological events (in addition to the destruction of the temple) known to have been written in advance of their fulfillment. There is *no doubt* that the writers of the New Testament were discussing these things prior to their occurrence.

The weight of the evidence leads to the conclusion that all of the New Testament was written prior to AD 70. Or at the very least, the key prophecies were recorded prior to their fulfillment in AD 70. In summary, we have at least three lines of evidence supporting this:

1. The events of AD 70 are always discussed as future events; that is, they were predictive prophecies.

2. These prophecies definitively pointed to AD 70, but did not have the embellishments and detail they would have had if they had been written after the fact.

3. At least some books in the New Testament, which scholars are certain were written prior to AD 70, contain prophecies of "last things" events which can be demonstrated to have occurred by AD 70.

The evidence goes deeper than this and we will consider related issues as we proceed. But more than adequate modern, scholarly research has been done on the dating of the New Testament. We need not go further here than to suggest that the historical record together with the internal evidence points to the conclusion that most if not all of the New Testament was written prior to AD 70. Thus, Jesus' prediction about the destruction of the temple and Jerusalem—in addition to related prophecies—were made and recorded *in advance of the events*. We can affirm this fact with the highest confidence. **Jesus was a true prophet**. Liberal Christians who teach that the Bible is tainted or in question are wrong.

We must address the second important challenge. This one comes to us primarily, but not exclusively, from *non*-Christians. In addition to the destruction of the temple, Jesus said that his Second Coming would occur during the lifetime of some of those who were living when He was actually speaking—in his own generation. This seems quite clear, for example, in Luke 21, which we quoted in part at the beginning of this chapter. So, the critics say that Jesus failed to come during the time frame that He predicted.

We have quoted certain verses from Luke's version of the Olivet Discourse to focus on certain key issues, but you can read the entire passage in your own Bible. The language of Jesus here, using the word *all* twice, clearly suggests that not only his Second Coming and related events would occur in his literal generation (verse 32), but that *all Old Testament prophecy* would be fulfilled in the same time frame—within the lives of some of those living in the first century (verse 22). Can this be right? Is God's Word so confusing that a plain statement by Jesus means something other than what it seems to mean? Did Jesus lie to, mislead, or deceive his disciples or the church? Is there some other way to interpret this passage? What if the straightforward meaning of this text is actually the correct meaning?

Jesus' words concerning the time frame of his Second Coming seem equally clear in numerous other passages. Consider this one from Matthew chapter 10, where Jesus tells us that He would come during the lifetime of some of those who were living when He spoke:

> For assuredly, I say to you, **you** will not have gone through the cities of Israel before the Son of Man **comes**. (*Matthew 10:23*)

If you ask your pastor about this passage, there is a good chance he will dance around it. He may say that it refers in some way to Jesus' First Coming. But Jesus was already upon the earth, so He could not have been talking about his First Coming. Jesus must have been predicting his Second Coming—that it would occur within the lifetime of some of those hearing his words. This would be consistent with the "this generation" language in the Olivet Discourse. We will consider this passage and numerous others in more detail in Chapter 7. This passage is not unique. The reader may want to glance at the list of imminence passages in Appendix A.

Many Christians dismiss these passages by assuming that Jesus must not have really meant what He seems to have said. However, in an apparent inconsistency, most Christians accept the notion that the *other* writers of the New Testament besides Matthew, Mark, and Luke (i.e., Paul, Peter, James, John, Jude, and the writer of Hebrews) also believed that Jesus would return in their own generation, that is, while some of them were still alive. The problem should be obvious. These modern Christians don't believe Jesus, but they admit that the *apostles* and other contemporaries of Jesus took Him at *face value* about when He would return.

C. S. Lewis is considered by many to be the premier Christian apologist of the twentieth century. He stated the apparent problem thusly:

> "Say what you like," we shall be told, "the apocalyptic beliefs of the first Christians have been proved to be false. It is clear from the New Testament that they all expected the Second Coming in their own lifetime. And, worse still, they had a reason, and one which you will find very embarrassing. Their Master had told them so. He shared, and indeed created, their delusion. He said in so many words, 'this generation shall not pass till all these things are done.' And He was wrong. He clearly knew no more about the end of

the world than anyone else." It is certainly the most embarrassing verse in the Bible.[13]

Lewis presented this as a straw man argument. Though he himself did not acknowledge that he shared the view of his straw man, Lewis failed to solve the dilemma he presented.

As we have mentioned, skeptics of various stripes weigh in on this too. They point to several passages by Jesus and his apostles to argue that Jesus did not return in the time frame He predicted (in his own generation)—so He was a false prophet. For example, Albert Schweitzer, the 1952 winner of the Nobel Peace Prize for philosophy, in his book, *The Quest of the Historical Jesus*, made this charge. Bertrand Russell also made such an accusation. Russell was one of the most influential philosophers of the twentieth century and the Nobel Prize winner for literature in 1950. He published a pamphlet entitled "Why I Am Not a Christian." In the pamphlet he explained that one of the reasons he rejected Christianity was that Jesus failed to return as He promised. Concerning Jesus, Russell wrote:

> He certainly thought that His second coming would occur in clouds of glory before the death of all the people who were living at that time. There are a great many texts that prove that. . . . and there are a lot of places where it is quite clear that He believed that His second coming would happen during the lifetime of many then living.

Jewish and Muslim critics make this charge as well. Consider this attack by the group Jews for Judaism:

> No amount of Christian theological acrobatics will ever solve the problems engendered by the historical reality that a promised imminent fulfillment made two thousand years ago did not occur as expected by the New Testament. Simply stated, Jesus is never coming back, not then, not now, not ever.[14]

The dilemma has tentacles in every direction. It arises with the cults too. Mormons use the notion that Jesus was a false prophet in order to excuse Joseph Smith for *his* wrong prophecies. (Since Jesus was wrong, Joseph Smith can be excused.) [15]

If Jesus was a false prophet, he could not be divine. He could not have even been a reliable teacher! Skeptics charge that the writers of the New Testament, who recorded the teachings of Jesus and received their instruction from our Lord himself (either first or second hand)—were also false teachers. Thus they could not have been inspired, and their status is reduced to a confused band of followers of another false Messiah.

If these charges against Christianity are valid for the pervasive and keynote issue of eschatology, the reliability of the rest of the New Testament comes into serious question. The Christian faith rests squarely on the reliability of the promises of Jesus. If the New Testament and the words of Jesus are not trustworthy, our *hope* is misplaced; *heaven* and *salvation* through Jesus are cruel illusions.

This problem is not trivial. Everything we know about Jesus and his teachings comes from the Bible. It is not our prerogative as Christians to ignore the biblical evidence, and invent a Jesus to suit ourselves. That would be idolatry. We cannot legitimately manufacture our hope from a false set of assumptions; we are limited to understanding Jesus and his teachings as presented in the Bible. Just as importantly, we must not present an unreliable Jesus to the world.

Some readers may suspect that perhaps this is simply about conservative or liberal Christianity, or perhaps over the question of inerrancy. It is not. These are challenges to all professing Christians. This matter is about the authority and divinity of Christ. A Christian cannot legitimately hold to the idea that Jesus was wrong.

These claims by skeptics, non-Christians, and cultists have perhaps been the most persistent attack against the Bible and Jesus that Christians have had to confront. But Christians are willing to just hide their heads in the sand. Adding to the derision are the failed end-times predictions of countless Christians through history. One can find plenty of attacks on the Internet against Christians for their falsified predictions.

All of this is detrimental to the Christian faith. If the skeptics are correct, Christianity falls on its face. Indeed, the critics of Christianity from all camps aim to discredit and destroy Christianity. Quoting Edward E. Stevens again:

The most critical weakness of the Futurist view, including Partial Preterists and especially Creedalists, is the issue of timing. This is precisely where the Islamic critics, Jewish critics, liberals, and skeptics are relentlessly attacking Christianity. It seems like every person in the world (except futurists) knows that Jesus and the apostles predicted the Parousia would occur in the first-century generation! Futurists shut their eyes and ears to this critical challenge—willfully blind and deaf to the war that is raging around us. "There is none so blind as he who WILL NOT see." [16]

Uncomfortable? Don't worry. We will thoroughly answer the charges by Christianity's critics in this book. Preterism is the view of eschatology that holds that Jesus was indeed correct. His prophecies were fulfilled in the *manner* He said they would be, and *when* He said they would be—during the generation of those living in the first century. The preterist message is one that restores the credibility of Jesus and God's Word. *This should be a tremendous comfort and reassurance to Christians—and it sends the skeptics packing.*

EXAMINING OUR PRESUPPOSITIONS

> "We do not start our Christian lives by working out our faith for ourselves; it is mediated to us by Christian tradition, in the form of sermons, books and established patterns of church life and fellowship. We read our Bibles in the light of what we have learned from these sources; we approach Scripture with minds already formed by the mass of accepted opinions and viewpoints with which we have come into contact, in both the Church and the world. . . . It is easy to be unaware that it has happened; it is hard even to begin to realize how profoundly tradition in this sense has molded us. But we are forbidden to become enslaved to human tradition, either secular or Christian, whether it be "catholic" tradition, or "critical" tradition, or "ecumenical" tradition. We may never assume the complete rightness of our own established ways of thought and practice and excuse ourselves the duty of testing and reforming them by Scriptures."
>
> —J. I. Packer [17]

There is clear truth in this statement by J. I. Packer. The fact of the matter is that theology, as many believe and practice it, is as much a matter of crowd psychology as biblical exegesis. The very existence of so much disagreement on almost every aspect of Christian doctrine is evidence in support of this charge. Shame on us.

In every generation after the apostles, there have been Christians who mistakenly believed that they were in the last days. They have thought that their generation was the one Jesus spoke of when He prophesied that "all these things" would happen in "this generation." Francis Gumerlock, in his book *The Day and the Hour: Christianity's Perennial Fascination with Predicting the End of the World,* lists end times prophecy predictions made by Christians beginning in the early centuries. Gumerlock wrote:

> I originally intended the chronicle to be an article, which I estimated would be about ten pages in length. Twenty-one chapters later, *The Day and the Hour* illustrates century after century, year after year, the perennial fascination of those in Christendom who predicted a date for the Rapture, the Resurrection, or the Return of Christ; those who calculated the nearness of Armageddon, the Last Judgment, or the Millennium; those who announced a contemporaneous identity for the Two Witnesses, a last-days Elijah, the Antichrist, or some Beast from the Book of Revelation; and those who believed that their sect was the 144,000 or their generation the last.
>
> In the course of this study, I have found that it was not only radicals and cultists who had engaged in this type of End-time date setting; almost no Christian denomination has been immune from it. Even some whom we consider heroes of the faith have mistakenly engaged in these sorts of vain speculations.[18]

Failed prognosticators have been a persistent embarrassment to Christianity. Gumerlock catalogued more than a thousand failed predictions since the early days of Christianity, beginning with the apostolic fathers. For example, Ignatius writes around the year AD 100 that "the last times are come upon us." Cyprian (200-258) writes that "the day of affliction has begun to hang over our heads, and the end of the world and the time of the Antichrist . . . draw near, so that we must all stand prepared for the battle."

Martin Luther made this statement: "I am satisfied that the last day must be before the door; for the signs predicted by Christ and the Apostles Peter and Paul have now all been fulfilled, the trees put forth, the Scriptures are green and flourishing. . . . We certainly have nothing now to wait for but the end of all things." [19]

Famous among predictors of the end of the world was Christopher Columbus. Columbus wrote a book entitled *Book of Prophecies* in which he called on many of the same passages of Scripture that false prophets cite today to predict the imminent end of the world. He apparently thought that his discoveries marked the beginning of the end.

The famous American Puritan preacher Cotton Mather believed Christ's return to be imminent and saw apocalyptic meaning in the conflicts and challenges of the American frontier. Mather was also a date setter. He predicted the Second Coming for 1697, then 1716, and finally 1736. The New Jerusalem, he believed, would be located in New England.[20]

In the more recent past, famous preachers such as Hal Lindsey, Jack Van Impe, and Tim Lahaye—as well as the pseudo-Christian cults or other religious figures in the culture—have all made predictions (including "on-or-around" year projections) of the Second Coming. Here are some examples of end-times dating:

- Ellen G. White (co-founder—Seventh Day Adventist Church): 1843, 1844, 1850, 1856.
- Joseph Smith (founder—Mormon Church): 1891.
- Jehovah's Witnesses: 1874, 1878, 1881, 1910, 1914, 1918, 1925, 1975, and 1984.
- Hal Lindsey: 1982, 1988, 2007, with contingency dates going as far as 2048.
- Jack Van Impe: 1975, 1992, 2000, 2012.
- Pat Robertson: 1982.
- Chuck Smith (founder of Calvary Chapel): before 1981
- Edgar C. Whisenant: 1988, 1989.
- Bill Maupin: 1988.
- J.R. Church: 1988.
- Charles R. Taylor: 1992.
- Benny Hinn: 1993.
- F. M. Riley: 1994.
- John Hinkle: 1994.

- Grant R. Jeffrey: 2000.

- Lester Sumrall: 1985, 1986, 2000.

- Kenneth Hagin: 1997 to 2000.

- Jerry Falwell: 2010.

- John Hagee (at age 71): before he dies.

- Harold Camping: 1994, 2011.

- Ronald Weinland: 2011, 2012.

- Perry Stone: 2009-2015

- Billy Graham: Even this venerable preacher began telling us in the 1930s to expect the soon return of Christ.

Pastors all across America's fruited plains have books of some of these authors proudly displayed in their office libraries. The same books, and videos too, fly off Christian bookstore shelves, and the money continues to flow to these authors and many others of the same ilk. While some of these authors may be good teachers on other subjects, their false predictions force us to doubt their views on eschatology. Many of the above people will be forgotten, but whenever you happen to be reading this book, you will probably be hearing from a new generation of false teachers.[21]

All of these people had something in common—they all thought they knew better than Jesus and/or the writers of the New Testament. Many Christians are going to have a knee-jerk reaction against the evidence provided here about fulfilled prophecy. They will simply brush off the evidence by insisting that the church settled this issue a long time ago. But the very fact of the many different and contradictory views of Bible prophecy that are still present in the church—not to mention the continued failed end times predictions—prove that the issue is not settled.

Some will first say that *preterism*—the view that most or all of biblical prophecy has already been fulfilled—is a modern idea without historical support. But they are wrong about that too.

Proponents of every eschatological view think they can find statements by apostolic fathers that tend to support their position. But such scholars as Francis X. Gumerlock, Gary DeMar, Kenneth L. Gentry, Jr. and others in their books and papers have adequately demonstrated that preterism, in varying degrees, has been a legitimate view of eschatology among Christians since the early days of the church.[22] Of course, this does not prove that preterist interpretations are correct, only that they are not novel. And while it is the minority view in the church today, it seems to be the fastest growing view.

Actually not much is known about the views of the early church fathers on eschatology. We do not have many writings about this from the early Christian leaders after the apostles (during the first 400 or so years of the church). We do know that they held differing views, and we know that some of them made the same foolish predictions about the end of the world that some Christians are making today.[23]

However, one prominent preterist commentator from the early church was the historian and church leader Eusebius of Caesarea (born c. AD 260/263; died c. AD 339/341). He is considered the Father of Church History and became the Bishop of Caesarea in about the year 314. In his work *Ecclesiastical History*, Eusebius specifically belittled the millennialist views of certain early writers, thoroughly rejecting the idea of a corporeal reign of Christ on earth during a literal millennium.[24]

Among Eusebius' other writings are these two works, *The Proof of the Gospel ("Demonstratio Evangelica")* and *Theophania*. In these books he touched on various aspects of fulfilled prophecy. By tracking the thread of eschatological comments throughout his writing, we can reasonably conclude that Eusebius believed that at least all of the following things were fulfilled by AD 70: [25]

- the Second Coming of Christ (at least in some sense)
- the Great Tribulation and the Day of the Lord
- the Abomination of Desolation
- the New Heaven, New Earth and the New Jerusalem
- the Days of Vengeance and judgment upon Israel
- the "time of the end"/ "end of the world"
- the ushering in of the new covenant/kingdom of heaven
- the Great Commission (gospel having been preached to the whole world)

We will discuss preterism in the early church further in Chapter 13. We preterists argue that our views are completely consistent with Jesus and his disciples. That is, the ideas which are represented by preterists were the views of the New Testament writers themselves, who expected the fulfillment of all biblical prophecy to take place in their generation. So we preterists feel that we are in good company!

We have already pointed out that most Christians acknowledge that the writers of the New Testament believed Jesus was coming back in their lifetime. We will show why it is indeed correct that the New Testament authors understood the Second Coming to be imminent. As we will see, the New Testament is chock-full of passages declaring the imminency of all the major eschatological events.

We further argue that almost *all* conservative Christians are preterists to a degree. That may seem like a surprising statement. But there is general agreement within biblical Christianity that Jesus predicted that the temple would be destroyed in his generation, and that it in fact happened while some who heard his words were still alive. So we are in agreement on the fulfillment of at least this one important event.

What is controversial is all the *additional* prophetic material given by Jesus that is found in the Olivet Discourse and elsewhere in the Bible, including the book of Revelation. We will show, if you will indulge us, that preterist eschatology is optimistic, beautifully consistent, and faithful to Scripture.

In this book we are not going to attempt to consider every passage of Scripture related to Bible prophecy. Our goal is to lay out a framework of the key passages so that the reader can understand the big picture. But we will not skip over the difficult passages. We hope to show how unified Scripture is on the subject of eschatology and give the reader a basis for further study.

We present our ideas with humility. We are called *to test all things and hold on to what is good* (1 Thessalonians 5:21), and *to search the Scriptures daily to find out whether these things are so* (Acts 17:11). While opinions from clearly biased sources sometimes test our patience, reasonable men can disagree. We believe that all true believers have the truth of the essential doctrines of the Christian faith, and in these there must be unity. However, no one man or denomination is without some measure of error. It would be difficult to find a Christian who will not admit that he has changed his opinion on certain matters. The Bible teaches:

> Oh, the depth of the riches both of the wisdom and knowledge of God! How unsearchable are his judgments and his ways past finding out! (*Romans 11:33*)

The Bible is the product of an infinite God and our understanding is finite. There are indeed mysteries from the mind of God that are "past finding out." But each of us should seek to grow in our knowledge and understanding. "The secret things belong to the LORD our God, but those things which are revealed belong to us and to our children forever, that we may do all the words of this law." (Deuteronomy 29:29)

Our agenda is Biblical Truth, so we are always open to any correction that is based on sound biblical exegesis, and would be thankful for your contribution to that end. We pray that the reader shares the same willingness to grow and learn.

How to Interpret the Bible

There are literally thousands of Christian denominations. American Christianity especially is separated into sects, giving the world the impression that we are confused and don't know what we are doing. Or even more alarming, our divisions give the impression that the Christian God is somehow confused and thus irrelevant. Some serious introspection is in order.

Some of our divisions are over trivial things. But some are over important doctrines. One major reason we divide is because we interpret the Bible differently. We have a tendency to make interpretations based on our extra-biblical presuppositions. Many Christians, sadly, are more interested in finding passages that support their sectarian ideas than in knowing what the Bible actually has to say. Human nature is such that there is tremendous pressure to acquiesce to a teaching in order to be accepted within one's community.

This is compounded by the system in which pastors are hired into a denominational or sectarian setting. (When was the last time you heard of a Baptist preacher being hired by a Lutheran congregation, for example?) Pastors cannot buck the establishment within their community without risking their job. In this environment, pastors and lay people conveniently overlook passages that don't fit their particular tradition. This often leads to biased interpretations. The church must work to overcome this.

Peer pressure can also outweigh good scholarship. But there is a related issue. People tend to seek an identity. They are comfortable with a label. They see themselves fitting in with a particular group: I am Catholic, or I am a Methodist, or I am Reformed, etc. There is a natural human tendency to seek *comfort* over *truth*.

Since 1999 we have been communicating through our FaithFacts.org website with all kinds of Christians, pseudo-Christians, and non-Christians. So we have some basis to make the following claim. Many Christians are either too lazy or simply afraid to deal with passages in the Bible that are challenging to them. Each group assumes that their leaders must have their theology right, and they fail to follow Paul's instructions in 1 Thessalonians 5:21 to test everything.

We Christians often prefer to ignore challenges to our preconceived notions about what the Bible teaches. We have built doctrines by picking and choosing the passages that fit our ideas and have ignored those passages that challenge us. We are really not interested in truth if it upsets our applecart. This has led to a shallow, lazy, distorted, and divisive Christianity.

In matters of prophecy, we have gravitated to fanciful popular books and movies about the end of the world. We have let ourselves be deceived by false prophets and teachers who have not done their homework. It is high time to open our minds to reasonable challenges to our thinking. Fortunately, with the Internet, the days of Christians being able to duck doctrinal challenges are gone.

Before we get deep into studying the Scriptures, we need to find some common ground about how to interpret them. Otherwise we will just be playing Bible ping-pong, each side throwing Bible passages at the other in an attempt to prove our preconceptions. Let's see if we can agree on some basic principles of interpretation.

Many conservative evangelical Christians, the group of which we consider ourselves to be a part, proudly say, "We take the Bible literally." But let's play "twenty questions" and consider a few passages:

1. When Jesus said that He is the vine (John 15:5), did He mean that He is a plant? Is God literally a rock (2 Samuel 22:3; Psalm 18:2, etc.)? Or is Jesus literally a stone (Acts 4:10-12) or a lamb (John 1:29)?

2. Should we literally hate our mother and father so that we can be Jesus' disciple (Luke 14:26)?

3. If your eye causes you to sin, should you literally pluck it out (Mark 9:47)?

4.   Must we sell everything we have and give it to the poor in order to inherit eternal life (Luke 18:18-22)?

5.   Is hell inside the earth (Ephesians 4:8-10)? Is heaven literally *up* and hell literally *down*?

6.   Is it necessary to literally eat Christ's body in order to have life (John 6:53)?

7.   Did the mountains and the hills really break into song and the trees clap their hands (Isaiah 55:12)?

8.   Did God literally hold out his hands to an obstinate people (Isaiah 65)? Does God have literal hands?

9.   Did Jesus mean that any Christian with faith like the grain of a mustard seed could literally move a mountain by voice command (Matthew 17:20)?

10.   Is David's throne literally extant forever (2 Samuel 7:13)? (Is it in a museum somewhere?) Did Jesus literally inherit David's physical throne (Luke 1:32)?

11.   Was Satan to fall literally from heaven like lightning (Luke 10:18)?

12.   Is it literally true that serpents and scorpions cannot harm Christians (Luke 10:19)?

13.   Would the moon literally turn to blood before the Day of the Lord (Joel 2:31)?

14.   When God judged Babylon, an event in actual history, did the stars and sun literally stop giving their light (Isaiah 13:10) and the heavens literally tremble (Isaiah 13:13)? When God judged Edom did the sky literally roll up like a scroll (Isaiah 34:4)? When God judged Israel according to Micah 1:2-16, did the mountains literally melt and the valleys split? Read these passages and numerous others like them in the Bible (for example, Isaiah 24:23; Ezekiel 32:7; Amos 5:20; 8:9; Zephaniah 1:15) and then consider what you think of Matthew 24:29.

15. Could stars literally fall to earth even though the smallest star is a thousand times bigger than earth (Revelation 6:13)?

16. Does Jesus literally hold seven stars in his right hand (Revelation 1:16)?

17. Did the locusts in Revelation 9 literally have crowns of gold and faces of men (v. 7)? Did the beasts in Revelation 13 literally have ten horns and seven heads (v. 1) or literally speak like a dragon (v. 11)?

18. Is the angel in Revelation 20 to have a literal key to a literal bottomless pit (verse 1)? Is the Book of Life in Revelation 20 literal, with paper or parchment pages (verses 12, 15)?

19. Do you really expect Jesus to be literally riding a white horse at his return (Revelation 19:11)?

20. Is the New Jerusalem a literal city with literal dimensions of 1,500 miles in length, breadth, and height, and resting in the air above Israel during the millennium (Revelation 21:16)?

In spite of how obvious most of these examples seem, some Christians may insist that these passages are to be understood literally. But certainly at least some of these are examples of how the Bible uses a variety of language techniques to describe real things in non-literal language. Note that Jesus himself often used hyperbole, for example, to make important points.

These questions could go on. Hopefully, we have not insulted you. We have a very conservative view of the Bible and believe that it is the inspired Word of God in its entirety, and that it communicates a literal sense even when it employs non-literal genres. But that does not mean that every word or phrase was meant to be taken in a wooden literal sense. The readers will hopefully be more attuned to figurative language in the Bible in the future. The fact is that nobody is a consistent literalist, nor should anyone be!

There are some Christians who hold "literalism" as a test for orthodoxy. In other words, they insist that those who do not hold to a "literal" interpretation are not faithful to Scripture or are "liberals." But these Christians are clearly inconsistent because they themselves do not and cannot possibly always interpret the Bible absolutely literally.

The New Testament *itself* has examples of people who erred by failing to recognize Jesus' use of figurative language. Here are some instances:

1. When Jesus referred to his body as a temple (John 2:19), the Jews misunderstood and sought his death based in part on a mistaken, overly literal interpretation (John 2:20).

2. Nicodemus' literal interpretation led him to question whether being "born again" meant to "enter a second time into his mother's womb" (John 3:4).

3. When Jesus spoke of "a fountain of water springing up into everlasting life," the Samaritan woman erred in wanting a literal drink of water (John 4:10-15).

In our everyday language, we use figures of speech so often that we do not even think about them. We sing metaphorically "A Mighty Fortress Is Our God." We say things like "I could eat a horse," "cat got your tongue," "the four corners of the earth," "the sky is falling," "coming apart at the seams," "he has a yellow streak down his back," etc. We use hundreds of such idioms that are not literal, but people in our culture understand exactly what is meant.

The Bible too uses a variety of literary devices. It uses parables, poetry, hyperbole, allegories, metaphors, and many other figures of speech. It is common in the Bible to use astronomical language to describe important prophetic events. There is Hebraic terminology that may be unfamiliar to us but was clearly understood by first-century Jews. Certain events described in the Bible in Hebraic apocalyptic language we know for certain have already been fulfilled, such as God's judgment upon Babylon (number 14 in the list above).

Consider further this passage from Ezekiel chapter 32:

"I will also water the land with the flow of your blood, even to the mountains; and the riverbeds will be full of you. When I put out your light, I will cover the heavens, and make its stars dark; I will cover the sun with a cloud, and the moon shall not give her light. All the bright lights of the heavens I will make dark over you, and bring darkness upon your land," says the Lord GOD. (*Ezekiel 32:6-8*)

Notes in *The Reformation Study Bible*,[26] a well-respected study tool, contain the following comments about this passage:

> The language of this section is similar to that used to describe the day of the Lord in Isaiah 13:10, Joel 2:30-31, Joel 3:15, Amos 8:9. . . . The appearance of God as a divine warrior is accompanied by convulsions in the created order. The universe dissolves into the chaos that existed before creation, when the heavens were dark. . . . Here the extravagant imagery is not meant literally but is used in connection with the death of a Pharaoh.

Now let's consider a couple of other questions:

1. Are Jesus' miracles to be taken literally? Why? See Matthew 11:4-6; Luke 7:22-23; John 10:25, 38; John 14:11, and John 15:24. Also see 2 Peter 1:16. It is clear from these passages that Jesus staked his ministry in part on his miracles. This confirms that we *are* to take the accounts of his miracles literally.

2. Did Jesus literally—really and truly—rise from the dead? Yes! See 1 Corinthians 15:1-11, where Paul made an impassioned argument that the resurrection was a fact of history attested to by many witnesses. Paul stakes all of Christianity on the *literal resurrection of Jesus*.

So, should we really interpret the Bible "literally" in every instance? Of course not. It is more faithful to Scripture to interpret each passage the way it *was intended to be interpreted* in its context and understood by its original audience.

We sometimes fail to appreciate how important it is to let Scripture interpret Scripture. Here's another quick example. We often see Jesus referring to himself as "the Son of Man." This designation has little meaning unless we understand that Jesus is referring to the Old Testament book of Daniel, in which "the Son of Man" is one who comes from heaven to receive everlasting dominion (Daniel 7:13-14). A person who has no knowledge of the Bible will likely think that Jesus is saying that He is nothing more than a man. But in fact, He is saying just the opposite! He is claiming divinity! To understand the Bible fully we often must cross-reference passages, which may require diligent study.

Matthew, in his gospel, has approximately sixty references to the Old Testament. And more than two-thirds of the passages in the book of Revelation contain references or allusions to Old Testament passages. While we study the Bible, we must be alert to such things.

It is also wrong to read into the Bible views or preconceived assumptions from secular society. For example, to assume out of hand that the miracles of the Bible could not have really happened is reading an atheistic or naturalistic assumption into the text.

The field of study concerned with biblical interpretation is called *hermeneutics*. Here is a definition from Henry Virkler: "In its technical meaning, hermeneutics is often defined as the science and art of biblical interpretation. Hermeneutics is considered a science because it has rules, and these rules can be classified in an orderly system. It is considered an art because communication is flexible, and therefore a mechanical and rigid application of rules will sometimes distort the true meaning of a communication. To be a good interpreter, one must learn the rules of hermeneutics as well as the art of applying those rules." [27]

Principles of Biblical Interpretation

Here are some overarching prerequisites and principles for biblical interpretation:

A.   acceptance of the Bible as the inspired Word of God, or at the very least acquiescence to the authority of Scripture, giving it the benefit of any doubt (2 Timothy 3:14-17, etc.) [28]

B.   a predisposition of faith and obedience (John 7:17-18; 8:43)

C.   seeing the parts in relation to the whole by means of proper interpretive methods, including those listed below

In the next three paragraphs, which discuss proper interpretive methods, you will see how these things are often discussed in theology textbooks. This may be a bit academic, but worth the effort. At the end we will summarize and simplify these principles.

1.   **Grammatico-historical method:** gathering from the Scriptures themselves the precise meaning that the writers intended to convey, taking into account the grammar and culture of their times and their primary audiences. This is not necessarily the "literal" meaning. We should remember

that the Bible was written for us today but not to us. Audience relevance is often the key to grasping what the writers intended. This is the antidote to the wooden literalism that is too often seen among Christians. The interpreter should apply to the sacred writings the same principles, as well as the same grammatical processes of sense and reason, which are applied to other books. In other words, we should use principles of language as well as standard reason to determine what the author intended and how the original readers would have understood it.

2. **Covenant-historical method:** paying careful attention to the development of the Kingdom of God in all its aspects throughout the course of biblical history, which is the central core and directing rudder of world history. Understanding the thread of God's covenantal history with mankind is the antidote both to the unbiblical legalism that flourishes in American Christianity, and to the prophetic speculations and fantasies that have diverted Christians from the real hope of the gospel.

3. **Redemptive-historical method:** interpretation of the Bible based on the principles that

    a. Scripture was written via progressive revelation.

    b. Scripture can only truly be understood Christologically throughout.

    c. The Old Testament people of God belonged to the same organic covenant community as the New Testament people of God.

Here is some practical guidance for earnest students of God's Word:

1. Interpreting the Bible for oneself, an important Protestant notion, but increasingly common with Catholics as well, does not mean that we should rely solely on our own judgments, ignoring the insights and research of others.

2. Interpreting the Bible for oneself does not mean that we have the right to "massage" the Bible in accordance with our own conceptions.

3. Interpreting the Bible for oneself does not mean that we can ignore the history of interpretation in the church, though we should keep in mind that the church is fallible and has not been unified on many points.

As we exercise our God-given responsibility to interpret the Scriptures, we must be aware of the elements of subjectivity and psychology that influence all interpretation:

- pride
- prejudice
- hidden agendas (personal and theological)
- cultural conditioning
- denominational distinctives
- peer pressure
- historical circumstances
- socio-economic factors
- unconscious expectations
- educational background
- personality distinctives
- occupational pressures
- interpersonal relational background
- wishful thinking

All of us who have become preterists have had to work through these issues. For example, in consideration of *pride*, our initial resistance was often based on an attitude of, "There is no way I could have been wrong for this long." And *prejudice*, "This view is new to me, therefore it is inferior." Or for pastors, "I cannot accept this view because I would lose my job in this denomination."

Here are ten guidelines for rightly handling the unified Word of Truth (2 Timothy 2:15):

1. **Doctrine must be squarely built upon Scripture**. Our doctrines must be erected from a proper interpretation or a legitimate inference from Scripture, and not from cherished traditions, or human creeds or confessions. While

there is a place for creeds and church traditions (some are clearly more biblically-based than others), the Christian's conscience is ultimately bound to Scripture. Creeds and traditions can and sometimes do contradict Scripture. A key proposition of the Protestant Reformation was "Sola Scriptura"—that is, Scripture Alone. Catholics also recognize that tradition may supplement but cannot *contradict* Scripture.

2. **Context is critical**. Every word, clause, sentence, and paragraph of Scripture comes to us in contexts—from the immediate passage to its place as part of a book, to the whole book, the author's identity, setting and purpose, and to the entire Bible, and even beyond to the cultural, socio-political, and historical contexts. Working outwardly to determine context in this manner is a helpful discipline for understanding anything we read in Scripture. Tunnel vision is perilous. Here's a simple example of taking something out of context: One can find the statement in the Bible that *there is no God* (Psalm 14:1). But the context of that statement is: *The fool says in his heart, "There is no God."* Context is crucial. While this is a simplistic example, properly relating to context is not always a simple task.

3. **Scripture is consistent and not contradictory**. A rule of logic is the so-called Law of Non-Contradiction, which states that two contradictory things cannot both be true at the same time and in the same relationship. Similarly, the "analogy of faith" is a hermeneutical principle which states that all Scripture is in agreement and will not contradict itself. Every proposed interpretation of any passage must be compared with what the other parts of the Bible teach. Therefore, though two or three different interpretations of a verse may be equally possible from a grammatical standpoint, any interpretation that contradicts the clear teaching of other scriptures must be ruled out from the beginning. Scripture interprets Scripture. While some Christians are willing to ignore these principles, we think the Bible deserves better.

4. **The clear should interpret the unclear**. A related principle that is very helpful in interpreting the Bible (prophecy and

apocalyptic literature in particular), is that "murky" passages can often be clarified by other scriptures that address the particular topic in a more straightforward way. For example, an interpretation of the highly symbolic visions of John's Apocalypse may never trump clear statements of Paul's epistles, which are more didactic (instructional or doctrinal) and less symbolic.

5. **Distinguish between what the Bible records and what it commands, commends, or approves.** We must recognize the difference between passages that are *pre*scriptive and those that are merely *de*scriptive. The saints in the Bible were sinful people. We are not to emulate their sinful behaviors. Emulation is not always synonymous with being obedient.

6. **Incidental or rare or otherwise exceptional events within Scripture should not necessarily be taken as normative for Christians today**. For example, Acts 1:26 says that the apostles drew lots in order to find the Lord's will as to who would replace Judas (whether Joseph or Matthias). But it is less than likely that this should be our approach when confronted with important decisions—especially since the drawing of lots occurred at the beginning stage of the church and was, apparently, not continued as a practice thereafter. (The New Testament records no other instances of drawing lots.)

7. **Recognize distinctive apostolic or cultural practices**. Distinctive apostolic practices that are rooted in theology, not in the culture of the day, may be taken as normative for the church, unless they were clearly temporary in nature. But we are not necessarily to emulate blindly or mindlessly (in legalistic or "patternistic" fashion) everything we see faithful people do in the Bible. The Bible teaches, for example, that Christians should greet one another with a "holy kiss." There is a cultural context for such commands that may not apply today.

8. **Don't build a doctrine upon a single verse or an uncertain textual reading**. In other words, we should not erect an entire teaching or system of doctrine upon a verse in

isolation from its context, or that has dubious manuscript support. Christian doctrine should be built upon passages which exist in the best manuscripts and can be confirmed through the science of textual criticism. An example is Mark 16:18, where we read that Jesus remarked to his immediate disciples that they would not be harmed if they took up serpents (or drank poisons). Some Christians, especially in the state of West Virginia and certain other states in the American South, have taken this to be a command for the church throughout history. Until outlawed by the government, some churches practiced the handling of poisonous snakes in church—to the regret of many. This passage of Scripture, however, does not appear in some early important manuscripts, and snake handling should not be considered either a command or normative.

9. **Be alert to figurative language**. The Bible uses multiple literary genres, and is filled with figurative language. This fact should cause the interpreter to take great care in his treatment of the Bible, and to make certain not to interpret in an overly literal sense that which was intended to be understood metaphorically or otherwise figuratively. All Scripture has a "literal" sense, but that sense is not always expressed in literal terms.

10. **Pray for the Holy Spirit's illumination**. The Holy Spirit's work is not only to show what the Bible means, but also to persuade Christians of its truth and how to live out that truth. Illumination is the Spirit's work. Pray that He will enable you to discern the meaning of the message, and to welcome and receive it as from God.

Finally, we emphasize three points. While the following concepts are important for any interpretive application, they are particularly appropriate for Bible prophecy:

1. **Objectivity.** As you let Scripture speak to you, do not over-rely on tradition, presuppositions, or peer pressure. And do not let wishful thinking cloud your judgment. Our goal should not be to get something for ourselves, that is, to read into the text what we want to find. What you have been taught may be correct, but it may not be. It is a biblical

principle to question what you have been taught. We are called *to test all things and hold on to what is good* (1 Thessalonians 5:21), and *to search the Scriptures daily to find out whether these things are so* (Acts 17:11). Beware. You may end up disagreeing with your favorite theologian or people in your fellowship. Sometimes truth is uncomfortable. To be faithful, we must value truth over personal comfort.

2. **Audience Relevance.** Remember that when you are reading the Bible, especially the New Testament, you are reading someone else's mail. It is crucial to think about how the original recipient of the communication would have understood it. While all Scripture has relevance to us today, it should be interpreted in light of how the speaker intended his original audience to understand it.

3. **Consistency.** When examining a doctrinal issue, make sure that your interpretation of all relevant passages is consistent. If the Bible is true, it is internally consistent and harmonious throughout. This implies that we should not arbitrarily dismiss passages we do not understand. Yes, some passages are more challenging than others. But we should attempt to reconcile them with all other passages on the same subject.

Question for your pastor, church leaders, and friends: "Should we interpret the Bible literally?"

---

3 — Different Views

E schatology is the study of the "end times" or "last things." Many Christians are unfamiliar with the word *eschatology* and are more familiar with the term "Bible prophecy." There are various aspects to this field of study. Included among these are: a violent disruption of life and theology, the "last days," a great tribulation, the Second Coming of Christ in judgment, the rapture, the gathering of believers, the resurrection of the dead, and a "new heaven and new earth." The study of eschatology can be complicated because of the numerous overlapping issues and terminology.

It has been estimated that one-fourth of the New Testament is about this. Indeed, it could be argued that the New Testament is *mostly* about eschatology! Every book in the New Testament except Philemon has some mention of these things. The Old Testament too has quite a bit of eschatological material, especially the books of Isaiah, Ezekiel, Daniel, Joel, and Malachi.

The word *eschatology*, interestingly, is not used in the Bible (though it is based on the New Testament word *eschatos*, which means "last").

Apparently the word was first used in English around the mid 16th century. There are primarily four different views of eschatology:

Futurism. The futurist believes that most eschatological events of the Bible still lie in our future.

Historicism. The historicist view seeks parallels between Bible prophecy and major events or people in history, especially those in church history. Various characters or events prophesied in the Bible are seen as parallels to historical people or events. For example, some of the Protestant Reformers saw the papacy or the Pope as the Antichrist. As crazy as this idea seems to most of us today, this was a popular view among even very learned scholars such as Calvin, Luther, and Wesley. This view is still around in some circles today.[29]

Idealism. The idealist views prophecies as timeless promises of hope, equally applicable to all generations. The idealist tends to see themes and concepts in biblical prophecy, rather than actual people and events. Thus prophecies do not have specific one-time fulfillments in history, but rather multiple fulfillments throughout the ages as God delivers his people and judges his enemies. This view sees in Revelation an allegorical struggle between good and evil. For example, the beasts in Revelation may represent various modern social injustices, which may be defined in liberal political terms such as exploitation of workers, the wealthy elite, materialism, etc. Idealism, at least in its purest form, is different from all the other views in that it does not see any of the biblical prophecies (with the possible exceptions of the Second Coming and final judgment) as being literally fulfilled either in the past or in the future.

Historicism and Idealism have both fallen out of favor. One reason for this is that one can read *anything* into the Bible by means of these schools of thought. Certainly the writers of the Bible (or the speakers whose thoughts were recorded by the writers) did not intend for their words to be understood in such a manner. They had specific events in mind when they wrote and spoke.

Historicist and idealist interpretations often violate a cardinal principle of biblical interpretation—the importance of audience relevance. These eschatological concepts would have had little or no meaning to the original readers. For these reasons, we find relatively few people who claim to hold to them now, even though they have been popular at various times in church history.

However, we do see many futurists, especially dispensationalists (see below), incorporating some similarly fanciful interpretive methods. They see the end of the world lurking behind every world event. But they have proven themselves to be wrong repeatedly. Yet dispensationalism is quite popular in American evangelical circles.

Preterism. Preterism is essentially a time perspective, the opposite of futurism. The preterist view is that most, if not all, prophetic events have already been fulfilled. The preterist believes that the Bible offers numerous time-reference statements that definitively tie fulfillment of prophesied events to the first century, in particular to the events surrounding the destruction of Jerusalem and the temple in AD 70. This is the view that we will argue as having the strongest biblical foundation.

The four eschatological views listed above have variously waxed and waned in popularity over the centuries. Today, the majority view is futurism. However, there is great disagreement even among futurists on the details. There are three primary camps within futurism:

- Premillennialism

- Postmillennialism

- Amillennialism

The "millennialism" aspect of futurism comes from Revelation, chapter 20, where we see mentioned a thousand-year period. Here are the first few verses of the chapter:

> Then I saw an angel coming down from heaven, having the key to the bottomless pit and a great chain in his hand. He laid hold of the dragon, that serpent of old, who is the Devil and Satan, and bound him for a **thousand years**; and he cast him into the bottomless pit, and shut him up, and set a seal on him, so that he should deceive the nations no more till the **thousand years** were finished. But after these things he must be released for a little while. And I saw thrones, and they sat on them, and judgment was committed to them. Then I saw the souls of those who had been beheaded for their witness to Jesus and for the word of God, who had not worshiped the

beast or his image, and had not received his mark on their foreheads or on their hands. And they lived and reigned with Christ for a **thousand years**. But the rest of the dead did not live again until the **thousand years** were finished. This is the first resurrection. Blessed and holy is he who has part in the first resurrection. Over such the second death has no power, but they shall be priests of God and of Christ, and shall reign with Him a **thousand years**. Now when the **thousand years** have expired, Satan will be released from his prison and will go out to deceive the nations which are in the four corners of the earth, Gog and Magog, to gather them together to battle, whose number is as the sand of the sea. (*Revelation 20:1-8*)

As you will note, the word *millennium* is not mentioned here, nor is it used anywhere in the Bible. It is a term used to refer to the thousand-year period mentioned in Revelation 20. We will cover aspects of this spectacular passage in detail in future chapters, but here are the basic systems of thought regarding the millennium:

Premillennialism. This is the view that takes Revelation 20 literally. Thus premillennialists believe that the millennium is a literal thousand-year period. They believe that a Great Tribulation will occur just prior to the start of the millennium. The tribulation is a period of vast upheaval which is mentioned in the Olivet Discourse and discussed similarly in Revelation. Such upheaval would include worldwide hardships, disasters, famine, and war. But Christ will literally and physically return to rule the earth in a worldwide kingdom of peace and righteousness, that is, in a utopian theocratic political kingdom on earth. Like other futurists, they call on such passages as Isaiah 2:1-5 (an expected time of peace in the latter days), Isaiah 11:1-10 (a time when "the wolf shall dwell with the lamb"), Isaiah 65:17-25 ("new heavens and new earth"), and Revelation 21:1-27 (new heaven/new earth/new Jerusalem) to support this position.

Premillennialism can be divided into various subcategories. Christ will come to rapture his saints either at the beginning of the tribulation ("pre-tribulationism"), in the middle of the tribulation ("mid-tribulationism"), or at the end of the tribulation ("post-tribulationism"). But the saints will return to the earth (or to the New Jerusalem city suspended above the earth) for the millennial period. The world as we know it will, in some sense, cease to exist at the end of the millennium. At that time, believers go to their eternal destination. There are variations in the details, as we shall consider later.

Another important twist to premillennialism is *dispensationalism*—or *dispensational premillennialism*. Dispensationalists hold that Israel and the church are distinct entities having different covenants. So Jews and Christians have distinct avenues to heaven. Dispensationalists put great weight in the idea that Israel will be restored and that the temple will be rebuilt. They think that when the modern state of Israel came into being in 1948 this was the beginning of these things. In Chapter 14 (as well as in Appendix C) we will consider dispensationalism and its particulars in detail.

Premillennialists who are not also dispensationalists call themselves "historic pre-millennialists." They do so to call attention to the fact that some Christians all the way back to the early church fathers held to variations of their ideas. They thus distinguish between their view and dispensationalism, which is a relatively recent addition to premillennial theories.

Amillennialism. The amillennialist considers the millennium to be figurative. Amillennialists note that the Bible often uses numbers in figurative ways. The number 1,000 is a figurative number for completeness. They hold that the millennium began with Christ's first coming (or at Pentecost which marked the beginning of the church) and that we are in it now. The millennium is not viewed as a future political order, but as the spiritual kingdom of Christ's rule in the church. So the millennium is the church age, also sometimes equated to the kingdom of God. There is not much in particular to look forward to this side of heaven in the view of amillennialists, as they tend to view mankind's sinfulness and rebellion against God as impossible to overcome to a great degree. However, the end of time holds the promise of restoration and heaven for believers. The Second Coming and final judgment also come at the *end* of the millennium, that is, at the end of time.

Postmillennialism. This view is something of a hybrid of premillennialism and amillennialism. Postmillennialists, like amillennialists, see Christ's Second Coming occurring at the *end* of the millennium, coincident with the end of the world. Some postmillennialists hold to a literal 1,000 year millennium, and understand that the beginning of the millennium is still in our future. Others see the millennium figuratively as a long period of time, and like amillennialists, understand that we are in the millennium now. Postmillennialists hold to a rather optimistic view of the future, believing that the world will tend to get better and better as more and more people come to Christ. In other words, the millennial age, while never reaching absolute perfection, will become beautifully Christianized.

So, like premillennialists they believe that a time will come on earth when peace and righteousness reign, but unlike premillennialists they believe this period will come *before* Christ returns, as a result of the worldwide preaching of the gospel. They also call on Isaiah 2, 11, and 65, as well as Revelation 21 in support of the idea of a literal worldwide golden age of peace and righteousness on earth.

Versions of postmillennialism have certain key elements in common with premillennialism. While postmillennialists deny any kinship with premillennialism, both schemes share a similar notion about the eschaton (last days). This concept is that all mankind will join together with Abraham and the other Old Testament saints in restored/resurrected physical bodies in a utopian paradise *on earth*.

There is not always a clear line of distinction among the various views. For example, a premillennialist can theoretically also be either an historicist or a futurist. A postmillennialist or an amillennialist may hold to certain aspects of preterism. The term *millennialism* is usually synonymous with premillennialism. But it could also refer to the version of postmillennialism which holds to a literal millennium.

Preterism. This is the view that we will present for your consideration. The term preterism comes from the Latin word *praeter*, which means *past*. Preterists hold that most if not all prophetic events have already been fulfilled with the events of the first century. While this is a minority view within Christianity, we believe that this is the only view that seriously considers the time-reference limitations given in Scripture for eschatological fulfillment. We will demonstrate why preterism is the view that best ties together all of the passages in the Bible about prophecy and is thus the most consistent.

Preterists teach that this view not only honors the Bible's time frame references but also the *manner* in which the Bible teaches prophecy being fulfilled. It is the only view that adequately considers the meaning of biblical apocalyptic language. We will carefully examine why we believe that an unbiased view of Scripture demands this conclusion. We will also discuss the objections to preterism, and let you be the judge as we attempt to make our case.

There are two distinct groups of preterists: *partial* preterists and *full* preterists. Full preterism goes by different names, including "realized eschatology," "covenant eschatology," "biblical preterism," "consistent preterism," or "fulfilled prophecy." As we get into the details, the reader will see why the term *covenant eschatology* is perhaps the best theological description, but *full preterism* is the most commonly used term. *Fulfilled prophecy* is probably the most descriptive term. We will demonstrate how eschatological passages do not refer to the end of time or the physical universe, but to the end of the Old Covenant Age. Eschatology is not about the end of the "world," but rather its **rebirth**, instituted by Jesus in the New Covenant order.

Full preterists believe that what most people think of as a future literal-physical coming of Christ to earth a second time has been misunderstood. We are of the studied opinion that the "Second Coming" of Christ was not to be a physical body appearance on earth, but rather a coming **in judgment** against the unbelieving Jews who perverted God's commandments and rejected Jesus and his church. Jesus discussed this over and over in his teaching, as we shall see. And as we will explore, a lot more happened at Christ's Second Coming than merely the judgment upon Israel.

His Second Coming in judgment and consummate completion of eschatological promises were fulfilled in AD 70. The apostles thought Jesus would return in their generation, and they were right. While this may seem foreign to you, we believe that numerous passages in both the Old Testament and New Testament prove the preterist view to be worthy of your consideration—so bear with us as we work through these passages.

To understand eschatology, it is important to understand the pattern repeated throughout the Bible in regard to God's "coming." The Old Testament teaches that God the Father *came down to earth* on multiple occasions. Though no one ever actually saw God, they definitely saw what He did. These "comings" were usually *in judgment* against the wayward Jews or their enemies. In the same way, Jesus came to judge the Jews in AD 70. We will demonstrate that Jesus discusses his future coming in precisely the same language that the Bible uses for God's comings in judgment in the Old Testament.

Full preterists disagree among themselves, however, on certain points. One of these is the millennium. While all full preterists believe that the millennium is figurative, some preterists believe (like amillennialists and some postmillennialists) that we are now in the millennium—that is, the church age. However, others believe that the millennium was symbolically the interim period between Christ's ascension and his coming in judgment in AD 70.

Unlike full preterists, partial preterists hold that in addition to the "metaphorical coming" of Christ in judgment in AD 70, there will be a literal-physical "consummate coming" of Christ at the end of time. Full preterists believe that the New Testament speaks only of one Second Coming, and that while some texts concerning the Second Coming have no clear time-reference associated with them, they must be interpreted in light of the texts that do have a time-reference constraint to the first century. Partial preterists argue on the basis of inference that because God came in judgment on multiple occasions in the Old Testament, it would be consistent for Jesus to have two "second" comings—one in AD 70 and one at the end of time. We will consider these things in more detail.

The End of the World or End of an Age?

I n this chapter we challenge a commonly held belief among Christians—that the Bible speaks of the end of the world, that is, the end of planet Earth and the physical universe. People point to four basic places in the Bible that they think refer to the end of the material creation:

- the "end of the world" as rendered in the King James Version of the book of Matthew
- the "last days" in various books including Acts 2 and Hebrews 1
- the "universe-burning" language in 2 Peter 3
- the "time of the end" in the book of Daniel

THE BOOK OF MATTHEW

In the King James Version of the Bible, the book of Matthew has Jesus speaking in several verses of "the end of the world" (Matthew chapters 13, 24, and 28). Here are these verses as we find them in the King James Version:

> Then Jesus sent the multitude away, and went into the house: and his disciples came unto him, saying, "Declare unto us the parable of the tares of the field." He answered and said unto them, "He that soweth the good seed is the Son of man; The field is the world [*kosmos*]; the good seed are the children of the kingdom; but the tares are the children of the wicked one; The enemy that sowed them is the devil; the harvest is the end of the **world** [*aion*]; and the reapers are the angels. As therefore the tares are gathered and burned in the fire; so shall it be in the end of this **world** [*aion*]. The Son of man shall send forth his angels, and they shall gather out of his kingdom all things that offend, and them which do iniquity; and shall cast them into a furnace of fire: there shall be wailing and gnashing of teeth. Then shall the righteous shine forth as the sun in the kingdom of their Father. Who hath ears to hear, let him hear. Again, the kingdom of heaven is like unto treasure hid in a field; the which when a man hath found, he hideth, and for joy thereof goeth and selleth all that he hath, and buyeth that field. Again, the kingdom of heaven is like unto a merchant man, seeking goodly pearls: Who, when he had found one pearl of great price, went and sold all that he had, and bought it. Again, the kingdom of heaven is like unto a net, that was cast into the sea, and gathered of every kind: Which, when it was full, they drew to shore, and sat down, and gathered the good into vessels, but cast the bad away. So shall it be at the end of the **world** [*aion*]: the angels shall come forth, and sever the wicked from among the just, and shall cast them into the furnace of fire: there shall be wailing and gnashing of teeth." (*Matthew 13:36-50, KJV*)

And Jesus said to them, "Do you not see all these things? Assuredly, I say to you, not one stone shall be left here upon another, that shall not be thrown down." And as he sat upon the mount of Olives, the disciples came unto him privately, saying, "Tell us, when shall these things be? And what shall be the sign of thy coming, and of the <u>end of the</u> **world** [*aion*]?" (*Matthew 24:2-3, KJV*)

And Jesus came and spake unto them, saying, "All power is given unto me in heaven and in earth. Go ye therefore, and teach all nations, baptizing them in the name of the Father, and of the Son, and of the Holy Ghost: Teaching them to observe all things whatsoever I have commanded you: and, lo, I am with you always, even unto the <u>end of the</u> **world** [*aion*]. Amen." (*Matthew 28:18-20, KJV*)

This is clear as could be, right? Jesus is talking about the end of the world—the end of the physical universe or at least of planet Earth. But hold on, most modern translations including the New King James Version say in each of these instances the "end of the **age**" instead of the "end of the **world**." This is a big difference! We'd better take a closer look.

When we examine the Greek we see that the word translated as "world" in the King James Version is *aion*, which in English is best translated as *age*. The King James Version mistranslated this word, or at best gave it a biased translation. *Readers of the King James Version of the Bible have been misled for 400 years!* While "world" is a possible translation of *aion*, if what Jesus meant was the end of the physical world, the Greek word *kosmos* would almost surely have been used here by Matthew.

But we note that even if we accept the King James translation, it does not necessarily mean the end of planet earth or the end of history. "World," even in English, often has a meaning closer to station or condition. For example, a dramatic event in someone's life might lead that person to say, "With that event, my world changed forever."

So to what *age* is Jesus referring? One of the passages above about the end of the age is in the Olivet Discourse (Matthew 24:3). In the preceding verse Jesus specifically mentioned the destruction of the temple (Matthew 24:2). As the chapter progresses, Jesus lists other events that were to happen. Then near the end of the chapter He gave a time constraint as to when *all* those things would happen—in his generation (Matthew 24:34). Since the initial thrust of the prophecy is the destruction of the temple at the end of age, it makes perfect sense that Jesus was talking about the end of the *Old Covenant Age*, sometimes called the Mosaic Age, or the Jewish Age.

This is confirmed in the parallel account in Luke 21, where in verse 24 we see the phrase "the times of the Gentiles." As we will explore later, the period between Jesus' earthly ministry and AD 70 was a transition period that fully grafted Gentiles into Christianity, which was initially a Jewish movement. The Old Covenant Age ended in AD 70 when the temple was destroyed, the important Hebrew genealogical records were destroyed with the temple, the nation of Israel ceased to exist, and *the ancient system of temple sacrifices for sin ended forever*.

There is broad agreement among Christians that in the Olivet Discourse Jesus predicted that the destruction of the temple would occur in his generation. Since the phrase "end of the age" appears in the verse (in Matthew's version) adjacent to the destruction of the temple prediction, they are logically tied together in time by their juxtaposition in the text. The temple destruction and the end of the age refer to the same time period, especially when put together with Jesus' declaration in Matthew 24:34: "Assuredly, I say to you, this generation will not pass away until all these things take place." (*English Standard Version*)

When we cover the Second Coming, we will examine objections to the Olivet Discourse having been fulfilled in the first century. One objection is that the phrase *this generation* does not necessarily have the obvious meaning of those living at that time. The second objection is that while some of the things in the Olivet Discourse were fulfilled in Jesus' literal generation, some are still future. We will address these objections.

We will also revisit Matthew 13 and show that the context is the judgment against the Jews in AD 70. But for now we merely want to point out that the book of Matthew speaks of *the end of the age* rather than *the end of the world*.

Next let's explore how the *end of the age* ties to the *last days*. Both terms present a consistent theme, and careful scrutiny supports the view that the end of the age and the last days culminated in AD 70.

THE LAST DAYS

Other places in the Bible where people think they find the universe's demise are in statements about the "last days" (or "last day" or "last hour" or "latter days"). The Old Testament speaks of the last days in such books as Joel, Isaiah, and Ezekiel. But only the New Testament writers proclaimed *themselves* to be living in the last days. Let's look at some of these passages.

In Acts 2, in his famous Pentecost sermon, Peter quotes the Old Testament prophet Joel to prove that he and his listeners were living in the last days. Here are his emphatic comments as he addressed the crowd:

> But Peter, standing up with the eleven, raised his voice and said to them, "Men of Judea and all who dwell in Jerusalem, let this be known to you, and heed my words. For these are not drunk, as you suppose, since it is only the third hour of the day. But this is what was spoken by the prophet Joel:
>
> > 'And it shall come to pass in the **last days**, says God,
> > That I will pour out of my Spirit on all flesh;
> > Your sons and your daughters shall prophesy,
> > Your young men shall see visions, Your old men shall
> >   dream dreams.
> > And on my menservants and on my maidservants I will
> >   pour out my Spirit in those days;
> > And they shall prophesy. I will show wonders in heaven
> >   above And signs in the earth beneath:
> > Blood and fire and vapor of smoke.
> > The sun shall be turned into darkness,
> > And the moon into blood,
> > Before the coming of the great and awesome <u>day of the
> >   LORD</u>.
> > And it shall come to pass
> > That whoever calls on the name of the LORD
> > Shall be saved.'" *(Acts 2:14-21)*

How could one mistake the time frame here? It is perfectly clear that Peter is declaring that they themselves were in the last days! Much more is contained in this passage—the cosmic language and also the term "the Day of the Lord," which people associate with the end of the universe. But clearly Peter is not speaking about the end of the world/universe, but rather the days in which he and his contemporaries were alive. (More on "the Day of the Lord" later.)

Now let's see what the writer of Hebrews has to say about the last days. We go to the opening verses of his letter:

God, who at various times and in various ways spoke in time past to the fathers by the prophets, has in **these last days** spoken to us by his Son, whom He has appointed heir of all things, through whom also He made the worlds. (*Hebrews 1:1-2*)

The writer of Hebrews used considerable space in his letter, as previously indicated, to explain how Christ's sacrifice ushered in the New Covenant, replacing the Old Covenant temple sacrifices for sin. The book of Hebrews is filled with preterist confirmations. We see in Hebrews chapter 8 this defining statement:

In that He says, "A **new covenant**," He has made the first obsolete. Now what is becoming obsolete and growing old is **ready to vanish away.** (*Hebrews 8:13*)

This is an important confirmation of what the other New Testament writers were conveying. The Old Covenant was *ready to vanish away* when the book of Hebrews was written. Hebrews imparts to the reader the sense that the New Covenant had already come, and that the Old Covenant was decaying and was soon to be ushered out. Of course, this would have to be AD 70 when the temple was destroyed, and the sacrificial system was abolished. Hebrews offers strong evidence, by the way, that the temple was still standing (Hebrews 9:8-10, see the *New American Standard Bible*), and that the temple sacrifices were still being practiced (Hebrews 10:2, 3, 11) as the book was penned. In another passage that unmistakably confirms this time frame, the writer of Hebrews adds a statement about the end of the ages:

He then would have had to suffer often since the foundation of the world [*kosmos*]; but **now**, once at the **end of the ages** [*aion*], He has appeared to put away sin by the sacrifice of Himself. (*Hebrews 9:26*)

In the above verse, the writer makes a distinction between the "world" (*kosmos*) and the "age" (*aion*). While these words can have a similar or overlapping meaning depending on the context, they are not quite the same thing. Paul makes a confirming statement about himself and his contemporaries living at the end of the ages in his first letter to the Corinthians:

Now all these things happened to them as examples, and they were written for **our** admonition, upon whom the **ends of the ages** [*aion*] **have come**. (*1 Corinthians 10:11*)

This confirms that "the end of the age" (singular), of which Jesus spoke in Matthew 24, is equivalent to the end of the ages (plural). It also confirms a consistent message with the writer of Hebrews, who many believe was Paul himself. It is the same Greek word in each instance—*aion*, even though it sometimes is translated as singular and sometimes as plural. For example, here is the same verse in the New Living Translation:

These things happened to them as examples for us. They were written down to warn **us who live at the end of the age**. (*1 Corinthians 10:11, New Living Translation*)

While we can easily get bogged down in the language, the critical thing is abundantly clear. Those first-century Christians were eye witnesses to the end of the age and the last days. This is definitive. But if you are not yet completely convinced that Peter, Paul, and the writer of Hebrews saw themselves as living in the last days and the end of the age, there is plenty more evidence. Here is another passage:

And let us consider one another in order to stir up love and good works, not forsaking the assembling of ourselves together, as is the manner of some, but exhorting one another, and so much the more as **you see the Day approaching**. (*Hebrews 10:24-25*)

In this verse we see another reference, this time by the writer of Hebrews, that ties to the statement by Peter (above) concerning the *Day of the Lord* (Acts 2:20). As promised, we will consider this term in more detail later. But we mention it here to confirm the imminency in this grand letter to the Hebrews and its consistency with other eschatological passages.

Audience relevance is again important. It would be impossible to miss that the writer of Hebrews expected that those to whom he wrote would be witnesses of the Day of the Lord, the approach of which they were seeing in real time. But there is *no mention of the end of the physical universe*. Those who think these passages refer to the end of the physical

universe are reading something into the text that is not there. What we
know today about a probable end to the physical universe comes from
science, and not from the Bible. Bear with us.[30]

Next we consider another statement by Paul in his second letter to
Timothy:

> But know this, that in the **last days** perilous times will come:
> For men will be lovers of themselves, lovers of money, boast-
> ers, proud, blasphemers, disobedient to parents, unthankful,
> unholy, unloving, unforgiving, slanderers, without self-control,
> brutal, despisers of good, traitors, headstrong, haughty, lovers
> of pleasure rather than lovers of God, having a form of godliness
> but denying its power. And **from such people turn away!** (*2
> Timothy 3:1-5*)

How could Timothy avoid such people if they were not going to be
in existence until 2000 years later? If *we* are living in the last days today,
then Timothy would have to be still alive in order for him to avoid these
men. Let's continue, now to the book of James, chapter 5:

> Come now, <u>you</u> rich, weep and howl for your miseries that are
> coming upon <u>you</u>! <u>Your</u> riches are corrupted, and <u>your</u> garments
> are moth-eaten. <u>Your</u> gold and silver are corroded, and their
> corrosion will be a witness against <u>you</u> and will eat <u>your</u> flesh
> like fire. <u>You have</u> heaped up treasure in the **last days**. Indeed
> the wages of the laborers who mowed <u>your</u> fields, which <u>you</u>
> kept back by fraud, cry out; and the cries of the reapers have
> reached the ears of the Lord of Sabaoth. <u>You have</u> lived on the
> earth in pleasure and luxury; <u>you have</u> fattened your hearts as
> in a day of slaughter. <u>You have</u> condemned, <u>you have</u> murdered
> the just; he does not resist <u>you</u>. (*James 5:1-6*)

Now we add James to the other apostles as proclaiming the last
days. Obviously, passages like this have tremendous lessons for people of all ages. We do not deny that such statements have meaning to
us today. But this passage, like the others, must be considered with
audience relevance in mind. The original readers of this letter would
have felt the historical weight of this passage upon themselves. James
was speaking to a particular audience. He said, "YOU" *have heaped up
treasure in the **last days***. Note that the verb is present perfect tense,
indicating fulfillment! So, again, the readers themselves would have

understood that **they** were in the last days. In complete agreement with all the other writers of the New Testament, there is the sense that the last days were present, but not quite over yet. The culmination of the prophetic events and the end of the age/ages was soon to come upon them.

The book of James may have been written early. Some believe that it may have been the first New Testament book written, perhaps in the mid 40s AD. So the events of AD 70 may have been a number of years off. Others think the book was written later, perhaps in the 50s or even early 60s AD.

Regardless, there seems to be even more urgency in the words of another New Testament writer which are thought to have been penned closer to AD 70. Let's look further, this time at another inspired apostle, John:

> And the **world** [*kosmos*] **is passing away**, and the lust of it; but he who does the will of God abides forever. Little children, **it is the last hour**; and as you have heard that the Antichrist is coming, even now many antichrists have come, by which we know that **it is the last hour**. They went out from us, but they were not of us; for if they had been of us, they would have continued with us; but they went out that they might be made manifest, that none of them were of us. (*1 John 2:17-19*)

Dating the book of 1 John is based on inferences drawn from the book itself. While some people place the book's writing years after AD 70, there is little to support that idea. It has the same tone as the other New Testament epistles, except that there is a greater sense of urgency about the time of the great consummation. This book was possibly written in the 60s AD, closer to the events of AD 70 than most or all of the other writers. James Stuart Russell, the author of a classic work on preterism, whom we will quote at various times in this book, had this to say, writing in 1878:

> It is impossible to overlook the fact, which everywhere meets us in this epistle, that the writer believes himself on the verge of a solemn crisis, for the arrival of which he urges his readers to be prepared. This is in harmony with all the apostolic epistles, and proves incontestably that their authors all alike shared in the belief of the near approach of the great consummation . . . .
> The last *times* become the last days, and now the last *days* become

the last *hour*. The period of expectation and delay was now over, and the decisive moment was at hand.[31]

Note the interesting statement in this passage in 1 John that the *world* [*kosmos*] *is passing away*. Unlike in Matthew where we saw the word *aion*, here we do see the Greek word *kosmos*. According to the online *Blue Letter Bible* lexicon, this word has 8 possible meanings. The first meaning is "an apt and harmonious arrangement or constitution, order, government." Another meaning is "the world, the universe." [32]

As always, context and cross-referencing determine how a word is to be understood. Which of these two meanings was John communicating as passing away? Using Scripture to interpret Scripture, we find Paul using a similar statement in the book of 1 Corinthians:

> For the **form** of this world [*kosmos*] is passing away. (*1 Corinthians 7:31*)

This passage helps to clarify what John, Paul, and the other New Testament writers were expecting. They were not expecting the end of the physical universe—but a very momentous change nonetheless. It would be the *form* of the world as they knew it that was changing. The *world order* in which they lived was passing away. The present tense used by both John and Paul in these last two passages tells us that they themselves were eyewitnesses to the change, and further, that the culmination of the change was imminent.

The message from each of the New Testament writers is consistent. They all point to an imminent first-century consummation. The last days and the end of the ages were upon *them*. Unless these writers were mistaken about the timing of the culminating events (and were thus not truly inspired), the events did in fact happen in the first century as they expected. In other words, if the apostles were anticipating the soon end of the physical universe, they were flat-out wrong. But if they were correct in their expectations, they were teaching something else—the imminent end of the *age*. About this they were indeed correct. The expected end of the age came in AD 70.

We further know that the apostles were not expecting the end of the physical universe, because they spoke of more distant ages to come. For example, the apostle Paul (who wrote two-thirds of the New Testament) in Ephesians 1:21 wrote of "the age to come," and in Ephesians 2:7 spoke of "the coming ages" in which Christ would show the riches of his grace. (Compare this to Hebrews 2:5). In Ephesians 3:21 Paul spoke of "all generations forever and ever." It does not make sense that Paul would speak of never-ending future ages if he expected the end of human history to take place in his generation. Nor does it make sense that the last days are in our future if the current New Covenant age has no end, which is indicated by these writers (Hebrews 13:20).

Confirmation that the "last days" ended with the destruction of the temple comes from an ancient writing called *The Epistle of Barnabas*. This was written after the destruction of the temple, perhaps near the close of the first century. The writer of this document considered the destruction of the temple to have occurred "in the last days." This letter is sometimes ascribed to Barnabas, who is mentioned in Acts, but its authorship is uncertain. The letter appeared as an appendix to the New Testament in some ancient compilations of the canon.[33]

An objection usually comes up at this point. Futurists say that "the last days," while *beginning* in the first century, are continuing today. *But it is not logical that the last (i.e., final, latter end) days could be longer than the period of which they are the end.* Here is what Russell wrote about this:

> The phrase, "the end of the ages" (Hebrews 9:26; 1 Corinthians 10:11) is equivalent to the "end of the age" (Matthew 13:39, 40, 49; 24:3; 28:20) and "the end" (Matthew 10:22; 24:6; 24:13-14; 1 Corinthians 1:8; 15:24; Hebrews 3:6; 3:14; 6:11; 1 Peter 4:7; Revelation 2:26). All refer to the same period, viz. the close of the Jewish age, or dispensation—that is, the Old Covenant—which was now at hand . . . . It is sometimes said that the whole period between the incarnation and the end of the world [i.e., the end of world history] is regarded in the New Testament as the "end of the age" [or the "last days"]. But this bears a manifest incongruity in its very front. How could the *end* of a period be a long protracted duration? Especially how could it be longer than the period of which it is the end? More time has already elapsed since the incarnation than from the giving of the law to the first coming of Christ: so that, on this hypothesis, the end of the age is a great deal longer than the age itself.[34]

So here is what we find in the New Testament. *There is not a single mention of "the last days" or the equivalent (last times, latter times, last hour) that clearly refers to any time outside the first century*—Acts 2:17; 1 Timothy 4:1; 2 Timothy 3:1; Hebrews 1:2; James 5:3; 2 Peter 3:3; 1 John 2:18; Jude 18.

FIRST AND SECOND PETER

The third place people think they find the end of the world is in Peter's epistles. These epistles are filled with eschatological expectations. You might want to take the time to read both books straight through. What he discusses is the expectation of a culminating cataclysmic event to happen very soon.

The language he used might seem to imply the total destruction of the visible creation. Peter used a variety of phrases in his epistles such as the "Day of the Lord," the "destruction of the heavens by fire," the "new heaven and earth," the "elements shall melt," etc. We will consider these terms in more detail in later chapters. But here we note that cosmic language was commonplace among the Old Testament prophets, speaking in *non-literal language about theological or covenantal events, and especially about actual judgments by God on guilty people—many of which are already fulfilled*! These previously fulfilled events in the Old Testament set the stage for understanding Peter's words.

Like the other writers, Peter gives us important time-reference statements. In his first epistle, Peter uses the phrase *last times* in a way that is consistent with his own comments in Acts 2:

> but with the precious blood of Christ, as of a lamb without blemish and without spot. He indeed was foreordained before the foundation of the world, but was manifest [has now revealed them to you, *New Living Translation*] **in these last times** for you. (*1 Peter 1:19-20*)

This declaration obviously cannot refer to a far distant time. Peter's statement indicates that the last days/last times included the time in which Christ was in the flesh; yet Peter was still in the last days as he spoke. Now consider this statement, which you may well have completely glossed over previously:

> **But the end of all things is at hand**; therefore be serious and watchful in your prayers. (*1 Peter 4:7*)

One can simply ignore such passages if he wishes, but one cannot ignore them and be faithful to God's Word. The imminence in Peter's mind is unmistakable. But Peter is not alone. The New Testament writers proclaimed with one voice that the "end" had drawn near. This will become increasingly clear as we continue.

In order for the Bible to be consistent, we must harmonize this statement with Peter's "astronomical" or "cosmic" language statements. The end of the physical universe was not at hand when Peter penned these words. Either Peter does not mean "at hand" in the normal sense of something close in time, or the cosmic language is not to be understood in the literal sense to describe the end of the physical universe. We think that the latter understanding is the only one consistent with Peter's words, as well as with the rest of the Bible.

The cosmic language does not describe the end of the physical universe but some other cataclysm that was close in time to Peter and the other writers of the New Testament. What Peter was expressing is that the end of all *old covenant* things was at hand. Peter was writing to the Israelites. He did not have to add the word "covenant" as this reference would have been understood by his readers at the time.

Remember that one of the precepts of biblical interpretation is that we interpret the less clear in light of the clear. *At hand* is clear; it means close in time—a meaning which is *confirmed by over 100 other imminency passages*. (Appendix A.) The astronomical language (which is less clear or at least less obvious to us moderns) must be interpreted in light of the clear imminency passages. So the cosmic language cannot be understood literally.

Our understanding of Peter's words should be interpreted in light of Hebraic apocalyptic language, which we will continue to examine throughout this book. But let's look in particular at 2 Peter 3:10 where Peter said, according to some translations, that the "elements" (Greek stoicheion) will be "burned up" (Greek katakaio). This passage is one that futurists rely on heavily. They say, "Look here! Obviously that has not happened yet." They think that "elements" refers to physics or chemistry—the elements of the periodic table (hydrogen, lithium, etc.).

The frame of reference for us today is what we learned in science class. But that was not the frame of reference for the first-century Hebrews. They were steeped in theology and Old Testament imagery.

The Bible is not a science book, but a religious book. The Scriptures throughout are about God's covenants with his people.

Let's consider how various versions of the Bible translate this verse, with particular notice of the Greek words *stoicheion* and *katakaio*:

> But the day of the Lord will come as a thief in the night, in which the heavens will pass away with a great noise, and the **elements** [*stoicheion*] will melt with fervent heat; both the earth and the works that are in it will be **burned up** [*katakaio*]. (*2 Peter 3:10, New King James Version*)

> But the day of the Lord will come like a thief, and then the heavens will pass away with a roar, and the **heavenly bodies** [*stoicheion*] will be burned up and dissolved, and the earth and the works that are done on it will be **exposed** [*katakaio*]. (*2 Peter 3:10, English Standard Version*)

> But the day of the Lord will come as unexpectedly as a thief. Then the heavens will pass away with a terrible noise, and the very **elements** [*stoicheion*] themselves will disappear in fire, and the earth and everything on it will be found to **deserve judgment** [*katakaio*]. (*2 Peter 3:10, New Living Translation*)

The first two versions, the New King James Version and the English Standard Version, are considered word-for-word translations. The third version, the New Living Translation, is a modern paraphrased translation.

We first note some distinct differences in how some of the words are translated. Let's consider first the word that is translated as "elements" in the first and third examples, and as "heavenly bodies" in the second example. This word in Greek is *stoicheion*. The online *Blue Letter Bible* lexicon gives various possible definitions of this word, including *heavenly bodies*. But the first definition given is "any first thing, from which the others belonging to some series or composite whole take their rise, an element, first principal."

Using the hermeneutical principle of using Scripture to interpret Scripture, let's consider every other use of *stoicheion* in the New Testament. We find that the apostle Paul also used this word (and never in reference to atomic elements) — first in Galatians 4:3 and 4:9. In Galatians, the word *stoicheion* is translated in the same above three versions of the Bible respectively as "elements," "elementary principles," and "spiritual principles." For example, here are these two verses from the English Standard Version:

> In the same way we also, when we were children, were enslaved to the **elementary principles** [*stoicheion*] of the world. . . . But now that you have come to know God, or rather to be known by God, how can you turn back again to the weak and worthless **elementary principles** [*stoicheion*] of the world [*kosmos*], whose slaves you want to be once more? (*Galatians 4:3, 9, English Standard Version*)

If you read Galatians 3, 4, and 5 you will find that the context is about how we are freed from the Law—the Old Covenant mandates! We are free from the Old Covenant, not from the material creation! Interestingly, Paul also used the word "world" (*kosmos*) in the same context—in reference to the Old Covenant world.

We find the word *stoicheion* used again by Paul in Colossians 2:8 and 2:20 in the same context—in reference to Christ freeing us from the Old Covenant mandates:

> Beware lest anyone cheat you through philosophy and empty deceit, according to the tradition of men, according to the **basic principles** [*stoicheion*] of the world, and not according to Christ. . . . Therefore, if you died with Christ from the **basic principles** [*stoicheion*] of the world, why, as though living in the world, do you subject yourselves to regulations— "Do not touch, do not taste, do not handle," which all concern things which perish with the using—according to the commandments and doctrines of men? (*Colossians 2:8, 20-22, New King James Version*)

The writer of Hebrews (Hebrews 5:12) used the term as well. The context is similar to the usage in Galatians and Colossians—Jesus is the new order of things that brings salvation. Hebrews 5:12-14 is titled "Spiritual Immaturity" in the New King James Version:

> For though by this time you ought to be teachers, you need someone to teach you again the **basic principles** [*stoicheion*] of the oracles of God. For everyone who partakes only of milk is unskilled in the word of righteousness, for he is a babe. (*Hebrews 5:12-13, New King James Version*)

These passages are the only ones outside of 2 Peter containing the word "elements" (*stoicheion*). *The interpretation of 2 Peter 3, therefore, becomes consistent and clear.* The "elements" are not physical world concepts, but spiritual things! Here is how Don K. Preston, a convert to preterism and writer of numerous prophecy books and articles, sums up the Bible's use of the word *stoicheion*:

> We thus have the passing of one world and the anticipation of another. The Old World is the Old Covenant World of Israel that anticipated and predicted the coming of the Messiah— these predictions were part of the elements, the first principles of Christ. The New World, the World to come, was initiated by the passion of Jesus and his work of atonement . . . . Hebrews then, agrees with Galatians and Colossians in its usage of the word "elements." It referred to the basic doctrines of Old Covenant Israel. In Galatians, Colossians and Hebrews the elements of that Old World (kosmos) were in the process of, and were ready to vanish away. Having observed all occurrences of the word *stoicheion* (elements), outside 2 Peter 3 we have seen that these references have nothing to do with physical creation. They refer exclusively to the basic doctrines and commands of the Old Covenant World of Israel. In each of the texts above the inspired writers predicted the passing of that Old World.[35]

But what about the words "burned up" (Greek *katakaio*)? If we have correctly identified the time frame as AD 70 and the "elements" as being about spiritual/covenantal issues, "burned up" also applies to AD 70 in a covenant context. Interestingly, "burned up" is literally correct about the destruction of the temple and Jerusalem. But other translations that say "exposed" or "found to deserve judgment" (or "laid bare" in the *New International Version*)—instead of "burned up"—would also be consistent with an AD 70 understanding. David A. Green points out the parallel between 2 Peter 3 and Isaiah 24:

> Peter's prophecy in 2 Peter 3 was a reiteration of Isaiah 24. In that chapter, Isaiah spoke of the time when the sun and the moon (the heavens) would be confounded and ashamed (Isaiah 24:23) and when the earth would be burned, broken down, dissolved, and would fade away (Isaiah 24:4, 6, 19-20). Isaiah was speaking of the destruction of Jerusalem (Isaiah 24:12).[36]

Some readers will stop and insist that the language of the heavens/ earth/burning, melting *just **sounds** too much like the end of the physical universe*. We will cover the concept of the new heaven(s) and new earth in more detail in Chapter 8, but let's preview one of the appropriate passages for that study, found in Matthew 5. Jesus is speaking:

> For assuredly, I say to you, till **heaven** and **earth** pass away, one jot or one tittle will by no means pass from the law till all is fulfilled. (*Matthew 5:18*)

If this is not clear, you might want to read it in other translations in addition to the New King James Version cited above. Jesus ties the passing of heaven and earth with the passing of the law. Reading this passage carefully reveals that unless "heaven and earth" have *already passed away*, every detail of the Law of Moses is *still in effect today*. Since the law has been replaced by the gospel, "heaven and earth" *must* have already passed away. This is perfectly consistent with Peter's statements of the heavens' and earth's imminent dissolution. It is confirmation from the lips of Jesus that "heaven and earth" is not a reference to the physical universe.

One verse that is always quoted in Peter's epistles to prove that the events are a long way off is 2 Peter 3:8, in which Peter compares a thousand years to a day. This passage cannot have a literal meaning, otherwise it would be nonsense. Thus it cannot mean that a short time really means a long time. If such an inference were possible it would be equally possible to infer the opposite, leaving only a logical nullity. Peter was likely referencing Psalm 90:4 to teach that God is sovereign over time and that his perspective on time differs from ours.

Peter may also have been quoting directly from the non-canonical Jewish book *Jubilees*, written about 200 years earlier. Jubilees, a book that was well-known to the early Christians, has this statement: "for one thousand years are as one day in the testimony of the heavens and therefore was it written concerning the tree of knowledge . . . ." This statement has a covenantal context. The thousand year period in Revelation, as we will see, also has a message concerning the completion of the Old Covenant order. These references are further evidences that Peter is describing the soon end of the Old Covenant Age.[37]

We will discuss the biblical usage of the number 1,000 when we consider the millennium. But suffice it to say for now that a "thousand" is a symbolic term of completeness. Peter is saying that covenantal completeness was coming soon. It also seems that scoffers (2 Peter 3:3) were deriding Christians, claiming that Jesus had not come soon as He had promised. Peter retorted, "The Lord is not slow to fulfill his promises." (2 Peter 3:9)

Peter was telling the scoffers that they should not make the mistake of believing Jesus had forgotten or overlooked his promise to return in their generation. He was warning the scoffers in no uncertain terms that "the Day of the Lord" would come and that *it would come upon those very scoffers* "as a thief in the night." The perceived delay or "slackness" was simply God's patience and longsuffering toward all who would come to repentance and be saved in the last generation of the Old Covenant Age (2 Peter 3:9).

Peter told his readers in verses 11-13 that *they* were to be looking for the coming Day of the Lord. If we are to receive a message as to the timing of the events in the statement about a thousand years being as a day, we submit that it means the opposite of what futurists think. Peter means that the expected events were a *short* time into the future, especially given the other imminency passages in his epistles.

In Peter's writings we have both a clear time-reference and a confirming exegesis from other parts of the New Testament that what is in view by Peter is the imminent end of the Old Covenant Age, not the end of the universe. This understanding is consistent with what we have considered so far about the *end of the age* and the *last days*. Remember, the Bible must be consistent if it is indeed God's Word. Go back and read 2 Peter 3 again and see if it doesn't make perfect sense now from a preterist perspective.

We will come back to Peter later and consider further the terms "Day of the Lord" and "New Heavens and a New Earth." We will see that these terms likewise are completely consistent with the preterist viewpoint. For now, we hope to emphasize that the last days are, in our judgment, not the end of the universe, but rather the days of cataclysmic events that surrounded the national judgment of Israel, the destruction of Jerusalem, and the end of the Old Covenant world.

Question for further discussion with your pastor, friends, and church leaders:

I couldn't help thinking about the prayer in church that we often hear for Jesus to come soon. Doesn't it seem misplaced that Christians find hope in the destruction of the planet and millions killed in a holocaust?

THE "END" TIMES

The Old Testament books of Isaiah, Ezekiel, Zechariah, Daniel, and Malachi are often quoted for their eschatological content. Of these, Daniel is perhaps most pertinent concerning the issue of the end of the world/ age. Daniel employs variations of the phrase "latter days" or "the end" in numerous instances.[38] A major theme of Daniel is the coming of the Messiah, the initiation of his kingdom, and the dissolution of the Jewish dispensation. You might find it helpful to go to your Bible and underline the phrases we mention in our discussion of Daniel 12. This chapter contains important eschatological references, and in many Bibles has the title: "The Time of the End." Well, the end of what?

We find many interesting prophetic terms to consider in this final chapter of Daniel, such as *the time of distress/trouble* (12:1), the *resurrection* (12:2), the *time of the end* (12:6, 9, 13), and the *abomination of desolation* (12:11). These tie together. Note that the text does not say, the "end of time," but rather the "time of the end." In fact, the Bible never speaks of the end of time! [39]

We discover also another important time-reference. Daniel gives us distinct clues as to when these things would take place. The revelation given to Daniel says:

> And he said, "Go your way, Daniel, for the words are closed up and sealed till the time of the **end**. Many shall be purified, made white, and refined, but the wicked shall do wickedly; and none of the wicked shall understand, but the wise shall understand. "And from the **time that the daily sacrifice is taken away**, and the **abomination of desolation** is set up, there shall be one thousand two hundred and ninety days. Blessed is he who waits, and comes to the one thousand three hundred and thirty-five days. "But you, go your way till the **end**; for you shall rest, and will arise to your inheritance at the **end of the days**." (*Daniel 12:9-13*)

When would the daily sacrifice be taken away? By now this should sound familiar to the reader. It would certainly fit the time frame of the Jewish War, in (or just before) AD 70 when the temple was destroyed and the age-old system of sacrifices for sin ended. It seems surprising to us that anyone could overlook this clear reference, but many do.[40]

We will consider more of Daniel in the next chapter. The "end" spoken of by Daniel is not the end of the planet. It is the end of the age—the Old Covenant Mosaic Age that ended in AD 70.

The reader is referred to Appendix B to the chart entitled "A Tale of Two Ages."

Here are some Questions for further discussion with your pastor, church leaders, and friends that will certainly generate some interesting conversation:

- Could you show me in the Bible where it clearly and unambiguously mentions the end of the universe or the end of the planet?

- The end time mentioned in the book of Daniel was to be when the burnt offering was taken away (Daniel 9:27 and 12:11). Since burnt offerings ended in AD 70, doesn't that mean the time of the end (and thus "the last days") was in the first century? [41]

- Does any mention of the last days (or last times, or last hour) in the New Testament clearly refer to any time outside of the first century (Acts 2:14-20; 1 Timothy 4:1; 2 Timothy 3:1; Hebrews 1:2; James 5:3-9; 1 Peter 1:5; 1 Peter 1:20; 1 Peter 4:7; 2 Peter 3:3; 1 John 2:18; Jude 18)?

- What does Peter mean by "The end of all things is at hand" (1 Peter 4:7)? Was Peter mistaken?

- What does the term "elements" (Greek *stoicheion*) in 2 Peter 3 refer to, given how the word is used in Galatians 4:3, 9; Colossians 2:8, 20, and Hebrews 5:12?

- Isn't the understanding of the New Testament writers about what was to happen explained by Paul when he said in 1 Corinthians 10:11 that the end of the ages had come, and in 1 Corinthians 7:29-31 when he said that it was the form (or fashion) of the world that was passing away—not the end of the physical universe?

- If you think there is more than one "end of the age" or "last day"—one in the first century and one thousands of years later—where is the scriptural support for that view?

5

The Great Tribulation and Judgment

In the book of Daniel we find these prophetic visions:

> And after the sixty-two weeks Messiah shall be cut off, but not for Himself; and the people of the prince who is to come shall **destroy the city and the sanctuary**. The end of it shall be with a flood, and **till the end of the war desolations** are determined. Then he shall confirm a covenant with many for one week; but in the middle of the week He shall bring an **end to sacrifice** and offering. And on the wing of **abominations** shall be one who makes **desolate**, even until the consummation, which is determined, is poured out on the **desolate**. . . . And there shall be a **time of trouble, such as never was since there was a nation, even to that time**. And at that time your people shall be delivered, everyone who is found written in the book. . . . And from the time that the **daily sacrifice is taken away**, and the **abomination of desolation** is set up, there shall be one thousand two hundred and ninety days. (*Daniel 9:26-27; 12:1b; 12:11*)

In the book of Malachi we find this prophecy:

> "Behold, I send my messenger, and he will prepare the way before Me. And the Lord, whom you seek, will suddenly come to his **temple**, even the **Messenger of the covenant**, in whom

you delight. Behold, He is coming," Says the LORD of hosts. "But who can endure the day of his coming? And who can stand when He appears? For **He is like a refiner's fire** and like launderers' soap. . . . And I will come near you for **judgment**; . . . "For behold, the day is coming, **burning like an oven**, and all the proud, yes, all who do wickedly will be stubble. And the **day which is coming shall burn them up**," says the LORD of hosts, "That will leave them neither **root nor branch**. But to you who fear my name the Sun of Righteousness shall arise with healing in his wings; and you shall go out and grow fat like stall-fed calves. You shall **trample the wicked**, for they shall be ashes under the soles of your feet on the day that I do this," says the LORD of hosts. "Remember the Law of Moses, my servant, which I commanded him in Horeb for all Israel, with the statutes and judgments. Behold, **I will send you Elijah the prophet before the coming of the great and dreadful day of the LORD**. And he will turn the hearts of the fathers to the children, and the hearts of the children to their fathers, lest I come and strike the earth with a curse." (*Malachi 3:1, 2, 5a; 4:1-5*)

Both of these passages are Messianic judgment prophecies. This latter prophecy from Malachi ties directly to John the Baptist. Jesus identified John as having fulfilled the prophecy of the return of Elijah. John the Baptist himself picked up on this prophecy with a prediction in Chapter 3 of the book of Matthew, using very similar language as in Malachi:

[7] But when he saw many of the Pharisees and Sadducees coming to his baptism, he said to them, "Brood of vipers! Who warned you to flee from the **wrath [about to,** Greek *mello*] **come**? . . . [11] I indeed baptize you with water unto repentance, but He who is coming after me is mightier than I, whose sandals I am not worthy to carry. He will baptize **you** with the Holy Spirit and **fire**. . . . [12] His winnowing fan is in His hand, and He will thoroughly clean out his threshing floor, and gather his wheat into the barn; but He will **burn up the chaff with unquenchable fire**." (*Matthew 3:7, 11, 12*)

The "time of trouble" of which Daniel spoke, and the "wrath [about to, Greek mello] come?" of which John the Baptist spoke, are generally considered by Christians—futurists as well as preterists—to be the so-called Great Tribulation. Supporting the preterist view, John the Baptist here specifically implicates the first-century Jews (the Pharisees and Sadducees) as the target of the coming wrath. Who was baptized with fire? It is not us today, but the first-century apostate Jews. The winnowing fan was in Jesus' hand; the events were imminent.

What were the crimes of the Jews of that generation that they deserved such vengeance? They persecuted the church, and of course, they ultimately rejected Jesus and had Him crucified. Jesus himself continually chastised the Jews for various offenses. But Jewish historian Josephus elaborates on the Jews in his time. He stated that they vied among themselves to come up with "new and unheard of paths of vice. They paraded their enormities and exhibited their vices as though they were virtues, striving daily to outdo each other in being the worst." Josephus further said that "since the world began" there had never been "a generation more prolific in crime." [42] These statements tie in with the words of Jesus in the Olivet Discourse:

Therefore when you see the "**abomination of desolation**," **spoken of by Daniel** the prophet, standing in the holy place" (whoever reads, let him understand), "then let those who are in Judea flee to the mountains. Let him who is on the housetop not go down to take anything out of his house. And let him who is in the field not go back to get his clothes. But woe to those who are pregnant and to those who are nursing babies in those days! And pray that your flight may not be in winter or on the Sabbath. **For then there will be Great Tribulation, such as has not been since the beginning of the world until this time, no, nor ever shall be.** And unless those days were shortened, no flesh would be saved; but for the elect's sake those days will be shortened. (*Matthew 24:15-22*)

We see that Jesus refers to Daniel and uses nearly identical language as Daniel to describe the coming holocaust of AD 66-70. We also look to Luke's parallel account for further clarification:

But when you see Jerusalem surrounded by armies, then know that its desolation is near. Then let those who are in Judea flee to the mountains, let those who are in the midst of her depart, and let not those who are in the country enter her. For **these are the days of vengeance**, that all things which are written

> may be fulfilled. But woe to those who are pregnant and to those who are nursing babies in those days! For there will be **great distress in the land** and **wrath upon this people**. And they will fall by the edge of the sword, and be led away captive into all nations. And Jerusalem will be trampled by Gentiles until the times of the Gentiles are fulfilled. (*Luke 21:20-24*)

Most Christians think that the Great Tribulation is still in our future. But we have shown that the words of Daniel chapter 12 and of Jesus in Matthew chapter 24 concerning the end times both relate to the first century, the end of the Old Covenant Age, and the wrath upon the Jews. And as we explore in detail in the next chapter, we find that Jesus clearly states that *all* of these things were to happen in his generation (Matthew 24:34; Mark 13:30; Luke 21:22, 32). This time frame is the obvious fit for all of these passages.

Interestingly, many Christians also think that the tribulation will be a global event. But notice that Jesus said that one could avoid the tribulation by fleeing to the mountains (Luke 21:21). So this desolation/tribulation would be a regional event, not global. Obviously, the region in view is Jerusalem and Judea, as Jesus stated plainly.

Luke's version makes it perfectly clear that the wrath that was to come was (a) about Jerusalem/Judea, (b) would occur when Jerusalem was surrounded by armies, and (c) would be the time when Jerusalem was trampled by the Gentiles. There cannot be much doubt that this was AD 70, can there?

But we have further confirmation. Note the term *abomination of desolation* used by both Daniel and Jesus. What is that about? The books of 1 and 2 Maccabees (books in the Roman Catholic Bible but not in the Protestant Bible) mention the term in reference to the actions of King Antiochus IV Epiphanes in the mid-second century BC.[43] The ruler set up an altar to Zeus in the Second Temple in Jerusalem, and sacrificed swine on it in 168 or 167 BC. This was a desecration of the temple. So the *abomination of desolation* referred there to the desecration of the temple. But Jesus and Daniel used the term to refer to a new abomination that would occur in the events of his Second Coming.

One thing that has intrigued Christians through the ages is the mention in Daniel's prophecy of various periods of days and weeks. All kinds of speculations surround the interpretation of these, which may require a literal understanding or may be merely symbolic. One such period mentioned in Daniel 12:11 is 1,290 days—which is approximately three and a half years. One possible starting point for this period is this: In a series of events during the war of AD 66-70, two groups of radicals—the Zealots and the Idumeans—stormed the temple and committed acts of mass murder. This could certainly be considered a desecration of the temple. While the timing of the events is uncertain, some think these assaults were about three and a half years before the burning of the temple in AD 70.[44]

Others argue that other events associated with the war better fit the timeline. One possible construct is outlined by authors Michael Fenemore and Kurt Simmons.[45] Vespasian began his Judean campaign in February, AD 67. The Temple burned in August, AD 70. The intervening period was exactly three and a half years.

The three and a half year period, interestingly, matches another curious statement just a few verses earlier in Daniel 12:7, which reads "that it shall be for a time, times, and half a time; and when the power of the holy people has been completely shattered, all these things shall be finished." The meaning of this statement is almost universally accepted to be three and a half years. ("Time" means one year; "times" means two years more; plus a "half of a time" means half of a year—totaling three and a half years.) [46]

Just to pique your interest to the many ties to Daniel we will find later in our exploration, in Revelation 11:2 we find this statement: "But leave out the court which is outside the temple, and do not measure it, for it has been given to the Gentiles. And they will tread the holy city underfoot for forty-two months." Forty-two months is also three and a half years. We will later prove that Revelation is covering the same events as Daniel. But let's not get ahead of ourselves.

We see the days/weeks schemata mentioned elsewhere in Daniel. What do these mean? Christians have proposed detailed systems to make them align consistently with historical (or speculative future) events. But we will avoid going down rabbit trails here and instead stick with what is the clearest information, and that is the time frame given to us by Daniel via his prophesied end of sacrifices. The end of temple sacrifices for sin ended at a known date—AD 70, a date that is critical in eschatology. So we will focus our attention on that.

By giving us the phrase from Jesus, *wrath upon this people* (Luke 21:23), Luke also helps us solidify that the desolation/tribulation was about God's judgment on the Jewish people in the first century. This is completely consistent with the words of John the Baptist in Matthew 3:7 (above), who specifically names the Pharisees and Sadducees as the targets of Jesus' coming wrath! It was not about a general judgment upon the world but upon a specific group of people in a specific place and time in Jesus' generation. (See also Ezekiel 5:5-12.)

But wait. Jesus said in Matthew's account that it will be the *worst tribulation ever*. Can the events of the Jewish-Roman War qualify for such a superlative statement? In Chapter 2 we demonstrated how Jesus often spoke in hyperbole. That is, He used exaggeration as a figure of speech to make a point. But in terms of Jewish history and covenant, the events surrounding AD 70 were without exaggeration the most horrific days ever to befall God's people. Recall the words of the historian Flavius Josephus, which we repeat here:

> Neither did any other city ever suffer such miseries, nor did any age ever breed a generation more fruitful in wickedness than this was, from the beginning of the world. . . . The multitude of those that therein perished exceeded all the destructions that either men or God ever brought upon the world.

This eyewitness account from Josephus, describing the catastrophe that befell Jerusalem, is uncannily close to the words of Jesus. Josephus' words, written after AD 70, strongly point to a fulfillment of the prophecies of Daniel, Malachi, John the Baptist, and Jesus. Now notice other details of descriptive statements that Jesus used to tell his listeners how terrible the coming disaster would be. Notice, for example, the mention of suffering women in Matthew 24:19, and remember the description we gave in Chapter 1 about the horrors of the war. Josephus described the woman named Mary, daughter of Eleazar, slaying her own infant son for food. Indeed, it almost sounds like Josephus had a copy of the Bible on his desk when he was writing his history.

In Matthew 24:28 Jesus prophesied of exposed carcasses. Here is what Josephus said about what he actually witnessed during the Jewish-Roman War:

> And indeed the multitude of **carcasses** that lay in heaps one upon another was a horrible sight, and produced a pestilential stench, which was a hindrance to those that would make sallies out of the city.[47]

Here is another quote from the writings of Josephus that tells just how devastating the war was:

There was no longer anything to lead those who visited the spot [where the city of Jerusalem had been] to believe that it had ever been inhabited.[48]

The prophecy of Jesus in the Olivet Discourse about this coming disaster was hardly an exaggeration. While Josephus was a Jew, not a Christian, his writings confirm that the prophecies of Jesus came to pass within the time frame that Jesus said they would. We will cover more of these prophetic events in the Olivet Discourse in the next chapter.

But here we focus on the tribulation and judgment. These two events are linked. Actually, the Bible speaks of different sorts of *judgments*. It speaks of the judgment that each of us will receive when we die. As we read in Hebrews: "It is appointed for men to die once, but after this the judgment" (Hebrews 9:27). But the Bible also speaks of judgments of nations and people groups in history. Prophecies of these events were fairly common in the Old Testament.

One thing in the section of Daniel above, on its face, seems to be a problem for the preterist view. It says in Daniel 9:26 that these events would come with a *flood*. But the events of AD 70 were not about a flood, but rather about the Roman army's destruction. However, in Luke chapter 17, where Jesus covers some of the same material as in the Olivet Discourse, we find him comparing the coming destruction with what happened to Noah!

> And as it was in the days of **Noah**, so it will be also in the days of the Son of Man: They ate, they drank, they married wives, they were given in marriage, until the day that **Noah** entered the ark, and the **flood** came and destroyed them all. (*Luke 17:26-27*)

So Jesus clarifies Daniel's words for us, teaching that the Great Tribulation would be a tremendous disaster for the unfaithful and unbelievers, in a sense comparable in biblical history to the Great Flood.[49] Also, the image of a flood is used in the Old Testament as a metaphor for an invading army overflowing its borders and invading another country.[50] All things considered, the prophecies of Daniel, Malachi, John the Baptist, and Jesus are amazingly consistent and "spot on" about the judgment that was to come upon the nation of Israel in AD 70. The Bible is proven to be a document that consistently predicts events ahead of time to a degree that no other prophetic material has ever accomplished. The skeptic cannot fail to be impressed that these men—Daniel and Malachi, and then John the Baptist and Jesus, writing hundreds of years apart about the same event, were so amazingly accurate in their predictions.

Many of Jesus' parables are clear warnings about the judgment that was about to come upon the Jewish nation in the end of the age. For example, let's look at the Parable of the Wicked Tenants (or sometimes called the Parable of the Wicked Vinedressers) found in Matthew 21:

> Hear another parable: There was a certain landowner who planted a vineyard and set a hedge around it, dug a winepress in it and built a tower. And he leased it to vinedressers and went into a far country. Now when vintage-time drew near, he sent his servants to the vinedressers, that they might receive its fruit. And the vinedressers took his servants, beat one, killed one, and stoned another. Again he sent other servants, more than the first, and they did likewise to them. Then last of all he sent his son to them, saying, "They will respect my **son**." But when the vinedressers saw the son, they said among themselves, "This is the heir. Come, let us kill him and seize his inheritance." So they took him and cast him out of the vineyard and killed him. Therefore, when the owner of the vineyard comes, what will he do to those vinedressers? They said to Him, **"He will destroy those wicked men miserably, and lease his vineyard to other vinedressers who will render to him the fruits in their seasons."** Jesus said to them, "Have you never read in the Scriptures: 'The stone which the builders rejected has become the chief cornerstone. This was the LORD's doing, and it is marvelous in our eyes'? Therefore I say to you, the **kingdom of God will be taken from you** and given to a nation bearing the fruits of it. And whoever falls on this stone will be broken; but on whomever it falls, it will grind him to powder." **Now when the chief priests and Pharisees heard his parables, they perceived that He was speaking of them.** But when they sought to lay hands on Him, they feared the multitudes, because they took Him for a prophet. (*Matthew 21:33-46*)

It is perfectly clear that the Jews were the target of God's wrath for rejecting his Son—the chief Cornerstone. The message was understood by the chief priests and Pharisees! Not only were they going to be judged and killed, but the kingdom would be given to others. This was not something that would happen two thousand years later. Those hearing Jesus' words were the target of the coming judgment!

No twisting of language, no double meanings, and no wishful thinking can deflect what Jesus was saying. There was a wrathful judgment coming upon the Jews who were hearing Jesus' words. This is not about the end of world history. It is about the first century. We must forcefully reject any idea to the contrary. Or as better stated by Russell: "The bearing of this parable on the people of our Savior's time is so direct and explicit, that it might be supposed that no critic would have to seek for a hidden meaning, or an ulterior reference." [51]

As put by David Chilton, "In the destruction of their city, their civilization, their Temple, their entire world-order, they would understand that Christ had ascended to His Throne as Lord of heaven and earth." [52] Just as God used the Babylonians to punish the Jews in an earlier time, God used the Romans to punish the Jewish nation in AD 70 for their crimes of commission and omission, including the murder of the saints and of the Son of God himself.

The nation of Israel ceased at the same time that the temple was destroyed. The priesthood ceased, as the genealogical tables and the important Levitical records were concomitantly destroyed. The age of offering animal sacrifices in the temple ended. It was an unprecedented time of upheaval in terms of transferring the custody of God's covenant away from the twelve tribes of ethnic Israel to believers in Israel's Messiah, the Lord Jesus Christ.

One cannot underestimate the meaning of this event. As the writer of Hebrews (8:13) said a few years before AD 70, the old covenant was obsolete and aging and was soon to disappear. As Russell elaborated, "The chosen people, the children of the Friend of God, the favored nation, with whom the God of the whole earth deigned to enter into covenant and to be called their King—were about to be overwhelmed by the most terrible calamities that ever befell a nation. . . . But there was also to be a glorious change in this world. The old made way for the new; the Law was replaced by the Gospel; Moses was superseded by Christ. The narrow and exclusive system, which embraced only a single people, was succeeded by a new and better covenant, which embraced the whole family of man. . . . The destruction of Jerusalem was not a mere thrilling incident in the drama of history, like the siege of Troy or the downfall of Carthage, closing a chapter in the annals of a state or a people. It was an event that has no parallel in history. It was the outward and visible sign of a great epoch in the divine government of the world. It was the close of one dispensation and the commencement of another. It marked the inauguration of a new order of things. The Mosaic economy—which had been ushered in by the miracles of Egypt, the lightnings and thunderings of Sinai, and the glorious manifestations of Jehovah to Israel—after subsisting for more than fifteen centuries, was now abolished." [53]

Let's consider a second parable, The Parable of the Wedding Banquet (or the Parable of the Wedding Feast), again from Matthew's Gospel:

And Jesus answered and spoke to them again by parables and said: "The kingdom of heaven is like a certain king who arranged a marriage for his son, and sent out his servants to call those who were invited to the wedding; and they were not willing to come. Again, he sent out other servants, saying, 'Tell those who are invited, see, I have prepared my dinner; my oxen and fatted cattle are killed, and all things are ready. Come to the wedding.'" But they made light of it and went their ways, one to his own farm, another to his business. And the rest seized his servants, treated them spitefully, and killed them. **But when the king heard about it, he was furious. And he sent out his armies, destroyed those murderers, and burned up their city. Then he said to his servants, 'The wedding is ready, but those who were invited were not worthy.** Therefore go into the highways, and as many as you find, invite to the wedding.' So those servants went out into the highways and gathered together all whom they found, both bad and good. And the wedding hall was filled with guests. But when the king came in to see the guests, he saw a man there who did not have on a wedding garment. So he said to him, 'Friend, how did you come in here without a wedding garment?' And he was speechless. Then the king said to the servants, 'Bind him hand and foot, take him away, and cast him into outer darkness; there will be weeping and gnashing of teeth.' For many are called, but few are chosen." (*Matthew 22:1-14*)

This parable so obviously fits what happened in AD 70—armies, destruction, burning city, etc.—that it might send chills down your spine. (At least it had that effect on this author, the first time he read it in the proper context.) This parable was aimed directly at the Jews of Jesus' generation. The weight of the charge by Jesus was felt by the Jews themselves, as the very next verse suggests:

> Then the Pharisees went and plotted how they might entangle Him in his talk. (*Matthew 22:15*)

Perhaps you have previously read these parables without the context we have brought to your attention. We are confident that when you go back and read the other parables of Jesus, you will often see AD 70 in them too.

Consider further this passage in Matthew 23, which is not in parable form, but an explicit indictment of the scribes and Pharisees by Jesus:

> **Woe to you, scribes and Pharisees, hypocrites**! Because you build the tombs of the prophets and adorn the monuments of the righteous, and say, "If we had lived in the days of our fathers, we would not have been partakers with them in the blood of the prophets." Therefore you are witnesses against yourselves that you are sons of those who murdered the prophets. Fill up, then, the measure of your fathers' guilt. Serpents, brood of vipers! How can you escape the condemnation of hell? Therefore, indeed, I send you prophets, wise men, and scribes: some of them you will kill and crucify, and some of them you will scourge in your synagogues and persecute from city to city, that on **you** may come **all the righteous blood shed on the earth**, from the blood of righteous Abel to the blood of Zechariah, son of Berechiah, whom you murdered between the temple and the altar. Assuredly, I say to you, **all these things will come upon this generation. O Jerusalem, Jerusalem**, the one who kills the prophets and stones those who are sent to her! How often I wanted to gather your children together, as a hen gathers her chicks under her wings, but you were not willing! See! Your house is left to you desolate; for I say to you, **you** shall see Me no more till **you** say, "Blessed is **He who comes** in the name of the LORD!" (*Matthew 23:29-39.* See also a parallel passage in *Luke 11:49-53*)

This is an amazing passage. It is a lead-in to the Second Coming section to follow immediately in Matthew 24, which we will consider in the next chapter. Here Jesus said that all the righteous blood ever shed on earth all the way back to creation would fall upon his generation! No one can doubt that *this generation* in this passage means those living at that time—since Jesus not only is laying the guilt and judgment upon the scribes and Pharisees to whom he is speaking, but is lamenting specifically for Jerusalem. This is about the national judgment that was soon to befall Israel in AD 70, at Jesus' *Second Coming* (Matthew 23:39).

The imminence of this great judgment is all over the New Testament. Consider these additional passages:

> the times, indeed, therefore, of the ignorance God having overlooked, doth now command all men everywhere to reform, because He did set a day in which He is **about to judge** the world in righteousness, by a man whom He did ordain, having given assurance to all, having raised him out of the dead. (*Acts 17:30-31, Young's Literal Translation*)

> but a certain fearful looking for of **judgment**, and fiery zeal, **about to devour the opposers**; (*Hebrews 10:27, Young's Literal Translation*)

> Do not grumble against one another, brethren, lest you be condemned. Behold, **the Judge is standing at the door!** (*James 5:9*)

> who shall give an account to Him who is **ready to judge living and dead** (*1 Peter 4:5, Young's Literal Translation*)

> **For the time has come for judgment to begin** at the house of God; and if it begins with us first, what will be the end of those who do not obey the gospel of God? (*1 Peter 4:17*)

God continues to judge individuals and nations (Numbers 32:23; 2 Chronicles 7:14; Job 12:23; Psalm 9:17-20; 33:12; 110:6; Proverbs 14:34; Ecclesiastes 12:14; Isaiah 2:4; 60:12; Micah 4:3; John 3:36; Acts 10:42-43; Romans 1:18; 6:23; 12:19; 14:12; 2 Corinthians 5:10; Galatians 6:7; Ephesians 5:3-6; Hebrews 9:27; 13:4; Revelation 2:10; 14:13; 21:8; 22:14-15). God did not retire in AD 70. Indeed, his wrath is mentioned some forty-six times in the New Testament. His righteous judgment against all ungodliness and unfaithfulness continues.

But the **Great Judgment**, of which the New Testament speaks repeatedly, came to pass in AD 70, just as it had been prophesied! The tribulation and judgment are inexorably linked to each other and to the first century. The subject of the great judgment will come up again in several places in our study as it is linked to still other events. As we consider these things further in Chapters 6 and 7, it will become even clearer that the tribulation and judgment are tied to the Second Coming.

Questions for further discussion with your pastor, church leaders, and friends:

- What do you think about the Great Tribulation?
- Do you think it is still future?
- Do you think it was to be a global disaster or a regional one?

---

6 The Second Coming of Christ in the Olivet Discourse

> *"If you believe what you like in the gospels, and reject what you don't like, it is not the gospel you believe, but yourself."*
>
> —*Saint Augustine*

A s we noted previously, the Olivet Discourse encompasses the largest body of New Testament prophecy outside of the book of Revelation. The discourse is contained in the parallel passages of Matthew 24-25, Mark 13, and Luke 21. Luke 17 contains some supporting material. When people talk about the Second Coming, they often go to the Olivet Discourse first.

For future reference in this book as well as in your own study, there are various Greek words used in the New Testament to describe the Second Coming. The primary word is the noun *parousia*. It is sometimes capitalized to be consistent with the English capitalization of Second Coming. It means presence, arrival, advent, or coming. Secondary nouns are *epiphaneia* (an appearing or appearance) and *apokalypsis* (a revelation, appearance, or unveiling). The primary verb is *erchomai* (to come). Secondary verbs are *phaneroo* (to make manifest), *optanomai* (to appear), and *heko* (to be present). *Parousia* is used for Jesus' Second Coming four times in Matthew's version of the Olivet Discourse (Matthew 24:3, 27, 37, 39). *Erchomai* is used for Jesus' Second Coming five times in Matthew 24 (Matthew 24:30, 42, 44, 46, 48) and five times in Matthew 25 (Matthew 25:6, 10, 13, 27, 31).[54]

"Second Coming" is actually not a term found in the Bible. That is, "Second" is not attached to "Parousia" (or the other nouns above). Parousia (pronounced pah-roo-see'-ah or pair-oo-see'-ah), when used in reference to Jesus' return, really means "presence" (as opposed to absence)—and this is exactly how it is translated in Young's Literal Translation. (Go to Bible Gateway online and look up Matthew 24 in Young's Literal Translation for confirmation.) The common rendering of the word simply as "coming" may be adequate but somewhat misleading. "Coming" is correct insofar as it describes God's effectual divine presence as found in the Old and New Testaments. The use of the word "coming" is justified because there is an assumption that there must be a coming in order for there to be a presence. This would be a correct assumption in the case of a human being, but an incorrect assumption on the part of deity. In other words, God's presence does not mean that He was absent previously.[55]

We propose the following terms as better translations for the Parousia. Any of these would be closer to the biblical meaning:

- Returning Presence
- Divine Presence
- Effectual Presence
- Effecting Presence

Partial preterists often use the term "metaphorical" to describe Jesus' coming in judgment in AD 70. But this term fails to describe the event adequately. Jesus' Second Coming was *real*. It was just not a visible *bodily* return that most Christians have in view. We are partial to the phrase *effectual divine presence* as describing Christ's Parousia.

It would at least be better to leave *parousia* in the Greek form in English translations rather than to translate *parousia* as "coming." However, we acquiesce to convention and use the term Second Coming.

The question is: *Did Jesus predict that his Second Coming would occur in the first century?* He clearly did, and his disciples thought that He clearly did. In opening verses of Matthew 24, the disciples asked Jesus a simple and direct question:

Then Jesus went out and departed from the temple, and his disciples came up to show Him the buildings of the temple. And

Jesus said to them, "Do you not see all these things? Assuredly, I say to you, not one stone shall be left here upon another, that shall not be thrown down." Now as He sat on the Mount of Olives, the disciples came to Him privately, saying, "<u>Tell us, when will these things be? And what will be the sign of your **coming** [*parousia*], and of the end of the age?</u>" (*Matthew 24:1-3*)

First notice that the disciples tied the Second Coming with the end of the age, which we have already, hopefully, successfully argued was the end of the Old Covenant Age which ended in AD 70. Even though a short break in time is implied between verses two and three, the flow of the discussion ties the destruction of the temple with the Second Coming. In verses 27 and 30, near the end of a list of details about the prophecy, Jesus confirms that his Parousia is the focus of the disciples' question:

For as the lightning comes from the east and flashes to the west, so also will the **coming** [*parousia*] of the Son of Man be. . . . Then the sign of the Son of Man will appear in heaven, and then all the tribes of the earth will mourn, and they will see the Son of Man **coming** [*erchomai*] on the clouds of heaven with power and great glory. (*Matthew 24:27, 30*)

Then, just four verses later, He gives us a time constraint for the fulfillment of his prophecies, which encompasses the Second Coming:

Assuredly, I say to you, **this generation** will by no means pass away till **all** these things take place. (*Matthew 24:34*)

Jesus never veers from the topic and does not lose his focus, which is his Second Coming and simultaneous judgment upon Jerusalem in the end of the age. No shift in the subject would have been discernible to the original audience. If our Lord said it, Christians ought to believe it; however, they often do not. **All** of Jesus' predictions were to be fulfilled in **his own generation**. There are over one hundred time frame references and implications in the Bible that support the idea that the last days and the Second Coming were to be in the first century. (Appendix A.)

In Luke's version of the Olivet Discourse (Luke 21:22), Jesus is recorded as making an even more sweeping statement that does not appear in Matthew's or Mark's versions of the Olivet Discourse. Here is verse 22 (along with verse 32, which is not unique to Luke's Gospel):

> For **these** are the days of vengeance, that **all** things which are written may be fulfilled. . . . Assuredly, I say to you, <u>this generation</u> will by no means pass away till **all** things take place. (*Luke 21:22, 32*)

In verse 22, we see Jesus proclaiming that ALL *Old Testament* prophecy would be fulfilled in his generation (in addition to his own additional prophecies, verse 32)! Verse 22 has been enough to convince some Christians to become preterists. While some people think "these" (days) really means "those," there is little doubt that Jesus was referring to his own time. This is confirmation that Jesus meant what He said about the timing of not only his Second Coming, but of all the other things He predicted in the Olivet Discourse and elsewhere in his teachings.

Also, some people say that "all" in these verses does not mean 100%. It is true that "all" is sometimes used hyperbolically in the Bible to mean "a very great number" rather than literally "all." The context determines its interpretation. The context here is clear. Jesus is referring to the days in which He and his contemporaries were living, in which all Old Testament prophecy plus every prophecy He uttered in the Olivet Discourse would be fulfilled.

Luke 21 further confirms the imminency of the prophesied events. Note verse 36, which is clearest in the New International Version. This version includes the correct interpretation of the Greek word *mello* which appears in the text. This word means "about to," proving the important sense of imminence of the prophesied events:

> Be always on the watch, and pray that you may be able to escape all that is **about** [Greek, *mello*] **to happen**, and that you may be able to stand before the Son of Man." (*Luke 21:36, New International Version*)

So, in Luke's version of the Olivet Discourse, there are *three verses* that express the radical imminence of the coming events: verses 22, 32, and 36. Nowhere does Jesus tell us that some events were imminent and others were in the far distant future. If you are a Christian with some familiarity with prophecy, as you read these things you may be thinking of objections to the preterist view. We welcome your challenges and will certainly cover the most common objections. But let us plainly state that there is nothing in the term "this generation" or the other imminence terminology found in the Olivet Discourse (or anywhere else in the Bible) that means our own generation 2,000 years later.

Does Jesus ever lie, mislead, or deceive? As we diligently work through what Holy Scripture has to say further about this matter, we will argue that many Christians have simply misunderstood what Jesus meant by his Second Coming.

The Parousia of Jesus was very real and historically discernible, but not in the way that most people assume. The effects of his coming would be clearly seen, but not his physical appearance. Yes, we know this may sound bewildering, and the reader's initial response may be a bit of discomfort. But please continue with us through this biblical adventure. We are confident that when you see how everything fits together, passages that may have previously been confusing to you will become clear. And your confidence in the consistency and truth of Scripture will increase.

Let us consider how *other prophecies* are presented in the Bible. In the previous chapter we looked at Malachi 4, which marks the end of the Old Testament. Let's return to this passage, where we will look more closely at the prophecy of the return of Elijah. God declared:

> "For behold, the day is coming, burning like an oven, and all the proud, yes, all who do wickedly will be stubble. And the day which is coming shall burn them up," says the LORD of hosts, "That will leave them neither root nor branch. But to you who fear my name The Sun of Righteousness shall arise with healing in His wings; and you shall go out and grow fat like stall-fed calves. You shall trample the wicked, for they shall be ashes under the soles of your feet on the day that I do this," says the LORD of hosts. "Remember the Law of Moses, my servant, which I commanded him in Horeb for all Israel, with the statutes and judgments. Behold, **I will send you Elijah** the prophet before the coming of the great and dreadful **day of the LORD**. And he will turn the hearts of the fathers to the children, and the hearts of the children to their fathers, lest I come and strike the earth with a curse." (*Malachi 4:1-6*)

God promised to send the prophet Elijah to Israel before the coming of the dreadful Day of the Lord. The Day of the Lord is a term we ran across in Peter's epistles, which we concluded must, in that instance, refer to AD 70. We will consider this term in more detail later, but for now we note that most Christians accept the idea that the Day of the Lord occurs with the tribulation, judgment, and the Second Coming. The question is when were these things to take place? *The Jewish people, based on this prophecy, expected to see Elijah return in a literal, physical, and visible way to signal these events. They were expecting to see a spectacular supernatural return which no one could mistake or misinterpret.*

2 Kings 2:11-12 relates the manner in which Elijah was taken away by God. He ascended on a chariot of fire. The Jews thought that Elijah might well return in exactly the same manner that he ascended, on a chariot of fire.

But in Matthew 11:13-15; Matthew 17:10-13, and Mark 9:11-13 Jesus identifies *John the Baptist* as the expected Elijah! What a confusing surprise. We could not possibly know that John the Baptist fulfilled this prophecy if Jesus hadn't told us so!

Even John the Baptist *himself* denied being the expected Elijah (John 1:21)! So Jesus had to sort it all out for us. Further clarification comes from the angel that appeared to John's father Zechariah. The angel explained in Luke 1:17 that John the Baptist would go before the Lord God in the *spirit and power of Elijah.* In spite of what Malachi seemed to be saying, and in spite of what the Jews saw as literal, the return of Elijah was not literal.

The reason this misunderstanding by the Jews was so important is that it was a major reason why the Jews rejected Jesus as the Messiah. This is critical. The Jews knew that Jesus could not possibly be the Messiah because they knew from the unmistakable (they thought) prophetic text of the "return of Elijah," that anyone who claimed to be the Christ before Elijah the Prophet had visibly and literally returned from heaven, would have to be a false prophet. Further, they expected Jesus to be a political figure who would free them from Roman domination. In *their* eyes, Jesus failed on both counts.

We can actually sympathize with the Jews here. Malachi's prophecy explicitly says that Elijah was going to return—not some other man. Instead of Elijah personally returning from heaven, what the rabbis actually got was John—a raggedy fellow who ate grasshoppers. He did not fit the picture. He did not come floating down from heaven in his former earthly body. Instead, he came like everybody else—from a mother and father. John was not even named Elijah. He had a different body, a different personality, and different teachings than Elijah. John the Baptist and Elijah were two different people.

The Jews made two interpretive errors about prophecy—one about Elijah and the other about the Messiah. The Jews did not have the insight to recognize the "second coming" of Elijah when they saw it. In fact, most Jews did not believe Jesus when He explained it. Today, most Christians expect *the same sort of future return* of Christ that the Jews expected for the second coming of Elijah—**a literal physical return in his self-same previous body**. This parallel, but mistaken expectation about Jesus' Parousia, should be enlightening to Christians today.

Further, the Jews expected the Messiah to be a political-military leader who would deliver them from their enemies, a savior to rule the world and set all things right on earth. This error is **another parallel** of what Christians expect of Jesus at his Second Coming. Christians expect Jesus to usher in an earthly golden age and to punish his enemies. The Jews were wrong about this expectation of the First Coming of Jesus, just as Christians are mistaken about the nature of the Second Coming!

Jesus told us *when* he would return—within a generation. And, as we will see below, He told us *how* he would return—in divine judgment. Christians don't believe Jesus now anymore than the Jews believed Him in the first century. Could the church (and your pastor) be just as mistaken about this as were the Jews in Jesus' day?

Before we leave the passage from Malachi, it is appropriate to again notice that there are other preterist clues in this passage. As we pointed out in the previous chapter, the passage prophesies the destruction and judgment of the wicked soon after the return of Elijah (i.e., the coming of John the Baptist). Sounds like AD 70, doesn't it?

In the Old Testament, God "came" to earth on multiple occasions. These occasions were often *in judgment* of Israel or her enemies, or to otherwise effect change. While people did not literally see God, they certainly saw what He did on earth. Consider this section from the first chapter of the book of Micah:

> For behold, the **LORD** is **coming** out of His place; He will **come down** and tread on the high places of the earth. The **mountains will melt under Him**, and the **valleys will split like wax** before the fire, like waters poured down a steep place. All this is for the transgression of Jacob and for the sins of the house of Israel. What is the transgression of Jacob? Is it not Samaria? And what are the high places of Judah? Are they not Jerusalem? Therefore I will make Samaria a heap of ruins in the field, places for planting a vineyard; I will pour down her stones into the valley, and I will uncover her foundations. All her carved images shall be beaten to pieces, and all her pay as a harlot shall be burned with the fire; all her idols I will lay desolate, for

she gathered it from the pay of a harlot, and they shall return to the pay of a harlot. Therefore I will wail and howl, I will go stripped and naked; I will make a wailing like the jackals and a mourning like the ostriches, for her wounds are incurable. For it has come to Judah; it has come to the gate of my people—to Jerusalem. . . . For the inhabitant of Maroth pined for good, but disaster **came down** from the LORD to the gate of Jerusalem. O inhabitant of Lachish, harness the chariot to the swift steeds (She was the beginning of sin to the daughter of Zion), for the transgressions of Israel were found in you. (*Micah 1:3-9; 12-13*)

Partial preterist Gary DeMar had this to say about this passage:

"The Lord is said to come 'forth from His place' to 'come down and tread on high places of the earth.' In what way did this take place? Was this a physical/bodily coming so people actually saw Jehovah? Did the mountains really melt? Did the valleys split? This coming of Jehovah in judgment is directed against the two seats of government in Israel, Samaria in the north and Jerusalem in the south, prior to the Assyrian and Babylonian captivities. The New Testament uses nearly identical language to describe Jesus' judgment-coming on Jerusalem in A.D. 70 (Matthew 24:27-31)." [56]

Here is a list of some other Old Testament references that speak of God's "coming," "coming down" to earth, "returning," or that speak of his presence on earth effecting change. The reader should look these up for a fuller understanding of how God "comes."—Genesis 11:5; 18:21; Exodus 3:8; 19:11; Numbers 11:17; Deuteronomy 4:11-14; 33:2; 2 Samuel 22:8-15; Psalm 50:3; 96:13; 97:5; 144:5; Isaiah 19:1-4; 26:21; 29:6; 31:4; 64:3; 66:15; Jeremiah 4:13-28; Ezekiel 1:28; Hosea 8:1; Zechariah 1:16; 9:14; 14:3-6. The language of God's comings is critical to understanding New Testament eschatology. Let all of this sink in!

The New Testament also uses language about God's or Jesus' coming in contexts other than a literal-physical or visible coming. Consider John 14:3; Revelation 2:5; Revelation 3:3, and Revelation 3:20. You may want to take time to look up these passages too. They teach that God *comes* to us in several senses—to judge us, to take us to heaven, or to join with us spiritually.

Now let's return to the Olivet Discourse and begin to unpack more of Jesus' teaching. Consider this Second Coming verse in Matthew 24 (verse 30) in slightly greater context, including the verses immediately before and the verse after the one we showed above. Remember, Jesus is speaking:

> For as the lightning comes from the east and flashes to the west, so also will the **coming** of the Son of Man be. For wherever the carcass is, there the eagles will be gathered together. Immediately after the tribulation of those days the sun will be darkened, and the moon will not give its light; the stars will fall from heaven, and the powers of the heavens will be shaken. Then the sign of the Son of Man will appear in heaven, and then all the tribes of the earth will mourn, and they will see the Son of Man **coming** on the **clouds** of heaven with power and great glory. And He will send his <u>angels</u> with a great sound of a <u>trumpet</u>, and they will gather together his elect from the four winds, from one end of heaven to the other. (*Matthew 24:27-31*)

This is packed with imagery. Included in this imagery are (1) lightning, (2) cosmic disturbances, (3) clouds, (4) angels, (5) trumpets, and (6) four winds. People who are not familiar with biblical imagery assume that such language is literal. When Jesus comes again He will literally appear riding a cloud with the fanfare of trumpets while angels wing around him; so they think.

But in the Bible, **clouds** especially are used symbolically to portray God's presence, judgment, or proclamation. Riding on clouds is a sure sign of deity. People did not see God literally, but saw what He did or perceived his presence in other ways. Consider these passages:

> And the LORD said to Moses, "Behold, I **come** to you in the thick **cloud**, that the people may hear when I speak with you, and believe you forever." (*Exodus 19:9*)

> Now the LORD **descended** in the **cloud** and stood with him there, and proclaimed the name of the LORD. (*Exodus 34:5*)

> and the LORD said to Moses: "Tell Aaron your brother not to come at just any time into the Holy Place inside the veil, before the mercy seat which is on the ark, lest he die; for I will **appear** in the **cloud** above the mercy seat." (*Leviticus 16:2*)

Then the LORD **came down** in the **cloud**, and spoke to him, and took of the Spirit that was upon him, and placed the same upon the seventy elders; and it happened, when the Spirit rested upon them, that they prophesied, although they never did so again. (*Numbers 11:25*)

These words the LORD spoke to all your assembly, in the mountain from the midst of the fire, the **cloud**, and the thick darkness, with a loud voice; and He added no more. And He wrote them on two tablets of stone and gave them to me. (*Deuteronomy 5:22*)

He bowed the heavens also, and **came down** with darkness under His feet. And He rode upon a **cherub**, and flew; He flew upon the wings of the wind. He made darkness his secret place; his canopy around Him was dark waters and thick **clouds** of the skies. From the brightness before Him, his thick **clouds** passed with hailstones and coals of fire. (*Psalm 18:9-12*)

Clouds and darkness surround Him; righteousness and justice are the foundation of his throne. (*Psalm 97:2*)

He lays the beams of his upper chambers in the waters, who makes the **clouds his chariot**, who walks on the wings of the wind, (*Psalm 104:3*)

The burden against Egypt. Behold, the LORD rides on a swift **cloud**, and will **come** into Egypt; the idols of Egypt will totter at his presence, and the heart of Egypt will melt in its midst. (*Isaiah 19:1*)

Blow the **trumpet** in Zion, and sound an alarm in my holy mountain! Let all the inhabitants of the land tremble; for the day of the LORD is coming, for it is at hand: [2] A day of darkness and gloominess, a day of **clouds** and thick darkness, like the morning **clouds** spread over the mountains. A people come, great and strong, the like of whom has never been; nor will there ever be any such after them, even for many successive generations. (*Joel 2:1-2*)

God is jealous, and the LORD avenges; the LORD avenges and is furious. The LORD will take vengeance on His adversaries, and He reserves wrath for his enemies; [3] The LORD is slow to anger and great in power, and will not at all acquit the wicked. The LORD has his way in the whirlwind and in the storm, and the **clouds** are the dust of his feet. (*Nahum 1:2-3*)

The great day of the LORD is near; it is near and hastens quickly. The noise of the day of the LORD is bitter; there the mighty men shall cry out. That day is a day of **wrath**, a day of trouble and distress, a day of devastation and desolation, a day of darkness and gloominess, a day of **clouds** and thick darkness, (*Zephaniah 1:14-15*)

In these passages we see it prominently expressed that clouds are God's figurative abode and figurative mode of travel. We also see trumpet and angel language as well as a judgment message in some of these passages. Jesus in the Olivet Discourse was claiming deity when He spoke of himself as coming with the clouds. So when we read Matthew 24 in light of this Old Testament language we understand that Jesus' Second Coming was a *literal judgment* upon Israel expressed in highly *figurative, but common prophetic language.*

We also see the cloud travel imagery applied to Jesus in Daniel. Recall that we showed in the previous chapter that the vision in Daniel chapter 12 applied to AD 70. In the passage below we also see reference to the commencement of the Messiah's *everlasting kingdom,* which as we will see in Chapter 10 of this book, had a first-century fulfillment:

I was watching in the night visions, and behold, one like the **Son of Man, coming with the clouds** of heaven! He came to the ancient of days, and they brought Him near before Him. Then to Him was given dominion and glory and a **kingdom** that all peoples, nations, and languages should serve Him. His dominion is an **everlasting dominion**, which shall not pass away, and his kingdom the one which shall not be destroyed. (*Daniel 7:13-14*)

Consider the presence of *angels* with Jesus in Matthew 24:31. It is common in Scripture for angels to be said to accompany God when He judges, even though people may or may not have seen the angels. See such passages as Deuteronomy 33:1-2; 2 Samuel 22:10-12; Psalm 78:49, and many instances in Revelation. And *trumpets* often accompany God. See Psalm 47:2-5 and Isaiah 18:3. *Four winds*, another interesting image, is found in Zechariah 2:6 and, again, in many instances in Revelation.

How do we know that this "coming" of Jesus is about earthly judgment? Much of Matthew has been leading up to this. We saw it in Jesus' parables and in his "this generation" warnings to the Jews, including the one in Matthew 23:36 just preceding the Olivet Discourse. We also saw it in Jesus' comparing his Second Coming to the Great Flood of Noah (Matthew 24:37, 39). Of course, in addition to the earthly judgment upon the nation of Israel, God would have judged each person individually who died during this upheaval, sending him to his eternal destiny. Later, we will also explore how God judged, at the same time, those who were long dead.

Verse 29 of Matthew 24 uses astronomical disturbances language — *sun and moon darkened, stars fall, heaven shaken*. This again is common judgment language in the Bible. Note this passage from Isaiah 13:

> Behold, the day of the LORD comes, cruel, with both wrath and fierce anger, to lay the land desolate; and He will destroy its sinners from it. For the **stars of heaven and their constellations will not give their light; the sun will be darkened** in its going forth, and the moon will not cause its light to shine. I will punish the world for its evil, and the wicked for their iniquity; I will halt the arrogance of the proud, and will lay low the haughtiness of the terrible. I will make a mortal more rare than fine gold, a man more than the golden wedge of Ophir. Therefore I will **shake the heavens, and the earth will move out of her place**, in the wrath of the LORD of hosts and in the day of his fierce anger. (*Isaiah 13:9-13*)

Isaiah 13 concerns the judgment upon Babylon, which was fulfilled in the sixth century BC. (Jeremiah 51:11, 28 and Daniel 5:30-31 tell us that the Medes conquered Babylon.) Please look up these *additional* passages that show God's judgments expressed in cosmic language or in terms of the destruction of the created order: Isaiah 19:1-22 (against Egypt); Isaiah 24:1-23 (against Jerusalem); Isaiah 34:1-17 (against Edom); Jeremiah 51:25 (against Babylon); Ezekiel 32:7-8 (against Pharaoh); Joel 2:10-31 (against

Israel, ref. Acts 2); Joel 3:15-16 (against the nations); and Micah 1:2-16 (against Israel and Judah). These are not end-of-the-planet judgments, but rather expressions of God's wrath upon wayward groups of people. While Isaiah 24 and Joel 2/3 point to the first century, the others were most certainly fulfilled in Old Testament times. The book of Revelation, by the way, is filled with nearly identical symbolic language.

Again, we call on the always eloquent Russell to offer insight about the language of prophecy. He stated:

"In prophecy, as in poetry, the material is regarded as the type of the spiritual, the passions and emotions of humanity find expression in corresponding signs and symptoms in the inanimate creation. . . . The earth convulsed with earthquakes, burning mountains cast into the sea, the stars falling like leaves, the heavens on fire, the sun clothed in sackcloth, the moon turned into blood, are images of appalling grandeur, but they are not necessarily unsuitable representations of great civil commotions—the overturning of thrones and dynasties, the desolations of war, the abolition of ancient systems, the great moral and spiritual revolutions. . . . As the dissolution of the material world is not necessary to the fulfillment of the Old Testament prophecy, neither is it necessary to the accomplishment of the predictions of the New Testament. . . . The moral and spiritual facts which they represent, the social and ecumenical changes which they typify, could not be adequately set forth by language less majestic and sublime." [57]

Here is something noteworthy. The judgments effected by God were usually administered by enemies of those who received the judgment. In the case of Isaiah 13, the judgment against the Babylonians (verses 1 and 19) was effected by the Medes (verse 17). In other words, God uses earthly people as an instrument of his judgment. This is exactly what happened in AD 70. God used the Roman army to exact punishment upon the Jews! We trust that the reader is beginning to see how this works.

The image of *lightning* in Matthew 24:27 is likewise interesting. In the Bible, lightning often signifies the presence of God and his coming in judgment. See Exodus 19:16-19; 20:18; Psalm 18:14; Job 36:29-33, and Zechariah 9:14. Some of these passages also have the *trumpet* calls similar to what we see in Matthew 24:31.

If you have a Bible next to you, open it up to Matthew 24, then keep your finger in that place and compare the structure of this passage to the parallel passages in Mark 13 and Luke 21. In many Bibles there are headlines before each section and you will note that the structure of the Olivet Discourse covers events in this general order: the prediction of the Destruction of the Temple, the Signs of the Close of the Age, the Abomination of Desolation, and the Second Coming (then the Lesson of the Fig Tree and Warnings). These are not things separated by thousands of years, but parts of the same event, or series of events. If this is not clear from simply reading the Olivet Discourse, it will become clear as we examine the text in greater detail.

The judgment here is clearly the judgment upon the nation of Israel. How do we know? If the temple destruction and the abomination of desolation description were not proof enough, notice that in verse 30 "all the tribes of the earth [also translated as "the land"] will mourn." This is clearly a reference to the twelve tribes of Israel. It is further confirmed by the Lesson of the Fig Tree. The fig tree is used in the Bible as a symbol for Israel. For example, in Jeremiah 24, the people of Israel are compared to figs, both good and rotten. When Jesus mentions the fig tree in the Olivet Discourse, He is symbolically referring to Israel.

By the way, the fig tree does not indicate Israel becoming a nation again in 1948 as dispensationalists think. Jesus had previously given the Jews warnings with the metaphor of a fig tree. Here are other mentions of the fig tree from Matthew and Luke:

> And seeing a **fig tree** by the road, He came to it and found nothing on it but leaves, and said to it, "Let no fruit grow on you **ever again**." Immediately the fig tree withered away. (*Matthew 21:19*)

> He also spoke this parable: "A certain man had a **fig tree** planted in his vineyard, and he came seeking fruit on it and found none. Then he said to the keeper of his vineyard, 'Look, for **three years** I have come seeking fruit on this fig tree and find none. Cut it down; why does it use up the ground?' But he answered and said to him, 'Sir, let it alone this year also, until I dig around it and fertilize it. And if it bears fruit, well. But if not, after that you can **cut it down**.'" (*Luke 13:6-9*)

In the passage from Matthew we notice that Jesus pronounced the fig tree to be cursed *forever*. In the passage from Luke, the three years corresponds precisely with the period of Jesus' earthly ministry! Each one of the major events covered by Jesus in the Olivet Discourse is about Israel and the end of the Old Covenant. And remember Matthew 23:29-39, which is the lead-in, or backdrop, if you will, to the Olivet Discourse—where Jesus clearly said that his judgment was against the Jews to whom he was speaking, and insisted that it would happen in their generation.

The reason for the curse is straightforward. The fig tree (Israel) failed to bear fruit (faith) even though its leaves indicated it was in season—for the appointed time of the coming of the Messiah. Due to its lack of fruit, the fig tree withered. Israel's lack of faith, even when presented with the Messiah *before their very eyes*, led to her eventual destruction at the hands of the Romans in AD 70.

The debate among Christians is about the timing of these events in the Olivet Discourse and whether they were to occur in the same era in history. But the disciples linked them together. The subject matter links them together. Jesus confirmed that they were linked together. The language itself links them together. To fix the time of one of these events is to fix the time of all of them.

Partial preterist R. C. Sproul wrestled with the futurist view in a 1993 conference on eschatology. He challenged his peers about the Olivet Discourse:

> Do you realize how powerful that language is? Jesus doesn't simply, in an ambiguous way, hint that the time is near for the fulfillment of these things. He gives a parable about seasons, about the time of ripening, and then He says that these things are near—and "near" is ambiguous? How near is near? I'll tell you how near it is—"at the door." It's that close. Doesn't it sound to you that our Lord is laboring something here? That He's calling them to this vigilance because of the radical nearness of all of these things, of this coming of which He's speaking? And then He says, "Be assured . . ." [Matthew 24:34] Now how much assurance can you have?

> Jesus gets done with His speech, and one of the disciples goes up to the other and says, "Man, did you hear that? Some of us aren't going to die until this comes to pass." "Don't read too much into that, you know, He may have a program here where this isn't going take place for 2,000 years." "Come on, did you hear what He said? He said it's near; it's at the door; I want you to be alert."

Is it even remotely conceivable that a disciple who heard this statement from Jesus would have even allowed for the possibility that that which He was talking about would take place 2,000 years later? I think we're straining at a gnat and swallowing a camel here. Now, don't get me wrong, I haven't landed. But I will never be satisfied with anything less than a full explanation of this that takes seriously both sides of it—the coming as well as the destruction of Jerusalem. We know the destruction of Jerusalem takes place. I know [another speaker] labored with the phrase *panta tauta* ["all these things"], and he tried to divide it up structurally and say that *panta tauta* refers to all the references to Jerusalem, and everything else refers to the coming of Christ. It's a nice little theory, but in my judgment it is contrived. It's artificial.[58]

COMMON OBJECTIONS

There are a few common objections to the idea that everything in the Olivet Discourse, especially the Second Coming, happened in AD 70, as full preterists teach. Let's consider these objections.

The first objection is that the word translated *generation* (Greek *genea*) is not always meant the way we commonly use it—that is, the multitude of people living at the same time, or generally a period of time of about forty years. Some Christians have attempted to get around the standard meaning of *generation* by forcing it to mean *race* in Matthew 24:34. Or they might say that the word means a kind, type, or sort of person—or possibly those of a similar frame of mind. Thus Jesus is portrayed as saying, "This *race*—the Jews, or the human race, or all believers, or even all unbelievers—will not pass away until all these things take place."

Excuse our bluntness, but this is eisegesis, not exegesis—and it borders on the dishonest. The Greek word for "race" is *genos*. Not all Greek dictionaries even offer "race" as a potential definition of *genea*. The word *genea* is used forty-three times in the New Testament and not once in any standard Bible is it translated as "race." Besides being a stretch of language in and of itself, there are at least twenty-three times in the New Testament outside of the Olivet Discourse (including multiple uses in parallel passages) that the word *genea* is found, and it is almost always translated as "generation" and it consistently means *the people living at the time*—especially, the Jewish people living in the first century.

We already presented one of these, Matthew 23:29-39. In this passage and others like it, when Jesus condemned "this generation" it is obvious that He meant the generation of people living at the time He was on the earth—his Jewish contemporaries. In fact, there is minimal debate about the other instances of *this generation* (outside of the Olivet Discourse). It is only in the Olivet Discourse that people try to pour a different meaning into the phrase.[59]

If you want to check this out, you can go to an online Bible search engine such as Bible Gateway or Bible Study Tools and do a word-search for "generation." Study how the word is used elsewhere in the New Testament. But especially, check out other "this generation" prophecies of Jesus in addition to those already mentioned in Matthew 23, Matthew 24, and Luke 21—namely Matthew 11:16; 12:38-45; Mark 8:12; 8:38-9:1; 13:30, and Luke 7:31; 11:29-32, 49-51; 17:25. "This generation" *always* means "this generation"—which means the generation of people alive at the time of Jesus. You may also see the excellent article referenced in the following endnote that explores the use of "generation" in the New Testament, along with other pertinent eschatological words, including the Greek words that express Jesus' Second Coming.[60]

Question for your pastor, church leaders, and friends: If generation in the Bible means "race," does that mean that forty-two "races" are spoken of in Matthew 1:17?

The second objection we hear is that "this" (as in "this generation") does not mean "this." Rather, it means "that," thus *that* generation"— implying some future generation. Such an idea is also an attempt to force a meaning into the Bible that is not there.

The use of "you" in the Olivet Discourse clearly identifies the generation as being that of those to whom Jesus was speaking. When speaking to his disciples Jesus said:

- Do **you** not see all these things? Assuredly, I say to **you**, not one stone shall be left here upon another, that shall not be thrown down. (*Matthew 24:2*)

- Take heed that no one deceives **you**. (Matthew *24:4*)

- And **you** will hear of wars and rumors of wars. See that **you** are not troubled. *(Matthew 24:6)*

- Then they will deliver **you** up to tribulation and kill you, and **you** will be hated by all nations for my name's sake. *(Matthew 24:9)*

- Therefore when **you** see the "abomination of desolation," spoken of by Daniel the prophet, standing in the holy place" (whoever reads, let him understand), "then let those who are in **Judea** flee to the mountains. *(Matthew 24:15)*

- But when **you** see Jerusalem surrounded by armies, then know that its desolation is near. *(Luke 21:20)*

- So you also, when **you** see all these things, know that it is near—at the doors! *(Matthew 24:33)*

- Assuredly, I say to **you**, this generation will by no means pass away till all these things take place. *(Matthew 24:34)*

- Therefore **you** also be ready, for the Son of Man is coming at an hour **you** do not expect. *(Matthew 24:44)*

These statements by Jesus are spoken directly to his disciples. Unless the reader injects futurist presuppositions into the text, the time frame for their fulfillment is unmistakable. The prophesied events would happen to Jesus' contemporaries. Nothing in these passages, when read straight-forwardly, speaks of anything thousands of years in the future. Russell put it thusly:

"It is impossible to read [the Olivet Discourse] and fail to perceive its distinct reference to the period between our Lord's crucifixion and the destruction of Jerusalem. Every word is spoken to the disciples, and to them alone. To imagine that the "you" in this address applies, not to the disciples to whom Christ was speaking, but to some unknown and yet non-existent persons in a far distant age, is so preposterous a supposition as not to deserve serious notice." [61]

It is universally accepted that in the Olivet Discourse Jesus predicted the destruction of the temple to occur in his generation. Yet many equivocate the term "this generation" in Matthew 24:34. When it concerns the destruction of the temple, "this generation" in that verse means Jesus' own generation in the first century. But when it concerns the fulfillment of "all these things," suddenly "this generation" in that verse means something entirely different!

It is certainly possible for a term to have different meanings or applications if used in different sentences or different contexts. But it is logically and linguistically impossible for a single instance of "this generation" to simultaneously have two opposite meanings! Do you catch the importance of this? If "this generation" in Matthew 24:34 is applied to the first-century destruction of the temple, then it must necessarily refer to the first century in every other application it modifies in the same context. You honestly can't have it both ways.

Yet, there is a third objection (or really additional nuances of the above objections) that people often raise. They still think that "this generation" does not modify everything in the Olivet Discourse—even though Jesus said *all* would happen in his generation. Thus, it is argued, part of the Olivet Discourse has already been fulfilled in the first century, but part of it is yet to be fulfilled. In other words, the events of the Olivet Discourse were *partially fulfilled* in the first century, and in part remain unfulfilled. However, what is unfulfilled varies from expositor to expositor. So as not to get too confusing, let's consider aspects of the partial fulfillment objection in parts.

PARTIAL FULFILLMENT CONSIDERATION A — DIVIDE THE TEXT

Some say that Matthew 24 speaks of two different time periods—some to near events (verses 1-34), and some to future events (verses 35 and following). A significant problem exists for this view. There are two primary words in Matthew's version of the Olivet Discourse used for the Second Coming—the noun *parousia* and the verb *erchomai*. Each word is used in both sections of the discourse! *Parousia* is used in Matthew 24:3, 27 (first section) and in Matthew 24:37, 39 (second section). *Erchomai* is used in Matthew 24:30 (first section) and in Matthew 24:42, 44, 46, 48 (second section). Are Jesus and his apostles aware of two different comings separated by thousands of years? There is not a hint that these words in the two alleged sections imply two different fulfillments thousands of years apart! [62]

Another serious problem with this idea is in Luke 17, where Jesus speaks of the same events. Luke mixes the events up, thus making a two-section reading of Matthew 24 impossible. Below is an explanation from full preterist Edward E. Stevens.[63] Stevens numbers certain things that appear in both texts to show in what order they are found.

Matthew 24	Luke 17
SECTION A (events associated with AD 70)	ALL ONE SECTION (one time period) AD 70

Matthew 24:1-34

1. vv. 17–18 – "let him who is on the housetop not go down…"

2. vv. 26–27 – "For just as the lighting comes from the east…"

3. vs. 28 – "Wherever the corpse is, there the vultures will gather."

SECTION B
(events still future to us)?

Matthew 24:35 ff

4. vv. 37-39 – "For the coming of the Son of Man will be just like the days of Noah."

5. vv. 40-41 – "Then there shall two men in the field; one will be taken, and one will be left."

2. vv. 23-24 – "For just as the lighting, when it flashes…"

4. vv. 26–27 – "And just as it happened in the days of Noah, so it shall be also in the days of the Son of Man."

1. v. 31 – "On that day, let not the one who is on the housetop…"

5. vv. 35–36 – "There will be two women grinding at the same place; one will be taken, and the other will be left."

3. v. 37 – "…Where the body is, there also will the vultures be gathered."

Notice in the chart above how Luke records the same events as Matthew, but in a different order. Matthew's order is 1-2-3-4-5, but Luke's order is scrambled 2-4-1-5-3! Luke has an event from Section A followed by one from Section B, then another from Section A followed by Section B, and finally one from Section A. This presents a problem: If Matthew 24 really has two sections (or two different time periods separated by thousands of years) under consideration, then Luke's account is incorrect, because he mixes the five events up as if they are all to happen in one time period. Either Luke is mistaken (and therefore uninspired), or it is wrong to divide Matthew 24 into two sections. Of course, the solution to this is that both Matthew and Luke speak of the same events which would all happen in the same time period. And Matthew 24:34 tells us when that time period was to occur: the "generation" alive when Jesus uttered the Olivet Discourse (the generation that was alive in the first century)!

PARTIAL FULFILLMENT CONSIDERATION B — PICK AND CHOOSE

Other people pick and choose certain events Jesus lists in the Olivet Discourse, without regard to order, which they think have not been fulfilled. We have already covered most of the major events—the close of the age (Matthew 24:3), the abomination of desolation (Matthew 24:15), particular hardship for women (Matthew 24:19), and the tribulation (Matthew 24:21). We have shown that these happened in the Jewish-Roman War from AD 66-70. But the Olivet Discourse contains other prophetic details that we should consider.

One that is a major consideration for many Christians is whether the gospel has been preached all over the world (Matthew 24:14). Jesus marked this as a distinct prerequisite to "the end." The Greek word the Bible uses here for what Jesus stated as "world" was *oikoumene*.[64] While the word can mean "the inhabited earth," it also sometimes implies (and may be translated/rendered as) "the Roman world"—for example Luke 2:1; Acts 11:28; Acts 17:6, and Acts 24:5.

But even more importantly—and this will come as a huge surprise to many Christians—the Bible itself, in multiple places, proclaims that the gospel **had already been preached in the *whole world/to every nation* in the first century**! See Acts 19:10; Romans 1:8; 10:18; 16:25-27; Colossians 1:6; 1:23; 1 Thessalonians 1:8; 1 Timothy 3:16. This specific prophecy of Jesus was fulfilled, if you believe the Bible, by the time Paul wrote his letters. Any honest reader must acknowledge this fact.

Gary DeMar, in his book *Last Days Madness*, does an excellent job covering in detail every aspect of Jesus' prophecies in the Olivet Discourse. Anyone who wants to go over these things with a fine-toothed comb can do so in DeMar's very helpful book.[65] In each case it can be verified that the prophecies of the Olivet Discourse were fulfilled in the first century. Below is a short summary.

- *wars and rumors of wars* (Matthew 24:6)—We know of wars and rumors of wars in the first century from general history, including from period historian Tacitus. Tacitus said of the period, "It was full of calamities, horrible with battles, rent with seditions, savage in peace itself."

- *famines* (Matthew 24:7)—Four famines occurred during the reign of the Emperor Claudius (AD 41-54). One of them was recorded in Acts 11:28.

- *earthquakes* (Matthew 24:7)—Notable earthquakes occurred during the reigns of Caligula and Claudius (AD 37-54). See also Matthew 27:54; Matthew 28:2, and Acts 16:26.

- *persecution of Christ's disciples* (Matthew 24:9)—This is a well documented fact in the Bible (Acts 4:3; Acts 4:17; Acts 5:40; Acts 7:54-60; Acts 8:1; Acts 9:1; Acts 11:19; Acts 12:1-3; Acts 14:19; 2 Corinthians 11:24-26; Revelation 1:9) as well as general history (Josephus, Tacitus, etc.).

- *a great apostasy* (Matthew 24:10)—Paul, John, and Peter's letters all refer to this fact during their lifetimes. As put by Don Preston, "The unbroken testimony of the epistles is one of the inspired writers attempting to stem the tide of apostasy and encouraging faithfulness! The Great Apostasy happened in the first-century generation as Jesus said it would! How much clearer could the Bible tell us it had already happened? Since the apostasy occurred as Jesus predicted and it was to be a sign of the coming of the Lord, then the coming of the Lord was to happen in that generation as well. If not, why not?" [66]

- *flee to the mountains* (Matthew 24:16)—According to the early church historian Eusebius, the Christians did in fact flee Jerusalem during the Jewish-Roman War. History does not record any Christians having perished in the siege of Jerusalem. So those who followed Jesus' instructions and fled were saved from the slaughter (Matthew 24:13). This passage, by the way, further confirms that the tribulation was to be a regional event rather than global. It makes little sense if this prescribed way of escaping the tribulation given by Jesus was an instruction for us 2,000 years later.

- *false prophets* (Matthew 24:24)—Josephus mentions many false prophets and false messiahs. See also Acts 5:36-37; Acts 13:6; Acts 20:29-30; 2 Corinthians 11:13; 1 Timothy 4:1 (note reference to the "latter times"); 2 Timothy 2:16-18; 2 Timothy 3:13; 2 Peter 2:1-3; 1 John 2:18-19; 1 John 4:1; 2 John 1:7.

- **astronomical signs** (Matthew 24:29)—In this verse we see *the sun and moon being darkened, the stars falling, and the heavens being shaken.* It is difficult for many people to get over the idea that this language is not about the end of the physical universe. We have already covered this topic and have shown that such language in the Old Testament is often symbolic language about literal events. At least some of such passages are widely acknowledged as having already been fulfilled (Isaiah 13:9-13; Isaiah 34:4-6; Isaiah 51:5-6; Jeremiah 4:1-28; Jeremiah 15:9; Ezekiel 32:7-8; Joel 2:1-10; Joel 3:15-16; Amos 8:9; etc.). But indeed, literal astronomical signs were reported by various historians in AD 66-70, including Josephus. And some have been confirmed by modern astronomy. Nevertheless, this was familiar language to those to whom Jesus was speaking, and they would have understood Him to be speaking about national judgment rather than the end of the universe. Note specifically Acts 2:15-21 where Peter quotes, as you will recall, astronomical language of the prophet Joel. Peter placed the fulfillment of that prophecy in his own day.

Russell had some poignant thoughts about those who pick and choose items in the Olivet Discourse, making some past and some future. He said:

"The disciples came to their Master with a plain, straight-forward inquiry, and it is incredible that he would mock them with an unintelligible riddle for a reply. In such a view, our Lord, in answering the question of his disciples respecting the destruction of Jerusalem mixes up different events—now to Jerusalem and now to the human race; now to events close at hand and now to events indefinitely remote—that to distinguish and allocate the several references and topics, is exceedingly difficult, if not impossible. Is this the manner in which the Savior taught his disciples, leaving them to grope their way through intricate labyrinths? There are no words too strong to repudiate such a suggestion." [67]

PARTIAL FULFILLMENT CONSIDERATION C — TYPES AND SHADOWS

There are those that say, "Well, okay. I can see that the events listed in the Olivet Discourse happened just as Jesus said they would in the first century. But these are only *shadows* of what is to come in the future."

But as put by author John Bray, "Who gives us authority to say that there is to be another fulfillment beyond what Jesus said would take place back in His generation?" [68] This double fulfillment argument has no basis in the Bible insofar as Jesus never hinted at such a thing. He never said anything like: "These events will come upon YOU, but will also come upon some generation long into the future. You will witness these specific things. But some far distant people will see these things repeated."

This idea suggests that there will be two Second Comings, two end times, two Days of the Lord, two Great Tribulations, two gatherings of the elect, and so forth. There is no indication in the New Testament of such double fulfillment. Jesus clearly had one time frame in mind and He stated it as clearly as language will allow. The time frame of fulfillment was his generation. And that is exactly how his disciples understood it. To suggest otherwise is make-believe based on wishful thinking or blind allegiance to a tradition. It is the root of false prophecy; it does a disservice to God's Word.

The double fulfillment idea is just not in the New Testament. It is true that there are "types and shadows" in the Old Testament. For example, the old covenant was a type or "shadow" of things to come—

the new covenant. However, the new covenant is not a shadow of still newer things to come. The only thing left to be fulfilled is each individual's entrance into heaven in our glorified body. The types and shadows of the Old Testament have been fulfilled once for all with Jesus' completed work in the first century.

PARTIAL FULFILLMENT CONSIDERATION D — SEPARATE QUESTIONS

Some argue that in Matthew 24:3, the disciples are asking two separate and unrelated questions: (1) When will the destruction of the temple happen? and (2) What will be the sign of Jesus' Second Coming and of the end of world history? But in the parallel passages in Mark 13:4 and Luke 21:7, we see that there is only one question with different parts. For example, here is the text in Mark: "Tell us, when will these things be? And what will be the sign when all these things will be fulfilled?" As we have already observed, Jesus' answer confirms this understanding—*all* prophecy was to be fulfilled in their generation.

PARTIAL FULFILLMENT CONSIDERATION E — MATTHEW 25

Some partial preterists argue that Matthew 25, even though it is part of the Olivet Discourse, refers to the end of time. They agree that Matthew 24 was entirely fulfilled in AD 70 but believe that Matthew 25 is yet unfulfilled. The primary reason for their argument is that Matthew 25:31-46 discusses the so-called *general resurrection*, which they <u>assume</u> has not happened yet.

First, we notice that Christ's coming, as expressed by the Greek word *erchomai*, appears in both sections. *Erchomai* is used for Jesus' Second Coming five times in Matthew 24 (Matthew 24:30, 42, 44, 46, 48) and six times in Matthew 25 (Matthew 25:6, 10, 13, 19, 27, 31). Unless the Second Coming in Matthew 25 is a different Second Coming than in Matthew 24, these two sections of the Olivet Discourse must be referring to the same event.

Further, there is mention of a *gathering* in both sections: Matthew 24:31 (gathering of the elect) and also in Matthew 25:32 (gathering of all the nations). We also notice that we have accompanying angels in both sections (Matthew 24:31 and 25:31). There is judgment/vengeance in both sections (Matthew 24:30, 37 and 25:32, 41, 46). Remember that there were no chapter separations in the original manuscripts of the Bible, and such separations by chapter are not inspired. Matthew 24 and Matthew 25 speak of the same events and cannot be separated by thousands of years. We ask the reader to bear with us on the meaning of the general resurrection until we get to Chapter 11 where we will discuss it in detail.

FINAL OBJECTION—DENIAL

> *"After the prediction of the destruction of Jerusalem, another trio of texts—Matthew 24:29-31; Mark 13:24-27 and Luke 21:25-28— speak of the Son of Man's return. So far as our problem is concerned, it is extremely important to note how these two aspects—the imminent destruction of Jerusalem and the Parousia—are temporally related. . . . The fall of Jerusalem is not the end of the world but the start of a new age in salvation history."*
>
> *—Joseph Ratzinger* [69]

In case you don't recognize the name Joseph Ratzinger, he became Pope Benedict XVI. Ratzinger, of course, is not a preterist. But this admission is astounding. It was not a passing consideration. It came from his book entitled *Eschatology*. He simply had to admit that the fall of Jerusalem in AD 70 and the Second Coming were **temporally related**, that is, they happened at the same time! While this was a "problem" for him, at least he was willing to put it on the table.

What is equally amazing is how Ratzinger spent the rest of his book ignoring the problem he presented at the beginning of his book, by merely appealing to "the tension between reality on the one hand and the literary schemata used by the word on the other. . . . the now naked word, duly divested of the Church's tradition, seems either meaningless or in need of a radical transformation to be brought into significant relation with the new look of reality." [70] (Theologians have a way with words, don't they?)

Perhaps the biggest objection to preterism is simply "Don't bother me with the facts." This is sometimes true among pastors because either they have really not studied the issues or they know that their job is at stake if they buck the system. Indeed, we have heard pastors say that they just cannot reveal what they really believe because they would lose their job and the opportunity to accomplish other things that are important to them. Hmmm.

We also hear the phrase, "I just think. . . ." What follows is usually some vague concept that replaces the facts with wishful thinking. It might be, "*I just think* that Jesus had something more in mind here." Christians, let's stick with the testimony of God's Word.

We have more to say, and indeed we will come back to the Olivet Discourse when we cover the rapture and other topics. For now, we reiterate that Jesus said all these things would come to pass in his generation, and *we believe Him.* His disciples also believed Him, as we will confirm. We have presented adequate evidence that Jesus was correct, proving Himself to be the most amazing prophet in history.

We close this chapter with two stanzas plus the refrain from the marvelous hymn, *'Tis So Sweet to Trust in Jesus,* by Louisa M. R. Stead (1882):

'Tis so sweet to trust in Jesus,
Just to take Him at his word;
Just to rest upon his promise,
And to know, "Thus saith the Lord!"

Yes, 'tis sweet to trust in Jesus,
Just from sin and self to cease;
Just from Jesus simply taking
Life and rest, and joy and peace.

Jesus, Jesus, how I trust Him!
How I've proved Him o'er and o'er;
Jesus, Jesus, precious Jesus!
Oh, for grace to trust Him more!

Questions for further discussion with your pastor, church leaders, and friends:

- *Even though Jesus said in the Olivet Discourse that all the things He predicted would be fulfilled in his own generation, do you think that any were not fulfilled as He predicted?*

- *If so, which specific ones, and why?*

- *If you were convinced that your church is wrong about prophecy, would you speak out?*

7 The Second Coming of Christ Outside of the Olivet Discourse

The Bible contains much more material concerning the Second Coming. Consider this passage in Matthew that we have already mentioned, which we will now consider in more depth. Jesus is speaking to his disciples:

> And you will be hated by all for my name's sake. But he who endures to the end will be saved. When they persecute you in this city, flee to another. For assuredly, I say to you, you will not have gone through the cities of Israel before the Son of Man comes. (*Matthew 10:22-23*)

Here Jesus made a clear statement about the timing of his Second Coming. Jesus stated to his disciples that He would come before they had completed going through all of the cities of Israel. Let's consider how some interpreters view this passage.

Some commentaries say that this statement is not about the Lord's Second Coming at all, but about his First Coming. But obviously, this passage cannot be about his First Coming; Jesus was already there!

Similarly, some say that the passage is referring to Jesus' own ministry in the cities of Galilee. But that does not fit the passage either. It is not about Jesus' ministry in the cities of Galilee; it is about the disciples who were going through the cities of Israel. The passage makes sense only if Jesus was looking ahead to the time when He was no longer on the earth and the disciples had the responsibility of carrying out their work of evangelism. Further, Jesus was giving the disciples themselves a timeline for what was going to happen in relationship to *their* work, not Jesus' own work.

Other commentaries acknowledge that Jesus is referring to the Second Coming. For example, the popular NIV Study Bible says, "The saying seems to teach that the gospel will continue to be preached to the Jews until Christ's Second Coming." Such an interpretation completely ignores the fact that Jesus is telling his disciples that they *themselves* will not finish their mission before his Second Coming. (It's amazing what otherwise good scholars can come up with in order to support a flawed presupposition.)

Matthew 10:22-23 is in the context of a longer statement by Jesus that extends from verse 5 to verse 42. Open up your Bible and read this entire section for the context. You will notice that in verse 15 Jesus said, "Assuredly I say to you, it will be more tolerable for the land of Sodom and Gomorrah in the day of judgment than for that city." So part of the context of the passage is the coming judgment. On multiple occasions Jesus uses the analogy of the city of Sodom to warn of the devastating judgment that would soon befall his generation. For example, read Luke 17:29. As we discussed in the previous chapter, in Luke 17 Jesus covers some of the same material that is in the Olivet Discourse.

Other commentators simply skip over the Matthew 10 passage without a comment. Why? The reason is simply because it does not fit their paradigm. (This would be a good passage to ask your pastor about to see if what he tells you makes sense.)

So what's left? What is left is the full preterist viewpoint—that the Second Coming would occur during the lifetime of some of Jesus' disciples who lived in his generation. This implies that the Second Coming was to be of a nature different from what most Christians think it to be. This passage makes little sense to someone who thinks that Jesus' Second Coming is still in the future. But it makes perfect sense to the full preterist. The "end" has to be the end of the age, as previously discussed. Let us continue—to see if we can find consistency in what the Bible teaches. Here is another interesting passage a few chapters later in Matthew 16:

²⁷ For the Son of Man will [*mello*] **come** [*erchomai*] in the glory of his Father with his angels, and then He will reward each

according to his works. [28] Assuredly, I say to you, **there are some standing here who shall not taste death** till they see [*eido*] the Son of Man **coming** [*erchomai*] in his kingdom." (*Matthew 16:27-28*)

This passage reads a lot like the previous one—Jesus was to come again while some of his disciples were still alive. Some interpreters attempt, in various ways, to explain away the obvious teaching here. Some will say that this prediction refers to the Transfiguration, which occurred just six days later (see Matthew 17). But think about this for just a moment. Unless Jesus thought that some of those with Him were going to die in those six days, this interpretation makes no sense. And Scripture gives us no indication that some actually did die in those six days.

Further, we notice that Jesus used some familiar terminology in this passage: *will come in glory with his angels.* Sound familiar? As we saw in the last chapter, Jesus used nearly identical language in the Olivet Discourse about his Second Coming (Matthew 24:31 and 25:31). The language in Matthew 16:27-28 does not sound like the Transfiguration, but does sound like the same events as described in the Olivet Discourse. And since He delivered the Olivet Discourse *after* the Transfiguration (at least according to the order of their presentation in the Gospels), we have another good reason why in Matthew 16:27-28 Jesus was not referring to the Transfiguration.

But there is more. Jesus said in Matthew 16:27 that *judgment* would accompany his coming. There was no judgment at the Transfiguration. Matthew 16:26-27 should be taken in the context of Jesus' comments beginning with verse 21, which the reader may wish to look up. It becomes clearer in this context that the *coming* of Jesus is about vindication for Jesus' suffering, as well as the suffering of his disciples, at the hands of the Jewish leaders. This suffering and vindicating judgment ties perfectly with Matthew 23:34-39, which is clearly a prophecy about the events that were to befall those in Jesus' own generation.

In Matthew 13:39-42, which we examined earlier, Jesus stated that the judgment would come at the *end of the age*. We have established beyond a reasonable doubt that the end of the age refers to the Old Covenant Age, which ended in AD 70. If the judgment about which Jesus spoke in Matthew 13 is AD 70, then the judgment three chapters later in Matthew 16, as well as the judgment three chapters earlier in Matthew 10, are about AD 70. The judgment and the end of the age and the Second Coming are consistently tied together. So the Second Coming and judgment both occurred in the end of the age in AD 70.

Matthew 16:27-28 is clearly not about the Transfiguration, so what are the other possibilities? Some Christians think that the verses will be fulfilled at the end of history. But note that the Greek word for *will* in verse 27 (*will* come) does not fit a time frame of 2000+ years in the future. The Greek word there is *mello* ("about to"). This is the same word that we encountered in Luke's version of the Olivet Discourse in Luke 21:36 ("all these things that are *about to* come to pass"). The context in both cases demands an imminent fulfillment, as is clear in Young's Literal Translation of Matthew 16:27, which reads, "For the Son of Man is **about to** come in the glory of his Father. . . ." [71]

Another view is that this passage refers to Pentecost (Acts 2). Pentecost is often considered to be the beginning of the new covenant church. Is Pentecost a possible fulfillment of Matthew 16:27-28? One might say that Jesus, in a sense, came in his kingdom when the church was established at Pentecost. But the Pentecost theory has the same flaws as the Transfiguration theory. Jesus did not come in glory with his angels to reward all men according to their works at Pentecost. The day of Pentecost witnessed the coming of the Holy Spirit, not the coming of Jesus to bring final judgment! [72]

Matthew 16:27-28 does not fit the Transfiguration. It does not fit Pentecost. It does not fit 2,000 years later. But it fits AD 70 perfectly.

Some may object that no one actually *saw* Jesus return in the first century (verse 28). We will discuss this objection in more detail in Chapter 12, but for now we note that the word "see" in verse 28 is the Greek word *eido*. Just as in English, the word "see" can have nuances of meaning. It does not necessarily mean literal, physical sight. The online Blue Letter Bible says that *eido* can mean "to perceive" or "to know." So the passage does not require seeing Jesus in physical form in the sky as most Christians assume. What people would have seen would have been the *effects* of Jesus' return in judgment rather than his physical body.

The only other argument that is offered in defense of a futurist interpretation of Matthew 16:27-28 is that the two verses refer to two different times. But such an idea cannot be taken seriously. There is no break in the prophecy. This is confirmed by the fact that verses 27 and 28 both have imminency language. These verses cannot be separated.

We also note that the Greek word for "to come"—*erchomai*—appears in both verses 27 ("the Son of Man is about *to come* in the glory of His Father") and in verse 28 ("There are some standing here who shall not taste of death till they see the Son of Man *coming* in His kingdom"). It seems preposterous that in recording Jesus' words, Matthew used the same word in adjacent sentences to describe two different events that would be separated by thousands of years. Jesus' listeners would *certainly* have understood that He was describing the same time and the same event in these adjacent sentences.

Don K. Preston further notes that verse 28 begins with the Greek phrase *amen lego hymin* ("verily I say to you"). He argues that this phrase is used some 95 times in the New Testament, and that it almost always calls the listener's attention to what is about to be said in order to reinforce something that has already been said. If it is used in this instance to introduce a new subject, thus breaking up the discussion, it would be an anomaly. Therefore, it is most reasonable to conclude that verse 28 is emphasizing what verse 27 says.[73] Preston summarizes Matthew 16:27-28 and its parallel passages thusly:

> Matthew 25:31 speaks of when Christ would come "in his glory, and all the holy angels with him, then he will sit on the throne of his glory." This is patently the time of judgment and parallel to Matthew 16:27-28. So when would Christ come IN HIS GLORY, with the angels, and judge? In Matthew 24:29-34 we are told "the sign of the Son of Man shall appear in heaven, and then shall all the tribes of the earth mourn, and they shall see the Son of Man coming on the clouds of heaven with power and great glory and he will send his angels with a great sound of a trumpet. . . ." Here is the coming of Jesus with the angels, in power and great glory. When was this to happen? Read verse 34: "Verily I say unto you, this generation shall not pass, till all these things be fulfilled." . . .
>
> Matthew 25 is but a continuation of the discourse in Matthew 24, therefore the same time statement applies there as well. . . . This means of course that Matthew 16:27-28 and parallels cannot be used as predictions of the end of time, a future establishment of the kingdom, nor of the establishment of the kingdom on Pentecost. What is in view is the coming of Messiah, in that generation, in the full exercise of his Messianic kingdom authority to judge the living and the dead. This is the only interpretation of this text which honors inspiration, satisfies the demands of the text, and is in harmony with the rest of scripture.[74]

Matthew chapters 10, 13, 16, 21, 22, 23, 24, 25 are all parallel and speak of the same events! The reader is invited to pause here and return to his or her Bible. Read the following passages from these chapters: Matthew 10:16-23; 13:36-43; 16:21-28; 21:33-46; 22:1-14; 23:29-39; 24:1-51; 25:1-46. This time, notice the common prophetic themes of the rejection and crucifixion of Jesus, the persecution of his disciples—and the imminent coming vengeance against the perpetrators at the return of our Lord.

The next passage for our consideration is from Matthew 26. This chapter continues the theme:

But at last two false witnesses came forward and said, "This fellow said, 'I am able to destroy the temple of God and to build it in three days.'" And the high priest arose and said to Him, "Do you answer nothing? What is it these men testify against you?" But Jesus kept silent. And the high priest answered and said to Him, "I put you under oath by the living God: Tell us if you are the Christ, the Son of God!" Jesus said to him, "It is as you said. Nevertheless, I say to you, hereafter **you will see the Son of Man sitting at the right hand of the Power, and coming on the clouds of heaven**." Then the high priest tore his clothes, saying, "He has spoken blasphemy! What further need do we have of witnesses? Look, now you have heard His blasphemy! What do you think?" They answered and said, "He is deserving of death." Then they spat in his face and beat Him; and others struck Him with the palms of their hands, saying, "Prophesy to us, Christ! Who is the one who struck you?" (*Matthew 26:60b-68*)

This is obviously more of the same. This passage contains identical language to the Olivet Discourse which just precedes this passage. But this time, Jesus was speaking to Caiaphas the high priest as well as the scribes and elders. Jesus was publicly proclaiming that *they* would witness the Second Coming. Was Jesus wrong? Either Jesus was wrong or the Jews did in fact see his Second Coming in some sense. (Again, whether or not Jesus was to come in a visible earthly body will be addressed directly in Chapter 12.) The power of the imminence of this passage was expressed well by nineteenth-century author Milton Terry:

> We maintain that this language cannot be naturally interpreted as a reference to an event belonging to a far distant period of time. It is something which the high priests and his associates are to see.[75]

Below is a brief summary of some of the other imminency passages in the New Testament, excluding the synoptic gospels (Matthew, Mark, and Luke), and excluding Revelation which we will consider separately. These passages concern not only the Second Coming but related events as well:

- Jesus said the judgment of the world was *"now"* (John 12:31).

- Jesus said He would come again to claim *his disciples* to whom He was speaking (John 14:3).

- The Christians were *eagerly waiting* for the glory *about to be* (Greek *mello*) *revealed* (Romans 8:18-23).

- The hour *had come*, and the prophesied events were *nearer/at hand* (Romans 13:11-12).

- The Christians were (*eagerly*) *waiting* for the *revealing* of Jesus in the Day of the Lord Jesus—at the end (1 Corinthians 1:7-8).

- The time was very *short* (1 Corinthians 7:29).

- The form of the world *was passing away* (1 Corinthians 7:31).

- The end/fulfillment of the ages *had come upon them* (1 Corinthians 10:11).

- Some *believers would be alive* at the Second Coming (1 Corinthians 15:51).

- The brethren were (*eagerly*) *waiting* for Christ's coming (Philippians 3:20).

- The Lord was *at hand* (Philippians 4:5).

- They waited for Jesus from heaven to grant *them* relief from their oppressors when Christ was revealed from heaven with his mighty angels in flaming fire (1 Thessalonians 1:8-10; 1 Thessalonians 2:14-19; 2 Thessalonians 1:3-10). The language mirrors that of the Olivet Discourse. Paul promised the Thessalonians that God would give them relief at Christ's Second Coming. If that relief did not come as promised, then Paul was either a false prophet or a liar. Are the Thessalonians still waiting today for relief from their first-century oppressors?

- Some of Paul's brothers to whom he wrote would be *alive* at the *Second Coming* (1 Thessalonians 4:15, 17).

- Paul told his brothers to be *watchful for the Day of the Lord* (1 Thessalonians 5:2-11). Why would they be told to be watchful if the events were 2,000 years later?

- Paul prayed that the *bodies of first-century believers would be preserved* until the Second Coming (1 Thessalonians 5:23).

- The Second Coming would occur during the *life of Timothy* (1 Timothy 6:14).

- The brethren were *waiting* for the glorious appearing of Jesus (Titus 2:13).

- Jesus would appear a second time to save those in the first century who *were eagerly waiting for Him* (Hebrews 9:28).

- The *Day was approaching/drawing near* (Hebrews 10:25).

- Jesus was coming again *in a very, very little while without delay* (Hebrews 10:37). "Very" appears twice in the Greek text. And nowhere in the Bible is "a little while" portrayed as being thousands of years.

- The coming of the Lord was *near/at hand* (James 5:7-8).

- The judge was standing *at the door* (James 5:9).

- Christ was *ready to judge* the living and the dead (1 Peter 4:5).

- The end of all things was *at hand* (1 Peter 4:7).

- It was *time for the judgment to begin* (1 Peter 4:17).

- The glory and Second Coming were *about to be* (Greek *mello*) *revealed* (1 Peter 5:1, 4).

- With the Lord a thousand years *is as a day* (2 Peter 3:8). While this passage is often translated as meaning a *long* time, given the imminency of Peter's other words in his epistles, it seems best to believe that he meant the Day of the Lord would come soon, as we will elucidate in the next chapter. The time was *short*.

- They were *looking for* and *hastening* the coming of day of God (2 Peter 3:12).

- The world *was passing away* (1 John 2:17).

- It was the *last hour* (1 John 2:18). If the fulfillment of this verse is still in the future, its fulfillment is about 17 million hours late!

The Old Testament expresses strong sentiment about false prophets. Deuteronomy 18:20-22 teaches that false prophets should be put to death. With one voice all of the writers of the New Testament prophesied the imminency of these coming events. According to Scripture, they were all guilty and worthy of death if these events did not come to pass when and how they prophesied they would!

We have heard a few Christians say the apostles did not expect a Second Coming in the first century. Obviously these Christians are grossly mistaken. We have heard other Christians say that, yes, the disciples did indeed expect the Lord to return in their lifetimes, but the disciples were simply wrong. But, if the writers of the New Testament were wrong, then they were not inspired. We have also heard Christians use what can only be described as theological double talk. This quote is typical of such:

> The primary thought expressed by the word "imminency" is that something important is likely to happen, and could happen very soon. While the event may not be immediate, or necessarily very soon, it is next on the program and may take place at any time.[76]

According to the online source Dictionary.com, synonyms for *imminent* include: *near, at hand,* and *impending.* Antonyms include: *distant, remote.* These events were not distant or remote. They were *near!* To try to explain this away is just not faithful to the text or to Jesus. The imminency of the Second Coming in the New Testament is adequately summed up by author Brian L. Martin:

> We have yet to find *a single verse in the whole New Testament* that even hints at a far-distant, future Second Coming.[77]

So what's the answer? Jesus and the New Testament writers did emphatically expect the Second Coming in their generation. And they were correct. Jesus came—*in judgment*—in AD 70, ushering out the Old Covenant Age and exacting wrath on the apostate Jews. But stay tuned; there is more that happened in AD 70.

You might email your pastor and ask him this question:

"Do you believe that the writers of the New Testament — Paul, James, John, Peter, and the writer of Hebrews — thought that the Second Coming would happen in the lifetime of some of their contemporaries?" This question should generate an interesting discussion.

Day of the Lord and New Heaven and New Earth

These two terms—*the Day of the Lord* and *New Heaven(s) and New Earth*—are found in prophetic literature in the Bible. They have different meanings, but we will consider them together in this chapter. They sometimes appear together in the same context, such as in 2 Peter 3. We have encountered both of these terms already in our study, but will consider them in more depth now.

THE DAY OF THE LORD

Some Christians see the term "Day of the Lord" and immediately think, "Ah, yes. The end of the world!" But those who think this have not studied how the phrase is used in the Bible.

The phrase *the day of the Lord* (or variations of the phrase) is used in seventeen or so passages in the Old Testament (Isaiah 2:12; Isaiah 13:6-13; Isaiah 34:2-10; Jeremiah 46:10; Lamentations 2:22; Ezekiel 13:5; Ezekiel 30:2-4; Joel 1:15; Joel 2:1; Joel 2:11; Joel 2:31; Joel 3:14; Amos 5:18-20; Obadiah 1:15; Zephaniah 1:2 to 2:3; Zechariah 14:1; Malachi 4:5)—and in at least five passages in the New Testament (Acts 2:20; 1 Corinthians 5:5; 1 Thessalonians 5:1-2; 2 Thessalonians 2:2; 2 Peter 3:10). It is also alluded to in other passages (Hebrews 10:25; Revelation 6:17; Revelation 16:14). The exact count of how many times "the day of the Lord" is found in Scripture may differ because we can include similar phrases such as "that day" or "day of his wrath."

The term does not always refer to the same time period. The Bible uses the term to mean *any time* that God brings judgment upon the godless or wicked, or brings blessing and salvation to the godly. We don't think anyone who has studied it would disagree with that. But the precise application of the term in some passages is a point of disagreement among Christians. The disagreements arise because the text in some cases may not be specific as to who the recipient of God's justice is, or because of the assumptions that different Christians bring to a given passage. And, as in other matters of prophecy, some people see multiple fulfillments of the same prophecy.

However, there is broad agreement that certain prophecies which predict "the day of the Lord" have already been fulfilled. For example Isaiah 13 is an instance in which the interpretation is clear. We have already looked at this passage. Here we consider a bit more of the context:

> The burden against **Babylon** which Isaiah the son of Amoz saw. Lift up a banner on the high mountain, raise your voice to them; wave your hand, that they may enter the gates of the nobles. I have commanded my sanctified ones; I have also called my mighty ones for my anger—those who rejoice in my exaltation. The noise of a multitude in the mountains, like that of many people! A tumultuous noise of the kingdoms of nations gathered together! The LORD of hosts musters the army for battle. They come from a far country, from the end of heaven—the LORD and His weapons of indignation, to destroy the whole land. Wail, for the **day of the LORD** is at hand! It will come as destruction from the Almighty. Therefore all hands will be limp, every man's heart will melt, and they will be afraid. Pangs and sorrows will take hold of them; they will be in pain as a woman in childbirth; they will be amazed at one another; their faces will be like flames. Behold, the **day of the LORD** comes, cruel, with both wrath and fierce anger, to lay the land desolate; and He will destroy its sinners from it. For the stars of heaven and their constellations will not give their light; the sun will be darkened in its going forth, and the moon will not cause its light to shine. I will punish the world for its evil, and the wicked for their iniquity; I will halt the arrogance of the proud, and will lay low the haughtiness of the terrible. I will make a mortal more rare than fine gold, a man more than the golden wedge of Ophir. Therefore I will shake the <u>heavens,</u> and the <u>earth</u> will move out of her place, in the wrath of the LORD of

hosts and in the day of His fierce anger. . . . Behold, I will stir up the **Medes** against them, who will not regard silver; and as for gold, they will not delight in it. . . . And **Babylon**, the glory of kingdoms, the beauty of the Chaldeans' pride, will be as when God overthrew Sodom and Gomorrah. (*Isaiah 13:1-13, 17, 19*)

Nobody doubts that this passage is about God's judgment upon Babylon, that it was to be administered by the Medes, and that it has been fulfilled.[78] It was fulfilled in the sixth century BC in a series of devastating attacks upon Babylon. Notice again the astronomical language in this passage which we discussed relative to New Testament imagery—in particular Jesus' pronouncements upon Jerusalem. Also note the *heavens and earth* language (verse 13) which we will consider below.

Here is a list of some of the other Day of the Lord passages that refer to judgments or warnings to specific groups of people. In addition to naming specific targets of God's wrath, some of these prophecies convey a sense of imminence, which confirms a past fulfillment:

- Isaiah 34—Here we find an oracle of judgment against Edom. This is probably the same prophecy against Edom as in Jeremiah 25:21, which was fulfilled at the same time as the judgment against Judah by Nebuchadnezzar, king of Babylon. The Jeremiah prophecy, like Isaiah 34, uses highly figurative and hyperbolic language about a judgment that every interpreter accepts was fulfilled in the past. (See also Ezekiel 25:12-14 and 35:15 for references to the judgment against Edom.) The apocalyptic language of Isaiah 34 cannot be understood literally as the end of the world because it describes animals surviving. Also, see Obadiah 15 below.

- Jeremiah 46:10—This is part of a series of judgment oracles in Jeremiah chapters 46-51 against the named nations that were surrounding Judah.

- Lamentations 2:22—This is a reference to a judgment upon Jerusalem that had already occurred at the time the book was written.

- Ezekiel 13:5—Here we have a warning specifically against Israel's false prophets. (Note verses 1, 6, and 7.)

- Ezekiel 30:2-4—This is about a judgment against Egypt by means of Babylon.

- Joel (various passages)—Because of the difficulty in knowing when Joel was written, it is not possible to say in each case to whom God's wrath is directed. Most commentators say that some passages in Joel refer to Israel while other passages refer to other groups ("the nations"). Futurists acknowledge that at least Joel 1:15 and 3:14 have been fulfilled in some sense. Peter, in Acts 2, references Joel 2, thus placing the "last days" in his own time. The phrase *the moon turning to blood* is noteworthy in that it was used by Joel and quoted by Peter as being fulfilled in the first century.

- Amos 5:18-20—Amos 5 and 6 is a prophetic oracle against the northern kingdom of Israel. Even futurists acknowledge that it has been fulfilled at least in some sense.

- Obadiah 15—Like Isaiah's prophecy in Isaiah 34, Obadiah's oracle concerns Edom. Futurists again acknowledge that this prophecy has been fulfilled at least in some sense. Since Edom no longer exists, this clearly falls in the category of past fulfillment.

- Zephaniah 1:2 to 2:3—Notwithstanding the universal language ("everything," "all") found at the beginning of this section— hyperbolic language common to biblical apocalyptic prophecies, the judgments are particularized to Judah and Jerusalem, and against Judah's enemies. We also see that the prophecy is accompanied by a time-reference statement of *near* or *at hand* (depending on the translation). Different interpretations of this passage are possible. Scholars are not certain when Zephaniah was written, so there is disagreement about when the judgments were actually fulfilled. There are multiple possibilities that could fit past fulfillment, including AD 70.[79]

- Malachi 3:1 to 4:5—We covered Malachi's prediction of a Day of the Lord judgment in Chapters 5 and 6. This prophecy is clearly Messianic. The identification by Jesus of the fulfillment of the return of Elijah by John the Baptist unambiguously places its fulfillment in AD 70. John the Baptist himself uses Malachi's words to predict the wrath that was soon to be poured out upon the Jews in his generation (Matthew 3:7-12; cf. Malachi 4:1).

In other instances in the Old Testament, God declared his judgment on specific people groups, but without the term Day of the Lord. For example, Isaiah 10, which is a prophecy of God's wrath against Israel by means of Assyria, uses the term *day of punishment*. Even though the terms are not exactly the same, the message is the same.

Since "the Day of the Lord" in the Old Testament at least sometimes refers to historical judgments that have already been fulfilled, it is reasonable to infer that the instances in the New Testament of this term may also refer to an already fulfilled event—specifically to the judgment on Israel in AD 70 that was prophesied numerous times in both the Old and New Testaments. Most of the uses of "the Day of the Lord" in the New Testament have strong time-reference statements associated with them that tie it to a first-century fulfillment—namely, Peter's Pentecost sermon and his epistles, and Paul's letters to the Thessalonians.

The Day of the Lord is primarily about God's judgment. We have seen that the judgment spoken of over and over in the New Testament, as well as some prophetic passages in the Old Testament, point to AD 70. (Note parallels between Zechariah 14 and Matthew 24.) We cannot find adequate biblical reason why any of the Days of the Lord remain unfulfilled. *Jesus does not allow for any unfulfilled prophecies past the first century* (Luke 21:22, 32; Revelation 1:1; 22:6).

The primary objection to this conclusion is the notion that we can expect a double fulfillment of some of these passages—one past and one future. But where is the Scriptural support for such a view? Is it enough to simply assume that since there are Old Testament types that were fulfilled in New Testament antitypes, we must therefore regard the New Testament prophecies as typical of some future antitypes?

Where in the Bible does it teach that we should expect more than one fulfillment of New Testament prophecy? It seems to us that the people who insist on a double fulfillment of the same passage are reading something into the text that is not there. Such a view is pure conjecture based on a futurist assumption, without satisfying an evidentiary burden. But we will consider this objection in more detail later.

Concerning the use of the term "the Day of the Lord" in the New Testament, we find that in each case the term is linked to imminency passages. We have already, in Chapter 4, covered passages where Peter used the term (Acts 2; 2 Peter 3). The writer of Hebrews saw "the Day approaching" (Hebrews 10:25). We will look at Paul's use of the term in 1 and 2 Thessalonians in Chapter 11 of this book. But suffice it to say now that the Thessalonians clearly did not see the Day of the Lord as many moderns do (as the end of the physical universe), because they were under the impression that the Day had already come—which necessitated Paul correcting them (2 Thessalonians 2:2-4). Another instance is in 1 Corinthians 5 ("the day of the Lord Jesus"), which is in the context of the soon coming judgment.

In summary, "the Day of the Lord" is a term that refers to any of God's judgments. The evidence supports the preterist view that all such uses of the term have been fulfilled.

NEW HEAVEN AND NEW EARTH

Have you heard your pastor mention the term *new heaven and new earth*? In some churches you may have never heard that term mentioned. In other churches you may have heard it often. And depending on which church you attend the pastor may mean vastly different things by the term.

There is much confusion about the term *new heaven(s) and new earth*—a term that we find in both the Old Testament and New Testament. To some Christians it simply means *heaven*. To others it suggests a future material cosmos after the coming of Christ. Some, namely Jehovah's Witnesses and some dispensationalists, separate it in two and think that the eternal destiny for some believers is a "new earth" while other believers go to a "new heaven." Some Christians think it could mean different things depending on the context. Some admit that they don't know what the term means. We will now attempt to shine some light on what is biblically correct, and will show that the *new heaven and new earth* is a covenantal/theological term.

Here are some significant places in the Bible where we find the term, or its approximate equivalent:

New Testament:

- Jesus—Matthew 5:18; Matthew 24:35
- writer of Hebrews—Hebrews 12:22-29
- Peter—2 Peter 3:7, 13
- John—Revelation 21:1

Old Testament:

- Isaiah—Isaiah 1:2-5; Isaiah 13:13; Isaiah 24:1-23; 34:4-9; Isaiah 51:5-6, 15-16; Isaiah 65:17; Isaiah 66:22

We will consider how the term is used in each of these passages, except for the one in Revelation. (We will look at the book of Revelation in the next chapter.) First of all, the idea of a *new* heaven must not refer to a *literal* "new" heaven, since heaven is eternal. If God lives in heaven, why does it need to change?

As regards the earth, the Bible indicates that the *earth will abide forever* (Ecclesiastes 1:4; Psalm 78:69; Psalm 104:5, and Psalm 148:4-6). These statements about the earth abiding forever are most likely figurative, comparative, or in reference to the everlasting nature of God's dominion—rather than about literal cosmology. The Bible, as we have already discussed, is at best, ambiguous about whether the physical universe might end (Psalm 102:25-26). So it gets more complicated than most Christians believe.

Now take a moment and turn to Hebrews 12:22-29 in your Bible. Notice that the writer uses language about the heavens and earth, and clearly sets the context as the change in the covenants! Another reason the new heaven and new earth cannot mean the replacement of the material creation is because of Jesus' statement in the book of Matthew:

> For assuredly, I say to you, till **heaven and earth** pass away, one jot or one tittle will by no means pass from the law till all is fulfilled. (*Matthew 5:18*)

Jesus tied the passing of "heaven and earth" to the fulfillment of the law. Unless in some sense *heaven and earth* have already passed away, every jot and tittle of the law of Moses is still in effect even today! We know that Jesus ushered in the New Covenant of grace, so why would every detail of the law still be in effect? Thus the passing of the details of the law has already occurred and the passing of *heaven and earth* has already been fulfilled. We must be in the *new* heaven and earth now!

Christians, while we have mentioned this passage previously, don't let this just go by without thinking about it. The passing of h*eaven and earth* is equated by Jesus to the passing of the Mosaic theocratic order inaugurated on Mt. Sinai. In other words, the concept of a *new heaven and earth* is a theological expression used by Jesus (and the biblical writers) that, while context determines its interpretation, generally refers to the New Covenant world or the events surrounding its initiation.

The language is covenantal language rather than physical world language. So if a "new heaven and earth" was ushered in at the final consummation of the Old Covenant—when the long-held Jewish custom of sacrifices for sins ended, and when the temple was destroyed in AD 70— then Jesus' statement makes perfect sense. It can be argued that most references to the *heavens and earth* are uses of Hebraic phraseology that refer to the religio-political government of a people group. The time frame is made clear in Matthew 24:29-35 of the Olivet Discourse (and parallel passages in Mark 13:24-31 and Luke 21:25-33), where Jesus put the context of the passing of heaven and earth (coincident with the Second Coming and national judgment upon Israel) in the generation that was then alive—*his* generation. Notice the connection:

> Assuredly, I say to you, **this generation** will by no means pass away till all these things take place. **Heaven and earth** will pass away, but my words will by no means pass away. (*Matthew 24:34-35*)

We have already considered Peter's epistles concerning the last days. Now we return to Peter in this new context. Peter's second epistle contains a prominent prophecy of the passing of the old heaven and old earth and the ushering in of the new heaven and new earth. Peter most certainly expected to see an imminent fulfillment of the events prophesied in his epistles—including the Day of the Lord, the judgment, the new heavens and new earth, and the Second Coming. Let's look again at the imminence context in key passages in his epistles. The first passage below contains the new heavens and new earth. Those that follow highlight the further imminence context of Peter's epistles:

> But **the heavens and the earth** which are now preserved by the same word, are reserved for fire until the day of judgment and perdition of ungodly men. . . . Therefore, since all these things will be dissolved, what manner of persons ought you to be in holy conduct and godliness, **looking for and hastening** the coming of the day of God, because of which the heavens will be dissolved, being on fire, and the elements will melt with fervent heat? Nevertheless **we**, according to his promise, look for **new heavens and a new earth** in which righteousness dwells. Therefore, beloved, **looking forward to these things**, be diligent to be found by Him in peace, without spot and blameless; (*2 Peter 3:7, 11-14*)

to an inheritance incorruptible and undefiled and that does not fade away, reserved in heaven for you, who are kept by the power of God through faith for salvation **ready to be revealed in the last time**. In this you greatly rejoice, though now **for a little while**, if need be, you have been grieved by various trials, that the genuineness of your faith, being much more precious than gold that perishes, though it is tested by fire, may be found to praise, honor, and glory at the revelation of Jesus Christ, (*1 Peter 1:4-7*)

He indeed was foreordained before the foundation of the world, but **was manifest in these last times for you.** (*1 Peter 1:20*)

They will give an account to Him who is **ready to judge the living and the dead**. (*1 Peter 4:5*)

But the end of all things is at hand; therefore be serious and watchful in your prayers. (*1 Peter 4:7*)

Beloved, do not think it strange concerning the fiery trial **which is to try you**, as though some strange thing happened to you; but rejoice to the extent that **you** partake of Christ's sufferings, that when His glory is revealed, **you** may also be glad with exceeding joy. (*1 Peter 4:12-13*)

For **the time has come for judgment** to begin at the house of God; and if it begins with **us** first, what will be the end of those who do not obey the gospel of God? (*1 Peter 4:17*)

The imminence of the coming eschatological events in these passages cannot be missed. Peter warned that those reading his letters would see these things happen. Peter's words are consistent with those of Jesus. The passing of heaven and earth must be referring to the end of the Jewish dispensation—the Old Covenant order—in AD 70.

In modern language, we use the idiom "move heaven and earth" to mean doing everything one can to achieve something. President Barack Obama, in a messianic moment, used this term in his third debate against Mitt Romney in 2012. He certainly did not mean to imply anything about the end of the world. It should not be surprising to us moderns that the ancients used similar terminology in theology to refer to something other than the physical world—and other than the heavenly residence of God. Thus the phrase "new heaven and new earth" or simply "heaven and earth" can be biblical idioms that are not the same thing as "heaven" itself.

To fill out our knowledge about the biblical heavens and earth terminology, let's turn to the book of Isaiah. This book contains language that futurists as well as preterists consider important in understanding the eschatological *new heaven and earth*. In the opening verses of Isaiah we see this:

> Hear, O **heavens**, and give ear, O **earth!** . . . Alas, sinful nation, a people laden with iniquity, a brood of evildoers, children who are corrupters! (*Isaiah 1:2a, 4a; cf. Deuteronomy 31:30-32:1*)

This proclamation is apparently addressed to the children of Judah/Israel concerning their sins. (Some would say that the prophet is telling all creation about the sins of Israel, but it does not seem likely that anyone would be addressed here other than the offenders themselves.) So it can at least be reasonably argued that "heavens and earth" here is Old Covenant Israel. Given this understanding, we can infer that the *new* heavens and earth refers to the New Covenant Church, the successor to Old Covenant Israel. Returning to Isaiah 13, we note this passage in which God is speaking:

> Therefore I will shake the **heavens**, and the **earth** will move out of her place, in the wrath of the LORD of hosts and in the day of His fierce anger. (*Isaiah 13:13; cf. Haggai 2:6, 21*)

As we discussed above regarding "the Day of the Lord," this verse is in the context of heavenly upheaval language—the sun and moon darkened, etc. It concerns the specific judgment that came upon historic Babylon. Christians agree that this prophecy has been fulfilled. So, Isaiah 13 uses the term in conjunction with the concept of *judgment*.

Peter's epistles are certainly speaking of a coming judgment, which we know accompanied the covenantal upheaval of AD 70. So the concepts of Old Covenant Israel and judgment fit hand in glove with the different uses of heaven and earth terminology. There is often contextual overlap between the terms (new) heavens and earth and the Day of the Lord, the connection being judgment. Peter was undoubtedly repeating the *new heaven and new earth* terminology of Isaiah (especially Isaiah 65 and 66) which itself points to AD 70. Here is Isaiah 51, which adds the concept of *salvation* to our understanding of heaven and earth:

> My **righteousness is near**, my **salvation** has gone forth, and my arms will judge the peoples; the coastlands will wait upon Me, and on my arm they will trust. Lift up your eyes to the **heavens**, and look on the **earth** beneath. For the **heavens** will vanish away like smoke, the **earth** will grow old like a garment, and those who dwell in it will die in like manner; but my **salvation** will be <u>forever</u>, and my righteousness will not be abolished. . . .For the moth will eat them up like a garment, and the worm will eat them like wool; but my righteousness will be forever, and <u>my salvation from generation to generation</u>. . . . But I am the LORD your God, who divided the sea whose waves roared—the LORD of hosts is his name. And I have put my words in your mouth; I have covered you with the shadow of my hand, that I may plant the **heavens**, lay the foundations of the **earth**, and say to Zion, "<u>You are my people</u>." (*Isaiah 51:5-6, 8, 15-16*)

This is not the end of the universe. The "heavens" vanish like smoke and the "earth" waxes old, but generations of people live on (verse 8). Unlike Isaiah 13, nothing concrete in this passage ties it to a specific time of fulfillment. Many futurists—millennialists—think this passage is about a literal millennium spoken of in Revelation 20 and that it is still in our future. However there are some clues that would seem to preclude a far distant fulfillment. Note that the prophet used the term *near* (verse 5). That would suggest that the further into the future one expects the fulfillment to come, the less likely that interpretation is correct.

Notice also the term *salvation*, mentioned twice in this passage (verses 5, 6). Salvation here could mean salvation in a limited sense and apply to salvation from a specific judgment in Old Testament times (like Isaiah 13). But since it mentions an enduring *righteousness and eternal salvation* ("forever," verse 6), with accompanying judgment, the best fit would be the first century and the coming Savior. (More on the salvation aspects of AD 70 in Chapter 10.)

This passage is clearly covenantal. ("You are my people.") Further confirmation comes from Isaiah 51 being sandwiched within four Messianic "Servant Songs": Isaiah 42:1-9; 49:1-7; 50:4-11, and 52:13-53:12. The preterist interpretation is consistent with other passages we have already considered from the New Testament, and thus we think Isaiah 51 looks forward to Christ's first and second advents in the first century.

Now Isaiah 65—an important eschatological section, which is titled in some Bibles, "New Heaven and a New Earth," or in others, "The Glorious New Creation":

> "For behold, I create **new heavens and a new earth**, and the former shall not be remembered or come to mind. But be glad and rejoice forever in what I **create**; for behold, I **create Jerusalem** as a rejoicing, and her people a joy. I will rejoice in Jerusalem, and joy in my people; the voice of weeping shall no longer be heard in her, nor the voice of crying. No more shall an <u>infant</u> from there live but a few days, nor an old man who has not fulfilled his days; for the <u>child</u> shall <u>die</u> one hundred years old, but the <u>sinner</u> being one hundred years old shall be accursed. They shall build houses and inhabit them; they shall plant vineyards and eat their fruit. They shall not build and another inhabit; they shall not plant and another eat; for as the days of a tree, so shall be the <u>days of my people</u>, and <u>my elect</u> shall long enjoy the work of their hands. They shall not labor in vain, nor bring forth children for trouble; for they shall be the descendants of the blessed of the LORD, and their offspring with them. It shall come to pass that before they call, I will answer; and while they are still speaking, I will hear. The wolf and the lamb shall feed together, the lion shall eat straw like the ox, and dust shall be the serpent's food. They shall not hurt nor destroy in all my holy mountain," says the LORD. (*Isaiah 65:17-25; cf. Isaiah 24:1-23; 34:4-9*)

This is an idyllic picture. There is to be no more weeping in Jerusalem. The wolf and the lamb shall feed together. Is this to be taken literally?

Many futurists think that it is indeed to be taken literally, but disagree as to when this will occur. Amillennialists think that this is a picture of heaven and/or of earthly restoration at the end of the world. Premillennialists think this is a picture of a future millennial paradise on earth. Preterists believe that this passage uses figurative language that refers to the covenant curses we no longer suffer in the New Covenant Age. What view makes the most sense?

There may be certain challenges for each viewpoint. Preterists point out that critical problems are evident for those who take the passage literally. First of all, we again remember that Jesus stated in Luke 21:22 that all Old Testament prophecy—which obviously means all prophecy remaining unfulfilled when Jesus spoke—would be fulfilled in his generation. That would certainly mean that Isaiah 65 has been fulfilled.

Various other reasons prompt us to reject the idea that this passage is about heaven (an amillennialist view). It cannot be the eternal state since it contains birth, death, building of houses, and planting of vineyards. People don't die in heaven. Particularly interesting is the mention of births and children. Jesus said in Matthew 22:23-33 that no marriage will take place in the resurrection. Amillennialists, at least, believe this means heaven, and tie it to Isaiah 65. If the amillennial view is correct, we will have to conclude that people will be having babies out of wedlock in heaven. Will there be conjugal relations in heaven? Will these children be illicit children? Or will these be virgin births?

Premillennialists don't seem to fare any better. They apparently tie "the resurrection" of which Jesus speaks in Matthew 22 (and elsewhere) to the *earthly* millennium along with Isaiah 65—rather than in heaven as amillennialists do. But the same problem exists. If there is no marriage in the resurrection/millennium (per Jesus), will the births at that time be illegitimate, etc.? Also, premillennialists believe that death will be very rare or non-existent in the millennium, but Isaiah 65 speaks of death. And by what manner of interpretation should we consider the wolf and lamb feeding together, or the lion eating straw, as literal? [80]

We are getting ahead of ourselves concerning the resurrection, which we will discuss later. The general resurrection does indeed tie to the new heaven and new earth and to the millennium, but none of these remain in our future (bear with us). The main point for now is that the *new heaven and earth* in Isaiah 65 refers to the New Covenant Age. The book of Hebrews confirms this. Hebrews 12:18-29 tells us this *newly created Jerusalem* of Isaiah 65:18, in the context of the new heavens and new earth, was the New Testament church victorious—that is, the new covenant kingdom. Here is a quote from partial preterist Andrew Corbett:

> The context of the latter portion of Isaiah is the coming new covenant. Within this context the Lord speaks of creating a new heaven and a new earth. The expression "heavens and earth" seems to speak of God's relationship with mankind. He is the God of the heavens and the earth (Genesis 14:19; Ezra 5:11). Actually He is the God of the entire cosmos—but the expression "heaven and earth" emphasizes His connection to mankind. And the expres-

sion "heaven and earth" may well refer to the covenant God has with mankind. When the Lord speaks of a new heaven and a new earth there may be some merit in regarding this as Biblical language for a new covenant.[81]

That Isaiah 65 is covenantal is further supported by the terms found in verse 22 about "my people" and "my elect." Don K. Preston sums up the preterist view thusly:

> The only view which does not pose serious interpretative snafus is that which sees the New Creation [of Isaiah 65 and Revelation] as the consummated Kingdom of our Lord in which those who believe in Him do not die (John 8:51); in which there is peace (Philippians 4:4-9); there is eternal life (1 John 5:13) . . . This New World was consummated when God destroyed his old people, the Old Jerusalem (Isaiah 65:13ff), the Old Heavens and Earth of Judaism (Isaiah 51:15-16)—bringing to a close the Old World Age (Matthew 24:3) and bringing to glorious perfection (1 Corinthians 13:8-10), the New World. That time was when Jesus returned and destroyed the capital and hub of the Old World, Jerusalem, in AD 70.[82]

The apparent problem for preterists in Isaiah 65 is the utopian language such as the wolf and the lamb feeding together. We will consider *restorationism* in Chapter 13, but all things considered, the best conclusion is that this language is symbolic. The sense in which Isaiah 65 describes a new created order is similar to the sense in which Paul described a Christian upon his conversion as a totally *new creation*, which we see here in Paul's second letter to the Corinthians:

> Therefore, if anyone is in Christ, he is a **new creation**; old things have passed away; behold, all things have become new. (*2 Corinthians 5:17*)

In Isaiah 65-66 we do not see the universe as dissolved, like many Christians think. In Isaiah 65:17ff we see that there are births, deaths, and even sin in the new heavens and new earth. In Isaiah 66, we see that God's enemies are killed, but regular human history continues. Indeed, survivors would be sent out to evangelize those who never heard of God (66:19). So there are still people who never heard of God! Here is an excerpt from Isaiah 66:

The sound of noise from the city! A voice from the <u>temple</u>! The voice of the LORD, who fully <u>repays his enemies</u>! . . . "Rejoice with <u>Jerusalem</u>, and be glad with her, all you who love her; rejoice for joy with her, all you who mourn for her; . . . Behold, I will extend peace to her like a river, and the glory of the <u>Gentiles</u> like a flowing stream." . . . For behold, the LORD will come with **fire and with his chariots**, like a whirlwind, to render his anger with fury, and his rebuke with flames of fire. For by fire and by his sword the LORD will <u>judge</u> all flesh; and the slain of the LORD shall be many. . . . "For I know their works and their thoughts. It shall be that I will gather all nations and tongues; and they shall come and see my glory. I will set a sign among them; and those among them who escape I will send to the nations. . . to those that have not heard my fame or seen my glory. And they shall declare my glory among the Gentiles [nations]. . . . For as the **new heavens and the new earth** which I will make shall remain before Me," says the LORD, "So shall your descendants and your name remain. And it shall come to pass that from one new moon to another, and from one Sabbath to another, all flesh shall come to worship before Me," says the LORD. "And they shall go forth and look upon the <u>corpses of the men who have transgressed against Me</u>. For their worm does not die, and their fire is not quenched. They shall be an abhorrence to all flesh." *(Isaiah 66:6, 10, 12, 15-16, 18-19, 22-24)*

No specific time-reference is found here, but there is not much that distinguishes this passage from the others we have considered. Isaiah chapters 65-66, considered together, speak of the destruction of God's old covenant people and the full establishment of his new covenant people in the new heaven and new earth.

Isaiah 66 further speaks of the final judgment, the end of the elements of Old Testament law, and the gathering of all nations. These are themes consistent with Jesus' Olivet Discourse. While AD 70 witnessed the horrors of God's judgment, it ushered out the old and decaying while ushering in the new. In Romans, Paul implies that Isaiah 65/66 is contrasting old covenant Israel with God's new covenant people (Romans 10:19-21; cf. Romans 9:21-33).[83]

There is one particularly interesting thing in this passage—the *Lord's coming with chariots*. Now, hold on to your hats. Josephus related a most spectacular event that occurred in AD 66:

Besides these [signs], a few days after that feast, on the one-and-twentieth day of the month Artemisius, [Jyar,] a certain prodigious and incredible phenomenon appeared; I suppose the account of it would seem to be a fable, were it not related by those that saw it, and were not the events that followed it of so considerable a nature as to deserve such signals; for, before sun-setting, **chariots** and troops of soldiers in their armor were seen running about among the **clouds**, and surrounding of cities. Moreover, at that feast which we call Pentecost, as the priests were going by night into the inner [court of the] temple, as their custom was, to perform their sacred ministrations, they said that, in the first place, they felt a quaking, and heard a great noise, and after that they heard a sound as of a great multitude, saying, "Let us remove hence." [84]

Perhaps we should take this with a grain of salt, but this is an astounding account of an event reportedly witnessed by many people. Other ancient writers also commented on it. It should not be discounted. It certainly lends strong support to the preterist view. More importantly, it supports the Bible—specifically the prophecies of Isaiah and Jesus. Note the cloud language. The sight of the soldiers and chariots in the clouds could be interpreted as the Second Coming.[85]

Another piece of evidence we find from Josephus is that he explained in his writings that in the Jewish mind, heaven and earth came together in the temple.[86] Of course, the temple was destroyed in AD 70. The New Heavens and New Earth, we conclude, arrived at that time. When we consider Revelation in the next chapter, we will see that the new heaven and earth theme in Revelation 21 fits perfectly with other biblical references to the new heaven and earth in the preterist context. The reader can look forward to our discussion of *restoration* in Chapter 13.

The reader is once again referred to Appendix B to the chart entitled, "A Tale of Two Ages."

Question for your pastor, church leaders, and friends: Since Jesus said that the law would remain in effect until heaven and earth had passed away, is the law still in effect?

Revelation:
The Apocalypse

R evelation is considered by many to be the most difficult book in the Bible. Scholars are often timid when it comes to this magnificent book. Even the great Reformation scholar John Calvin wrote separate commentaries about every book of the Bible except Revelation. Preterists don't claim to have every detail figured out either. However, some significant conclusions can be drawn which should be very clear. While details of Revelation are challenging and in dispute, the big picture is not so difficult, once you begin to see the patterns developing.

The ideas we present in this chapter are going to be particularly shocking to the typical American fundamentalist steeped in millennialism and wooden literalism. We will present our case that Revelation is, foremost, a covenantal book. It is not about a whole new set of concepts, nor is it about fanciful phenomenon at the end of the world. It teaches the same things the rest of the Bible teaches, being completely consistent with the rest of the Bible.

While Revelation is a timeless book with universal relevance (Revelation 5:9; 7:9; 10:11; 13:7; 14:6), we note that it was written specifically to Christians living at the time John wrote it. As is clear in the early chapters, Revelation was a letter written to specific historic churches in Asia Minor, and would have been read out loud by the Christians there. It is also evident from the letter that it was to be *understood* by the Christians reading it. As the name of the book implies, it is *revealing* something important to the first-century readers. John states to his readers, "He who has an ear, let him hear" (Revelation 2:7, 11, 17, 29; 3:6, 13, 22).

One of the main purposes of the book was to give comfort to the saints of that day in the face of their suffering, and to remind them that

Christ was still in charge and would soon triumph. In fact, the book specifically says it is about events that **must** (not *might*) *take place shortly* (Revelation 1:1; 22:6). One thing that is often missed by Christians today is that John told us that *he and his readers were already in the tribulation!* He states, "I, John, both your brother and companion in the **tribulation**. . . ." (Revelation 1:9a). John and his readers were suffering real persecution and tribulation. What a cruel joke it would have been to use the promise of the imminent Second Coming as a ruse, to get the church to endure in its tribulations, when the Second Coming was actually not going to happen till thousands of years later.

By the way, a detail we have not yet mentioned is that the tribulation period had two phases. There was a time of intensified persecution of Christians under the Jews and Nero during the period of approximately AD 62-68. Then there was the period of Rome's war against the Jews from AD 66-70. Depending on when John was writing, he may have been referring to either. It is quite possible, as we will explore, that John was writing in about AD 64, so he may have been referring to the period of Christian persecution.[87]

This is not to say the book of Revelation has no relevance to us today. It is certainly relevant in a similar way that Paul's epistles to various first-century churches also have relevance to all of us in all times. But John's Revelation was first of all specific to his times and to his first-century readers.

But if the book is all about events long into the future, then it had little relevance to those to whom it was written. So it cannot be talking about nuclear weapons or the Chinese or the Iranians in the twenty-first century. As Russell put it when he was writing in the nineteenth century,

"Is it conceivable that an apostle would mock the suffering and persecuted Christians of his time with dark parables about distant ages? . . . If it spoke, as some would have us believe, of Huns and Goths and Saracens, of mediaeval emperors and popes, of the Protestant Reformation and the French Revolution, what possible interest or meaning could it have for the Christian churches of Ephesus, and Smyrna, and Philadelphia, and Laodicea? . . . It may be safely affirmed that on this hypothesis [Revelation] is incapable of interpretation: it must continue to be what it has so long been, material for arbitrary and fanciful speculation." [88]

As we explore below, we will find that Revelation gives us some firmly established time-references that tie its fulfillment to the first century. Our conclusion, stated up front, is that the book of Revelation is John's expanded, dramatized, and "transfigured" version of the Olivet Discourse. It uses much of the same language and time-references. We note that the three synoptic gospels—Matthew, Mark, and Luke—all contain the Olivet Discourse. The Gospel of John curiously does not. John places his version of it in a separate book—Revelation.

Revelation parallels the Olivet Discourse at many points. They both contain these themes: war, strife, famine, earthquakes, persecutions, judgment of a sinful city following completion of the world mission, the Great Tribulation, the abomination of desolation, urging of the faithful to flee from the city, false prophets, Jesus' return on clouds, sounding of the trumpet at the time of the end, salvation of the elect, gathering of the birds of the air to feast on the carcass of the dead, etc. The parallels are too numerous to be coincidental, and they begin to solve the mysteries of Revelation.[89]

Here's an interesting question for your pastor, church leaders, and friends: Was John already in the tribulation when he wrote Revelation?

When Was Revelation Written?

The dating of Revelation is important to our discussion. Many Christians understand the book to have been written around AD 95 or 96 (or more broadly between AD 90 and 110). If this is correct, preterists may be mistaken about Revelation. But there is strong and convincing evidence that the book was written prior to AD 70. Over sixty authors, from different theological persuasions, have been identified as holding to a pre-AD 70 date.[90]

An important and compelling book that argues for a pre-AD 70 date for Revelation is by conservative scholar Kenneth L. Gentry, Jr., and is entitled *Before Jerusalem Fell: Dating the Book of Revelation*. Another noteworthy book is by *liberal* scholar John A. T. Robinson entitled *Redating the New Testament*. Other helpful books about the dating of Revelation include *Who is this Babylon?* by Don K. Preston, and *The Early Church and the End of the World* by Gary DeMar and Francis X. Gumerlock. Preston takes the reader step-by-step through Revelation and conclusively argues for an early date, while DeMar and Gumerlock examine the views of early church writers on the subject. R. C. Sproul discusses the dating of Revelation in a book entitled *The Last Days according to Jesus*. In his book, Sproul discusses the scholarship concerning the early dating. Drawing on the research of Gentry and others, Sproul said:

> Though conceding that in twentieth-century scholarly circles the majority have placed the writing of Revelation well after A.D. 70, Gentry lists numerous scholars who place it earlier. This list includes Greg L. Bahnsen, Adam Clarke, F. W. Farrar, John A. T. Robinson, Henry Barclay Swete, Milton S. Terry, Wilhelm Bousset, F. F. Bruce, Rudolf Bultmann, Samuel Davidson, Alfred Edersheim, Johann Eichhorn, Joseph A. Fitzmyer, J. B. Lightfoot, C. F. D. Moule, and August H. Strong, to name but a few. Two things can be said of this list. First, it represents scholars from every point on the theological spectrum. And second, the list, in itself, does not prove an early-date theory, as the theory cannot be demonstrated by counting noses. The list does reveal, however, that the notion of an early date for Revelation is by no means a novelty.[91]

The argument for the late date of Revelation rests principally on an ambiguous, third hand remark by Irenaeus (c. AD 180). The weight of the evidence is against the Irenaeus citation. Irenaeus is known to have made other historical errors, which Gentry explores. While none of the church fathers are totally reliable in this matter, Gentry cites others that, at least, imply a pre-AD 70 writing of Revelation. Papias (c. AD 100) purportedly said that John was killed by the Jews. This would have been when the Jews could have accomplished the execution—before AD 70. Or, Nero may well have had him executed at Patmos. If John had lived many years past AD 70, his influence in church matters would have been powerful. Instead, there is silence. John is not even listed in the Catholic records as being in the papal succession.

We will not dissect the Irenaeus issue here, other than to say that dozens of scholars who have studied this issue, have concluded that either Irenaeus was mistaken or that he has been misunderstood. As we progress, the open-minded reader will agree, we believe, that Revelation had to have been written prior to AD 70. It does not matter what Irenaeus may have thought if it conflicts with Holy Scripture.[92]

We must go to the book of Revelation itself for internal evidence. One interesting thing is that the period of time where there were *only* seven churches in Asia was during the few years from the early sixties AD to the time prior to the Jewish War. It is also critical to note that the destruction of Jerusalem and the temple are not mentioned. Sproul comments on this:

> If the Book of Revelation was written after the destruction of Jerusalem and the temple, it seems strange that John would be silent about these cataclysmic events. Granted this is an argument from silence, but the silence is deafening.[93]

Actually, the testimony in Revelation about the temple is not mere silence. In Revelation 11:1-8 John was told to measure the temple. He was also told not to measure the outer court of the temple because Jerusalem was going to be trampled for forty-two months. These would be most bizarre instructions if John wrote the book after the time of the destruction of Jerusalem and the temple.

We will consider further evidence as we continue. So far we have referenced primarily modern Protestant scholars. Here is a quote from a nineteenth-century Roman Catholic source:

> The book of Revelation will probably never now admit of a wholly luminous exposition, in consequence of the histories we have of the times to which it refers not corresponding to the magnified scale of its prophecies. But the direction in which it is most wise to seek for a solution of its enigmas is from that standing-point which considers that it was written before the destruction of Jerusalem, to encourage those whose hearts were then failing them for fear of those things which were then speedily coming upon the earth; that is, taken up primarily and principally with events with which its first readers only were immediately interested; that it displays a series of pictures doubtfully chronological, and perchance partly contemporaneous, of events all shortly to come to pass. . . . [94]

IMMINENCY AND TIES TO THE REST OF THE BIBLE

We will not attempt to cover every detail of Revelation. There are some 300 references in Revelation to the Old Testament, and the book ties everywhere to other parts of the New Testament. But we do want to get a solid understanding of the big picture. We will present some of the important time-reference texts for the reader's consideration. We will also attempt to identify the major themes of the book.

Some two dozen passages in the book of Revelation tie the date of the events of Revelation to first-century Israel, either (a) by specific time-reference, (b) by correlating to other texts that are limited by a time-reference (some of which we have studied in previous chapters), (c) by pointing specifically to Jerusalem or the nation of Israel, or (d) by being confirmed by actual historical accounts of first-century Jerusalem as the place and time of the apocalypse. Here is a list of such passages:

> Revelation **1:1; 1:3;** 1:7; 1:9-10; 1:19; 2:10; **2:16;** 2:25; 3:10; **3:11;** 4:1; 6:12-17; 8:13; **10:6-7;** 11:2; 11:8; 11:15-19; 12:5; 14:7; 14:14-20; 15:5-8; 16:6; 16:19; 17:8; 18:19, 24; 20:7-10; 20:11-15; **22:6; 22:7; 22:10; 22:12; 22:20.**

If the reader takes the time to look up each of these passages he will note familiar language that we have already discussed. The passages in bold specifically say that the events in view, including the Second Coming, were to happen **soon** or were **near** or were going to take place **without delay** ("must shortly take place."). In addition, certain of these passages (1:19; 3:10; 8:13; 10:7; 12:5; 17:8) contain the Greek word *mello*, which, as we have already noted, is translated in Young's Literal Translation and in interlinear translations as "about to" (happen). These time-texts are definitive, and they are noteworthy by being consistent with the imminency passages in the rest of the New Testament. We strongly suggest that any eschatology that denies a plain literal interpretation of the New Testament time-texts, has adopted an overly elastic and, frankly, unscriptural position that damages the Bible's integrity.

Some interpreters believe that Revelation is to be divided into sections, some to near events and some to distant events. But we see imminency language and other references that tie to first-century Israel at the beginning, the middle, and the end of the book. Riley O'Brien Powell, on her website, comments:

> The letter of Revelation itself says nothing about a shift in audience or subject matter. It says nothing about a delay in timing or a change in intended audience. EVER. Revelation is *one letter, one message*, written to seven churches in Asia Minor—*from beginning to end*. Chopping the letter up is an arbitrary idea forced onto the text. It is the result of a misunderstanding about when or why it was written and how it was fulfilled to its original audience. Once we see WHEN and WHY Revelation was written, much of the mystery of its content is solved.[95]

Also of note, Revelation 22:7 applies imminence to the entire book of Revelation. Jesus states: "Behold, I am coming quickly! Blessed is he who keeps the words of the prophecy of this book." The message of Revelation is consistent throughout and applies to the events that were about to happen.

The placing of the time statements at both the beginning (Revelation 1-3) and the end of the book (Revelation 22) demands that the fulfillment of its prophecies rise or fall together. They simply cannot be bifurcated. And we will show that a strong case can be made that fulfillment of the entire prophecy of Revelation occurred in association with the Jewish-Roman War of AD 66-70 and the destruction of Jerusalem and the temple.

When we have asked futurists whether they are bothered by this soon/near language in Revelation, we typically get a deer-in-the-headlights stare, or a response that does not address the issue. "Well, it can't mean what it says. It doesn't agree with what I've been taught." At this point we are reminded of a line in Simon and Garfunkel's song, The Boxer: "A man hears what he wants to hear, and disregards the rest." And like Jacob, futurists find themselves boxing with God.

Some people say that when Jesus said He was to come soon or quickly, He meant that when He does come thousands of years hence, He will come swiftly. Well, that would be like calling an ambulance and hearing them say that they are coming quickly, and then years later they show up going 100 miles an hour. It makes no sense. (Ask your pastor about these imminency passages and pay attention to what he says.)

Dispensationalists especially accuse other Christians of not taking the Bible literally. But we think their accusation is hypocritical. They take the spectacular language of Revelation literally—Jesus returning on a white horse and all of that—but refuse to take straightforward language of soon and near literally.

Can all references to soon or near throughout the Bible mean the far distant future? Can all references to love mean hate? Can references to happy mean sad? This makes a mockery not only of language, but of the Bible. Jesus said he was coming soon; we ought to believe Him. Let us quote Kenneth Gentry:

> . . . First, we should note that [John] carefully varies his manner of expression, as if to avoid any potential confusion as to his meaning. A brief survey of the three leading terms he employs will be helpful in ascertaining his meaning. The first of these terms to appear in Revelation is the Greek word *tachos*, translated "shortly."

(Revelation 1:1; 2:16; 3:11; 22:6-7, 12, 20) . . . Another term John uses is *eggus*, which means "near" (Revelation 1:3; 22:10). . . . The final term we will note is *mello*, which means "about to" (Revelation 1:19; 3:10). . . . John was telling the seven historical churches (Revelation 1:4, 11; 22:16) in his era to expect the events of his prophecy at any moment. He repeats the point time and again for emphasis.[96]

It is absolutely clear that whenever the book of Revelation was written, there must have been events soon afterward that matched the description of the events in the book! Included in these events was the Second Coming (Revelation 1:7; 22:12)! If you were trying to sound the alarm about something to happen soon, how many times and in how many ways would you have to say it for people not to deny it: the time is near, must shortly take place, coming quickly, at hand, it's the last hour, etc.?!

In an article from the Catholic Archdiocese of Washington, Monsignor Charles Pope offered ten reasons why he believes that Revelation was written prior to AD 70:

Most of the Book of Revelation is drawn directly from Old Testament Prophets such as Joel, Daniel and Ezekiel. Since this is done, it is important to learn what their historical context and concerns were. Most of the O.T. sources from which John and the Holy Spirit draw, have the historical context of the destruction of Jerusalem and the Temple which took place in 587 BC. If that was the original context of the texts from which John borrows, then it is strongly probable that John is saying, what happened then (in 587 BC) will happen again unless there is Jewish repentance and faith. This is what the passages meant in the Old Testament time and now John borrows them for the current time of 70 AD, wherein the Temple and Jerusalem were prophesied by Jesus to be destroyed again. Thus parallel events are being described and point to the context in which John writes. The minority view [pre-AD 70 authorship] fits nicely with this historical perspective.[97]

We also note that the book of Revelation is consistent with the other books of the New Testament. Let's look at some interesting passages:

- *coming with clouds, every eye to see Him, even those who pierced Him, all the tribes of the earth [land] to mourn because of Him* (Revelation 1:7)—The first thing that should jump out at you here is the cloud language. It is the same language used in the Olivet Discourse where Jesus says all prophecy would be fulfilled in his generation. "Tribes" (also in the Discourse, Matthew 24:30) can only mean the tribes of Israel (who pierced Him), so this ties to Israel in the first century. The word translated as "earth" is the Greek word *ge*. In other places it is translated as "country," "district," or "land," thus having a regional connotation (Matthew 9:31; Acts 7:3; etc.). So clearly, the events John saw were to be local rather than global.

What about "every eye will see Him?" This statement connects to statements of Jesus such as in Matthew 26:64 where He tells the Jewish leaders that *they* would see Him coming on the clouds of heaven. Given this setting, it seems best to understand *seeing* in the sense of *revelation* rather than literal sight. Isaiah 40:5 says, "And the glory of the Lord shall be *revealed*, and all flesh shall see it together." Elsewhere we find the concept of "to look upon" God in the sense of profound earnest regard or to "look to the Messiah as the source of salvation." See Zechariah 12:10. In a similar way many passages in John's gospel speak of faith in terms of "seeing" (John 6:40, etc.). Yet, in a more literal sense, recall the chariots seen in the sky in AD 66 (Chapter 8), which could be a literal fulfillment of Jesus' prophecy in the first century. (As promised, we will consider in more detail in Chapter 12 the issue of a literal-physical return of Christ.) [98]

- ***the great day of Christ's wrath had come*** (Revelation 6:16-17)—In Russell's lengthy discourse on Revelation, he points out the reiterations in Revelation of other prophetic passages in the Bible. For example, the dramatic Sixth Seal (Revelation 6:12-17) parallels perfectly with the Olivet Discourse—earthquake, sun and moon darkened, stars fall to earth, heavens shaken, the fig tree image, etc. The many visions of warfare throughout the book depict the same wrath that Jesus spoke of in the Olivet Discourse. But in the book of Revelation, it is revealed that He himself participates in the destruction of Jerusalem. In addition to the obvious urgency in Revelation 6:16-17, we can see how this passage ties back to Malachi chapters 3 and 4, which predicted the national judgment that would come upon the Jews at the Messiah's Second Coming. ("The Lord, whom you seek, will suddenly come to his temple; and the messenger of the covenant in whom you delight, behold He is coming. . . .

Then I will draw near to you for judgment.") All of this leads us inevitably to an AD 70 fulfillment.

- *earthquakes, stars falling from heaven, angels sound their trumpets, eagle cries "woe"* (Revelation 8:6-13)—This passage echoes the Olivet Discourse. The eagle (sometimes translated *angel*) in Revelation 8:13 is a striking parallel to the judgment upon Israel in Hosea 8:1. Again, because of the ties to the Olivet discourse, the time-texts in Revelation, and the references to judgment on Israel, we conclude that the book of Revelation was to be fulfilled in our Lord's own generation.

- *the temple court being given over to the Gentiles who would trample it underfoot for forty-two months* (Revelation 11:2)—This ties well with the events of the Jewish-Roman War. Recall in Chapter 5 when we considered the statements in the book of Daniel about the tribulation period, specifically the 1,290 days—which we noted is three and a half years. Here we see John in Revelation predicting the time period as forty-two months, which is also three and a half years! (The two periods do not have to be the same three and a half years. Some would argue that the forty-two months may tie to the period of Neronian persecution that ended with Nero's death in AD 68.) [99]

- *dead bodies in the city where the Lord was crucified* (Revelation 11:8)—This location, of course, was old covenant Jerusalem. Along with identifying markers in other passages, this reveals the place where the wrathful events of Revelation took place.

- *the 144,000 were the first fruits to God and the Lamb, and they were the ones coming out of the Great Tribulation* (Revelation 7 and 14)—Remembering that there were twelve tribes of Israel, the 144,000 can be understood for what it signified. The number 1,000 is symbolic of "fullness." So 12 times 12 times 1,000 equals 144,000. As the *first* fruits, the 144,000 represents the first-generation Christians (the righteous remnant of the twelve tribes of Israel) who experienced the Great Tribulation, that is—the desolation of Jerusalem and the Jewish holocaust in AD 66-70! Revelation is a book that contains highly symbolic imagery throughout. The 144,000 is clearly not to be taken literally—as, for example, Jehovah's Witnesses think. Romans 8:23; 16:5; 1

Corinthians 16:15; 2 Thessalonians 2:13, and James 1:18 further identify the first fruits as first-century believers.

- *no one could enter the sanctuary until the events of Revelation were finished* (Revelation 15:5-8) — This verse seems to be a parallel with Hebrews 9:8 and its context, where we read that Jesus would come a second time at the end of the Old Covenant Age in order to make manifest the heavenly holiest of holies.

- *the new Jerusalem and new heaven and new earth, the former things having passed away* (Revelation 21:1-4) — This is consistent with the new heaven and new earth discussion that we presented in the previous chapter, as well as the statements by Paul, the writer of Hebrews, Peter, etc. concerning the passing away of the old form of the world, and the changing of the imperfect old covenant order into the perfection of Jesus. Revelation 21:1-4 is symbolic of the AD 70 full establishment of God's kingdom, and depicts the same event as Isaiah prophesied (65, 66). The New Covenant order fully arrived when the Old Covenant order was removed and abolished in AD 70 (Hebrews 8:13; 12:18-29).

- *instructions not to seal up the words of the book for the time was near* (Revelation 22:10) — This passage is a *remarkable bookend* to the statements in Daniel 8:26 and 12:4. These passages in Daniel say respectively: "Therefore **seal up** the vision, for it refers to many days in the future." and "But you, Daniel, shut up the words, and **seal** the book, *until the time of the end*." Can there be any reasonable doubt that Revelation speaks of the time of the end of which Daniel spoke? This completes the picture. Daniel was told to seal up the book because the time of the end was far off. In Revelation, John was told *not* to seal the book because the time was near. Daniel's prophecy was to be sealed up until the time of its fulfillment. We have already tied Daniel's prophecy to the time when the burnt offering was taken away. When John penned Revelation, the time was near for the destruction of the "city and the sanctuary" (Daniel 9:36), and the end of the Old Covenant Age. Even without all of the many other imminence passages in Revelation, this reference alone concludes, irrefutably, the imminence of the events of Revelation.

JUDGMENT UPON BABYLON

There is universal agreement that the major theme of Revelation is the judgment upon Babylon. The disagreement is about who Babylon is, and, when her judgment takes place. Consider this excerpt from the magnificent section of Revelation, chapters 18 and 19:

> Alas, alas, that **great city Babylon**, that mighty city! For in one hour your **judgment has come**. . . . For in one hour she is made desolate. Rejoice over her, O heaven, and you holy apostles and prophets, for God has avenged you on her! . . . And in her was found the **blood of prophets and saints**, and of all who were slain on the earth. . . . After these things I heard a loud voice of a great multitude in heaven, saying, "Alleluia! Salvation and glory and honor and power belong to the Lord our God! For true and righteous are his judgments, because He has judged the great **harlot** who corrupted the earth with her fornication; and He has avenged on her the blood of his servants shed by her." . . . Now I saw heaven opened, and behold, a white horse. And He who sat on him was called Faithful and True, and in righteousness He judges and makes war. . . . And He has on his robe and on his thigh a name written: KING OF KINGS AND LORD OF LORDS. (*Revelation 18:10b; 19b, 20, 24; 19:1, 2, 11, 16*)

You might want to stop and read chapters 16-19 in their entirety. The great city Babylon is judged at the coming of the Lord. Who is this great city called Babylon? We have plenty of information to identify her as none other than old covenant Jerusalem. The term *great city* is used in other places in Revelation, for example, in chapter 11:

> And their dead bodies will lie in the street of the **great city** which spiritually [*symbolically* in some versions] is called Sodom and Egypt, where also our **Lord was crucified**. (*Revelation 11:8*)

Jesus was crucified in Jerusalem. So "the great city" (Babylon) is clearly identified. For further confirmation, we find that the only city referred to symbolically in the Bible as Sodom is old covenant Jerusalem (Deuteronomy 32:28-33; Isaiah 1:9-10; Jeremiah 23:14, and Ezekiel 16:46-57). Paul, in 1 Thessalonians 2:14-16, stated that it was the Jews who killed Jesus, and upon whom God's wrath had come "to the uttermost." We also note that in Revelation 18:20, 24 (above) the apostles and prophets rejoiced at the impending judgment of Babylon for her persecution of them. No other city in history can be identified with persecuting the prophets: "It cannot be that a prophet should perish away from Jerusalem" (Luke 13:33). The reader will also remember from Chapter 5 that Jesus himself said that the blood of all the prophets in history would fall upon Jerusalem in *his own generation* (Matthew 23:29-39; Luke 11:49-53). Compare Jesus' words with Revelation 18:24: "And in her [Babylon] was found the blood of prophets, and of saints, and of all that were slain upon the earth." Babylon could not refer to any other city in any other time period. Author Don K. Preston also points out that ancient extra-biblical Roman and Jewish commentators referred to Jerusalem as "the great city." These are undeniable proofs that point to Jerusalem and AD 70.[100]

It is also significant that the Babylon of Revelation is described as being a harlot (Revelation 17:1, 15; 19:2). As pointed out by Gary DeMar, "Throughout the Bible, when Israel is unfaithful, she is characterized as a 'harlot' and an 'adulterer' (Ezekiel 16). She played the harlot with the Egyptians and the Assyrians (Ezekiel 16:26, 28). Both Israel and Judah played the harlot with the idolatrous nations surrounding them (Jeremiah 3:6-9)." [101] See also, Deuteronomy 31:16-18; Isaiah 1:21; Jeremiah 2:20; Ezekiel 16:14-15; Hosea 9:1.

There are other markers that identify Jerusalem as Revelation's Babylon, but the point is adequately proven. Over and over the same picture emerges. It is Jerusalem in the generation of Jesus, Paul, and John that is the target of John's revealed judgment. Jerusalem was to be judged for the specific crimes listed in Revelation 18. The judgment was to come upon Jerusalem *soon,* and it did. Jerusalem was judged in the first century for her historic crimes. There is no reason to believe she will ever be judged again for those crimes.

THE BEAST

Except for the millennium, probably no part of Revelation has garnered more speculation than the Beast of Revelation 13. But we suspect that many who throw around accusations as to who or what the beast is in our day (or who the antichrist is, or what 666 means), have probably never read or seriously studied the text. Here is what the Bible says about the beast:

> Then I saw a **beast** rising up out of the sea. It had seven heads and ten horns, with ten crowns on its horns. And written on each head were names that blasphemed God. . . . And the beast was allowed to wage war against God's holy people and to conquer them. And he was given authority to rule over every tribe and people and language and nation. And all the people who belong to this world worshiped the beast. They are the ones whose names were not written in the Book of Life before the world was made—the Book that belongs to the Lamb who was slaughtered. Anyone with ears to hear should listen and understand. . . . He [the second beast] was granted power to give breath to the image of the beast, that the image of the beast should both speak and cause as many as would not **worship** the image of the beast to be killed. He causes all, both small and great, rich and poor, free and slave, to receive a mark on their right hand or on their foreheads, and that no one may buy or sell except one who has the mark or the name of the beast, or the number of his name. Here is wisdom. **Let him who has understanding calculate the number of the beast,** for it is the number of a **man**: His number is **666**. (*Revelation 13:1, 7-9, 15-18*)

Actually, there are two beasts. The first beast came from the sea; the second beast came from the earth. The first beast is the primary actor, with the second beast appearing in a supporting role as a propagandist for the first beast. We doubt that anyone can establish an absolutely airtight interpretation of all this. But one interpretation makes more sense to us than any other. John was telling his readers that the beast was a man, and that they could figure out who the man was by calculating his number.

Since the book of Revelation was written to a first-century audience, around AD 62-67, we should expect the first-century readers to have been able to calculate the number. For the beast to be someone thousands of years in the future would have made no sense to the readers in the first century, and would have made the calculation of the number impossible for them. Remember, the Bible was written *for* us but not *to* us. Audience relevance is critical to understanding the sacred text.

As every school child knows, the Romans used letters to represent numerals. Similarly, the Greeks and Hebrews assigned numerical values to their letters. Since Revelation was written by a Jew in a Hebrew context, and with numerous allusions to the Old Testament, we should expect the solution to deciphering the meaning of 666 to be Hebraic. It turns out that when Nero's name is translated numerically into Hebrew we find something very interesting. One version of Nero's name—Neron Caesar (*Nrwn Qsr*)—provides us with precisely the value of 666! While we will not go into detail here, you can check this out in various places. One book that goes into it is Gary DeMar's *Last Days Madness*.[102] Another one is R. C. Sproul's *The Last Days according to Jesus*.[103] You can also find this discussed online in various places. (Do an Internet search for "beast and Nero.")

It is plausible that the Beast was Nero. Nero was ruler of Rome from AD 54-68, during the time when Revelation was written. The life of Nero perfectly fits the description; he was indeed a beastly man. He was a ruthless, insanely cruel murderer of many, including members of his own family—and the first Gentile persecutor of Christians. There were other ghastly tyrants in the ancient world, but nobody distinguished himself any more in violence, brutality, and debauchery than Nero (though Caligula came close in AD 37-41). Period secular historian Apollonius of Tyana made note of the fact that Nero was indeed referred to as a "beast." [104]

Another aspect of Nero that fits the description in Revelation is that Nero insisted on being worshipped as a god, which was antithetical to Christians. So Christians would have considered him a beast not only for his ruthless persecution of Christians and his murderous ways, but also for his insistence on being worshipped.[105]

There is an interesting twist on this story. Many ancient manuscripts of the Bible have the number 616 instead of 666! In fact, perhaps the oldest manuscript available uses 616.[106] This will surprise a lot of Christians who are wrapped up in 666 numerology speculation. The intriguing thing is that 616 spells Nero in *Latin*, the way 666 spells Nero in *Hebrew*! Some scholars believe that the change in the number was done purposely. Since Latin was the Roman language of the region that included Judea, the change was made so that Latin readers of the Bible would also have understood that the beast was Nero.

We again call on Kenneth Gentry to shed even more light as to the identification of the beast: [107]

John wrote to be understood: "Blessed is he that readeth, and they that hear the words of this prophecy, and keep those things which are written therein: for the time is at hand" (Revelation 1:3). In fact, he specifically points out here that the wise one will understand: "And here is the mind which hath wisdom. The seven heads are seven mountains, on which the woman sitteth" (Revelation 17:9). The referent is beyond doubt: Rome is alluded to in this vision of the seven-headed Beast. The original recipients of Revelation lived under the rule of Rome, which was universally distinguished by its seven hills. How could the recipients, living in the seven historical churches of Asia Minor and under Roman imperial rule, understand John's vision as anything other than this geographical feature?

. . . We learn further that the seven heads also have a political referent: "And there are seven kings: five are fallen, and one is, and the other is not yet come; and when he cometh, he must continue a short space" (Revelation 17:10). . . . Of the seven kings "five have fallen." These emperors are dead, when John writes. But the verse goes on to say "one is." That is, the sixth one is then reigning even as John wrote. That would be Nero Caesar, who assumed imperial power upon the death of the fifth emperor, Claudius, in October, A.D. 54. Nero remained emperor until his suicide in A.D. 68, a period of over thirteen years.

John continues: "The other is not yet come; and when he cometh, he must continue a short space." As the Roman Civil Wars broke out in rebellion against Nero, Nero committed suicide on June 8, A.D. 68. John informs us that the seventh king was "not yet come." That would be Galba, who assumed power upon Nero's death in June, A.D. 68. But he was only to continue a "short space." As a matter of historical fact, his reign lasted but six months—until January 15, A.D. 69. He was one of the quick succession of emperors in the famous era called by historians: "the year of the four emperors."

Gary DeMar sums it up: "Nero Caesar fits three essential criteria in determining the identity of the sea beast who will 'make war with the saints' (13:7): the time of his reign (AD 54-68), the numerical value of his official name and title, and his character as a persecutor of the saints." [108] So we see how everything ties together. Revelation is speaking of the events of the first century—the same eschatological events as the rest of the Bible. It all fits.[109]

Many Christians believe that the beast and the antichrist of John's epistles are the same. To figure out one is to figure out the other. This connection may or may not be correct as the antichrist is not even mentioned in Revelation, nor is the beast mentioned outside of Revelation (except Daniel 7). Here is what we know about the antichrist:

> Little children, it **is the last hour**; and as you have heard that the **Antichrist** is coming, even now many antichrists **have come**, by which we know that it is the **last hour**. . . . Beloved, do not believe every spirit, but test the spirits, whether they are of God; because many false prophets have gone out into the world. By this you know the Spirit of God: Every spirit that confesses that Jesus Christ has come in the flesh is of God, and every spirit that does not confess that Jesus Christ has come in the flesh is not of God. And this is the spirit of the **Antichrist**, which you have heard was coming, and is **now already in the world**. You are of God, little children, and have overcome them, because He who is in you is greater than he who is in the world. (*1 John 2:18, 4:1-4*)

John refers to multiple antichrists which had already come. This reference may mean anyone who had opposed Christ. But *the* antichrist—or at least his spirit—was already in the world. This too fits the time frame of a first-century fulfillment. Since John insisted that they were in the *last hour*, the imminency of the message precludes a yet-future fulfillment. To say that a bogeyman antichrist is still in our future is simply not biblical. John's epistles are the only place in the Bible that the antichrist is mentioned. It is best to simply rely on John's description of the antichrist, which is altogether different from the modern image. John's antichrist is:

1. false believers who went out from the church (1 John 2:19)

2. anyone who "denies Jesus is the Christ" (1 John 2:22)

3. anyone who "denies the Father and the Son" (1 John 2:23)

4. "every spirit that does not confess Jesus" (1 John 4:3)

5.   "deceivers who do not acknowledge that Jesus Christ came in the flesh" (2 John 7)

So who was the *second* beast (the "land beast")? It seems probable that this was apostate Judaism, who had become subservient to the Roman state. This beast is described as "exercising authority of the first beast" (Revelation 13:12) and "deceiving those who dwell on earth" (Revelation 13:14).

THE MILLENNIUM AND BEYOND

Revelation chapter 20 contains details that are perhaps the most controversial in the entire Bible. It is a magnificent section. But the study of the differing views of the millennium is daunting. We will not resolve all of the disputes to the complete satisfaction of the reader who wants precision in every jot and tittle. We will only try to give a critical perspective. Revelation 20 will come into greater focus in our discussion about resurrection in Chapter 11. Here is the entire chapter of Revelation 20 printed for your convenience, with the section titles as shown in the New King James Version:

Satan Bound 1,000 Years

[1] Then I saw an angel coming down from heaven, having the key to the bottomless pit and a great chain in his hand. [2] He laid hold of the dragon, that serpent of old, who is the Devil and Satan, and bound him for a **thousand years**; [3] and he cast him into the bottomless pit, and shut him up, and set a seal on him, so that he should deceive the nations no more till the **thousand years** were finished. But after these things he must be released for a little while.

The Saints Reign with Christ 1,000 Years

[4] And I saw thrones, and they sat on them, and judgment was committed to them. Then I saw the souls of those who had been beheaded for their witness to Jesus and for the word of God, who had not worshiped the beast or his image, and had not received

his mark on their foreheads or on their hands. And they lived and reigned with Christ for a **thousand years**. (⁵ But the rest of the dead did not live again until the **thousand years** were finished.) This is the first resurrection. ⁶ Blessed and holy is he who has part in the first resurrection. Over such the second death has no power, but they shall be priests of God and of Christ, and shall reign with Him a **thousand years**.

Satanic Rebellion Crushed

⁷ Now when the **thousand years** have expired, Satan will be released from his prison ⁸ and will go out to deceive the nations which are in the four corners of the earth, Gog and Magog, to gather them together to battle, whose number is as the sand of the sea. ⁹ They went up on the breadth of the earth and surrounded the camp of the saints and the beloved city. And fire came down from God out of heaven and devoured them. ¹⁰ The devil, who deceived them, was cast into the lake of fire and brimstone where the beast and the false prophet are. And they will be tormented day and night forever and ever.

The Great White Throne Judgment

¹¹ Then I saw a great white throne and Him who sat on it, from whose face the earth and the heaven fled away. And there was found no place for them. ¹² And I saw the dead, small and great, standing before God, and books were opened. And another book was opened, which is the Book of Life. And the dead were judged according to their works, by the things which were written in the books. ¹³ The sea gave up the dead who were in it, and Death and Hades delivered up the dead who were in them. And they were judged, each one according to his works. ¹⁴ Then Death and Hades were cast into the lake of fire. This is the second death. ¹⁵ And anyone not found written in the Book of Life was cast into the lake of fire.

Numbers in the Bible are often symbolic, especially in apocalyptic texts. The number seven in the Bible is symbolic for *completeness*. Even numbers (as opposed to odd numbers) have their own symbolism. The number ten in the Bible is symbolic for *manyness.* The thousand years is a symbolic term for many years. The Greek word translated "thousand" is *chilioi.* According to the online Blue Letter Bible, the root word of *chilioi* means "plural of uncertain affinity." Linguists tell us that *chilioi* is an "indefinite plural."

As put by Steve Gregg, "The number 'a thousand' is frequently used in Scripture without the intention of conveying statistical information. It is given as the number of generations to which God keeps His covenants (Deuteronomy 7:9), the number of hills upon which God owns the cattle (Psalm 50:10), the number of enemy troops that one Israelite shall chase (Joshua 23:10), the number of those who shall fall 'at your side' as opposed to the ten thousand who will fall at 'your right hand' (Psalm 91:7), etc. Furthermore, the expression 'a thousand years' is never used elsewhere in Scripture for an actual number of years, but only to suggest the idea of a very long time (cf. Psalm 90:4; Ecclesiastes 6:6; 2 Peter 3:8)." [110]

The usage of a thousand years is not necessarily a long period of time, as it can also be understood symbolically in context to mean "completeness" or "fullness" (Psalm 50:10-12). According to Anthony A. Hoekema, "The number 'thousand' which is used here must not be interpreted in a literal [straight forward] sense. Since the number ten signifies completeness, and since a thousand is ten to the third power, we may think of the expression 'a thousand years' as standing for a complete period. . . . of indeterminate length. . . . We may conclude that this thousand-year period extends from Christ's first coming to just before his Second Coming." [111]

There seems to be an almost limitless number of permutations on how to interpret this chapter of the Bible. Every word in Revelation 20 may be subject to interpretation. Every commentator makes certain assumptions that influence how he or she views the millennium.[112]

You can read commentators of different persuasions who think they have every detail of Revelation 20 figured out. The confidence they express in their view may be convincing—until you read someone else with an opposing view with equal confidence! We suggest caution and humility. Revelation 20 is the most symbolic section of the most symbolic book in the Bible. Futurists and preterists disagree even among themselves. Every view has significant challenges.[113]

The first question one should ask is this: Why isn't the millennium mentioned anywhere else in the Bible? Why didn't Jesus or his apostles mention it? Is it likely that John revealed something entirely new that no other gospel writer (or Old Testament saint or prophet) ever knew or spoke about?

Full preterists can be categorized in two groups, depending on their interpretation of whether the Second Coming was before or after the millennium. We could call these two groups "premillennial preterists" or "postmillennial preterists." Postmillennial preterists believe, based on the overwhelming number of references and time statements in Revelation, that the book was *entirely* fulfilled by AD 70, when Jesus returned. But premillennial preterists see it differently. They see this chapter teaching that the millennium *began* in the first century with Jesus' Second Coming in AD 70, and continues into our future. (Technically, premillennial preterists are not "full" preterists, but are nearly so.)[114]

Included in the significant events depicted in Revelation 20 are death and resurrection. The reader should keep something in mind as he or she works through this next section, as well as the more in-depth discussion of the resurrection that follows in Chapter 11. The Bible speaks of two kinds of death—*physical* death and *spiritual* death. Thus there are two types of resurrections—physical and spiritual. Spiritual death and resurrection are described in such passages as this one in Ephesians:

And you He **made alive**, who were **dead** in trespasses and sins, in which you once walked according to the course of this world, according to the prince of the power of the air, the spirit who now works in the sons of disobedience, among whom also we all once conducted ourselves in the lusts of our flesh, fulfilling the desires of the flesh and of the mind, and were by nature children of wrath, just as the others. But God, who is rich in mercy, because of His great love with which He loved us, even when we were **dead** in trespasses, **made us alive together with Christ** (by grace you have been saved), and **raised us up together**, and made **us** sit together in the heavenly places in Christ Jesus, that in the ages to come He might show the exceeding riches of His grace in his kindness toward us in Christ Jesus. (*Ephesians 2:1-7*)

Other similar passages include: Luke 15:32; John 5:24-25; Romans 6:11; Colossians 2:12-13; 3:1; 1 John 3:14. Now let's jump in and consider Revelation 20, point by point.

We will cover the major points as simply and clearly as we can, and offer considerations for alternative views. The reader can use this discussion as a basis for further study.

1. Most, if not all of Revelation has been fulfilled. The full preterist (postmillennial preterist) position is the best fit of the evidence. As put by Joseph M. Vincent, "John limits the time frame of fulfillment for the entire book of Revelation to having its consummation or completion in his near future." [115] The millennium was thus the approximately forty-year period from Christ's ministry in the flesh till his Second Coming in AD 70.[116] Thus the thousand years is a *qualitative* symbol rather than a *quantitative* designation of time. The Second Coming and second resurrection occurred at or near the *end* of the millennium in AD 66-70, "in the dispensation of the fullness of times" (Ephesians 1:10).

2. We recall the use that Peter made of a "thousand years" in 2 Peter 3. We concluded that his use of the term was in regards to the imminent fulfillment of God's covenant promises. Consistency points us in the same direction in Revelation 20. It marks the soon end of the Old Covenant Age and the ushering in of the New Covenant Age at the end of the millennium.

3. The reference to Gog and Magog (verse 8) probably points to AD 70 as well. Gog and Magog in the Old Testament are in the context of when all nations would know God (Ezekiel 38:16, 23; 39:21)—certainly a reference to the New Covenant Age. Ezekiel 38:16 states that Ezekiel's prophecies would be fulfilled in the last days ("latter days"). Ezekiel often uses the term "on that day" (Ezekiel 38:10, 18, 19; 39: 8, 11, 13, 22), which is a prophetic reference to the Day of the Lord.[117] According to Ezekiel, this day would mark the judgment against Israel (Ezekiel 38:18).

It is likely that these are all references to AD 70. The apostle Peter proclaimed that *all the prophets from Samuel forward were pointing to the days in which Peter spoke* (Acts 3:24), so we can only infer that Ezekiel was pointing to the first century as well. And Jesus stated that all prophecy would be fulfilled in his generation (Luke 21:22, 32; Revelation 1:1; 22:6). We

cannot project Gog and Magog past the first century without
dancing around Peter's and Jesus' clear statements. Whatever Gog and Magog refers to, it is certainly not modern Russia
(or some other bad-boy nation in our day) as some dispensationalists teach—an idea we think is pure invention.

4. Key to understanding the rest of Revelation 20 is placing the
    famous "Great White Throne" judgment recorded in Revela-
    tion 20:11-15 in its proper time period. This refers to the Second
    Coming events of AD 66-70 described elsewhere in the Bible.
    Death was destroyed (verse 14) at the end of the millennium,
    which is a parallel to 1 Corinthians 15:19-26, 54-56 where Paul
    said the last enemy, death, would be put down at Christ's
    Second Coming. Revelation 22:12 confirms that the judgment
    was to be at the *soon* coming of Christ. As put by Russell,

"There is no reason to doubt that the judgment scene depicted here
is identical with that described by our Lord in Matthew 25:31-46. We
have the same 'throne of glory,' the same gathering of all the nations,
the same discrimination of the judged according to their works, and
the same 'everlasting fire prepared for the devil and his angels.' . .
. It follows that it is not the 'end of the world,' but that which is so
frequently predicted as accompanying the end of the age, or termina-
tion of the Jewish dispensation. That great consummation is always
represented as a judgment-epoch. It is the time of the Parousia, the
coming of Christ in glory to vindicate and reward His faithful servants, and to judge and destroy His enemies. There is a remarkable
unity and consistency in the teachings of Scripture on this subject." [118]

5. Confirming fulfillment at the AD 66-70 Parousia, Revelation
    20:11-15 refers to the *imminent* general resurrection predict-
    ed elsewhere in Scripture. The term "general resurrection"
    refers to the bodily resurrection and judgment of everyone
    who had died prior to that time. The Bible only refers to one
    general resurrection of the physically dead that includes the
    righteous and the wicked. The faithful received their new im-
    mortal heavenly bodies at that time. Per Jesus: "When the Son
    of Man comes. . . . He will separate them one from another,

as a shepherd divides his sheep from the goats. . . . For the hour is coming in which all who are in the graves will hear his voice and come forth—those who have done good, to the resurrection of life, and those who have done evil to the resurrection of condemnation." (*Matthew 25:31-32; John 5:28-29*)

Revelation 20:13 refers to the general resurrection to which Jesus and Paul refer—which by implication is the *second resurrection*. Note from the text that both the righteous dead and the wicked dead were raised at this second resurrection. There is no limiting categorization of those resurrected, so it must refer to all of the dead, consistent with what Jesus said. This is confirmed by Revelation 22:12, where Jesus said He was coming soon to repay **everyone** for what they had done. **Everyone** would be raised on the **last day** (John 6:39-40; 54). Other passages confirm that the general resurrection, judgment, and Parousia occurred in AD 70 at the **end** of Israel's Old Covenant world. Consider such passages as: Daniel 12:2-13; Matthew 13:36-43; 16:27-28; 24:31-34; 25:30-46; Acts 24:15 (*mello*); 2 Timothy 4:1 (*mello*); 1 Peter 4:5, 17.

6. However, there was a prior (first) resurrection event described in verses 4-6. While we can be confident of what happened in verses 11-15 (and when they happened—AD 66-70), full preterist interpretations of verses 4-6 are all over the map. One view is that the first resurrection is actually part of the second resurrection, that is, part of the bodily resurrection on the last day. In this view, John's description of events in Revelation 20 is not strictly chronological, but rather is a series of recapitulations of the various events. Such recapitulations are common in Revelation.

Another view is that the first resurrection is about earlier events surrounding the resurrection of Jesus—his descent into hades, and an associated resurrection of the saints (Matthew 27:52-53). From ancient times among the Jews, there was a strong belief that the martyrs would have priority status in the last days at the resurrection and judgment.

However, some are inclined to think that the first resurrection is different in *nature* from the second resurrection, and verses 4-6 should not be taken strictly literally. The often symbolic nature of Revelation makes this a possibility. One argument that the first resurrection was a metaphorical one is that it does not seem reasonable that only those beheaded as a separate class would be resurrected, which seems to be implied. Why would those beheaded receive mention over other martyrs, especially when beheading was relatively rare?

Taken on its face, the first resurrection comes at the beginning of the millennium. Since it appears from various texts that *everyone* would be raised on the *last day*, perhaps this first resurrection was a different *type* of event. And, there is no apparent theological reason why anyone would have been raised to heaven prior to everyone else. According to this idea, the group of beheaded saints is possibly representative of a larger group of faithful who were *living*. We recall from Matthew 5:10-11 that all believers in some sense suffer persecution. So, this passage possibly speaks of *living* believers all during the millennial transition period, as the "reign" of believers "with Christ" was underway (verse 4).

7. The coming to life of the saints (first resurrection) and the *reigning of the saints with Christ* during the millennium (verses 4, 5b) is consistent with Paul's similar statement in Ephesians 2:1-7 which declares that *God made Paul and his fellow first-century believers (who had been spiritually dead in their trespasses) alive together with Christ and **raised them up with him**—seating them with Him in the heavenly places*. This parallel gives confirmation that the first resurrection was a metaphorical one, and that the millennium began earlier in the first century. This understanding—that the first resurrection means the co-resurrection of believers with Christ—is consistent with Colossians 2:12-14 in which Paul said that **you were raised with him through faith**. It *perhaps* could also be that Jesus' "born again" statement in John 3 (cf. 1 Peter 1:22-23) is about the identical thing.[119]

8. There is a further powerful parallel in Revelation 6:9-17, in which the slain saints were given white robes of righteousness and royalty (i.e. they were *reigning with Christ*) and were told to "rest a little longer" until the great day of God's wrath had come to avenge the blood of the righteous.[120] The phrase "reigning with Christ" is a metaphorical expression. It is the New

Testament image for the eternal glory that Christians receive through Christ. See also Matthew 19:28; Romans 5:17; Revelation 5:10; 20:6; 22:5. While some people think that "reigning with Christ" is talking about heaven, in the context of these passages it is really about salvation and elevation of status in God's eyes. This is supported by the concept that all believers are priests (1 Peter 2:5, 9; Revelation 1:6; 5:10). Notice that those in the first resurrection only "reigned with Christ" for only a thousand years. Why only a thousand years if they were indeed dead and in heaven? Indeed, do souls literally reign? So the millennium was a short period ("a little longer"), not a long period—ending in AD 70 in the Day of the Lord.[121]

9.   An interesting passage is Revelation 20:5a, "The rest of the dead did not come to life until the thousand years were ended." This could imply that both resurrections were similar in nature. However, this sentence may be spurious, and was added hundreds of years after-the-fact. It does not appear in the Codex Sinaiticus manuscript, which is a very early manuscript. Indeed, this manuscript, which dates to the fourth century, is the oldest extant manuscript that contains Revelation 20. And it does not appear in many manuscripts subsequent to that one. It seems that someone added the phrase—probably a confused millennialist, who felt that he was living in the millennium and was concerned that there were no apparent resurrections occurring, as should have been happening per his millennial theory. Some modern translations put this phrase in parentheses. If you remove this phrase, the circular and wordy nature of the text is cleared up. The entire verse thus becomes: "This is the first resurrection."

10.   Whether or not the "first resurrection" of Revelation 20:4-5 is the same as the "resurrection" delineated in such passages as John 5:24-25; Ephesians 2:1-7, and Colossians 2:12-14, these latter passages describe a type of resurrection. The "resurrection" described in these passages was soteriological (that is, salvational). The resurrection of Revelation 20:13 was **eschatological** (glorified body). Physically dead believers residing in hades at AD 70 had already received spiritual/metaphorical "resurrection" *prior to their physical death*—when they first believed (Romans 4, etc). They didn't need to receive (again)

something they already possessed! Thus, the resurrection of the physically dead was qualitatively different the from "resurrection" of living persons. This dual resurrection is reflective of what we believers experience today: We get saved while we are alive, and we go to heaven when we die.

11.   Satan was *bound* at the beginning of the millennium, that he might not deceive the nations any longer (verse 2). This clearly indicates that certain limitations were placed on Satan at the beginning of the millennium—that is, *during Christ's ministry*. This is consistent with numerous passages such as Matthew 12:28-29; Mark 16:17; Luke 10:17-19; 11:22; John 12:31; Colossians 2:15; Hebrews 2:14, and 1 John 3:8—where the demons became subject to Christ during the time of his First-Coming. These passages along with Revelation 20:2 confirm that the beginning of the millennium was at that time. Full preterists, amillennialists, and postmillennialists agree that the beginning of the millennium was at Christ's First Coming (or shortly thereafter at Pentecost), but disagree on when it ends.

12.   The binding of Satan suggests that he cannot reverse the expansion of the gospel and God's kingdom. However, while Satan was "bound" at the First Coming, he retained some power during the millennium (Ephesians 2:2; 1 Timothy 3:7; 1 John 5: 19). He was bound; he was not in the Lake of Fire.

13.   Satan was temporarily loosed for a short time (verse 3) near the end of the millennium (probably while Peter was writing about the influence of the devil in 1 Peter 5:8)—until Christ's Second Coming in AD 70. This is consistent with 2 Thessalonians 2:1-12, which discusses the Man of Lawlessness, who would be revealed as an agent of Satan before the Day of God's wrath.

14.   Satan was *defeated* at the end of the millennium (verse 10). Paul (Romans 16:20) and John (Revelation 12:12) both anticipated that the *crushing* of Satan was **near to them in time** ("soon/time is short"). Therefore, the end of the millennium was near. At the Second Coming and judgment in AD 70, Christ fully implemented his power and reign (verses 10-15), fulfilling these prophecies. Satan was indeed crushed ("thrown into the lake of fire," verse 10).[122]

Some believe that Satan is still alive and may wield some power even today—that he tempts us and is able to blind the minds of some (2 Corinthians 4:4)—presumably those who are weak or not among the elect. But if Satan still exists today, he has no real spiritual power over us now. He has been cast out (John 12:31); he has lost "authority" over us (Colossians 1:13); he cannot "touch" a Christian (1 John 5:18). It seems more biblically correct to believe that we are tempted by our own desires rather than by Satan, per James 1:12-15. (Even in Bible times, it was not normative to be tempted by Satan. We remember that Jesus taught that it is what is on the *inside* of us that defiles us per Mark 7:14-23.) But the final crushing of Satan is consistent with the AD 70 institution of the eternal reign of Christ per Revelation 11:15:

> Then the seventh angel sounded: And there were loud voices in heaven, saying, **"The kingdoms of this world have become the kingdoms of our Lord and of his Christ, and He shall reign forever and ever!"** And the twenty-four elders who sat before God on their thrones fell on their faces and worshiped God, saying: "We give You thanks, O Lord God Almighty, the One who is and who was and who is to come, because You have taken Your great power and reigned. The nations were angry, and your **wrath** has come, and the **time of the dead, that they should be judged**, and that You should reward your servants the prophets and the saints, and those who fear your name, small and great, and should destroy those who destroy the earth." (*Revelation 11:15-18*)

This passage is consistent with such passages as Isaiah 9:7 which speaks of the coming Messiah: "Of the increase of his government and peace there will be no end, upon the throne of David and over his kingdom, to order it and establish it with judgment and justice from that time forward, even forever." We do not wait for an unfulfilled event for Christ's victory. *It is difficult to comprehend that a Christian would deny that Christ has already been victorious, and would deny that He reigns today, as many premillennialists do.*

And, by the way, Revelation 20 does not say there will be peace on earth during the thousand years. Nor does it say that Jesus Christ will rule during the thousand years from the present city of Jerusalem. These common ideas of premillennialists are simply absent from Revelation 20, which is the only place in the Bible that we find the millennium.

Hades—the temporary abode of the dead—(verses 13 and 14) has been done away, as it was emptied at the general resurrection in AD 70. The righteous dead were raised to heaven; the wicked dead were raised to their eternal destiny and experienced the "second death"—that is, to hell/the lake of fire (variously interpreted as eternal conscious punishment or destruction). There is no second death for believers (verses 6 and 14), who have eternal life. Believers today go to heaven in their glorified body immediately after they die, without an intermediate state. Further, Satan has been crushed. "The devil made me do it" is not a valid excuse for our waywardness!

However, an interesting alternate view is offered by those holding to premillennial preterism, in which the millennium only *begins* in the first century. There are various iterations of this, but some think Revelation 20 ties to 1 Thessalonians 4:16 ("the dead in Christ will rise first"), which occurred sometime after Paul was writing to the Thessalonians.

That is to say, if the text refers to actual beheadings that occurred between AD 30 and AD 70 (or more specifically during the Neronic persecution from AD 64-68) then the resurrection of these saints (the first resurrection) must have occurred in or about AD 70 and not in circa AD 30. Revelation 20:4 says that this first resurrection is when the millennium *began*. So this pushes the *end* of the millennium past AD 70 well into the future.[123]

In this view, Revelation 20:1-4 and then Revelation 20:11-15 were fulfilled in AD 66-70. But part or all of the intervening passages are a parenthetical digression that describes the end of history—rather than AD 70. Christ came in judgment in AD 66-70 to raise the dead and usher out the Old Covenant order, but there remains some unfinished business. While Satan was bound per Revelation 20:2 in the first century, he will not be finally destroyed until the end of time per Revelation 20:10. There will be a future end to evil at the close of the millennium, that is, at the end of history. The battle of Gog and Magog is a future contest of some sort with the church. James Stuart Russell was a proponent of this view. Duncan McKenzie is a modern proponent.[124]

There is yet another approach to explaining the timing and nature of the millennium—*bimillennialism*. This approach holds that John contemplated *two separate non-literal millennial periods*. Full preterist Kurt

Simmons, concludes that there are two "thousand-year" periods that cannot be precisely parallel. In his system, the two millennial periods—the detention of Satan and the reign of the saints—are slightly different, but the fulfillment of all prophecy was completed at the conclusion of the destruction of Jerusalem.

Another bimillennial approach is by Douglas Wilkinson. In his system, there are two separate non-literal periods that do not overlap. The symbolic thousand-year detention of Satan starts in Christ's ministry and ends with the beginning of the Jewish War in AD 66. He points out that in Revelation 20, only one of the two symbolic thousand-year periods is predicted to end. In Wilkinson's view, the millennium of the saints extends to the whole of human history since the founding of the church. Wilkinson's system is a version of premillennial preterism, and like other versions relies on Daniel 7 for support. But instead of the Gog/Magog business happening in the distant future per Russell/McKenzie, it is the millennium of the saints that extends past AD 70, and indeed, continues today. In Wilkinson's view, there was only one resurrection (rather than two) which happened in AD 66-70. Note that the text only *implies* a second resurrection and does not specifically say it.[125]

These schemata may hold some interesting promise. If you re-read the text, you will note that the English translation uses the indefinite article "a" three times with "thousand years" and the definite article "the" three times. Leading theologians of the past (notably Augustine and John Wesley) have worked on the possibility of two millennia, but failed to grasp the preterist context of Revelation. We predict that more work will be done on this by scholars in the future.

Concerning the millennium, could it really only be the "forty-year" period between "Pentecost and the Holocaust" that full preterists think? Here is an interesting consideration. According to research done by Edward E. Stevens, many rabbis expected a period of travail in which the Messiah would have enemies to defeat before his reign was established and his kingdom consolidated. Some thought it would be a thousand years, but most agreed that it would probably be about forty years, like the transitional period of wandering in the wilderness and the forty-year preparatory reign of David before his son Solomon built the temple! [126]

To grasp the millennium as an interim period in the first century, it is helpful to understand just how Jewish the first few years of Christianity were. Initially, Christianity was almost exclusively a Jewish movement. Gradually, with much debate and struggle, the apostles began to understand that Gentiles would participate as heirs to the kingdom, and that circumcision and law-keeping would pass away as the New Covenant took hold (Acts 10:9-11:18; Acts 21:17-36; Ephesians 2:11-3:13). Jesus was saying in Matthew 24:32-35 that for a period of time yet, the Jews, both believing and unbelieving, would continue to closely observe the law. Jesus himself, of course, conducted his ministry in the flesh within the confines of Israel. Indeed, the first Jewish Christians kept the ancient law-keeping practices, including animal sacrifices for sin—until the destruction of the temple in AD 70. The millennium was this transitional period in which Judaism gave way to Christianity.

Full preterists understand this "millennial" period similarly to the majority of rabbis—as a "transition period" between the time of the ascension and the end of the Jewish age in AD 70—a period of about forty years in which the Old Covenant and the New Covenant existed side-by-side. Paul speaks of the great "mystery" being revealed (Ephesians 1-3) which was the grafting of the Gentiles into Israel's spiritual things. This mystery is in the context of "uniting all things in heaven and on earth" (Ephesians 1:9-10) in preparation for the world which was to come (Ephesians 1:21). The millennium was the period in which the kingdom was being built. This is consistent with the previously discussed idea that the new heaven and new earth marked the transition from the Jewishness of the Old Covenant to the inclusion of Gentiles in the New Covenant.

Okay. Now let's move on to Revelation 21 to consider some additional interesting and important points:

- *new heaven and new earth, New Jerusalem, no more death or crying or pain as the former things have passed away, Christ is seated on the throne and makes all things new* (Revelation 21:1-27)

We have examined the preterist implications of some of this language previously. In chapters 4 and 8 we showed that the new heaven and new earth symbolically refers to the new covenant world. The passing away of heaven and earth (the old covenant world) appears in Revelation 21:11. These are first-century events. But we should spend some more time here.

The New Jerusalem, of which Christians are citizens, is certainly the New Covenant church. It is the Israel of God (Romans 2:28-29; 4:1-25; 9:6-8; 11:11-32; Galatians 3:6-8, 29; 4:28; 6:14-16; Ephesians 2:11-3:13; Hebrews 8-12). Hebrews 12:22 states, "But you have come to Mount Zion and to the city of the living God, the heavenly Jerusalem." The New Jerusalem was already becoming a reality for the first-century readers of Hebrews. The New Jerusalem is the bride (Revelation 21:2), which means the bride of Christ (John 3:29; Ephesians 5:22, 23, 31, 32; Revelation 19:7-8). Its foundations were the "twelve apostles of the Lamb" (Revelation 21:14; cf. Ephesians 2:19-22). The building/city motif is Pauline theology concerning the church (Ephesians 2:19-22).[127]

The picture that is painted for us by John is that Israel was a harlot (Revelation 17:1, 5, 15; 19:2). For her marital unfaithfulness she received divorce and punishment. Then we see the new bride—the church—coming to take her place. Jerusalem is destroyed and replaced by the New Jerusalem of which first-century Christians were citizens. The church is the New Jerusalem that takes over for the old Jerusalem. The church no longer needs a temple because Christ brings the presence of God to his people (Revelation 21:22).

The text also says that *God will wipe away every tear from their eyes; there will be no more death, sorrow, or crying.* This at first glance could be a problem for preterists, and the reader at this point may close our book in disgust. Obviously we still suffer death, pain, and sadness.

The statement about *no more death* in Revelation 21:4 ties to the statement in Revelation 20:14, which tells us that death and hades were thrown into the lake of fire. But if Jesus has already returned, and death has been done away, why then do we still see death all around us? The answer is simple: the end of death applies only to Christians, who only *appear* to die as they are transferred into the heavenly realm when they expire. Put another way, Christians are transferred into the presence of Jesus when they die their earthly death. Jesus said, "I am the resurrection and the life. He who believes in Me, though he may die, he shall live. And whoever lives and believes in Me shall never die." (*John 11:25-26a*) Michel Fenemore explained it thusly:

> The book of Revelation was addressed to God's servants. So, everything in the book must be understood from *their* perspective. Death has been destroyed for Christians, not unbelievers. Revelation was not intended for the masses who hate God. They might read it, but will never understand it. God's Old Testament servants died and went to Hades. This was necessary because Jesus had not yet been sacrificed for their sins. However, once the plan of salvation was complete, death and Hades became unnecessary for God's people.[128]

Amillennialists believe that Revelation 21 is referring only to heaven. Premillennialists believe it only begins with a literal utopian thousand years on earth. But we conservative evangelical preterists believe that it begins with the life of the believer in Christ, ushered in with Christ's first-century work, and that it corresponds to the same state depicted in Isaiah 65. But, our life in Christ here on earth is but a spiritual foretaste of truly realizing (in a literal sense) *no more death or suffering*—in heaven.

So, just as the individual believer is a "new creation" (2 Corinthians 5:17), there is a present reality for the Christian that death has been abolished (John 11:25-26; 1 Corinthians 15:26, 55-57; 2 Timothy 1:10)! We were once dead in our sins (Ephesians 2:1; Colossians 2:13a), but are now alive in Christ (Romans 6:1-14; Ephesians 2:5-6; Colossians 2:11-14)! We do not "sorrow as others who have no hope" (1 Thessalonians 4:13). "No tears" refers to statements in the Bible about the long-awaited Messiah; Jesus has "borne our griefs and carried our sorrows" (Isaiah 53:4; cf. Isaiah 25:8; 35:10)! **The Messianic promise of no more weeping of Isaiah 65 and Revelation 21 is fulfilled with Jesus in the context of his living water (John 4:10-15; Revelation 7:9-17; 21:5-7).** The living water is not just meant for those who die physically. The water is here now and we no longer need to thirst or mourn. Indeed, for the Christian, "old things have passed away; behold, **all** things have become new" (2 Corinthians 3:18; 5:17; Revelation 21:5).

With the emphasis on "all things," the Christian is not simply given a ticket to heaven and a new set of religious rituals, but every area of life is targeted for renewal as the result of his participation in the new life. How many times does Jesus have to make things new for it to be effective? All things are indeed new now! Revelation 21 is, we argue, referring to the new covenantal order ushered in once for all in AD 70. We must not forget the large number of imminency passages at the beginning, middle, and end of Revelation that teach us that the events described would come to fruition shortly.

Remember the difficulty of interpreting prophecy literally, as we have demonstrated in previous chapters. Related to the issue of "no more death" is the concept of "no more sin." **The Bible repeatedly says that Jesus has already put an end to sin and ushered in everlasting righteousness (Daniel 9:24-27; John 1:29; Romans 6:1-14; Colossians 1:22; Hebrews 9:26; 1 John 3:5).** But certainly we see sin all around us today. So these declarations must be taken in the sense that they were intended. It is about the blood of Jesus making his people *sinless in God's sight.* So, when Revelation 21 says that death and tears will be vanquished at the Second Advent, and when 2 Peter 3:10-13 says that the Day of the Lord will usher in a new heaven and new earth in which righteousness dwells, preterists say that these statements should be cast in the same figurative light.

Terms such as "will wipe away every tear" or "wherein righteousness dwells" are statements about Jesus and his unprecedented accomplishments—and our new life in Him, on earth and in heaven. Duncan McKenzie gives us reasons why Revelation 21 is not describing heaven:

> The new heaven and earth in Revelation (and Isaiah) is not heaven. Notice, it still has unrighteous people in it, those outside the New (covenant) Jerusalem (Revelation 22:14-15). The new heaven and new earth is a symbolic representation of the post AD 70 spiritual order of this planet. The old covenant order (the old heaven and earth) flees and the new covenant order (the new heaven and earth) is established (Revelation 20:11; 21:1-2). One has to constantly remember that the truths of Revelation are communicated by way of symbols (Revelation 1:1). In the new heaven and earth those who are part of the New Jerusalem bride have access to the tree and water of life (Revelation 22:1-2); those outside of the new covenant city do not. The New Jerusalem is a picture of the bride of Christ (Revelation 21:9-10); only those who are in the Lamb's Book of Life are part of her (Revelation 21:22-27). Those who are not part of the New Jerusalem are not part of the new covenant. There is no more death for those inside the city (Revelation 21:1-4); those outside the city are already dead (spiritually separated from God). Unless they turn to the Lord and become part of the new covenant bride, [they] will end up in the lake of fire (Revelation 20:15; 21:7-8, 27; 22:14-15).[129]

Dr. Kelly Nelson Birks, in a response to a challenge by postmillennialist Keith A. Mathison, said this:

> The passage in Revelation 21: 4, "And God will wipe away every tear from their eyes. . . . " is a passage that I'm sure Mr. Mathison would agree, must be interpreted according to its context. The fact of the matter is, that the descriptions of what is going on in the 21st and 22nd chapters of Revelation, have primarily to do with the spiritual facts of life in the church, the New Jerusalem, the Bride of

Christ. It all speaks of the finishing up of the Old Covenant system, and the bringing in of the New Covenant in its fullness. This is our present experience NOW. The phrase, "God will wipe away every tear from their (our) eyes," is a reference to the fullness of personal relationship that each believer has with God. That He is personally attending to our pains and sorrows. No more death! That is, no more separation from God in the full spiritual realities of experiencing the present age.[130]

Premillennialists see all of this happening in the literal millennium that has not yet begun. They see the reign of Christ as wholly future. David Chilton had some particularly strong words about this: "The notion that the reign of Christ is something wholly future, to be brought in by some great social cataclysm, is not a Christian doctrine. It is an unorthodox teaching, generally espoused by heretical sects on the fringes of the Christian church." [131] While Chilton was unnecessarily harsh, his point is that it really is blasphemous to say that Christ is not reigning today.

The ending chapters of Revelation describe a series of events that are consummated together: the new heaven and new earth and New Jerusalem which are the New Covenant church order, the dissolution of hades, the final defeat of death and Satan, and the Parousia—marking the beginning of the established and victorious eternal reign of Christ. Repeating for emphasis, Satan was *limited* at the First Advent of Jesus, which Jesus proved by casting out demons (Matthew 12:28; Luke 11:17-20; Revelation 20:2). Satan was then *crushed* at the Second Coming (Romans 16:20; Revelation 20:10). The message of the New Testament is that Satan was absolutely defeated in the life, death, resurrection, ascension, and then finally at the Parousia of Jesus Christ (cf. Colossians 2:15; Hebrews 2:14-15). The reader might want to take the time to revisit these passages, especially Romans 16:20. Christ reigns victorious.

Amillennialists, postmillennialists, and preterists join on this point of Christ's current reign and ruling authority against the premillennialists. But amillennialists and postmillennialists fail to connect the dots. If Christ is reigning today, then the Parousia and other events associated with it have already taken place. Only preterism offers assurance of Christ's reign now.

We will discuss more fully in Chapter 11 the biblical meaning of the death which overcame mankind at the Fall. And we will resume other aspects of this discussion in Chapter 13 under the topic of *Restoration*.

- *no temple, Jesus as the light, gates open to all nations, etc.* (Revelation 21:22-27)—This section relates to Isaiah 60 which discusses the Gentiles (the "nations") coming into the light, as well as to other passages about the Gentiles that we have already mentioned. Revelation 21:22-27 is a strong preterist passage—no physical temple, which is replaced by "the Lord God the Almighty and the Lamb," (a clear reflection of Jesus' predictions in Matthew 24:2 and John 4:21, thus AD 70). The opening of the gates to the nations depicts the ushering in of the New Covenant world wherein Jews and Gentiles are now one people in Christ in the New Jerusalem.

As we leave Revelation 21 we come to the end of the book in Revelation 22. In this chapter, John reiterates the prophecy of the soon coming of Christ (events that *must* soon take place, Revelation 22:6-20). In the final words of the Bible—Revelation 22:19—we are warned not to take away from the words of his prophecy. Christians, let us heed that warning.

The reader is referred to Appendix B to the chart entitled "Millennium."

Question for your pastor, church leaders, and friends:
*"What do you think of the fact that Revelation teaches that the events therein **must** happen **soon**?" Then listen carefully to see if his answer is faithful to the text, or whether it contains assumptions alien to the text.*

10

Completion and the Kingdom of Heaven

COMPLETION

Consider this passage from Hebrews:

> He then would have had to suffer often since the foundation of the world; but now, once at the **end of the ages**, He has appeared to put away sin by the sacrifice of Himself. And as it is appointed for men to die once, but after this the judgment, so Christ was offered once to bear the sins of many. To those who **eagerly wait for Him** He will appear a **second time**, apart from sin, for **salvation**. (*Hebrews 9:26-28*)

Chances are that you have never heard a sermon on this passage. The reason is that it can be alarming for the futurist paradigm. Why? Because it implies that your salvation is not altogether effective until the Second Coming.

Are you certain that your salvation is secure *now*? Most Protestant Christians, at least, would say YES! But this passage might put some doubt in that confidence, if you hold to futurist eschatology. The passage certainly makes it clear that Christ's death took our sins away. But there is a sense in which our salvation was not quite complete at the cross. The writer of Hebrews taught that the completion of our salvation was imminent. This point should be emphasized. In greater context from the book of Hebrews (chapters 8-10) the writer argued that

Christ's work of salvation would be completed at the doing away of the Old Covenant order, i.e., at his imminent Second Appearing.

Russell said this: "The New Testament always speaks of the work of redemption being incomplete until the Parousia. . . . There was still incompleteness in His work until the whole visible fabric and frame of Judaism were swept away. This fact is clearly brought out in the Epistle to the Hebrews. . . . "[132] There are multiple other places in the New Testament where we see similar statements about the imminent completion of Christ's redeeming work at the end of the age. Consider the words of Jesus found in Luke:

> Now when these things begin to happen, look up and lift up your heads, because your **redemption draws near.** (*Luke 21:28*)

This passage, as you will note, is in the Olivet Discourse, and refers to events to happen at the AD 70 Parousia. When you have read this passage in the past, you may have jumped right over it. If you thought about how the New Testament uses the term redemption, you probably assumed that redemption only refers to the cross. But this passage is smack-dab in the middle of Second Coming material. The Second Coming, then, is when our redemption becomes complete. Consider further this passage from Romans 8:

> For I reckon that the sufferings of the present time are not worthy to be compared with the glory **about to be revealed in us**. . . . For we know that the whole creation groans and labors with birth pangs together **until now.** Not only that, but we also who have the firstfruits of the Spirit, even **we** ourselves groan within ourselves, **eagerly waiting for the adoption**, the **redemption** of our body. (*Romans 8:18, 22, 23, Young's Literal Translation, New King James Version*)

Those who are waiting for a *future* second coming, though they may be imbued with a firm assurance that God is not slack concerning his promises, must nonetheless accept that Christ's work toward their salvation is not yet complete! Only with the understanding that Christ came in finality in AD 70 can we be biblically assured that his work of salvation *is* complete. This is glorious good news for Christians — a source and confirmation of our *hope.*

We could call this the *completed redemption.* So while our salvation was secured and guaranteed at the cross, it was completed at the Second Coming. Perhaps an analogy might be a dying patient receiving a life saving injection. The injection from the needle guarantees that the patient is spared, but it takes a little while for the medicine to work inside the body to kill the infection.

These passages do not minimize the importance of the cross. The Bible is clear that Christ's perfect life, and death on the cross, paid the penalty for our sins (Romans 5:9-10; 8:1-4; 1 Corinthians 15:3; 2 Corinthians 5:17-21; Hebrews 9:12-22; Revelation 1:5; 5:9; etc.). And his resurrection provided hope for eternal life (1 Corinthians 15:1-19, etc.). Nevertheless, the Bible teaches us that at the Parousia, Christ's work of redemption and salvation was completed.

These passages, in part, hold a promise specifically for the first-century Christians of being saved in an earthly sense from persecution and tribulation, similar to salvation of the Jews from specific instances of worldly bondage in the Old Testament (such as their escape from Egypt or from Babylonian captivity per Exodus 14:13; Isaiah 41:14; 56:1). But there is also the definite sense that the Parousia *sealed*, that is finalized, the personal salvation of every Christian.

The salvation from *worldly* bondage by God in the Old Testament foreshadowed the ultimate salvation from the *spiritual* bondage of *sin*, *death*, and the *Law* brought by the Messiah (Romans 11:25-27; 1 Corinthians 15:26). This salvation was initiated at the cross but was not quite finished. The Exodus from Egypt and the forty-year period of wandering in the wilderness, foreshadowed the forty-year transition period of the first century, until full deliverance in AD 70.

> This is a remarkable parallel that the reader should not miss. The Hebrew children escaped the *worldly* bondage of slavery in Egypt at the Exodus, but they did not reach their new home for forty years, after much trial and tribulation. In the first century, believers received their promised escape from *spiritual* bondage at the cross, but would enter their *new spiritual dwelling place* — the New Jerusalem/New Heaven and Earth (Revelation 7, 21) — about forty years later, after much trial and tribulation! (Acts 14:22)

The cross purchased our hope; the Parousia sealed and delivered it. Futurists acknowledge the hope of salvation at the Parousia. But, sadly, they miss the good news of Christ's final work toward the believer's salvation.

Other passages in Scripture relate to the same concept as those above. Consider these:

> So Jesus answered and said, "Assuredly, I say to you, there is no one who has left house or brothers or sisters or father or mother or wife or children or lands, for my sake and the gospel's, who shall not receive a hundredfold now in this time—houses and brothers and sisters and mothers and children and lands, with persecutions—**and in the age to come, eternal life**." (*Mark 10:29-30*)

> And do this, knowing the time, that now it is high time to awake out of sleep; for now our **salvation** is nearer than when we first believed. The night is far spent, **the day is at hand**. Therefore let us cast off the works of darkness, and let us put on the armor of light. (*Romans 13:11-12*)

> In him you also, when you heard the word of truth, the gospel of your **salvation**, and believed in him, were sealed with the promised Holy Spirit, who is the guarantee of our inheritance **until we acquire possession of it**, to the praise of his glory. (*Ephesians 1:13-14, English Standard Version*)

> Are they not all spirits of service for ministration being sent forth because of those **about to inherit salvation**? (*Hebrews 1:14, Young's Literal Translation*)

> Blessed be the God and Father of our Lord Jesus Christ, who according to his abundant mercy has begotten us again to a living hope through the resurrection of Jesus Christ from the dead, to an inheritance incorruptible and undefiled and that does not fade away, **reserved in heaven for you**, who are kept by the power of God through faith for **salvation ready to be revealed in the last time**. In this you greatly rejoice, though now for a little while, if need be, you have been grieved by various trials, that the genuineness of your faith, being much more precious than gold that perishes, though it is tested by fire, may be found to praise, honor, and glory at the revelation of Jesus Christ, whom having not seen you love. Though now you do not see Him, yet believing, you rejoice with joy inexpressible and full of glory, receiving the end of your faith—the **salvation of your souls**. (*1 Peter 1:3-9*)

Then I heard a loud voice saying in heaven, "Now **salvation**, and strength, and the kingdom of our God, and the power of his Christ have come." (*Revelation 12:10*)

Additional New Testament passages that relate to this issue include Matthew 24:13; Romans 11:25-27; 1 Corinthians 15:51; Ephesians 1:13-14; 4:30; Colossians 3:4; 2 Timothy 4:8; Titus 2:13-14; Hebrews 9:8-11 (*mello*); 1 Peter 5:4, and Revelation 15:8; 22:3. Look up these passages to see how the writers predicted a coming change of status to *living, first century* believers. The language includes salvation, day of redemption, receive the crown of glory/righteousness, changed, and gain the ability to enter the most holy place/sanctuary.

An appropriate Old Testament passage that ties to this is Daniel 9:24-27. This is the famous seventy-weeks passage. We considered aspects of this passage in Chapter 5 when we covered the AD 70 judgment upon Jerusalem. In this passage we also find the prophetic statement about the Messiah putting "an end to sin and to atone for iniquity" in the context of the ending of the sacrificial system and the abomination of desolation. So while our sins were forgiven at the cross, the completion of Christ's work to cover our sin happened in AD 70.[133]

Another aspect of our salvation is atonement. Atonement, in Christian theology, refers to how God makes possible the reconciliation between Himself and creation. We commonly think of atonement occurring at the cross, which is correct. But that is not the full picture. As we have already observed, in order to capture the fullest meaning of Christian concepts, we must understand their Old Testament context. In the Old Testament, we find that *atonement* is related to *judgment*. Notice this powerful passage from Deuteronomy:

"Now see that I, even I, am He, and there is no God besides Me; I kill and I make alive; I wound and I heal; nor is there any who can deliver from my hand. For I raise my hand to heaven, and say, As I live forever, If I whet my glittering sword, and my hand takes hold on **judgment**, I will render **vengeance** to my enemies, and repay those who hate Me. I will make my arrows drunk with blood, and my sword shall devour flesh, with the blood of the slain and the captives, from the heads of the leaders of the enemy." Rejoice, O Gentiles, with his people, for He will **avenge the blood** of his servants, and render **vengeance** to his adversaries; He will provide **atonement** for his land and his people. (*Deuteronomy 32:39-43, cf. Numbers 35:30-34*)

Final judgment upon God's nation did not happen at the cross, but in AD 70. Point in fact, the ultimate biblical judgment occurred in AD 70. Remember the astounding statement made by Jesus as He confronted the Jews:

That upon **you** may come **all** the righteous blood shed on the earth, from the blood of righteous Abel to the blood of Zechariah, son of Berechiah, whom you murdered between the temple and the altar. Assuredly, I say to you, all these things will come upon **this generation**. (*Matthew 23:35-36*)

Jesus was prophesying that his vengeance upon the Jews of his generation would reach all the way back to the murder of Abel! This decidedly puts an exclamation point to what happened in AD 70. The Jews could not have missed the finality of what Jesus was saying.

The ultimate judgment marked the completion of Christ's work of atonement. Perhaps we should not carry this point too far. There is a need to differentiate the ideas of atonement for individuals and the atonement/judgment relationship that here operates at a corporate or national level vis-à-vis God's people. But there is a relationship, an association.

Also, we remember that in Revelation 20:14, *death* was overcome at the Great White Throne judgment. As a preview to the next chapter in our book, per Paul in 1 Corinthians 15:19-26 the last enemy, *death*, would be put down at Christ's Parousia. So *everything* was coming to a head in AD 70. This was the culmination of Israel's covenantal history. Together, these passages speak of the soon culmination of:

Salvation, Adoption, Redemption, and Atonement
—thus Completion.

The implication of these passages can be a bit unnerving to some Christians because they have never seriously contemplated these statements from God's Word. But we are seeking to honor Scripture in its fullest. In the past, the author simply skipped over most of these (as well as many other passages in Scripture) because he did not know how to fit them into his futurist presuppositions. Perhaps the reader has done the same thing.

We continually hear Christians talk about their hope being in a *future* Second Coming. Preterists argue that our salvation is already complete. Our hope comes from Christ's finished work on the cross and his ushering in of the age of redemption in AD 70. We do not need to wait for a future Second Coming to be assured that our salvation is complete! For this reason, preterism is a *very optimistic* eschatology. In fact, we would go even further. To teach that the completeness of our salvation is still in the future is not only unnecessarily discouraging, but also biblically inexcusable.

In what is our **ultimate hope**? Go back up to the passage from 1 Peter. He tells us plainly wherein our hope lies. Ultimately, it is an inheritance in **heaven**!

We appreciate how much the expectation of a "new heaven and new earth" has permeated the thinking of many Christians. It may be at first disappointing to learn that the new heavens and new earth are not a future utopian state on planet earth. But the truth is even more optimistic. If preterism is true, we do not have Armageddon or a Great Tribulation or the burning of the planet in front of us. The Great Tribulation is history, having occurred in AD 62-70, and included Christian persecution by the Jews and Nero, and also especially the Jewish-Roman war period. During this period more than a million Jews were killed, the nation of Israel ceased to exist, the temple was destroyed, and the age-old system of temple sacrifices for sin (the system of the old heaven and earth) was abolished forever. The burden of Old Covenant legalism has been replaced by grace.

There is still another reason why preterism is wonderfully optimistic. The preterist view holds that when we die, we do not have to wait in some state of limbo until the end of time. When believers die today we immediately go to be with the Lord in heaven in our glorified body. We touched on this in the previous chapter and will examine this issue further in the next chapter when we discuss the resurrection.

Understanding that finality has come, we find that preterist completion resolves other problematic passages in the Bible as well. For just one example, consider the issue of speaking in tongues. In 1 Corinthians 13:8-13 Paul teaches that speaking in tongues—a practice that many Christians view with suspicion—was to *cease*. It was never to be a permanent part of Christianity, but it was a last-days sign to apostate Judaism and a tool with which to build the church of the first century

(1 Corinthians 13-14). 1 Corinthians 13:10 tells us that tongues were to cease "when that which is perfect has come." Clearly, the perfection of which Paul speaks here is the same perfection that he and the other New Testament writers foresaw immediately ahead of them (Hebrews 7:18-19; 9:9; 10:1-4). All prophecy would be fulfilled (Luke 21:22, 32, 36; Revelation 1:1-3; 22:6-7); the Old Covenant would be ushered out (Hebrews 8:13); and our redemption would be complete and perfected with finality (Luke 21:28; Hebrews 9:28).[134]

THE KINGDOM OF HEAVEN

The theme of *the kingdom of heaven* or *the kingdom of God* is one that is pervasive in the New Testament. *Kingdom of heaven* occurs, if we have counted correctly, at least thirty-two times in the New Testament. *Kingdom of God* appears at least sixty-eight times. At other times the Bible simply uses the term *the kingdom*. The terms are used interchangeably and refer to the same concept, as you can clearly see as you examine the passages below.[135]

We shouldn't confuse this terminology with the fact that God's rule in all things has been in effect forever. "Kingdom of heaven" in the New Testament is a covenantal term—a precursor to heaven itself.

Preterists, amillennialists, and postmillennialists generally agree that the kingdom of God was instituted in the first century with Jesus, and that it continues today. Premillennialists think the kingdom of God is essentially the same thing as the future millennium. The evidence is overwhelmingly against the premillennialists. Jesus (and John the Baptist and the apostle John) said that the kingdom was at hand for their hearers. Here are some examples:

> In those days John the Baptist came preaching in the wilderness of Judea, and saying, "Repent, for the **kingdom of heaven** is at hand!" (*Matthew 3:1-2*)

> Now after John was put in prison, Jesus came to Galilee, preaching the **gospel** of the **kingdom of God**, and saying, "The **time is fulfilled,** and the **kingdom of God** is **at hand**. Repent, and believe in the **gospel**." (*Mark 1:14-15*)

Whatever city you enter, and they receive you, eat such things as are set before you. And heal the sick there, and say to them, "The **kingdom of God has come near to you**." (*Luke 10:8-9*)

But if I cast out demons with the finger of God, surely the **kingdom of God has come upon you**. (*Luke 11:20*)

And I also say to you that you are Peter, and on this rock I will build my church, and the gates of hades shall not prevail against it. And I will give **you** the keys of the **kingdom of heaven**, and whatever you bind on earth will be bound in heaven, and whatever you loose on earth will be loosed in heaven. (*Matthew 16:18-19*)

For the Son of Man will come in the glory of His Father with his angels, and then He will reward each according to his works. Assuredly, I say to you, **there are some standing here who shall not taste death** till they see the Son of Man coming in his **kingdom**. (*Matthew 16:27-28*)

So you also, when you see these things happening, know that the **kingdom of God is near**. (*Luke 21:31, Note that this is in the Olivet Discourse.*)

We would like the reader to notice that the kingdom was instituted progressively. John the Baptist announced its soon arrival even before Jesus began his ministry (Matthew 3:1-2). Then shortly afterward, Jesus Himself confirms the arrival of the kingdom coincident with his announcement of the gospel (Mark 1:14-15). Later, we see Jesus marking the kingdom with healing miracles and his casting out demons (Luke 10:8-9; 11:20; 17:21). Then, Jesus projects his kingdom forward until after his resurrection (Luke 22:15; 24:30-32). Next we can infer that Jesus marks the continuing steps of the kingdom's progression with Pentecost and the granting of salvation to the Gentiles, when He said that He would give Peter the keys to the kingdom (Matthew 16:18-19, cf. Acts 2:14-41; Acts 10-11). Then finally we see the kingdom consummation at the Second Coming in AD 70 (Matthew 16:27-28; Luke 21:31). Revelation further confirms that the kingdom had come by the end of the "millennium" and that it would continue forever (Revelation 11:15; 12:10; 22:5).

> Then the seventh angel sounded: And there were loud voices in heaven, saying, "The kingdoms of this world **have become the kingdoms of our Lord** and of his Christ, and He shall reign forever and ever!" (*Revelation 11:15*)

> Then I heard a loud voice saying in heaven, "Now salvation, and strength, and the **kingdom of our God**, and the power of his Christ **have come**, for the accuser of our brethren, who accused them before our God day and night, has been cast down." (*Revelation 12:10*)

So we understand that at the Second Coming the kingdom of God arrived in its fullness. The kingdom was thus instituted, or at least revealed, in a *progressive* manner. This is consistent with the previous section where we saw how Christ's salvation work was, in a sense, a progressive work culminating at the Second Coming.

In the passages above we can easily see that the kingdom was instituted with Jesus' first-century work and that its consummation was imminent. Premillennialists and some postmillennialists think that the kingdom is still future, that it will be a *worldly kingdom* instituted on earth in the millennium, i.e., the very kind of rule the Israelites wanted. This seems like a frightening misinterpretation to us. Jesus made it clear that his kingdom was not an earthly kingdom at all, but a spiritual one:

> Jesus answered, "My kingdom is **not of this world**. If my kingdom were of this world, my servants would fight, so that I should not be delivered to the Jews; but now my kingdom is not from here." (*John 18:36; cf. Luke 17:20-21*)

An objection that millennialists give to the kingdom being a spiritual kingdom is a statement in Revelation 5:10: "And have made us kings and priests to our God; and we shall reign on the earth." Millennialists argue that God's people have never physically reigned on the earth, so this passage cannot have been fulfilled. But, of course, there is an assumption that the passage speaks of a physical reign. Our discussion of Revelation and our arguments elsewhere in this book should be adequate to dispel this assumption. And, certainly, this one verse cannot be used to explain away every time reference in Revelation. God's people are to reign not in the sense of worldly power, but as priests dispensing the gospel to the nations and bringing sinners to God.

The insistence of millennialists of a future utopian kingdom on earth is a man-centered theology that diminishes, we think, the finished work of Christ. Notwithstanding the view of some postmillennialists that the Holy Spirit will impart utopian perfection in each of us, we think it also gives too much credit to man's ability to overcome his deep-seated sinful nature. It is a carnal Christianity that understands God's promises as a future earthly kingdom ushered in by human effort (postmillennialists) or sustained by human effort (premillennialists).

One thing that confuses millennialists is that the coming kingdom is associated with the Second Coming and judgment, which they incorrectly *assume* is still future. But, as we have seen, the Second Coming and judgment were imminent events for the writers of the New Testament. All of these things were fulfilled in AD 70. Note how Paul put it:

> I charge you therefore before God and the Lord Jesus Christ, who will [*mello*, is about to] judge the living and the dead at his **appearing and his kingdom.** (*2 Timothy 4:1*)

Russell sums it up thusly:

> The *coming*, the *judgment*, the *kingdom*, are all coincident and contemporaneous, and not only so, but also *nigh at hand*. . . . So long as the Theocratic nation existed, and the temple, with its priesthood and sacrifices and ritual, remained, and the Mosaic law continued, or seemed to continue, in force, the distinction between Jew and Gentile could not be obliterated. But the barrier was effectually broken down when law, temple, city, and nation were swept away together, and the Theocracy was visibly brought to a final consummation. That event was, so to speak, the formal and public declaration that God was no longer God of the Jews only, but that He was now the common Father of all men. . . . [136]

Brian L. Martin sums up the error of premillennialists in expecting that national Israel must be restored in splendor in an earthly millennial kingdom:

> We find no such compulsion in the New Testament. After Pentecost, there is no mention of a future physical kingdom. After describing the Church as the temple of God, there is no mention of a future physical temple. After stating that true Israel is made up of spiritual Jews circumcised of the heart, Paul never says that

being a true Israelite will ever be dependent upon a bloodline and physical circumcision.[137]

Amillennialists separate the kingdom and judgment by putting the coming of Christ's kingdom in the past but his judgment in the future. Preterists argue that the coming of his kingdom and the judgment are inseparably linked in the past. As we recall, both Jesus and John the Baptist linked the kingdom advent and the judgment to the first century:

> For the Son of Man will come in the glory of his Father with his angels, and then He will **reward** each according to his works. Assuredly, I say to you, there are **some standing here** who shall not taste death till they see the Son of Man coming in **his kingdom**. (*Matthew 16:27-28*)

> In those days John the Baptist came preaching in the wilderness of Judea, and saying, "Repent, for the **kingdom of heaven is at hand**!" . . . But when he saw many of the Pharisees and Sadducees coming to his baptism, he said to them, "Brood of vipers! Who warned you to flee from the **wrath** [*mello, about*] **to come**?" (*Matthew 3:1, 2, 7*)

Once again, preterism helps us understand how consistent the Bible is. It is reasonable to believe that Daniel 7 was fulfilled in the first century (especially in light of Daniel 12 which we have already considered). An excerpt from Daniel 7 that contains kingdom language reads thusly:

> I was watching in the night visions, and behold, one like the Son of Man, **coming with the clouds of heaven**! He came to the Ancient of Days, and they brought Him near before Him. Then to Him was given dominion and glory and a **kingdom**, that all peoples, nations, and languages should serve Him. His dominion is an **everlasting dominion**, which shall not pass away, and his **kingdom** the one which shall not be destroyed. (*Daniel 7:13-14*)

Daniel's prophecy does not mention a bodily visible return, but rather a coming on clouds—the Second Coming. Neither does it say anything about a limitation on how long the kingdom would last— i.e. a millennium, as is commonly thought by many evangelicals. Rather, the gist of Daniel's prophecy is the ushering in of an *everlasting dominion*.

Jesus came in glory in AD 70 to once-for-all usher in the New Covenant Age and his kingdom, which puts Daniel 7 in conformity with the many other eschatological passages throughout the Old and New Testaments.

As we have moved through the Bible, we have seen over and over that the various aspects of eschatology consistently tie together with the events of AD 70. We hope the reader has come to a sense of appreciation for the consistency, the accuracy, and the reliability of Holy Scripture.

If you are in a dispensational church that teaches that the kingdom is still future, you might ask your pastor about some of the above passages, especially the ones that announce the imminency of the kingdom of heaven.

11 Challenges for Preterism: Resurrection, Rapture

I f you think our previous material is controversial, the next two chapters will be particularly exciting—or offensive. Out of a hundred prophetic passages that are clear as to the timing of fulfillment, a few offer interesting challenges: 1 Corinthians 15 (resurrection), 1 Thessalonians 4 (rapture), and Acts 1 (Jesus to come "in like manner"). Certain mentions of The Last Day (various passages) are also noteworthy. We consider the first two in this chapter and the second two in the next chapter.

Christians have a lot of presuppositional emotion wrapped up in these subjects. They have a picture of Christ floating down to earth on a literal cloud to snatch his flock into the air, and corpses flying out of their caskets at the end of time to be united with their spirits. But is this a correct understanding?

The above passages often separate partial preterists from full preterists. Here is a common way that partial preterists separate past and future events:

Past fulfillment in AD 70: a "metaphorical" coming (*parousia*) of Christ, a Day of the Lord, the judgment upon Jerusalem, the end of the Old Covenant Age, and perhaps a resurrection of some sort

Still Future: the "consummate" coming of Christ, the final Day of the Lord, the resurrection of the dead, the "rapture" of the living, the final judgment of the living and the dead, the end of history [138]

Note: In this chapter we express our vigorous disagreements with certain partial preterist theologians who are currently writing on eschatology. Because these disagreements are not meant as personal attacks, we considered removing their names from the text, leaving only their views. After all, names and faces of theologians come and go. Only the Bible is constant. After consideration, we have left the men identified with their teachings, which is the standard method of scholarship.

187

RESURRECTION

> "The Christian faith knows that human life is life in a higher and more comprehensive sense than mere biology grants. . . . The only sufficient answer to the question of man is a response which discharges the infinite claim of love. Only eternal life corresponds to the question raised by humans living and dying on this earth."
>
> —Joseph Ratzinger (Pope Benedict XVI) [139]

Various passages link the resurrection to other eschatological events, such as the judgment and the Second Coming. There is a great deal of tradition about the resurrection and the afterlife that may be more difficult to support from the Bible than one might imagine. The primary focus of this section will culminate on the controversial passage 1 Corinthians 15. The interpretation of this chapter of the Bible is hotly contested.

What is the nature of our eternal existence in the afterlife? The Bible tells us very little indeed about what we will experience in heaven. Much of what Christians believe is based on inference or even speculation. When one begins to think about this, innumerable questions arise: What age will we be in heaven—the age when we were in our "prime" or the age at which we died? Will someone who died as an infant be an infant in heaven? Will there be any semblance at all to our old life on earth in our fleshly bodies? Can we sin in heaven? If not, what kind of life would that be?

First, let's consider briefly some background about what the Bible says happens after biological death. There is confusion among Christians on this point. The majority view is that when believers die, our soul goes to "be with the Lord," but our bodies await the end of time to be raised and united with our souls in heaven. Exactly what "being with the Lord" means is hazy, though. It may or may not be heaven, but is sometimes thought of as a "temporary" or "intermediate" place or state. Some hold that after death, everyone "sleeps" until the final judgment, after which everyone will be sent to heaven or hell.

But it is particularly confusing because what we hear preachers say at funerals is not consistent. A preacher may say that the deceased, if he was a believer, "is in heaven now." Or he may say that he is "with God." Even when he says that the deceased is in heaven, if he explains it further in another setting, he may say that the person is really not in heaven but in a temporary state until the end of time. The church has entertained variations on this theme throughout history. And Roman Catholics have the concept of purgatory (a place in which the souls are purified of certain sins), but such an idea is rejected by Protestants.

If you attempt to prove any of the standard views by Scripture you will have a labored time of it. While we will get resistance to this, we suggest that the majority views are put together with baling wire and chewing gum. In other words, they are believed on weak inference or tradition with only sketchy biblical support, and are heavily influenced by extra-biblical philosophy. There is evidence that the concept of the immortality of the soul, as understood by many Christians, may be more from Greek thought than from the Bible. We have added a few comments about the soul in Appendix D, should the reader want to explore this. In any case, let's try to get a basic understanding of what the Scriptures teach happens after death.

Jesus states in John 3:13 that "No one has ascended to heaven but He who came down from heaven, that is, the Son of Man who is in heaven." If no one went to heaven prior to Jesus' messianic work, where did people go when they died? We contend that they went to *hades*. In the Old Testament, the Hebrew counterpart for the Greek word hades is *sheol*. The Hebrew word *sheol* is used numerous times and in different ways in the Old Testament, including to describe a place in the earth, the abode of the dead, oblivion, a place of consciousness (Isaiah 14:9-10; Ezekiel 31:16-17), or simply as the grave. Of note, sheol is not always a place of punishment, as we see such faithful servants as Jacob there (Genesis 37:35; 42:38; 44:29, 31). Righteous Job also longed for it in Job 14:13. David spoke of going to sheol in Psalm 29:15, and Jesus apparently went there (Psalm 16:10; Acts 2:24-31).[140]

Now for the New Testament. This topic is another area in which the King James Version has confused readers for a long time. The Greek language (Greek being the language of the New Testament) has different words for hades and hell, but the King James Version translates both of them as "hell." Most modern translations have made a partial correction, and you will see both words *hades* and *hell* in English versions of the New Testament. Thus in most modern translations, the Greek word *hades* is usually kept as "hades" in English, while the Greek word *gehenna* is substituted (not translated) with the word "hell."

Our discussion will focus on hades, as it has the most eschatological significance. Our conclusion must necessarily rest partly on inference, because the New Testament is not perfectly clear on just what hades is. Hades appears in the New Testament eleven times. The more significant passages that seem to relate to the concept of hades, even if the word is not specifically mentioned, are Luke 16:22-23 (Abraham's side/bosom), Luke 23:43 (paradise), Acts 2:24-32 (Jesus was not held by it), Ephesians 4:8-10 (descended to the lower parts of the earth), 1 Peter 3:18-20; 4:6 (Christ's proclamation to the spirits in prison), and Revelation 20:13-14 (death and hades thrown into the lake of fire). You might want to take the time to look up each of these passages. You can check out all of the mentions of hades at the Blue Letter Bible.

It seems that sheol/hades is (*was*) a temporary abode of the dead. People resided in hades until Jesus' Second Coming. If they were dead at the Second Coming in AD 70, they left hades and went to either heaven or hell (gehenna) for eternity. The area (region) of hades where the *faithful* resided is "Abraham's bosom" or "paradise" (Luke 16:22-23). The area of hades where the *condemned* resided is (apparently) called tartarus (2 Peter 2:4). Jesus apparently announced to the faithful in Abraham's bosom the good news that they would be raised to heaven (Ephesians 4:8-10; 1 Peter 3:18-20).

Now, this gets even more interesting but quite controversial. Some Christian scholars are convinced from a comprehensive analysis of the Bible that hell is not, in fact, a place of eternal conscious punishment as is the standard view. Gehenna, the Greek word rendered "hell" in English, was an actual place outside of Jerusalem where waste was deposited and burned. So, some argue that *Jesus used gehenna/hell as a metaphor for the total destruction or annihilation of the damned*, rather than a place of eternal conscious punishment.[141]

In this book we take no position on this view, which is usually called *annihilationism*. Preterism does not rest on this in any way. Many if not most preterists hold to the standard view of hell being eternal conscious punishment, while others hold to annihilationism. We at least agree that *gehenna* is probably inappropriately rendered as "hell" and should be brought into English simply as gehenna, just as hades is now generally left in the Greek form in many English Bibles. We simply suggest that the reader keep an open mind on annihilationism until having studied it. It does appear to be gaining adherents from Christians of all eschatological persuasions. Check the endnotes for sources for study.[142] Our focus in this discussion is the temporary abode of the dead—hades.[143]

As we considered in Chapter 9, Revelation 20 reveals that hades was abolished at the Second Coming in AD 70. Here is the text:

And I saw the dead, small and great, standing before God, and books were opened. And another book was opened, which is the Book of Life. And the dead were judged according to their works, by the things which were written in the books. The sea gave up the dead who were in it, and **Death and Hades delivered up the dead** who were in them. And they were **judged**, each one according to his works. Then **Death and Hades were cast into the lake of fire**. This is the second death. And anyone not found written in the Book of Life was cast into the lake of fire. (*Revelation 20:12-15*)

The text indicates that there was a resurrection and judgment of the dead. This is what is referred to as the *general resurrection*. When would this happen? This vision is placed just *after* a vision of Jesus' return (Revelation 19) and *after* the millennium (Revelation 20:1-7), but just *prior* to the vision of the new heaven and earth (Revelation 21). All of this ties to the overwhelming number of imminency statements in Revelation, such as Jesus' promised imminent Parousia in AD 70 (Revelation 22, etc.). Everybody who was in hades at the Second Coming was raised to their ultimate judgment. Those people who die subsequent to AD 70 go *directly* to heaven or to the Lake of Fire (either eternal conscious punishment per the standard view, or are destroyed according to the annihilationist view).

Hebrews 9:27 says that "And just as each person is destined to die once and after that comes judgment," (NLT). This passage, which is in the context of the end of the age, further confirms that after the end of the age men no longer go to hades, but rather go directly to their ultimate judgment, which would be consistent with Revelation 20:12-15 above. Thus men do not wait in a temporary place until the end of time to be judged.

We are concerned in this discussion about what the Bible teaches as to both the *timing* of that general resurrection as well as the *nature* of that resurrection. There is more room for doubt about *what* exactly happened at the "general resurrection" than the *timing* of that event, which we think is definitive. We are persuaded that the Bible teaches that at or near the end of the age in AD 70, the resurrection of the Old Testament saints, along with the deceased Christians, occurred. Certain other passages of Scripture are pertinent. Here is one from the Old Testament:

¹ "At that time Michael shall stand up, the great prince who stands watch over the sons of your people; and there shall be a **time of trouble**, such as never was since there was a na-

tion, even to that time. And at that time your people shall be delivered, everyone who is found written in the book. ² And **many of those who sleep in the dust of the earth shall awake, some to everlasting life, some to shame and everlasting contempt.**" . . .⁷ . . . and when the **power of the holy people** has been completely shattered, all these things shall be finished. ⁸ Although I heard, I did not understand. Then I said, "My lord, what shall be the end of these things?" ⁹ And he said, "Go your way, Daniel, for the words are closed up and sealed till the time of the end. . . . ¹¹ And from the time that the **daily sacrifice is taken away,** and the abomination of desolation is set up, . . . ¹³ But you, go your way till the **end**; for you shall rest, and will **arise to your inheritance at the end of the days.**" *(Daniel 12:1-2, 7b-9, 11a, 13; cf. Job 14:7-14, 19:26; Psalm 49:15; Isaiah 26:19)*

Daniel chapter 12 is the most important passage in the Old Testament about the resurrection. We previously showed in Chapters 4 and 5 that Daniel 12 was fulfilled in AD 70. This passage contains the "time of trouble" (12:1—the tribulation) and the "end" (12:13—end of the Old Covenant order). The timing is confirmed by the "power of the holy people" being shattered (12:7, 11—end of the sacrificial system). Remember that in Luke 21:22 Jesus states, "For these are the days of vengeance, that all things which are written may be fulfilled." This understanding of a first-century fulfillment of ancient biblical prophecy was confirmed by Peter in Acts 3:24, where he stated that all the Old Testament prophets from Samuel onward were pointing to Peter's own time. Thus, if you believe Jesus and Peter, there is no way that the general resurrection is still future.

Daniel chapter 12 ties the resurrection (12:2, 13) to the great tribulation (12:1), to the judgment (12:2), and to the end of the Old Covenant Age (12:7, 11, 13). As we have labored to show previously, Jesus in the Olivet Discourse (and elsewhere) ties the great tribulation to the judgment against Jerusalem and end of the Old Covenant Age in his generation. This patently puts the resurrection in AD 70. For further confirmation, let's look at some additional texts. Remember that in Chapter 4 we concluded that the end of the age had to have happened in the first century. Here are Jesus' words about the end of the age relative to the resurrection and/or judgment:

The enemy who sowed them is the devil, the **harvest** is the **end of the age**, and the reapers are the angels. Therefore as the tares are **gathered** and burned in the fire, so it will be at the **end of this age**. The Son of Man will send out his angels, and they will gather out of his kingdom all things that offend, and those who practice lawlessness, and **will cast them into the furnace of fire**. There will be wailing and gnashing of teeth. Then the righteous will shine forth as the sun in the kingdom of their Father. He who has ears to hear, let him hear! (*Matthew 13:39-43*)

Jesus answered and said to them, "The sons of **this age** marry and are given in marriage. But those who are counted worthy to attain **that age**, and the **resurrection** from the dead, neither marry nor are given in marriage; nor can they die anymore, for they are equal to the angels and are sons of God, being sons of the **resurrection**." (*Luke 20:34-36*, see also a parallel passage in *Matthew 22:23-33*)

In this latter passage Jesus is imparting some information about both the timing and nature of the resurrection. He said that the resurrection was not available to them in "this age" (the Old Covenant Age) but would be available to them in "that" age (the New Covenant Age), implying that the general resurrection would occur at the conclusion of the Old Covenant Age.

Preterists are sometimes challenged with this passage, by the way. It is charged by some that to be consistent, preterists should teach that because we are in the new age now we should not marry. We certainly do not teach that and the passage does not demand that. This passage does not mean that after AD 70 marriage is abolished for subsequent generations of earth-dwellers. Jesus was merely teaching certain Jews that their concept of a physical nature of the kingdom was wrong. The Jews were of the mindset that their kingdom was expanded by marrying and having children. The kingdom of God, however, is a **spiritual** kingdom (John 18:36) and is spread by faith not by blood (Romans 9). Jesus may also have been suggesting that those who are in heaven after the resurrection of the dead in AD 70 (the Old Testament saints) will not marry because they are "like angels," i.e., spirits, in heaven. Spirits do not marry. Thus there is no marriage *in heaven*.[144]

Next, consider these words from the lips of Jesus from Matthew 25. This passage is often labeled in Bibles as "The Final Judgment":

When the Son of Man comes in His glory, and all the holy angels with him, then He will sit on the throne of his glory. All the nations will be gathered before him, and He will separate them one from another, as a shepherd **divides his sheep from the goats.** And He will set the sheep on his right hand, but the goats on the left. Then the King will say to those on his right hand, "Come, you blessed of my Father, inherit the kingdom prepared for you from the foundation of the world:" . . . Then He will also say to those on the left hand, "Depart from me, you cursed, into the **everlasting fire** prepared for the devil and his angels. . . **And these will go away into everlasting punishment, but the righteous into eternal life."** (Matthew 25:31-46)

This prophecy is the ending section of Matthew's version of the Olivet Discourse. We see in the passage that at Jesus' Second Coming in judgment, the sheep and the goats, the just and the unjust, were judged and sent to their final destination—either heaven or hell. We showed in Chapter 6 that Matthew 25 cannot be separated from Matthew 24 and its imminency context. Both "sections" of the Olivet Discourse were fulfilled in AD 70.

So now we have arrived at the next level of our understanding of what happened in AD 70. *Jesus not only judged the nation of Israel in AD 70, but He also judged those in hades at the same time.* We were introduced to this idea in our study of Revelation 20. But now we begin to see that this conclusion is inescapable as we examine additional pertinent passages including those below.

24 Most assuredly, I say to you, he who hears my word and believes in Him who sent me has everlasting life, and shall not come into judgment, but has passed from death into life. 25 Most assuredly, I say to you, **the hour is coming, and now is** ["is here now," *New Living Translation*], **when the dead will hear the voice of the Son of God; and those who hear will live**. 26 For as the Father has life in Himself, so He has granted the Son to have life in Himself, 27 and has given Him authority to execute judgment also, because He is the Son of Man. 28 Do not marvel at this; for **the hour is coming in which all who are in the graves will hear his voice** 29 **and come forth**—those who have done good, to the **resurrection**

of life, and those who have done evil, to the **resurrection** of condemnation. *(John 5:24-29)*

In this important prophecy, we agree with many futurists that Jesus was speaking of two different events. Verses 24-25 speak of a spiritual/metaphorical "resurrection" that is progressively accomplished in history as people believe in Christ and "live." Verses 28-29 teach a second, literal, resurrection of the deceased. In the preterist view, the second resurrection was fulfilled in AD 66-70, not at the end of history as futurists believe. [145]

The first resurrection (John 5:24-25) is the **soteriological** "resurrection" of the *living*, consistent with Romans 6:11; Ephesians 2:1-7; Colossians 2:12-13; 13:1, and 1 John 3:14. Jesus put this resurrection event in the *present tense* and applied it to "those who hear," thus applying it to the living. But Jesus put the second resurrection (John 5:28-29) specifically in the *future tense*. This most certainly was the **eschatological** bodily resurrection "out of their graves" to heaven in AD 66-70, consistent with Daniel 12, Matthew 25, and Revelation 20:11-15 — at the harvest at the end of the age (Matthew 13:36-43).

As discussed previously, these resurrections are different in nature! The first resurrection is spiritual/metaphorical. The second resurrection was the general resurrection of the physically dead from hades. Jesus, by the way, spoke of two types of death elsewhere. When Jesus said, "Let the dead bury the dead." (Matthew 8:22; Luke 9:60), He was referencing both types of death. The second death is physical-body death; the first death is spiritual death. Since there are two types of death, there are two types of resurrections. This makes perfect sense out of Revelation 20:6: If you have been resurrected spiritually, that is *saved*, by virtue of your faith, physical death has no power over you.

Biblical consistency demands that the source of many New Testament teachings on the resurrection was Daniel 12, which incontrovertibly was fulfilled, per Jesus, at the end of the age, that is, in AD 70 when old covenant Jerusalem was surrounded by armies, etc. (Luke 21). Paul confirms the preterist view that there was only one time of general resurrection and that its consummation was imminent in his day:

> But this I confess to you, that according to the Way which they call a sect, so I worship the God of my fathers, believing all things which are written in the Law and in the Prophets. I have hope in God, which they themselves also accept, that there **will**

be [*mello*] a **resurrection** of the dead, both of the just and the unjust. (*Acts 24:14-15*)

Paul here is certainly referencing Daniel 12 to tell his readers that the fulfillment of Daniel's prophecy was imminent. In this passage Paul uses the Greek word *mello*. While this word is translated "will be" in many translations, similar to what we have previously noted in other passages, the word in context frequently carries an immediacy connotation. It means *about to be*. Compare the New King James Version above with the same passage from Young's Literal Translation here: [146]

having hope toward God, which they themselves also wait for, [that] there is **about to be** a rising again of the dead, both of righteous and unrighteous; (*Acts 24:15, Young's Literal Translation*)

Other passages confirm the imminency of the resurrection and/or the judgment. For example, consider these passages from Matthew, Acts, Romans, 2 Timothy, 1 Peter, and Revelation:

For, the Son of Man is **about to come** in the glory of his Father, with his messengers, and then he will **reward each**, according to his work. Verily I say to you, there are certain of those standing here who shall not taste of death till they may see the Son of Man coming in his reign. (*Matthew 16:27-28, Young's Literal Translation*)

because He did set a day in which He is **about to judge** the world in righteousness, by a man whom He did ordain, having given assurance to all, having raised him out of the dead. (*Acts 17:31, Young's Literal Translation*)

And do this, knowing the time, that **now** it is high time to awake out of **sleep**; for now our salvation is nearer than when we first believed. The night is far spent, the **day is at hand**. Therefore let us cast off the works of darkness, and let us put on the armor of light. (*Romans 13:11-12, compare to Daniel 12*)

I do fully testify, then, before God, and the Lord Jesus Christ, who is **about to judge living and dead** at his manifestation and his reign. (*2 Timothy 4:1, Young's Literal Translation*) but they will give account to him who is **ready to judge the living and the dead**. . . . For it is **time for judgment to begin** at the household of God; and if it begins with us, what will be the outcome for those who do not obey the gospel of God? (*1 Peter 4:5, 17*)

"And behold, **I am coming quickly**, and my **reward** is with Me, to give to every one **according to his work**." (*Revelation 22:12*)

These passages confirm with certainty that the judgment of the dead—both the pious and the wicked—was imminent when the New Testament was written.

Don Preston offers another argument that the general resurrection was in AD 70. He points out that the time of the resurrection per Isaiah would be when the blood of the martyrs was avenged at the coming of the Lord (Isaiah 26:19-21). But the time when the blood of the martyrs was to be avenged was to be in Jesus' generation (Matthew 23:34-36). Therefore the time of the resurrection at the coming of the Lord was to be in Jesus' generation.[147]

Now let's consider what is probably the most famous passage on the resurrection—1 Corinthians 15. This passage further confirms that the general resurrection occurred at the Second Coming:

[19] If only for this life we have hope in Christ, we are of all people most to be pitied. [20] But now Christ is risen from the dead, and has become the firstfruits of those who have fallen asleep. [21] For since by man came death, by Man also came the **resurrection** of the dead. [22] For as in Adam all die, even so in Christ all shall be made alive. [23] But each one in his own order: Christ the firstfruits, afterward those who are Christ's **at His coming** [*parousia*]. [24] Then comes the **end**, when He delivers the kingdom to God the Father, when He puts an end to all rule and all authority and power. [25] For He must reign till He has put all enemies under His feet. [26] The last enemy that will be destroyed is death. . . . [35] But someone will say, "How are the dead raised up? And **with what body do they come**?" [36] Foolish one, what you sow is not made alive unless it dies. [37] And what you sow, you do not sow that body that shall be, but mere grain—perhaps wheat or some other grain. [38] But God gives it a body as He pleases, and

to each seed its own body. . . .[39] All flesh is not the same flesh, but there is one kind of flesh of men, another flesh of animals, another of fish, and another of birds.[40] There are also celestial bodies and terrestrial bodies; but the glory of the celestial is one, and the glory of the terrestrial is another.[41] There is one glory of the sun, another glory of the moon, and another glory of the stars; for one star differs from another star in glory. [42] So also is the **resurrection of the dead**. The body is sown in corruption, it is raised in incorruption.[43] It is sown in dishonor, it is raised in **glory**. It is sown in weakness, it is raised in power. [44] It is sown a natural body, it is **raised a _spiritual_ body**. There is a natural body, and there is a **_spiritual_ body**.[45] And so it is written, "The first man Adam became a living being." The last Adam became a life-giving spirit.[46] However, the **_spiritual_** is not first, but the natural, and afterward the **_spiritual_**.[47] The first man was of the earth, made of dust; the second Man is the Lord from heaven. [48] As was the man of dust, so also are those who are made of dust; and as is the heavenly Man, so also are those who are heavenly. [49] And as we have borne the image of the man of dust, we shall also bear the image of the heavenly Man.[50] Now this I say, brethren, that **flesh and blood cannot inherit the kingdom of God**; nor does corruption inherit incorruption.[51] Behold, I tell you a mystery: **We shall not all sleep**, but **we** shall all be **changed**— [52] in a moment, in the twinkling of an eye, at the **last trumpet**. For the trumpet will sound, and the **dead will be raised incorruptible, and we shall be changed**.[53] For this corruptible must put on incorruption, and this mortal must put on **immortality**.[54] So when this corruptible has put on incorruption, and this mortal has put on immortality, then shall be brought to pass the saying that is written: "Death is swallowed up in victory.[55] O Death, where is your sting? O Hades, where is your victory?" [56] The sting of death is sin, and the strength of sin is the law.[57] But thanks be to God, who gives us the victory through our Lord Jesus Christ. (_1 Corinthians 15:20-26, 35-57_)

Isn't this a marvelous and hopeful section? There are at least two issues to consider from this passage—the _nature_ of the resurrection as well as the _timing_ of its occurrence. There are certain things that lead to various controversies over this passage. Among these things are the assumptions that people bring to its interpretation. But also, many people fail to understand that the **Bible uses _resurrection_ in different senses**.

As pointed out in our discussion of Revelation 20, individuals die both *bodily* and *spiritually*. So they can experience both bodily and spiritual resurrection. In addition, there is an important, but often overlooked biblical theme about *Israel's national* rebirth/resurrection/restoration. The concepts of both individual and corporate resurrection converge in 1 Corinthians 15. As put by Derrick Olliff, "There is a clear analogy between Israel's rebirth/resurrection and our own (with both flowing from the foundational resurrection: the resurrection of Jesus)." [148]

Considering that Paul is discussing, at least in part, the resurrection of individual bodies to heaven, i. e., the second resurrection, he is arguing for a view of what our heavenly body will be like that is different than what most Christians think. Christians often have the idea that our resurrection body will be flesh and bone. But Paul forcefully disavows such a view and argues that our eternal body will be a *spiritual* body. Paul uses the adjective "spiritual" four times for emphasis! (Compare to "spirits in prison" in 1 Peter 3:19.) Though it is said to be a body, it is not a natural body but a supernatural body.[149]

He argues this in different ways. He says that there will be a correlation of sorts to our old physical body, using the seed illustration to say that what is sown will be different from its seed—but implying a degree of continuity with our earthly body. The outer shell of a seed always stays in the ground. We can also see in 1 Corinthians 15 that there will be personal identity in our resurrected bodies. If one does not like the conclusion that our resurrected bodies are spiritual rather than physical, his argument is not with preterists but with St. Paul.[150]

The common idea that our resurrected bodies will be our old biological bodies is based on a false assumption. That assumption comes in part from a bad interpretation of verse 22, which says that "For as in Adam all die, even so in Christ all shall be made alive." The standard view *assumes* that since Adam had a physical body, and died a physical death at the Fall—and further that Christ rose in his biological body—therefore *we* will have a physical/biological body in the resurrection.

Let's check the reference Paul makes about Adam. In Genesis 2:17 we read that God told Adam, "But of the tree of the knowledge of good and evil you shall not eat, for in the day that you eat of it you shall surely die." Yet when Adam ate of the fruit he did not die biologically that day! He was 930 years old when he finally died (Genesis 5:5). So the death that Adam experienced in Genesis 3 at the Fall was *spiritual* death rather than *physical* death.[151]

It is incorrect that mankind was created to physically live forever, and that only at the Fall became mortal. Jesus' body was the only one promised not to decay (Acts 2:27, 31; 13:35). Hebrews 9:27 indicates that man was mortal from the beginning. Our physical bodies return to dust (Genesis 2:7; 3:19; Psalm 90:3). Samuel G. Dawson argues accordingly:

> Not only were Adam and all the living creatures *living souls* before Adam sinned, but they also were subject to death before he sinned. After his creation, God placed Adam in the garden and gave him access to the tree of life to *sustain his life*. This fact alone tells us he wasn't immortal, but subject to death before he sinned. Some suggest that the fact Adam had to eat at all (much less of the tree of life), showed he was mortal (as are all other living creatures who eat to survive). Would he have starved to death if he had not eaten, like all other living creatures? If not, why did he need a stomach with a complete digestive system? When he sinned, he lost access to the tree of life, "lest he stretch out his hand, and take also from the tree of life, and eat, and live forever." (Genesis 3:22).[152]

Dr. Kelly Nelson Birks put it this way:

> Physical death is not a result of the fall of Adam. Adam was designed to physically die according to Genesis 3:19 and 2:7. Because man was taken from the ground, before the fall had occurred, then to the ground, or to dust he was always destined to return. Compare this with the fact that Hebrews 9:27 says that it is appointed for every man (including Adam), once to die. . . . Cross reference this with passages like Job 14:5 and Psalm 139:16, and you have a clear, contextual explanation as to why men die physically. So goes another tradition that seems to be guiding the exegesis of the doctors of the church as opposed to the teachings of scripture. Men suffer from physical death, brought on by sickness or otherwise, by the eternal decree and providential actions of God.[153]

Some Christians, namely young-earth creationists, teach that even animals did not die prior to Adam's Fall. But we remember that God provided food for the beasts of the earth before the Fall (Genesis 1:30). We must infer that animals as well as humans would have died without food, and thus God created both mankind and animals as mortal beings.[154]

The understanding that the death experienced by Adam at the Fall was *spiritual* death helps us understand what the Bible teaches in Genesis 3—when Adam and Eve's eyes "were opened" and they became embarrassed and covered their nakedness. This is a verse that made little sense to the author until he understood what was going on here. They died in the sense of being separated from God, and they knew it. They reacted with fear of God approaching them, and attempted to hide from Him. This was Adam's sin-death. Dawson continues:

> In Roman 6:23, Paul taught that the wages of sin is death. If this is physical death, and we're forgiven, why do we still die physically? What more needs to be paid than what Christ paid, if physical death is the subject? What did Christ accomplish if he paid for our sins, yet we still pay our own way? What kind of substitutionary death is that? Why do we still have to pay our own wages by dying physically if Christ paid for our sins? The answer, of course, is that Paul didn't speak of physical death, but the death we suffer like Adam did: spiritual death, the death of his fellowship with God the day he ate of the forbidden fruit.[155]

However, spiritual death resulting from the Fall certainly had far-reaching implications. What was lost at the Fall was not biological death, but rather life *after* death, which was restored for believers by Christ. Spiritual resurrection is related to bodily resurrection in that one must experience the former in order to gain the latter.

As to our heavenly bodies, they will be real bodies, but will have a spiritual aspect. There is, at least, a strong implication in the Bible that Jesus has a body in heaven (Mark 16:19; Luke 24:50-51; Acts 1:9-11; Ephesians 4:8-10; Colossians 2:9; Philippians 3:21; 1 Timothy 3:16; Hebrews 1:3; 10:12; 1 Peter 3:22; Revelation 1:9-18). This sets the pattern for us. Our heavenly bodies will be like Jesus (Romans 6:5; 1 Corinthians 15:49; Philippians 3:10-11;). Paul used the terms "immortal," "imperishable," and "glorified" to explain the nature of our heavenly bodies (1 Corinthians 15:35-55; 2 Corinthians 4:17; Philippians 3:20-21; cf. 1 Timothy 3:16).

The Transfiguration (Matthew 17:2) gives us a hint of what heavenly bodies might be like. Jesus said that our bodies will be like angels (Luke 20:36; cf. Luke 24:4, 23; John 20:12-13). Even though angels have sometimes appeared on earth, they usually exist outside of time and space. Revelation 1:12-20 also gives us a glimpse of Jesus' heavenly body, which our own heavenly bodies will resemble. This all adds to our understanding that our eternal bodies will have physicality—corporeal and personal in some sense. We just have to be satisfied with what information we have been given, as it is impossible to put into language what existence is like outside of time and space.

Many Christians read into 1 Corinthians 15 that because Jesus was physically raised from the dead, so must we be raised in the same physical manner. But that is not Paul's eschatology. We should remember that Jesus is different from us. He was fully God (John 1:1-18) as well as fully man. Unlike us, He was born without sin (Romans 3:21-26; Romans 5:12-21; Romans 7:4-11). Christ is the only one promised that his flesh would not suffer decay (Acts 2:27, 31).

Christ was raised in his physical body. There is no question about this fact. The evidence is overwhelming. The disciples ate with Him and touched his wounds. Jesus made it perfectly clear that his risen body was the same flesh-and-bone body in which he lived and died (Luke 24:39-43). Preterists are sometimes accused of teaching a non-physical resurrection of Christ. That is an absolutely false charge.

While Jesus resides in heaven in bodily form (Acts 7:56), the body of the *heavenly* Christ seems to be different from the *resurrected* Christ. Certain things point to this conclusion.

At some point Christ changed—probably at the ascension. After his ascension, Jesus appeared to Paul on the road to Damascus in a manner that Paul could see a light and hear the voice of Jesus, but neither he nor his companions actually saw Jesus in physical form (Acts 9:3-9; Acts 22:6-11; Acts 26:12-19; cf. John 17:5; Hebrews 5:7). In Acts 26:19 Paul described what he saw as a "heavenly vision." This would seem to be an appearance by Jesus in his glorified state. That Jesus' body had changed into an immortal/glorified one is confirmed by such passages as 1 Corinthians 15:45 and 2 Corinthians 3:17. So our heavenly body will be more like that of the glorified ascended Jesus, rather than the earthly flesh-and-bone Jesus. Quoting Dr. Edward J. Hassertt, Jr.:

> It is obvious to even the casual reader of scripture that the resurrection of Jesus is different in kind than our resurrection, since he appeared on earth three days after his death, and not some thousands of years after his death. So any claim that a human resurrection should be in the exact same form as Jesus is absurd, since people who have been dead for thousands of years have returned to dust and their atoms have been scattered to the ends of the world. So obviously it never had the potential to be the SAME kind of resurrection regardless of where the rhetoric leads. Unless we are raised after only three days in the grave, our resurrection would be physically different from that of Jesus even in your futurist account![156]

Futurists often argue that because Christ rose physically, so must we. That notion is as false as saying that because Christ was literally crucified, we must also be literally crucified (Galatians 2:20) in order to have eternal life. The physical work of Christ (crucifixion, death, burial, and resurrection) was *spiritually* reproduced in his people.

There are other legitimate questions when comparing Christ's resurrection and subsequent ascension and our own resurrection. Christ was raised with all wounds and scars intact. Must we necessarily assume by this fact that a blind or lame person would be resurrected blind or lame? Most Christians assume the opposite; the infirmities of this life will *not* appear in the afterlife. So there are clear differences between the resurrection of Jesus and our own resurrection body! Upon reflection, most will admit that Paul is not teaching that our resurrection will be physically *identical* to that of Jesus.

Joseph Ratzinger made this statement concerning 1 Corinthians 15:35-53:

> Paul was decidedly opposed to the prevailing Jewish view whereby the risen body was completely identical with the earthly body and the world of the resurrection simply a continuation of the world of the present.[157]

Our resurrection, then, is *not* the same as Jesus'. The word "same" does not appear in the text. There is more evidence that Paul taught a spirit-body resurrection rather than a physical one. Consider this:

> And their message will spread like cancer. Hymenaeus and Philetus are of this sort, who have strayed concerning the truth, saying that the resurrection is already past; and they overthrow the faith of some. (*2 Timothy 2:17-18*)

If the early Christians had believed that the resurrection would involve fleshly bodies coming out of the graves, as is taught today—coincident with the rapture, every eye beholding the physical Christ, and the burning of the planet, etc.—Hymenaeus and Philetus could never have convinced anyone that the resurrection had already happened. When Paul corrected Hymenaeus and Philetus, he said nothing about those men getting the *nature* of the resurrection wrong. Paul disagreed only with their *timing* of the resurrection, which Paul taught was soon but not yet. The first-century Christians must have believed in the type of resurrection that we are describing—a resurrection into new bodies, leaving the old ones behind. They must also have believed that life on earth would go on without material change for people living after the resurrection. So they did not believe that they would be transported from a decaying planet earth![158]

We must further consider how 1 Corinthians 15 speaks of a *corporate* sense of resurrection. Resurrection in this sense is the "salvation of Israel" (Romans 11:25-27). This view harkens back to the dry bones passage in Ezekiel 37ff in which God resurrects his people (Ezekiel 37:11-14) into the new covenant (Ezekiel 37:26-28). Ezekiel 37 was specifically fulfilled in the restoration of Israel from captivity back to its land, per the books of Ezra and Nehemiah. But in the Old Testament, there is sometimes a *sensus plenior*, that is, a fuller meaning. Ezekiel's prophecy looked beyond the return from physical captivity to a time of spiritual restoration.

In 1 Corinthians 15:54-55, Paul is quoting Isaiah 25:8 and Hosea 13:14 (cf. Hosea 2:18-19; 3:4-5; 6:1-3) as fulfillment of the Old Covenant doctrine of the "resurrection" of Israel. Some preterists emphasize the language of "reproach" and "salvation" in Isaiah to argue that Paul is speaking of a future restored relationship with Old Covenant Israel. So resurrection refers, in part, to the hope of Israel (inclusive of all believers) to life in Christ. In this sense, resurrection is recovery of relational death between man and God that stood since the Garden of Eden.

This interpretation of resurrection is referred to as the "corporate (collective) body view" (CBV). This contrasts with the "individual body view" (IBV)—which is also stated as the "immortal body at death" view (IBD).

The CBV paradigm was developed by Max R. King (born 1930), who applied resurrection *principally, if not exclusively*, as a corporate occurrence. In this view, resurrection is *merely* a metaphorical event (renewal, regeneration, restoration, rebirth, relationship).[159]

IBV advocates consistently acknowledge that there is an element of corporate resurrection in Scripture. However, CBV advocates may or may not accept that there is also an element of individual bodily resurrection. This is a point of debate among full preterists. Even the contributors to this book hold to widely differing views on this, as excellent Bible students reach different conclusions.

The corporate view, **as a stand-alone doctrine,** in the author's opinion, over-simplifies and over-spiritualizes resurrection. If resurrection is nothing more than relationship, what happens to the doctrine of heaven? Some conclude that heaven is on earth, or that heaven offers nothing better than we have on earth!

At the very least, the **CBV-only** paradigm muddles and minimizes our afterlife hope. This diminution of classical Christianity's doctrine of heaven is an error of *"hyper-preterism"* and should be soundly rejected. There is a big difference between saying we have "heaven now" (a serious error) and saying we have been given "eternal life now" (which is correct). This error is a contributing factor to further distortions of the faith, including universalism and antinomianism.

This error is so obvious to most Christians, that its discussion seems unnecessary. But such is the current state of affairs in the eschatological debate. These extreme versions of preterism, unfortunately, are responsible for steering some Christians away from the preterist view.

So, is there nothing really better to look forward to in heaven? Tell that to the quadriplegic that cannot feed his family. Tell that to the Christian living in a 7x7 tin shanty in Delhi, Rio, or Mogadishu. Tell that to the Christian who lives in fear for his life in Pakistan or Syria, who has had loved ones murdered and mutilated by Muslims! Let's tell all these people that if they accept Jesus as their Lord and Savior, they can look forward to an obscure afterlife, or even one no better than they have now. Paul clearly refuted this in Philippians 1:23.

CBV-only advocates suggest that resurrection is purely collective, spiritual, and covenantal—and, thus by extension, is only individual and bodily in a limited (or murky) sense. These good folks think that the second resurrection is the same thing as the first resurrection—the two resurrections only being separated by time, and not by nature. The implication is that resurrection of the living is the same thing as resurrection of the dead. This defies reason.

As CBV advocates insist, resurrection doctrine draws from the Old Testament. But the most prominent text in the Old Testament about the resurrection is Daniel 12:2: "And many of those who sleep in the dust of the earth shall awake, some to everlasting life, and some to shame and everlasting contempt" (cf. Job 14:7-14; 19:26; Psalm 49:15; Isaiah 26:19). This is the general resurrection of the physically dead from hades in AD 70—the harbinger of the entry into heaven of every believer at death, as most Christians believe.

CBV proponents point out that, in the New Testament, Paul refers to resurrection as the "hope of Israel" (Acts 24:14-15, 21; 26:6-8, 22; 28:20). Was the hope of Israel limited to some concept of metaphoric relationship? Certainly not. The New Testament is clear that the hope of Israel was the Messiah to secure the blessings of heaven through the forgiveness of sins for all individuals who believe.

What was the "hope of Israel?" Answer: salvation from death (Isaiah 25:8-9), the grave (Isaiah 26:19; Daniel 12:2) and Sheol (Hosea 13:14), brought by Messiah—through forgiveness of sins (Isaiah 52-53; 59:17, 20; Romans 11:26-27). Who receives this? Answer: believers (John 3:16; 11:25-26) who confess Jesus (Romans 10:11-13)—i.e. the new "Israel of God" (Romans 11:20-27; Galatians 6:16). This confirms the traditional interpretation: Jesus promised that after biological death, believers will live forever in a better existence with *personality* and *identity* in heaven.

Certainly, this is how the original hearers would have understood resurrection. Consider the rich young ruler (Luke 18:18), Martha (John 11:24), and the disciples (John 14:2-3; cf. Luke 7:22; 9:7). A plain reading of other passages (Acts 26:8; Romans 8:11; 2 Corinthians 4:14-5:10; Philippians 1:22-24; 3:20-21, and many other places) demands an understanding of the promise to have an identifiable "persona" or "body" in heaven, albeit not the self-same body as our earthly body of flesh.

Jesus personalized all of theology. A reasonable case can be made that, with Messiah's advent(s), the IBV paradigm gained ascendency once for all over the CBV paradigm, and became dominant into perpetuity. Numerous passages in the New Testament explain that one's personal salvation is *by grace through a living faith in Jesus Christ alone.* It should be evident that the numerous passages about salvation are immensely personal in nature—not about corporate salvation. After all, corporate entities don't sin; individuals do. I fear that some CBV-only advocates have lost sight of the gospel.

God's covenants were developed corporately through Israel, but are applied individually. Was the eternal reward of the Old Testament saints connected to the group? The New Testament corrected any such understanding by teaching that we are saved not by blood, by works, by the law, or even of the will (John 1:13; Romans 9:13-33; Ephesians 2:8-10). We understand that even the Old Testament faithful were saved as *individuals*—through the vehicle of their personal *faith* (Romans 4:13; etc.). CBV national resurrection was fulfilled to teach a typological lesson about individual resurrection.

God used Israel as a corporate entity for *service* to bring the Messiah to the world. It was the Messiah as an individual that brought salvation to other individuals. Of course, the Old Testament faithful did not have the benefit of knowing Jesus in a personal way as we do today. They were saved by faith in the totality of God's promises, including the promised Messiah. But, not every individual Jew possessed that faith.

As pointed out by Jerel Kratt, CBV-only advocates are missing how "spiritual body" should be understood. Research by various scholars reveals that the ancients did not make the sharp distinction between physical and spiritual as we moderns do. Today, we think of the word "spiritual" as meaning non-physical, immaterial, or metaphorical. But the dominant view in the first century was more that "spiritual" (Greek, *pneuma*) meant *physical but invisible*. The spiritual could not be divorced from the physical. This is confirmed as a New Testament concept in such passages as Romans 8:9-11 and 1 Corinthians 2:15 (cf. Romans 1:3-4; 1 Corinthians 10:1-4; 1 Peter 3:18). Of interest, modern science has a parallel in that physical atoms are actually understood to be made up of invisible non-physical energy.[160]

Part of the CBV conclusion also seems to stem from a confusion of terms. The idioms "new heaven and new earth" and "kingdom of heaven" are different from heaven itself. "New heaven and new earth" and "kingdom of heaven" are about new covenant realities. Heaven (the "third heaven" per 2 Corinthians 12:2) is the "place" we go when we die. The biblical writers used the terms "heaven and earth," "heavens," and "heaven" in different ways, just as we do in modern English.

While the corporate body view is an element of what Paul describes in 1 Corinthians 15, it is inadequate to fully explain resurrection. Paul, in 1 Corinthians 15:12-20 (cf. 2 Corinthians 4:14-5:10; Philippians 1:21-24; 1 Peter 1:4) sets this earthly life over against the resurrection life in heaven, confirming his teaching of our personal life after bodily death. It also seems impossible to miss that in verses 35 to 55 Paul was describing the nature of *individual bodies* in heaven. And after all, the corporate church body is merely a collection of individual bodies, as Paul himself explains in 1 Corinthians 12:27.

The word "body" (Greek, *soma*) is used some 142 times in the New Testament. Relatively few of these are indisputably only about the collective body (the church). CBV advocates may respond that "the Bible uses physical body language to explain spiritual realities." The reader can decide for himself if this is treating the text fairly.

In sum, it is myopic to assume that biblical resurrection is **either/or** (CBV or IBV). Correctly understood, resurrection is not *either/or*. It is **both/and**. Resurrection is individual *and* corporate, bodily *and* spiritual. In order to reach heaven *bodily* after death, one must first be saved *metaphorically* while alive.

Because of the confusion of other terminology, a better paradigm is proposed: the **Personhood View** of the resurrection ("**PV**"). This view recognizes that we do not know just what our existence in the afterlife is like. But we are confident, based on what information we have been given in the Bible, that we will have *personality* and *identity* in our heavenly existence. <u>We reject both the fleshly-body paradigm of some futurists and the Gnostic-like CBV-only paradigm of some preterists</u>.

The PV paradigm is consistent with our theme of *evangelical preterism*. We will further discuss our glorious resurrection hope of heaven in Chapter 15.

> At the Second Coming to occur during the lifetime of Paul's contemporaries, there would be a culmination of the eschatological hope of the world. God's Suffering Servant would bring salvation to Israel and to the world (Isaiah 49:1-7; 52:13-53:12; 56:1-8; Luke 21:28; Romans 11:25-26; 13:11; Ephesians 1:13-14; Hebrews 1:14; 9:28; 1 Peter 1:3-9). The promised new heavens and earth would include the *gathering of the elect and of all nations* into the covenant as promised in Isaiah 40:5; 49:5-6; 56:8, by Jesus in the Olivet Discourse (Matthew 24:31; 25:32), and reiterated by Paul in 2 Thessalonians 2:1. Israel would be reborn and restored, and this would include immortal-body resurrection of the righteous — and ultimately eternal life *in heaven* as promised to believers in Christ's own resurrection (1 Corinthians 15:1-4, 19).

Let's jump in here and consider the question of when the resurrection was to take place. The book of 1 Corinthians is filled with imminence statements. See 1 Corinthians 1:7-8; 2:6; 3:22; 7:26-31; 10:11, and 16:22. Chapter 15 is consistent with that urgency of the coming last things events. The Bible describes the Parousia, the judgment, and the resurrection as being inseparably connected. We have shown that the Parousia and judgment occurred in AD 70 — so the general resurrection, whatever the nature of it, also occurred at that time.

Disagreement exists between full preterists and partial preterists on details of 1 Corinthians 15. Most partial preterists think it is *all* (or almost all) about events that are future to us living today; full preterists say that this passage is about AD 70. It mentions Jesus' Second Coming (the Parousia, verse 23), and verse 51 implies that some of those to whom Paul spoke would be alive at Christ's coming. In verse 52 we see the trumpet call, reminding us of Matthew 24:31. Unless this is a different trumpet call than the one Jesus referred to in the Olivet Discourse, 1 Corinthians 15 is tied to the same Parousia as in the Olivet Discourse (Matthew 24:3, 27, 37, 39), which was fulfilled in AD 70.

Full preterists argue that the Bible has only one Second Coming (Hebrews 9:28, etc.) And since other passages are tied in time to AD

70, 1 Corinthians 15 must be speaking of the one Second Coming. It is argued by Russell, "Why should Paul think of the distant future when it is certain that he considered the Parousia to be imminent?" [161]

Paul's statement in verse 51, "*we* shall all be changed," requires some additional comment as it appears that Paul changes in mid-sentence from discussing what would happen to dead believers at the Second Coming to the effect on living believers at that same time. There are (at least) two views. The first view is that the "we" of which Paul speaks is referring exclusively to living believers in his day, and was thus completely fulfilled in AD 70. It is clear that Paul expected those of his contemporaries who were alive at the Second Coming to be changed in some way. It was not to be their physical removal, but rather a spiritual change. They would enter the state of eternal life in Christ. The word "changed" (Greek, *allasso*) means "to exchange." At that time their "natural"/"mortal" bodies would be exchanged into bodies with "spiritual"/"incorruptible" properties (cf. Romans 8:11-23). [162]

This theme of change awaiting the first-century believers at the Second Coming is certainly not unique to 1 Corinthians 15. Consider these other passages, which offer further insight into both the nature and timing of the change that was about to come to the saints:

For I reckon that the sufferings of the present time [are] not worthy [to be compared] with the **glory about to be revealed in us**; (*Romans 8:18, Young's Literal Translation*)

and when the Chief Shepherd appears, **you will receive the crown of glory** that does not fade away. (*1 Peter 5:4*)

See also Colossians 3:4 and 1 Peter 5:1 (in Young's Literal Translation). Think about these verses when we consider the "rapture" below. These passages are consistent with the Christian's final salvation/redemption as discussed in the previous chapter. This "change" of which Paul speaks would thus be a spiritual change to the living, effected at the Parousia. Believers *were being transformed into the image of Christ*, such transformation being consummated with the changing of the covenants (2 Corinthians 3:7-18).

So for first-century believers, the transformation was already but not quite yet. Unlike them, we today do not have to wait until a future Second Coming for our transforming redemption to be completed. Our redemption/salvation/renewal occurs at the point of our faith. That is, we receive our new covenant promise (of Christ's life and righteous-ness) at the point of belief.

If you have studied the various references we have given so far about the resurrection, you may have noticed that both Jesus and Paul discussed the resurrection of the physically dead in the same texts as they discussed the spiritual or covenantal renewal of the living. They taught them as being interrelated. The same is certainly true in 1 Corinthians 15 (cf. 2 Corinthians 5 and Philippians 3). While resurrection of the physically dead is part of the text, in our opinion, the reader will see that spiritual transformation of the living is also in this text. Consider verses 22, 51, 52, 56, and 57.

It seems likely that 1 Corinthians 15 is speaking not only of the spiritual transformation of living believers at the AD 70 Parousia, but also of believers who would face future physical death (even those yet unborn believers). In this view, there is a final trumpet call for every be-liever when they die, at which time they will gain their new immortal bodies as they enter heaven. We are inclined to believe that Paul had all these things in mind. Living believers were changed spiritually at the Second Coming redemption; all subsequent believers are changed spiritually on conversion—and will gain their new heavenly bodies when they die.

Since Paul was speaking specifically of heaven, he was looking into the future even beyond the Parousia to each believer's death. Paul was certainly anticipating his own death, and was concerned for other be-lievers beyond his own generation. In his letters, he focused his atten-tion on the imminent Parousia, but had more distant things in view as well as he spoke elsewhere of the coming ages (Ephesians 1:21; 2:7; 3:21; cf. Hebrews 2:5).

We should understand that Paul, while inspired, did not know precisely what was in store. Jesus never divulged all the details. Paul was merely emphasizing that with the coming dramatic events, what-ever they might bring, all believers—past, present, and future—would be taken care of.[163]

Here's still another thing to think about. Christians agree that sin, death, and the law are related. Here are some thoughts of Tina Rae Collins that summarize the thinking of the above authors:

> Some who do not believe all prophecy has been fulfilled, and there-fore that sin and death have been abolished, nevertheless under-stand that we are not under law. I am not sure how they think that

is possible as the end of the law happened at the abolishment of sin and death, 1 Corinthians 15:51-57.[164]

This is pretty deep theology. The reader might want to go back over this section when his head is not spinning as it may be now. And it is admittedly complicated because so many concepts converge in 1 Corinthians 15, but hopefully we have added clarity. We are confident that we will be seeing a lot more written in the future concerning the theology of the resurrection. The topic is re-emerging in theological circles.

In any case, 1 Corinthians 15 is affirmation of the culmination of Christ's first century Parousia work to usher in once-for-all the New Covenant Age in AD 70. Thus, resurrection is entrance into the kingdom for all believers. As put by the writer of Hebrews, the promise of the *eternal inheritance was fulfilled with the New Covenant mediated by Christ* (Hebrews 9:15)—when He would come to *save those who were eagerly waiting for him* (Hebrews 9:26-28).[165] This is confirmation of the promise that Jesus himself made in Luke 21:28—that our redemption would come at the Second Coming, which itself would happen in Jesus' own generation. The promise would be fulfilled in just *a very, very little while* after the writer of Hebrews penned his book (Hebrews 10:37).

Consistent with what we have already considered in previous chapters, the full preterist view is that the general resurrection of the Old Testament saints, as well as deceased Christians, occurred in AD 70. When believers suffer biological death after AD 70, they go directly to heaven.

Most Christians think that the promise of an immortal, resurrected life is only a reality either in a future millennial kingdom or at the end of time. But Paul sees no such protracted delay. This is wonderful news for the believer. This promise is a current reality. As put by Stevens:

> If the general resurrection is past, it would stand to reason that the believer already has immortality available to him in the inner man, and only needs to rise into his immortal body when he sheds his outer shell at physical death. . . . But the transition period saints did have "eternal life" which was a "down-payment, earnest, or pledge" of the "about to come" [AD 70] immortality. . . . We Christians today still have the same hope for an immortal body and a heavenly afterlife that the first-century Christians had. It was the Cross which guaranteed that hope, and the Parousia which fulfilled

that hope and made all the benefits immediately available after our physical death.[166]

> The dead in Christ were raised to heaven in their glorified bodies from hades at the Parousia in AD 70, and the blessed afterlife of all believers was sealed in that day. The living believers were thus guaranteed their own future inheritance in heaven when they pass from this world. The time of the general resurrection, the "gathering," and the "rapture" was when all God's people—living and dead, past and present—were brought together into a single consummate everlasting kingdom at the Parousia.

It seems to us that if 1 Corinthians 15 is internally consistent as well as consistent with the rest of the Bible, the preponderance of the evidence suggests that this passage was at least *essentially fulfilled* in AD 70. Here is a summary of that evidence:

- Christ's Parousia (verse 23) must be the same Parousia as elsewhere in the New Testament, especially the Olivet Discourse (Matthew 24:3, 27, 37, 39), which we have argued was fulfilled in AD 70.

- *The trumpet* call (verse 52) confirms that this Parousia is the same as that of the Olivet Discourse (Matthew 24:31).

- The *end* (verse 24) is consistent with references to the end of the age, which we discussed at length in Chapter 4 as having taken place in the first century (Daniel 12:1-2, 9-13; Matthew 13:39, 49; 24:3, 6, 13, 14; 28:20; 1 Corinthians 10:11; Hebrews 8:13; 9:26; 1 Peter 4:7). Especially note Matthew 13:36-43, where the resurrection and judgment are tied to the same "end of the age."

- There is a thread of passages that run through the Bible which consistently ties the general resurrection and the final judgment to AD 70. These passages include Daniel 12:1-13; Matthew 13:36-43; 24:31-34; 25:31-46; John 5:28-29; John 6:39-40; Acts 24:15; 1 Corinthians 15:23-24; 50-54; 1 Thessalonians 4:13-16; 2 Timothy 4:1; Revelation 10:5-7; 11:15; 20:11-15; 22:12. In these passages the trumpet sounds at Christ's Parousia, the resurrection occurs, and God takes his resurrected people into

Christ's presence where they loudly proclaim the kingdom world of Jesus Christ. We have already discussed most of these at some length. No convincing evidence exists that there is more than one general resurrection, and no convincing evidence exists to conclude that the general resurrection is still in our future. To divide these passages, as some attempt to do—some to AD 70 and some to the distant future—is arbitrary and inconsistent.

- Paul's expectation was that the resurrection would happen while some of his contemporaries were still alive—before they all had "slept" (verse 51), a biblical term for death.

- The reference to the *law* (verse 56) connects the resurrection of the dead to the end of the Old Covenant Age and the coming New Covenant Age (Hebrews 8:13; 9:26-28). Paul is clearly speaking in a covenantal context.[167]

- Paul nowhere in his writings expresses expectations that the major prophesied events would occur far in the future. The prophetic events of 1 Corinthians 15 are tied by the time-texts not only within this section itself but by the many imminency passages elsewhere in the New Testament.

- The notion of two Second Comings, i.e. a double fulfillment (an AD 70 fulfillment being a shadow of a final future fulfillment) cannot be documented in the New Testament other than by unnecessary and unsupported inferences. A similar double fulfillment theory of the general resurrection is likewise problematic. Those who teach this are more about Houdini than biblical exegesis, it seems to us.

Concerning the dead being raised in AD 70, Russell simply questions why any Christian reader would doubt what the text says: "What, then, hinders the conclusion that such events might have taken place without observation, and without record?" Because there is confusion on this point among Christians, we repeat for emphasis. The general resurrection of the Old Testament saints was not a visible event since those in the grave went to heaven, not to earth. They entered heaven in their new resurrection bodies, leaving their old "worn out" bodies behind.

This should be marvelous good news to every Christian. We are surprised, frankly, at the resistance of many Christians to the belief that the general resurrection has already occurred. It is biblically accurate and it makes perfect sense. The Old Testament saints had to wait in hades until Christ finished his work at the Second Coming in his generation. What biblical purpose would it serve to make them wait beyond that appointed time for their promised reward? What reason would God have to make believers today sleep until the end of time to fully enter heaven in our glorified bodies?

Here is how Michael Fenemore powerfully argued:

> Paul wrote, "In Christ all shall be made alive. But each one in his own order: Christ the firstfruits, afterward those who are Christ's at His coming" (1 Corinthians 15:22b-23). So clearly, all the Old Testament saints, including Daniel and David, were to be "made alive" at the second coming. We all agree Christ has been resurrected and is now in heaven. However, there is no allowance for anyone else to be "made alive" before the second coming. So if Jesus has not returned, *none* of God's people could be in heaven with Christ. Only full-preterism offers an [adequate] interpretation allowing for Christians to be "alive" after death!
>
> Christians enduring severe trials would be tremendously encouraged if they could confidently anticipate their eventual *transfer* into the spirit realm at death where their redemption will be *complete* upon receipt of their new incorruptible bodies. Friends and relatives left to grieve might be greatly comforted by such clarity. Instead, some Christians picture themselves and their loved ones lying unconscious in the cold ground—possibly for centuries—waiting for the second coming. Others are confident they will go to heaven when they die, but wonder what it might be like to be there with no body and what difference it will make when they finally get one, which also, might not occur for centuries. Surely, these confusing, contradictory, uninspiring and sometimes bizarre beliefs must weaken the faith of some. . . .[168]

A final issue that is worth considering is the resurrection event that was coincident with the death of Jesus. It is described in Matthew 27:52-53, which says, "And the graves were opened; and many bodies of the saints who had fallen asleep were raised; and coming out of the graves after His resurrection, they went into the holy city and appeared to many." To some, this passage confirms that our resurrection will be a physical one. But this rather strange passage is vague, no matter what eschatological position one holds.

We never hear about these people again. What happened to them? Where did they go? What did they do? Did they die again? Are we all to be resurrected and then die once again? Did Jesus take them to heaven per Revelation 6:9-11? Some preterists see this group as being the ones in the first resurrection, per Revelation 20:4.

No matter where one goes with this passage, it provides little hard support against the full preterist view. It seems more consistent with a past resurrection than a futurist view. This event should be taken as a sign of the imminent resurrection, rather than the substance or beginning of the resurrection itself.[169]

In summary, we think it is clear that the general resurrection of the dead, the ushering out of the Old Covenant order, and Christ's Second Coming in judgment, were all fulfilled in AD 70. Hades, the temporary abode of the dead, was abolished (Revelation 20). The Old Testament saints were in heaven as of that time. Believers who die now do not wait until the end of time to go to heaven, but instead go to heaven immediately upon their death in their incorruptible, immortal, glorified, supernatural bodies to join the saints of all time in heaven (2 Corinthians 5:1-10). As for the damned, they too go immediately at their death to their eternal destiny—hell/destruction, fulfilling God's perfect will.[170]

Question for your pastor, church leaders, and friends:
1 Corinthians 15 says four times that in the resurrection we have a spiritual body. Do you believe that?

THE RAPTURE

The idea of the "Rapture" is taken primarily from 1 Thessalonians chapter 4:

> 13 But I do not want you to be ignorant, brethren, concerning those who have fallen asleep, lest you sorrow as others who have no hope. 14 For if we believe that Jesus died and rose again, even so God will bring with Him those who sleep in Jesus. 15 For this we say to you by the word of the Lord, that **we who are alive and remain until the coming of the Lord** will by no means precede those who are asleep. 16 For the Lord Himself will descend from heaven with a shout, with the voice of an archangel, and with the trumpet of God. And the dead in Christ will rise first. 17 Then **we who are alive and remain** shall be **caught up together** [*harpazo*] with them in the clouds to meet [*apentesis*] the Lord in the **air** [*aer*]. And thus we shall always be with the Lord. 18 Therefore comfort one another with these words. (*1 Thessalonians 4:13-18*)

We will consider this passage in light of both of Paul's letters to the Thessalonians, and in light of other related passages of Scripture. For example, the reader will inevitably note some themes in this passage common to 1 Corinthians 15. In this study we will draw from contemporary scholarship in an effort to understand what the Greek text means, and above all else, to reconcile these passages with other passages in the Bible. Remember that Scripture, properly understood as God's Word, must be thoroughly consistent.

Rapture is a word not found in the Bible. The term is derived from the Latin translation of the Greek word *harpazo* ("caught up," verse 17), the Latin word being *rapiere*. The understanding of "rapture" by many evangelicals is the idea of a secret snatching of the church out of this world before a future tribulation. Interestingly, this is a relatively new idea. John Nelson Darby is often credited with originating, or at least popularizing, the idea in the 1830s. Darby reportedly got the idea from a charismatic utterance from a fifteen-year old girl named Margaret McDonald. While in a trance, the girl received a vision that only a select group of believers would be removed from the earth before the days of the antichrist. Whether that story is true or not, prior to the invention of the modern rapture doctrine, many published commentators understood this passage to be referring to the resurrection! [171]

There are legitimate debates about exactly *what* St. Paul is communicating in 1 Thessalonians 4. Amillennialists, postmillennialists, premillennialists, and preterists all have different views. But there should be less doubt, we think, about *when* the events described would happen. We have strong exegetical reasons to conclude that the idea of a still future physical rapture of the church—as especially premillennialists understand it—is a concept that is not found in this text.

This may send shock waves among many American evangelicals who have become entrenched in their thinking about this, in part because of the popular *Left Behind* novels. As we have complained, the biggest problem we face in discussing these things with Christians is that many simply do not *want* to know the truth if it challenges their assumptions. (Don't confuse me with the facts.) But please stay with us here. Let's dig for the truth.

It is clear enough from 1 Thessalonians 4 (as well as other statements in both 1 and 2 Thessalonians which we will consider) that Paul expected the Second Coming and the meeting with Jesus (the "rapture") to occur while some of his friends were still alive. One cannot read this text with an open mind and miss this. Paul did *not* say: "Those who are alive centuries from now and remain until the Lord's coming. . . ." Paul's expectation here parallels his expectation in 1 Corinthians 15:51 when he said that *"we* shall not all sleep" until the resurrection and change would take place.

That Paul's first-century audience is who is in view here is further clarified by verses 9 to 12 leading up to 13 to 18 shown above. The "you" and "we" were the brothers in Christ at the time of Paul's writing. Paul was so certain of what he was telling the Thessalonians that he repeated his words. He had said once in verse 15, *"we* who are alive and remain until the coming of the Lord. . . ." Then in verse 17 he repeats: "*We* who are alive and remain shall be caught up together with them in the clouds. . . ."

Paul also expected that the "dead in Christ" would be raised just prior to the meeting with Jesus—the *gathering* spoken of elsewhere in the Bible (Matthew 13:40-43; 24:31; 25:32; Mark 13:27; 2 Thessalonians 2:1; etc.). The gathering, final redemption, resurrection, and judgment were contemporaneous events (or parts of the same event), as we pointed out in our discussions of Revelation, 1 Corinthians 15, and other passages. This time frame is perfectly consistent with everything else we have considered. These things would happen while many first-century Christians of Paul's day were still alive.

But the other details in 1 Thessalonians 4 are puzzling at first glance. How can the rapture have already occurred? There are two key words in 1 Thessalonians 4:17— (1) caught up, i.e. *"raptured"* (Greek *harpazo*), and (2) air (Greek *aer*). Dr. Kelly Birks argues that these two words have taken on meanings in translation that are not accurate from the Greek.[172] He points out that *harpazo*, which is used fifteen times in the New Testament, does not necessarily indicate a physical removal. In his view, the translators have added a directional sense (up and away) incorrectly. So the sense of this word is better understood somewhat like we would say in English, "I was so caught up in the novel that I saw myself in the story."

The online *Blue Letter Bible* lexicon offers varying definitions of *harpazo*. One such definition would be consistent with the common understanding of the rapture: "to seize, carry off by force." But another definition given is "to seize on, to claim for oneself eagerly." This second definition would be consistent with numerous other passages in the Bible in which God pursues or chooses or protects his elect. While the first definition has the sense of being snatched out or away, the second one does not. It is this second one that seems to best fit the context given other considerations. It is consistent with the usage of the word elsewhere in the Bible.

An interesting example of another use of *harpazo* in the Bible is 2 Corinthians 12:2-6. In this passage Paul speaks in the third person but clearly is speaking of a personal experience. Paul tells how he was "caught up [*harpazo*] to the third heaven." It was such a traumatic event for Paul that he said that he did not even know whether it was an in-body or out-of-body experience. While we do not know exactly what happened in this experience, perhaps he was in a trance (Acts 10:9; 22:17). But we do know that Paul remained on earth to tell the story.

Birks' further opinion is that in order for *harpazo* to unambiguously mean "up and away" in Greek, it would necessarily have been a compound word from the base word *harpazo*. So, for example, the word *anoharpazo* would have given the "up and away" sense.

Nor does **aer** (which is used seven times in the New Testament) really mean "way up in the sky," which is what most people think. If this were the meaning, Birks argues that Paul would have used the Greek word *ouranos* instead of *aer*. *Aer* is a close-to-earth thing, not the upper atmosphere. The online *Blue Letter Bible* lexicon defines *aer* as "the air, particularly the lower and denser air as distinguished from the higher and rarer air." While *aer* does have the meaning of literal "air," Birks argues that the usage elsewhere in the Bible suggests that it can also be used in a spiritual context rather than a physical context. This is especially evident in Ephesians 2:2 when Paul used the phrase "the prince of the power of the air [*aer*], the spirit that is now at work."

In a related sense, the *aer* is the air we breathe. So, as Birks postulates, Paul "is speaking of a spiritual meeting with the Lord, 'within' ourselves, within our spirits." Thus Paul was speaking in 1 Thessalonians 4:17 of a *spiritual* meeting with the Lord—a poignant moment at Christ's Parousia when the expected events (tribulation, judgment, gathering, resurrection) take place. This passage is not saying that we will (or that the first-century believers would) disappear from the earth! One's feet do not need to leave the earth to get "caught up" with the Lord in this air (*aer*).

Premillennialists think that the purpose of the rapture was to escape a future tribulation. But this does not fit. We showed that the tribulation happened in the first century. We recall that Jesus told his followers in the Olivet Discourse that in order to escape the tribulation, they could retreat to the mountains. (There is no record, by the way, of any Christians being killed in the war, as they apparently took Jesus' advice and fled to the mountains.)

Also notice the statement that Paul makes in verse 17: "And thus we shall always be with the Lord." This statement seems to wrap up what Paul means. The first-century believers bore the weight of the fact that Christ had left them. Just a few years earlier Christ was literally with them in the flesh on the earth, but now He was in heaven. They sensed the loss, and were fearful of the promised coming tribulation and judgment that would soon engulf them. Paul comforted his friends that Jesus was soon to return, never to leave again!

Rapturist eschatology would have us believe that we are now somehow separated from the Lord, and only after our removal from the planet will we be with Him forever (1 Thessalonians 4:17b). This must mean we are now serving an absentee Lord. Contrary to what the rapturists are forced to conclude, Christians are now indeed with Christ in a very real sense here on earth! This is great news for both Christians who lived through AD 70 and for us today! Michael Sullivan summarizes the rapture by showing parallels with other passages, which the reader may want to cross check:

> Since our Lord came *"with His saints"* and destroyed the earthly temple in AD 70 (Hebrews 9:8), the church of all ages lives and

reigns in glory with Him forever (Romans 6:8; 2 Corinthians 13:4; 2 Timothy 2:11-12). Now whether we are alive or asleep, we *"live together with Him"* (1 Thessalonians 5:10).[173]

The Thessalonians had been concerned that the saints who had died might miss their place in the kingdom when the Lord came, and they were worried about themselves in the coming wrath to be poured out upon the Jews and the nation of Israel. Paul was merely reassuring the Thessalonians that the Lord would take care of both the living and the dead. So, the force of the passage is pastoral, and intended to offer assurance and comfort to the grieved Thessalonians. Interestingly, in some Bibles, the title given to this section is "The Comfort of Christ's Coming" rather than something about the rapture.

N. T. Wright, while he is not a consistent preterist, in his book titled *Paul: In Fresh Perspective* added some helpful color to the interpretation of this passage. He stated, concerning the "meeting" (Greek *apantesis*) to which Paul refers in 1 Thessalonians 4:17:

> [It] evokes the scene, familiar from much Hellenistic and Roman writing, of a king or emperor paying a state visit to a city or province. As he approaches, the citizens come out to meet him at some distance from the city, not in order to hold a meeting out in the countryside, but to escort him into the city. "Meeting the Lord in the air" is not a way of saying, "in order then to stay safely away from the wicked world." It is the prelude to the implied triumphant return to earth where the Messiah will reign, and his people with him, as Lord, savior and judge. And in that context *Parousia [1 Thessalonians 4:17]* means what it means in imperial rhetoric: the royal presence of the true Lord or emperor. . . . Paul was saying that Jesus was Lord, and that Caesar was not.[174]

Don K. Preston reinforces that *apantesis* ("meet," verse 17) means the exact opposite of what modern rapturists think. The destination is earth![175] The Greek word *apantesis* is found in only two other places in the New Testament, and in both places it has this same usage. In Acts 28:15, believers from Rome went out to "meet" Paul and escort him back to their city. Similarly in Matthew 25:1-10, the virgins went out to "meet" the bridegroom and escort him back to the wedding hall. Thus, the image evoked in 1 Thessalonians 4:15-17 is that of believers being spiritually caught up to go out to meet and escort Jesus back to earth to begin his rule on earth. The idea of believers being physically transported to heaven in a literal rapture is exegetically foreign to the New Testament.

Okay, so you have some lingering doubts about what we have presented so far. The proof comes in the further context. Just when were these events in Thessalonians to take place? *This question determines whether or not the passage speaks of a literal removal of the church from the earth.* We shall now look at more evidence that the timing of these events is bound by certain constraints of Scripture.

Some people think that these events will occur before a literal future millennium. Others think that they will come at the end of the physical universe. But we think both of these views are mistaken. We think the context proves that these events have already taken place. We find no clear or compelling evidence in the Bible for either a literal millennium or a literal end of the universe.

We must understand 1 Thessalonians 4 in the context of both of Paul's letters to the Thessalonians. In 1 Thessalonians 1:9-10; 2:14-19; 3:3-4; 5:9, and in 2 Thessalonians 1:3-12, we see that **Paul's first-century readers** were to *wait for God's Son from heaven* who would deliver them from the persecution they had been experiencing as well as from the coming wrath which would befall their countrymen. Such persecution had been predicted by Jesus to occur before the end of the age (Matthew 24:9).

The wrath here is certainly the same wrath as in Luke 21:20-28 which Jesus said would befall "his people" and would be identifiable by his statement that "when you see Jerusalem surrounded by armies, then know that its desolation is near." Note especially in 2 Thessalonians 1:3-12 we see that Jesus would come to give *relief* to **Paul's first-century readers** even as He would inflict vengeance on those who were persecuting the Christians in the early 50s (when Paul was writing this letter) and who did not heed the gospel—obviously the Jews. Unless Paul was misleading his readers, they were going to witness the eschatological events in the near future. It might be helpful for the reader to go to his Bible and underline each of the aforementioned passages to see how they connect.

It is quite clear that whatever events Paul was referring to in these passages, they were to happen during the lifetimes of some of those to whom he was speaking. **It would make no sense for Paul to reassure those to whom he was speaking that relief would arrive in**

thousands of years. We remind the reader once again that the Bible was written *for* us but not *to* us. We must interpret the Bible in strong measure from the perspective of the original audience. If the relief promised by St. Paul to the Thessalonians never came to them, he was a false prophet.

In 1 Thessalonians 5:1-11 we see that the *brothers should be watchful for the Day of the Lord coming like a thief in the night.* Russell challenges us: "Why urge men in A.D. 52 to watch, and be on the alert, for a catastrophe which was not to take place for hundreds and thousands of years?" [176] As we have learned, the Day of the Lord is a phrase used in the Old Testament in reference to any day in which God came in judgment. There was not just one Day of the Lord, but multiple occurrences in the Bible. It does not refer to the end of the world. In this case, it refers to the *culminating* Day of the Lord that was rapidly approaching the first-century believers.

In 2 Thessalonians 2:1-8 we note that Paul was refuting those who were saying that the Day of the Lord (in conjunction with Christ's Second Coming) had already come. If the first-century Christians thought that the Day of the Lord would be a literal burning of the planet like many Christians today think, their concern would make no sense whatsoever. As put by Glenn Hill, "If Paul taught his followers that the coming of Jesus was going to be like this, then how could any one of the Thessalonians ever have been deceived into thinking Jesus had already come?" [177]

In these passages we also note certain language found elsewhere in the Bible which we can tie to a clear time frame. Certainly Paul got his ideas, as did the other writers of the New Testament, from the prophetic words of our Lord, found principally in the Olivet Discourse (Matthew 24-25, Mark 13, and Luke 21). Note the following ties in 1 and 2 Thessalonians with Matthew 24-25 (and other scriptures):

- Christ's **Parousia** (1 Thessalonians 2:19; 3:13; 4:15; 5:23; 2 Thessalonians 2:1, 8; Matthew 24:3, 27, 37, 39).

- Christ returning *from heaven* (1 Thessalonians 4:16; Matthew 24:30).

- Christ coming with a **shout** (1 Thessalonians 4:16; Matthew 25:6).

- Christ descending with a **trumpet** (1 Thessalonians 4:16; Matthew 24:31).

- Believers will *meet* the Lord (1 Thessalonians 4:17; Matthew 25:6).

- A *gathering* of the saints (1 Thessalonians 4:17; 2 Thessalonians 2:1; Matthew 24:31; 25:32. Compare to Matthew 13:39-43 where the gathering is placed at the end of the age and the final judgment).

- The *cloud* language (1 Thessalonians 4:17; Matthew 24:30).

- Christ being revealed with *angels* (1 Thessalonians 4:16; 2 Thessalonians 1:7; Matthew 24:31; Matthew 25:31).

- Christ coming like a *thief* (1 Thessalonians 5:2; Matthew 24:43. Compare to Revelation 3:3 and 16:15).

- Labor pains imagery and unexpected sudden *destruction* (1 Thessalonians 5:3; Matthew 24:8, 39, 44).

- Instruction for believers to be *watchful/awake* (1 Thessalonians 5:6; Matthew 24:42).

- Exhortation against *drunkenness* (1 Thessalonians 5:7; Matthew 24:49).

- Promise of *salvation* for some (1 Thessalonians 5:8; Matthew 24:13).

- *Judgment/vengeance* by Jesus (2 Thessalonians 1:5-9; Matthew 13:39-43; 23:29-39; 24:30, 37; 25:32, 41, 46.

- *Apostasy* (2 Thessalonians 2:3; Matthew 24:10-11).

- *Man of lawlessness/false Christs* (2 Thessalonians 2:3; Matthew 24:4).

- Mystery of *lawlessness* (2 Thessalonians 2:7; Matthew 24:12).

- *Deception* (2 Thessalonians 2:9-11; Matthew 24:24).[178]

Paul was clearly speaking point-by-point about the same events that Jesus foretold in the Olivet Discourse, which were limited in time to Paul's generation! Indeed, Paul indicates in 1 Thessalonians 4:15 that what he was saying was from Jesus himself. To repeat for emphasis, the term "this generation" is used numerous times outside of the Olivet Discourse, and consistently *without serious debate* means "the generation of those living at the time of Jesus." There is no rationale for giving it a different meaning in the Olivet Discourse without seriously twisting Scripture—and thus no valid reason for placing the "rapture" in a different time frame. Paul does not use the term "this generation" in these letters, but clearly communicates the same.

So, the events of 1 and 2 Thessalonians were in anticipation of the events surrounding the coming destruction of Jerusalem in AD 70 when Jesus came—not physically, but *in judgment against the apostate Jews and to rescue the saints,* just as He had promised! The language Paul used in these letters is so close to that of Matthew's version of the Olivet Discourse that it seems probable that the source for Paul was Matthew's material, either in oral or written form.

Some partial preterists think that the Olivet Discourse was fulfilled in AD 70 but that the "rapture" and the rest of 1 and 2 Thessalonians are still future. This seems to us to be an impossible conclusion. Paul and Jesus were speaking of the exact same event, which was to occur while many of those living in the first century were still alive.

Other partial preterists attempt to divide Thessalonians into different periods of fulfillment—some in AD 70, some at the end of time. For example, Samuel M. Frost has suggested that Paul is bouncing back and forth between an AD 70 coming in 1 Thessalonians 2:19 and 3:13, to a yet-unfulfilled "final coming" a few verses later in 4:15—and then back again to AD 70 in 1 Thessalonians 5:2 and 5:23.[179] This stretches credulity. We have conclusively demonstrated how picking and choosing sections of Matthew 24—some past, some future—collapses on close inspection. The same is true for Thessalonians.

We call out the partial preterists on their inconsistencies. The partial preterist method of interpretation is erratic. While the same word *can* refer to two different things, Paul offers no hint of such bifurcation. Frost's "exegesis" is desperate. We think he is reaching for something that is simply not there.

Other partial preterists' attempts are no less curious. Kenneth L. Gentry has stated that the coming of Jesus mentioned in 2 Thessalonians 1:10 is talking about a bodily final coming at the end of time. But he said that the coming of Jesus mentioned just three verses later in 2 Thessalonians 2:1 refers to the metaphoric past coming in AD 70.[180] Here is the section in question:

> [7] and to give **you** who are troubled **rest** with **us** when the Lord Jesus is revealed [*apokalypsis*] from heaven with his mighty angels, [8] in flaming fire taking vengeance on those who do not know God, and on those who do not obey the gospel of our Lord Jesus Christ. [9] These shall be punished with everlasting destruction from the presence of the Lord and from the glory

of His power, [10] when He **comes** [*erchomai*], in that Day, to be glorified in His saints and to be admired among all those who believe, because our testimony among you was believed. . . . [1] Now, brethren, concerning the **coming** [*parousia*] of our Lord Jesus Christ and our gathering together to Him, we ask **you**, [2] not to be soon shaken in mind or troubled, either by spirit or by word or by letter, as if from us, as though the day of Christ had come. [3] Let no one deceive **you** by any means; for that Day will not come unless the falling away comes first, and the man of sin is revealed, the son of perdition, [4] who opposes and exalts himself above all that is called God or that is worshiped, so that he sits as God in the temple of God, showing himself that he is God. (*2 Thessalonians 1:7-10; 2:1-4*)

Dr. Gentry attempts to convince us of his view by pointing out, in part, that in the first case (chapter 1) the word for Jesus' coming is *erchomai*. In the second case (chapter 2) the word for Jesus' coming is *parousia*. He also argues that there are elements mentioned in chapter 1 that are not mentioned in chapter 2. But such reasoning is seriously flawed, which the reader by now may notice. Here are some obvious issues:

- In the original manuscripts, there were no chapter and verse separations, so the chapter separations are not inspired elements of the text. Chapters one and two are not to be understood as separate sections. They are one continuous thought.

- Paul is writing to the Thessalonians to *clear up their confusion*, not to make things more confusing.

- That Paul would describe different elements surrounding the same event in the two adjacent passages should not be surprising.

- The different words used in 2 Thessalonians 1:10 and 2:1 can be simply explained by Paul's selection of a verb in 1:10 (*erchomai*) and a noun in 2:1 (*parousia*) to describe the same event.[181]

- Dr. Gentry apparently has no problem with both *erchomai* and *parousia* being used in Matthew 24 to refer to the same time— AD 70! As charged by Don Preston, "Every constituent element that Gentry links to the AD [70] *parousia* in Matthew is present in Thessalonians. Yet in Thessalonians he sees two comings separated by millennia." [182]

- In 2 Thessalonians 1:7, immediately *prior* to the verses in question (1:10 and 2:1), Paul promises relief (in some versions, "rest") to the first-century Christians. It is conclusive that this is a reference to the relief that would come to *them* in their own generation at Christ's Parousia, as Paul said that "you" and "us" were the ones who would receive the relief. Then immediately *after* the verses in question we see that Paul again confirmed that his message was directed exclusively to his first-century audience, as he said "you" twice (2:13-14) and "us" once (2:16). He never said anything that had so much as an implied reference to some far distant generation. Thus, these two verses (2 Thessalonians 1:10 and 2:1) are sandwiched between statements that have a clear first-century context.

- If we are to believe Dr. Gentry, Paul jumps out of a first-century context to a future end of history fulfillment in 2 Thessalonians 1:10. Then just three verses later in 2 Thessalonians 2:1 he switches back to the first century. This is arbitrary, inconsistent, and erratic.

- While Dr. Gentry has placed Christ's Parousia in 2 Thessalonians 2:1 in AD 70, elsewhere he places the Parousia at the end of history. For example, back in Paul's first letter to the Thessalonians (1 Thessalonians 4:15, the rapture section) Gentry has stated that the Parousia there is at the end of history. So, like Frost, he uses the identical word (*parousia*) as evidence that two *different* events are under discussion—and elsewhere uses two different words (*parousia* and *erchomai*) as evidence that two different events are under discussion. [183]

Did Jesus, the writers of the New Testament, or the first-century audience have any concept of two Second Comings—two *Parousias*? No.

> The Parousia of Christ is consistently used in the New Testament with a definite article—*the, his,* or *your*. This is true in Paul's letters to the Thessalonians, where Christ's Parousia is mentioned seven times. This leads to the incontrovertible conclusion that the writers of the New Testament saw but a single Parousia ahead of them. There is no hint of multiple Parousias or any hint that Paul was communicating an elastic dual fulfillment that would stretch from the first century to thousands of years later.[184]

We hope that the reader followed this. If you feel energetic, you could go into your Bible and make little marks at the identified passages to show which ones are, by these men's reckonings, future and which are past. All partial preterists, by the way, do not divide 1 and 2 Thessalonians in the same way. There is no shortage of confusion and inconsistency among partial preterists as to which verses in the Bible remain unfulfilled.

There is also inconsistency by partial preterist writers *depending on whom they are addressing.* They argue for preterist interpretations when debating premillennialists, battling off charges of heresy against their own views. But then they turn around and argue for futurist interpretations (even at times of the same passages!) when debating and condemning full preterists as heretics.[185]

Dr. Gentry is an admired scholar within the Reformed community. He has a well-deserved following. We are challenged by his thinking and agree with most of his conclusions. He has helped lay the groundwork that has brought many of us to consistent preterism. But let's lay it on the table. One has to wonder just how much even brilliant scholars bend to peer pressure and to their allegiance to certain extra-biblical traditions.

It is reasonable to ask if any given scholar has reached labored conclusions resulting from *a priori* commitments or from peer pressure. Dr. Gentry has openly stated that his views are influenced by an overarching commitment to the creeds, for example. (We will examine whether such a commitment is warranted in Chapter 13.) We cannot judge whether positions he might take are influenced by peer pressure too, but you can bet that such pressure is significant.

It is hard for us to find in Paul's letters to the Thessalonians anything that demands a far-distant fulfillment—unless one is influenced by pre-commitment. Partial preterists seem committed to finding a future Second Coming somewhere; so they will find it—even if it needs to be forced onto the text. The analyses of 1 and 2 Thessalonians by Dr. Gentry and Mr. Frost are so labored that we predict this type of argumentation will be abandoned or altered in the future. It can no longer escape the attention of other scholars. Indeed, we have noticed a recent trend that when asked to tell us which Second Coming passages are future and which ones are past, partial preterists dodge or ignore the question.

We note that the field of eschatology is undergoing a dynamic process of re-examination, change, and correction. By the time you read this book, these men may have changed their opinions. We reserve the right to change our minds, and give others the same courtesy. While we have presented the arguments of particular men, we do so to cite representatives of the partial preterist camp in general, rather than to single out anyone.

But we see the partial preterist camp as confused and unsure of itself. Frost, in particular, is already famous in preterist circles for his fluctuant and self-contradictory views. He has written in *favor* of consistent preterism, then *against* it. Even when writing against the consistent preterist view, he made this rather amazing admission: "Classic orthodox preterism [i.e., partial preterism] has **not done the work** that needs to be done in order to rescue [partial preterism] from full preterist attacks. . . . **I do not at all deny that many presentations of [partial] preterism are indeed 'inconsistent.'** They are not perfect. Not all the I's are dotted, or the T's crossed." (Emphasis added.) [186]

Such transparent inconsistency seems particularly strange coming from a scholar like Dr. Gentry. You will recall that in Chapter 9 we presented his detailed arguments that Revelation was written before AD 70 and that the beast of Revelation was the first-century figure Nero. Dr. Gentry understands the critical preterist context of the New Testament, and has argued forcefully for other preterist interpretations. He has also been a brave critic of dispensationalism, and we are with him in this effort.[187]

We see many wise men teaching vastly different things with the greatest of passion. But irrespective of any particular situation, it is a fact that denominational scholars do not always have complete freedom of expression. The wagons are circled. If they walk over the line set by their denomination, they risk not only losing their job, but also being literally *put on trial*, just as in a court of law. We have personally witnessed such a trial in the local congregation of a conservative Reformed denomination. While the offense was unrelated to eschatology, the process was ugly. These risks must be terrifying to a pastor or theologian.

Even those persons not in a denomination risk losing their constituency and all of the associated consequences (influence and financial support) by bucking the establishment—even if on strong biblical grounds. Indeed, the consequences in money and esteem for public Christian teachers are significant. The pressures to conform are quite real. The Protestant Reformation theoretically opened theology to "the priesthood of all believers," but *ecclesiastical tyranny* re-emerged in different forms. Some of this pressure may be healthy, but it also is a hindrance to good scholarship. The good news is that the days are over for even brilliant scholars to easily escape legitimate challenges; the pace of modern communications is turning the tide toward truly open debate. The result is the *surging preterist challenge to eschatology.*

This, *of course*, does not mean that a particular person's views are incorrect or dishonest just because he might be subject to these pressures. Partial preterists presumably believe firmly in what they are teaching. But here is what *appears* to be happening in partial preterist circles: Outstanding scholars have done their homework and have concluded that preterism has merit. But peer pressure has stopped them in their tracks. They have taken the preterist view as far as they can within their circles.

There is often a lingering question about potential biases that may be wrapped up in any particular view. Even great scholars invest their egos in doctrinal positions. No one is without biases. Looking at church history, opposing forces sometimes have expressed their views viciously. But the established views within the church have been wrong before. The church could be wrong again. The student should at least be aware of this consideration.

But let's get back to the rapture. Here is another passage we ought to consider. Futurists, especially dispensationalists, often tie 1 Thessalonians 4 with this passage in Matthew 24:

> For as in the days before the flood, they were eating and drinking, marrying and giving in marriage, until the day that Noah entered the ark, and did not know until the flood came and took them all away, so also will the coming of the Son of Man be. Then two men will be in the field: one will be taken and the other left. Two women will be grinding at the mill: one will be taken and the other left. (*Matthew 24:38-41*)

This is the only other passage outside of 1 Thessalonians 4 (or 1 Corinthians 15) that futurists hold out as talking about the rapture. But it does not fit. Those *taken away* would be the *unrighteous*, not the believers as rapturists suppose. Jesus is emphasizing how many deaths would occur during the tribulation (a high percentage of the population). Matthew 24:38-41 is about the tribulation that would occur in the first century, not a rapture thousands of years later. Those "left" in Matthew 24:40-41 are those who would be spared from God's wrath. 1 Thessalonians 4, on the other hand, is a reassurance that ultimately Christ is in control and that whatever happens, believers will enjoy a positive outcome—either in heaven, or on earth in the New Covenant Age for those who would survive.

Did Jesus ever say anything about a rapture? Actually Jesus prayed *against* any rapture in the sense of physical removal. In John 17:15 we see his prayer to the Father: "I do not pray that You should take them out of the world, but that You should keep them from the evil one." If Jesus asked for such, would the Father deny his request?

This discussion does not resolve all of the issues with 1 Thessalonians 4. Even full preterists have various views. For example, a few full preterists think that the saints living in or shortly before AD 70 were indeed *literally* raptured to heaven at that time. They have arguments to support their view.[188] But the preponderance of the evidence is against such a view. Daniel E. Harden, in his book *Gathered Into the Kingdom*, very effectively eliminated the literal rapture view as a serious possibility.[189]

There is complete consistency with 1 Thessalonians 4 and 1 Corinthians 15. In them Paul discusses the same impending events. They were both fulfilled by AD 70.

The Bible teaches that Jesus would return to **claim victory** (Romans 16:20; Revelation 12:7-12; 20:10), to **redeem his people** (Luke 21:28; Romans 8:18-23; 13:11-12; Ephesians 1:13-14; 4:30; Hebrews 1:14; 9:26-28; 1 Peter 1:3-21; Revelation 12:10), and to **be with us** forever (Revelation 21:3). And it would happen while some of the first-century disciples **were still alive** (Matthew 10:23; 16:27-28; 26:64; Luke 21:22, 27, 28, 32, 36; etc.). The rapture is describing these same events.

The reader is referred to Appendix B to the charts entitled, "The Same Events: Matthew 24, 1 Thessalonians 4 & 1 Corinthians 15" and "Resurrection."

Questions for further discussion with your pastor, church leaders, and friends:

- *How can the so-called rapture still be in our future when Paul clearly thought it would be in his generation?*

- *Did Jesus come to give relief to the Thessalonians as promised by Paul in 2 Thessalonians 1:7?*

- *Are you familiar with the circumstances surrounding John Nelson Darby's invention of the rapture doctrine in the 1830's?*

12 Challenges for Preterism: Ascension, Last Day

THE ASCENSION: WAS JESUS TO RETURN VISIBLY?

Now when He had spoken these things, while they watched, He was **taken up [*epairo*]**, and a **cloud received Him out of their sight**. And while they looked steadfastly toward heaven as He went up, behold, two men stood by them in white apparel, who also said, "Men of Galilee, why do you stand gazing up into heaven? This same Jesus, who was taken up from you into heaven, will so come **in like manner as [*hos tropos*]** you saw Him go into heaven." (*Acts 1:9-11*)

The single biggest objection to preterism is this: "Give me a break. If Jesus had really returned in the first century, somebody would have seen Him." This passage in Acts is the most important rallying point for anti-preterists. In Appendix A we list 101 imminency passages confirming a first-century fulfillment of the Second Coming and surrounding events. It does not matter to futurists if 100 passages point to a past fulfillment; if only one passage could support a future fulfillment, they are going with the one.

Partial preterists put a great deal of weight on relatively few passages, as discussed in this chapter and the previous one, to say that there are two *parousias* of Christ in the New Testament—a metaphorical one in

233

AD 70 and a literal one which is still future. We grant that this could be a possibility, at least apart from any serious exegetical considerations of the New Testament. Since God came in judgment in the Old Testament multiple times, it is *possible* that the New Testament could speak of two future comings of Jesus. But "could" is a weak reed on which to hang a doctrine, and an exceedingly poor interpretive tool.

The problem with the "two future comings" idea is that the Bible gives no hint of it. The Bible speaks only of one Second Coming. And Jesus told us when it would be—before some of those who were living in his generation had died. His *coming* (or "coming again") consistently refers to one particular event and one particular period. Any separation of a future coming that was near in time to the New Testament writers, and another in their far distant future, is arbitrary and based on presuppositions superimposed onto the text. So, we argue that as straightforwardly as Acts 1:9-11 seems to be teaching a physical, literal Second Coming, maybe there is something in this passage that many Christians, including your pastor, have been missing.

Another passage may shed some light on what our expectations of Jesus' return should be. This passage is a statement by Jesus found in the book of John:

> A little while longer and **the world will see me no more**, but you will see me. Because I live, you will live also. (*John 14:19*)

Most Christians interpret Acts 1:9-11 to mean that Jesus would return visibly so that everyone would literally see Him in the flesh. But since Jesus himself plainly stated per John 14:19 that the world would see Him no more, the standard interpretation of a world-wide visible return is suspect.

Let's take a closer look at the passage in Acts. Notice that it says that a *cloud received him out of their sight*. **The disciples did not really see Jesus go to heaven. He entered the heavenly realm hidden from their eyesight in the cloud of God's glory. His ascension was veiled by the cloud!** Christian artwork has added to the confusion of this passage. Many paintings incorrectly show Jesus visibly standing *on top* of a cloud as He ascends into the sky.[190]

Secondly, consider the Greek word that is translated as "taken up" (sometimes translated as "lifted up") in verse 9—*epairo*. The online *Blue Letter Bible* lexicon gives two definitions of this word:

1.   to lift up, raise up, raise on high

2.   metaphorically to be lifted up with pride, to exalt one's self

The sense in which *epairo* is used in this passage really may tell us more about Jesus' glorification or exaltation, and less about a visible physical ascent. Christians use similar phraseology, but in a more modest sense, all the time. When we "lift up" a brother, we encourage him, we ask for his special attention from God, etc. Or we "lift up" a person in the sense of elevation in honor and dignity. While *epairo* can mean the physical action of lifting an object, such as one's hands in prayer (1 Timothy 2:8), the word has a broader and more important connotation in this passage.

Note that the two men (presumably angels) challenged the disciples about looking toward heaven. This statement by the angels always puzzled the author until he considered the deeper meaning of this passage. Sometimes what *appears* to be obvious is not correct. The angels were apparently correcting the understanding of the disciples, a correction that is valid to us today. Where is heaven, anyway? Is it merely far away into space? Consider how other passages describe the same event:

So then, after the Lord had spoken to them, He **was received up** into heaven, and sat down at the right hand of God. (*Mark 16:19*)

And He led them out as far as Bethany, and He lifted up his hands and blessed them. Now it came to pass, while He blessed them, that He **was parted** from them and **carried up** into heaven. (*Luke 24:50-51*)

And without controversy great is the mystery of godliness: God was manifested in the flesh, justified in the Spirit, seen by angels, preached among the Gentiles, believed on in the world, **received up in glory**. (*1 Timothy 3:16*)

Therefore He says: "When He ascended on high, He led captivity captive, and gave gifts to men." (Now this, "He ascended"—what does it mean but that He also **first descended** into the lower parts of the earth? He who descended is also the One who **ascended** far above all the heavens, that He might fill all things.) (*Ephesians 4:8-10*)

We naturally think of heaven as "up." But is heaven a faraway place in space and time? Is hell *literally* "down" in the directional sense? Is heaven really *literally* "up"? While we commonly speak of these things in this way, aren't these really spiritual realities rather than spatial? Doesn't God live in heaven outside of time and space? Isn't He in reality just as present here on earth as in heaven, even though we cannot see Him? We think of God, or Jesus, as sitting on a literal throne in the clouds, but that vision is an attempt to apply our finite human understanding of an infinite God.

The point is that most Christians have a mental image of Jesus' ascension and his return that is, at least in part, extra-biblical. As we think about the above passages, we can understand that they emphasize Jesus' exaltation or glorification more than directional movement. They are not about the disciples watching him fly up and away, getting smaller and smaller in their view until He disappears from site — the view that many people have. The sense is more that Jesus *disappeared from their view*, and then went to heaven. He was **glorified** — <u>*received* into heaven</u>. We also note that there is nothing in these other passages suggesting the manner of Jesus' future Parousia.

We believe that the Bible is absolutely true and without error (at least in the original manuscripts). But we have already proven that we should use care about taking everything in a wooden literal sense. We should take the Bible in each passage as it was intended to be taken so that each passage is consistent with all others on a particular topic. In ordinary language we describe non-physical things in physical ways.

Insisting that the Bible is always to be taken in a precise, literalistic sense causes significant problems. If we see Acts 1 as true in the wooden literal sense in conjunction with other passages of the Bible, how far do we take it? If "in like manner" means "in exactly the same physical way and in every literal detail the same as he left," then consider these questions posed in an article by Joseph Vincent: [191]

- Only a small group of people saw Him glorified. Does this mean that only a small group — the same group of people — will see Him return?

- How does Jesus come from heaven riding on a white horse (Revelation 19:11) if He didn't leave that way?

- How does He come "with ten thousand of His saints" (Jude 1:14) if He didn't leave that way?

- How does He come "as the lightning comes from the east and flashes to the west" (Matthew 24:27) if He didn't leave that way?

- How does He come "with a loud command [shout] . . . and with the trumpet call of God" (1 Thessalonians 4:16) if He didn't leave that way?

- How does He come "in blazing fire with his powerful angels" (2 Thessalonians 1:7) if He didn't leave that way?

- How does He come "with his angels in the glory of his Father . . . to repay each person according to what he has done" (Matthew 16:27) if He didn't leave that way?

Vincent points out that "in like manner" in the sentence structure itself does not refer to Jesus' physicality. It refers to the *manner* of his coming, in a glory cloud. As we have seen before, God's comings were not always visible, yet they were said to be in a "cloud" of judgment.

And here's more. The phrase translated "in like manner" is *hos tropos* in Greek. This phrase is used elsewhere in the New Testament. Consider this passage:

O Jerusalem, Jerusalem, the one who kills the prophets and stones those who are sent to her! How often I wanted to gather your children together, **as** [*hos tropos*] a hen gathers her chicks under her wings, but you were not willing! (*Matthew 23:37*)

The word in English here "as" is the Greek phrase *hos tropos*. In this passage, *hos tropos* does not connect Jesus to a hen literally.

Randall E. Otto notes similarities in the accounts of the ascension of Jesus with Moses and Elijah, and quotes other authors on the subject:

The similarities between the account of Moses' departure in Josephus (*Antiquites* 4.8.48) and Jesus' ascension are striking: the event occurs amongst followers on top of a mountain and, while the leader is addressing his company, a cloud suddenly overshadows him and he disappears, vanishing out of their sight. The similarities to the account of Elijah's departure are also worth noting (2 Kings

2:9-12), where again, while the teacher speaks with his pupil(s), a storm cloud sweeps down and takes him away on the vehicle associated with the divine presence, signifying his exaltation with God. As with Elijah and the tradition of Moses, while the disciples were looking on, a cloud suddenly came down and completely enveloped their master, removing him from their sight. The cloud, of course, symbolizes the divine glory of God which must always be hidden from humanity due to its incapacity to see God in his unveiled splendor. Sproul says, "That Jesus ascended in a cloud suggests the presence of the Shekinah, which is manifest glory and splendor." The Shekinah (Hebrew, *presence*) was always veiled within the cloud, however, since no man can see the glory of God and live. The manifestation, then, was the cloud, hiding the splendor which would destroy any in its midst.

Guthrie rightly notes, "The focus falls on the screening cloud, precisely as it does in the Transfiguration account." Perhaps the traditions surrounding the exaltation of Moses and Elijah were at play in their involvement with Jesus at his Transfiguration, where he momentarily unveiled his glory in anticipation of his exaltation. In any case, just as the Transfiguration instilled great fear in Peter, prompting him to suggest building the three tents to shield him, James, and John from the splendor they could not bear, so the splendor of the risen Christ at his ascension would have required the veil of the cloud to shield the disciples from the glory they could not bear. Thus he was hidden in the cloud while he was exalted in glory. "In the same manner" he would come again (Acts 1:11). If, as Blaiklock says of understanding the ascension, "some of the difficulty encountered arises from an over-literal interpretation," the same may be said of understanding the manner of Christ's return.[192]

In studying different translations of the 2 Kings text, we conclude that it is not precisely certain what Elisha actually saw. The text indicates that he was indeed a witness to Elijah's disappearance, but it is not clear whether he saw Elijah literally ascend or merely saw the "whirlwind" and/or the chariots and charioteers. The Greek word for "whirlwind" can also be translated as "tempest" or "storm." The text says that *Elisha saw Elijah no more*. The text also indicates that a fire was involved in the scene, which may have hidden the details. In any case, the *return* of Elijah, as we discussed in Chapter 6 , *did not match the expectations that the Jews had, based on the 2 Kings text.*

All things considered, there is at least reasonable doubt that the Parousia of Christ should be understood as a return to earth in the way that Christians have usually read Acts 1—that is, as a visible return in the same physical body in which He left earth. Milton Terry (1898) had this to say about Acts 1:

> Acts 1:11 is often cited to show that Christ's coming needs be spectacular, in like manner as ye beheld him going into heaven. But in the only other three places where *what manner* [Greek, *hos tropos*] occurs, it points to a general concept rather than the particular form of its actuality. Thus, in Acts 7:28, it is not some particular manner in which Moses killed the Egyptian that is notable, but rather the certain fact of it. In 2 Timothy 3:8, it is likewise the fact of strenuous opposition rather than the special manner in which Jannes and Jambres withstood Moses. And in Matthew 23:37 and Luke 13:34, it is the general thought of protection rather than the visible manner of a mother bird that is intended.
>
> Again, if Jesus did not come in that generation and immediately after the great tribulation that attended the fall of Jerusalem, his words in Matthew 16:27-28; 24:29, and parallel passages are in the highest degree misleading. **To make the one statement of the angel in Acts 1:11, override all the sayings of Jesus on the same subject and control their meaning is a very one-sided method of biblical interpretation.** But all the angel's words necessarily mean is that as Jesus has ascended into heaven so he will come from heaven, and this main thought agrees with the language of Jesus and the prophets.[193]

Vincent sums up the issue thusly:

> To be quite honest, there is really nothing in the passage [Acts 1:9-11] as to the manner of coming in any physical sense (not at all a reference to the physical bodily nature of how Jesus left, and how He would again return), rather, the passage is a positive declaration that he would come in glory as He promised, just as He left. Remember, Jesus formerly promised them that when he would return, it would be with the glory of his angels. He never said anything regarding the physical manner of his coming. While it would certainly be a physically discernible event, it certainly would not be a physical body that every eye would see. While this verse (Acts 1:11) is generally cited to prove that the glorified Jesus will himself

be *personally and bodily* visible at his second coming, it is in fact the case that the glorified Jesus cannot be seen by any man because His glorified person is veiled, hidden, and enveloped within the cloud of God's presence. Just as the disciples had not seen Christ going up to heaven, rather, they saw Him disappear into the cloud which veiled him and his Divine Glory, so *in the same manner*, e.g., hidden within the cloud, He would also return.

Remember, if we are going to suggest that "in the same manner" must mean the exact physical manner, then we must argue that his coming would be invisible, not physical. It cannot be stated too strongly that the glorified Jesus Himself would *not* be visible in His second coming because He was not visible in His ascension, but rather hidden. This is not to say that His second coming would not be a visible event with a visible judgment, or visible action, or even with a visible cloud, rather, the "manner" in which Jesus was to return would be in the same Glory in which He ascended, i.e. IN A CLOUD OF GLORY! . . .

We must emphasize that the Lord himself is invisible and is only made visible by the symbolic and representational cloud which reveals the presence of His Divine Glory. This was the case all throughout the Old Testament, and it was the prediction of Jesus Himself when He stated that He would come again "on clouds of glory" (cf. Matthew 24:30; 26:64; Revelation 1:7). . . . For Jesus to retake the form of a human, even in a semi-glorified bodily state *per se* would be to leave His throne in heaven and His glory which cannot be seen by the naked eye of any human being (this is why His glory had to be veiled by a cloud at His departure and again by His return).[194]

Jesus lived in a physical, human body—mortal, perishable, natural—albeit a very special one. He was raised from the grave in that body. Even after his resurrection He declared his body to be physical and not spiritual (Luke 24:39). He proved that his body was physical by eating broiled fish (Luke 24:43). But by the time He "appeared" to Paul after his ascension, we really must infer that his earthly body had been glorified—that is, transformed into his *heavenly body*. This is critical. The commonly held futurist view is that Jesus resides today in heaven in the self-same earthly/fleshly body as He had on earth. This assumption does not hold up to evident reason or biblical scrutiny, no matter how much the Christian would prefer to imagine it that way. The understanding that Jesus is not now still in an earthly body in the heavens in no way diminishes our understanding of Him and his glory! In fact, it enhances it!

As discussed in the previous chapter, Jesus has a glorified body in heaven. There is no indication that Jesus' body disintegrated beyond recognition, as some CBV preterists suggest. His body changed, but it was not annihilated.

We have no reason to think from Acts 1:9-11, or any other passage of the Bible, that Jesus will return in his former physical human body. Witnesses saw the power of his wrath upon the nation of Israel and the temple in AD 70. These events fulfilled his Second Coming prophecies in judgment in a cloud of glory.

The reader may be thinking that there must be another side to this argument. And, of course, there is. So let us consider other passages that futurists offer in addition to Acts 1 to argue for a visible bodily return of Christ. As representative of the futurist view, here is an excerpt from comments in *The Reformation Study Bible*: "Christ's return will be personal and physical (Matthew 24:44; Acts 1:11; Colossians 3:4; 2 Timothy 4:8; Hebrews 9:28), visible and triumphant (Mark 8:38; 2 Thessalonians 1:10; Revelation 1:7)." [195]

Let's briefly examine these passages that are cited as proof texts. Below, we show the text of the passages, and add our comments in bold. But as you read these passages, consider that using them to prove a visible physical return of Christ may result in committing multiple logical fallacies, including these:

- **Begging the Question.** This logical fallacy *assumes* something to be true that one is trying to *prove* to be true. It is also called "circular reasoning."

- **Non Sequitur.** This is an argument in which the conclusion does not follow from the premise.

- **Argumentum ad populum.** This is urging the hearer to accept a position because a majority of people hold to it. It is also called "an appeal to the popular."

- **Appeal to Tradition.** This is trying to get someone to accept something because it has been believed for a long time.

- **Red Herring**. This means introducing a topic not related to the subject at hand.

Therefore you also be ready, for the Son of Man is coming at an hour you do not expect. (*Matthew 24:44*) **This passage says nothing at all about a visible, physical-bodily coming of Christ. The use of this passage to prove a visible physical coming merely *assumes* a visible physical coming, and does not support it. It is also an argument in which the conclusion does not follow from the premise. This is typical of much of the futurists' arguments. It commits at least two logical fallacies—Begging the Question and Non Sequitur.**

When Christ who is our life appears, then you also will appear with Him in glory. (*Colossians 3:4*) **This verse is similar to 1 Corinthians 15 and 1 Thessalonians 4 in the previous chapter. There is no support in this passage for an appearance of Jesus in his former earthly body.**

Finally, there is laid up for me the crown of righteousness, which the Lord, the righteous Judge, will give to me on that Day, and not to me only but also to all who have loved His appearing. (*2 Timothy 4:8*) **The Bible teaches that our righteousness comes from faith in Christ (Romans 3:22; 2 Corinthians 5:21). The reference to the Day of the Lord is a reference to Christ's judgment coming in AD 70, as we discussed in Chapter 8. His AD 70 Parousia sealed our salvation (Luke 21:28; Romans 13:11; Hebrews 9:26-28; 1 Peter 1:5), which was effectively our crown of righteousness. And certainly there is nothing in this passage that speaks of a visible physical return.**

Christ was offered once to bear the sins of many. To those who eagerly wait for Him He will appear a second time, apart from sin, for salvation. (*Hebrews 9:28*) **This passage has nothing to do with a physical appearance of Christ either, so again it is a logical fallacy to use this as a proof text. In context, this passage was fulfilled at the end of the age (Hebrews 9:26). Unless Christians are not already saved, this is a past fulfillment, as discussed in Chapter 10, and consistent with Luke 21:28; Romans 13:11, and 1 Peter 1:5.**

For whoever is ashamed of Me and my words in this adulterous and sinful generation, of him the Son of Man also will be ashamed when He comes in the glory of his Father with the holy angels. (*Mark 8:38*) **This passage again says nothing about a visible physical return.**

When He comes, in that Day, to be glorified in his saints and to be admired among all those who believe, because our testimony among you was believed. (*2 Thessalonians 1:10*) **Jesus is glorified in and admired among all of us who believe today. But that does not lend support to a future physical Parousia. In context, the strong time-texts in 1 and 2 Thessalonians argue for a past fulfillment, as we have discussed.**

Behold, He is coming with clouds, and every eye will see Him, even they who pierced Him. And all the tribes of the earth will mourn because of Him. Even so, Amen. (*Revelation 1:7*) **We discussed this last passage when we covered Revelation, but it is worth some more discussion here:**

Futurists either assume that Revelation 1:7 means that those who pierced Him would see Him again either briefly at the end of time on earth (or perhaps in the millennial kingdom) or in heaven, or perhaps in hell. However, this passage hearkens back to other parts of the New Testament that we have already considered. Remember especially Matthew 23:29-39 in which Jesus condemns the scribes and Pharisees telling them that *they* will see Him again in their generation when He comes to judge *them*. In Matthew 26:57-67 Jesus tells the chief priests and the whole council that *they* will see Him coming on clouds of heaven.

Does Revelation 1:7 really mean that those who pierced Jesus will only see Him on judgment day at the *end of time*? That cannot be the correct interpretation because John just four verses earlier (and numerous other times in Revelation, as we considered in Chapter 9), stated that these events were to happen *shortly*. Further, the *coming with clouds* is the same language that Jesus used in the Olivet Discourse, which is clearly established as a non-physical coming in AD 70. And we note that "Behold, he is coming" (Revelation 1:7) corresponds to "Behold, I am coming quickly (soon)" in Revelation 22:7.

If these facts are not sufficient evidence that John was speaking of a first-century fulfillment, it is noted that the "tribes of the earth" must mean the twelve tribes of Israel.[196] Giving us confirmation, Jesus used the "tribes of the earth" (tribes of the land) phrase in the Olivet Discourse (Matthew 24:30). So Revelation teaches—just as we saw in Matthew—that Jesus would come again in the near future. So, either John's revelation was wrong or Jesus did come again as He said (in AD 70). If John was inspired, the preterist view must be the correct one.

It is worth reminding the reader of the reports by Josephus of the chariots in the sky. Here is how Edward E. Stevens sums it up:

> The commander of the angelic hosts (Christ) was present with His angelic armies on that occasion (AD 66), just like Revelation 19:11-21 pictures for us. This was the visible return of Christ with his angels to judge His enemies and reward His saints, as both Revelation 1:7 and Acts 1:11 had predicted. Matthew 24:29-31 and Luke 21:25-28 also indicated there would be visible "signs" accompanying the return of Christ with His angels to raise the dead out of Hades, perform the judgment, and reward His faithful saints. This fulfills the "in like manner" terms of the Acts 1:11 text. Both Revelation 1:7 and Acts 1:11 fit the Matthew 16:27-28 "visibility" pattern.[197]

The full preterist interpretation is that the first-century living Christians were going to overcome what Christ overcame by his resurrection from the dead and his ascension. They were going to be like Him in the sense that they would be able to overcome physical death. They would experience the salvation promised to occur at the Second Coming (Matthew 24:13; Luke 21:28; Romans 8:18; 11:25-27; 13:11; Ephesians 4:30; Titus 2:13-14; Hebrews 1:14; 9:28; 1 Peter 5:4; 2 Peter 1:5; Revelation 12:10; 15:8). They would be transformed into his image (1 Corinthians 15:49; 2 Corinthians 3:18). They would become the full grown "new man" (Ephesians 4:13). They would see the reigning Jesus "face to face" (that is, intimately), and no longer see Him through the dark "glass" of shadows and prophecies (1 Corinthians 13:12). Christ's work in them and for us would be fully effectual.

We want to remain humble as to God's Word. We do not purport to say that the interpretations presented in this book are the last word. But it seems to us that in order for Acts 1:9-11 to be consistent with all the others we have considered, it was fulfilled in AD 70. And the fulfillment means that the Father, and the Son, and the Holy Spirit live in us today (John 14:23; 2 Corinthians 6:16; Galatians 4:19). What great news!

More questions for further discussion with your pastor, church leaders, and friends:

- *If we expect Jesus to come visibly, why is it that Acts 1:9-11 says that Jesus' ascension was not visible but was veiled by a cloud?*

- *If Jesus comes visibly to reign in Jerusalem, do you expect Him to be seen physically by all people everywhere?*

THE LAST DAY (SINGULAR)

This is the will of the Father who sent Me, that of all He has given Me I should lose nothing, but should **raise it up at the last day**. And this is the will of Him who sent Me, that everyone who sees the Son and believes in Him may have **everlasting life**; and I will raise him up at the **last day**. (*John 6:39-40*)

No one can come to Me unless the Father who sent Me draws him; and I will **raise him up at the last day**. (*John 6:44*)

Whoever eats my flesh and drinks my blood has eternal life, and I will **raise him up at the last day**. (*John 6:54*)

Martha said to Him, "I know that he will rise again in the **resurrection** at the **last day**." (*John 11:24*)

These four passages are about the "last day" (singular)—in contrast to the "last days" (plural). It is a reasonable inference that the "last day" is the final day of the "last days." However, if one looks at these passages in isolation, that is, taken out of the context of the rest of the Old and New Testament eschatological passages, one might argue that "last day" and "last days" do not necessarily refer to the same time period. Thus, some argue, that "the last day" is still future to us while "the last days" are past.

We showed in Chapter 4 that *last days* in the Bible clearly refers to the first century. In spite of the overwhelming imminency of the prophetic events that we have seen in previous chapters, many believe that Jesus (and Martha) in John 6 and 11 could be referring to a yet-future time. The last day here could be whenever the believer dies. Or it could refer to the end of time. It could also potentially refer to a literal rapture in our future.

While no time-reference is clearly given in these three passages, we notice that each of these passages is about the *resurrection*. We argued extensively in Chapters 6, 9, and 11 that the general resurrection occurred in the first century. Again considering the *nature* of the resurrection, Kurt Simmons emphasized:

> The idea that the "self-same" physical bodies are to be raised up at the last day is every bit as erroneous as the "visible, bodily" return of Christ. Not *one* reliable verse of scripture can be marshaled to establish such claim. Jesus' statement that all who are in the graves would hear his voice and come forth (John 5:25-29) neither says nor implies the resurrection of physical bodies. The redemption of men's bodies is no part of the redemptive work of Christ. Those holding this view place the resurrection on the *wrong* side of eternity. They place the resurrection in the temporal realm of the flesh, rather than the eternal realm of the spirit where it should be.[198]

Next, consider this passage which ties the last day to the *judgment*:

> He who rejects Me, and does not receive my words, has that which judges him—the word that I have spoken will **judge** him in the **last day**. (*John 12:48*)

We argued conclusively in Chapters 5, 6, 7, and 9 that the general judgment occurred in AD 70. So everything ties together for a first-century fulfillment.

Many think that "the last day" refers to the last day of the Christian age. But the Bible teaches that the Christian age has no end (Isaiah 9:6-7; Daniel 7:13-14; Luke 1:32-33; Ephesians 3:20-21). Therefore, the Christian age has no last days, nor does it have a last day! However, the Mosaic age had an end, last days, last day, and a last hour. The resurrection and Judgment of which Jesus, Moses, Daniel, Paul, and all the other prophets taught occurred on that day when the temple was destroyed, and the power of the holy people was completely shattered (Daniel 12). Everything ties together—judgment, resurrection, Second Coming, tribulation, "rapture," end of the age, last days, last day, and the last hour. All of these refer to AD 30-70. The preterist view is consistent.

Restoration and Other Objections

RESTORATION

Many Christians await the Second Coming in which Jesus restores all earthly things to an idyllic world with no sin and no more death, crying, or pain—from a literal reading of Isaiah 11:1-9; 65:17-25 and Revelation 21:1-4. These Christians challenge full preterists with this statement: "Jesus cannot have come yet because we still see sin, suffering, evil, and death all around us."

Let's consider this challenge. Concerning sin, the Bible says that Jesus appeared at his First Advent *to put away/remove sin* (Hebrews 9:26; cf. Daniel 9:24-27; Matthew 1:21; John 1:29; Acts 5:31; Romans 6:1-14; Colossians 1:22; Titus 2:14; Hebrews 1:3; 1 Peter 2:24; 1 John 3:5; Revelation 1:5), and to *destroy the works of the devil* (John 12:31; 1 John 3:8). Did Jesus fail? Think about that for just a moment.

Jesus did not fail. He conquered the REIGN of sin over us, not the EXISTENCE of sin (Romans 6:6, 11, 14, 22)! This was the promise all along from Isaiah and Revelation regarding the new covenant world of heaven and earth—and it has been fulfilled. Sin continues to exist in the new age (Matthew 12:31-32; 1 Timothy 5:20 (ref. 4:8); Revelation 22:14-15), but it is no longer master over God's people. It is only in heaven where we will get relief from death and suffering.

The Last Enemy (spiritual death, condemnation, alienation, or separation from God), which is the result of sin's reign over us, has been conquered. We now have access to the presence of God (Hebrews 9).

Even though we may still sin, it can no longer hold the true believer in its web. The objection of sin still being in the world not only fails to understand what needed to be restored (our relationship to God), but also fails to appreciate the depth of man's *earthly sinful nature*, and *fails to understand what Jesus has already accomplished.*

Concerning death, the Bible says that Jesus *destroyed/abolished death* (2 Timothy 1:10; cf. Romans 6:23; Hebrews 2:14-15). Did He fail? Again, no.

Indeed, not only spiritual death but also bodily death has been conquered. Jesus said, "If anyone keeps my word, he shall never see death." (John 8:51) As discussed in Chapter 11, Jesus made several such statements as found in the book of John, including, "Whoever lives and believes in Me shall never die. Do you believe this?" (John 11:26) Every Christian understands this on one level, so should not have to ask the question: Why do we see death all around us? Jesus assured the believer that he *will never die.* Physical death on this earth is but a step into the afterlife for the faithful believer.

Let us first speak specifically to amillennialists here. Amillennialists have a knee-jerk reaction against preterism that is often somewhat vague, and curiously ignores the imminency passages. We reference here a document by the Lutheran Church Missouri Synod, a highly respected amillennial denomination that prides itself on faithfulness to the Bible. This document is entitled "The 'End Times': A Study on Eschatology and Millennialism." [199] It states that Christians "await the Messiah's second coming when the kingdom of God will be made fully manifest. . . . Christians eagerly anticipate the consummation of the New Covenant when they will perfectly know the Lord and sin no more." [200] The document goes on to explain:

> When Christ returns, God will create new heavens and a new earth (Isaiah 65:17; 66:22; 2 Peter 3:13; Revelation 21:1). The Scriptures indicate that a continuity and a discontinuity will exist between the present world and the new world, just as there is a continuity and discontinuity between the Christian's present body and the resurrection body. The future new creation will in some sense involve the present creation and will be the culmination of Christ's redemptive work. Romans 8:19-23 speaks of creation as waiting with eager longing and groaning in travail for the time when it will be set free from its bondage to decay. One of the results of Adam's fall is that the ground is cursed and brings forth thorns and thistles (Genesis 3:17-18). Just as human beings who return to

dust at death will one day be raised, so creation itself will be set free from its bondage.[201]

This document, which is apparently a major position statement on eschatology by the denomination, is representative of the amillennial position. When we reviewed it, we noticed that in all of its 65 pages, the eschatological imminency passages were not even considered once. Respecting the otherwise excellent reputation of this church body, this is plainly irresponsible scholarship—but is typical of many church organizations that continually mislead the flock about these things.

We also noticed the vagueness of the new heaven and new earth. It is not the millennium; nor is it heaven. It is apparently something in between. The document correctly says that Christ's redemptive work culminates at the Second Coming, but obviously misses the timing.

The document references Genesis 3 and the Fall. From the document and from speaking to those who hold to the amillennial view, we have concluded that they have an overriding hope that God will restore the world to a pre-Fall utopia. Of course, this is exactly what premillennialists as well as postmillennialists hope for. But amillennialists have a less well-defined sense of this earthly utopia. It is vague and has no indicated length of existence.

Consider this passage from Acts 3 in which Peter speaks of *restoration*:

[17] Yet now, brethren, I know that you did it in ignorance, as did also your rulers. [18] But those things which God foretold by the mouth of all His prophets, that the Christ would suffer, He has thus fulfilled. [19] Repent therefore and be converted, that your sins may be blotted out, so that times of refreshing may come from the presence of the Lord, [20] and **that He may send Jesus Christ**, who was preached to you before, [21] whom heaven must receive **until the times of restoration of all things**, which God has spoken by the mouth of all his holy prophets since the world began. [22] For Moses truly said to the fathers, "The LORD your God will raise up for you a Prophet like me from your brethren. Him you shall hear in all things, whatever He says to you. [23] And it shall be that every **soul who will not hear that Prophet shall be utterly destroyed** from among the people." [24] Yes, and all the prophets, from Samuel and those who follow, as many as have spoken, have also **foretold these days**. [25] You are sons of the prophets, and of the covenant which God made with our fathers, saying to Abraham, "And in your seed all the

families of the earth shall be blessed." [26] To you first, God, having raised up his Servant Jesus, sent Him to bless you, in turning away every one of you from your iniquities. (*Acts 3:17-26*)

At least some commentaries acknowledge that this section refers to the Second Coming (verse 20), which we have argued was in AD 70. The passage (verses 18, 21, and 24) is reminiscent of the statement by Jesus in Luke 21:22, in which He said that all prophecy would be fulfilled in his generation. Peter confirms this time frame, and places these events specifically in *his* day—reinforcing what he *just stated a few verses earlier in Acts chapter 2* about the last days being in his time—as well as similar statements he would later make in his epistles.

Peter seems to be lumping together the First Coming and the Second Coming and applying them to his own time. This was the time of the *restoration of all things* (verse 21)! If this seems impossible, perhaps you have had in your mind a concept of restoration that is not biblically accurate. The word translated in some Bibles as "restoration" (verse 21) is translated as "restitution" in others, including Young's Literal Translation. Restitution, defined as *compensation* for what was lost rather than *returning* what was lost, better captures what happened in AD 70. Restitution is about *justice*! Verses 23-25 are clearly about justice and judgment. So, what some Christians consider to be restoration of the planet, at least from this passage, is really about restitution in AD 70. Restoration, in a fuller sense, is about restoring our fellowship with God, as Adam and Eve had before the Fall. Author Glenn Hill argues the case for past fulfillment thusly:

1. Since the "times of restitution" were prophesied by the prophets (Acts 3:24), and

2. Since their prophecies have all been fulfilled (Luke 21:22; Acts 3:24),

3. Then the prophesied "times of restitution" have been fulfilled too.

4. Since Jesus would return when "the times of restitution" arrived (Acts 3:21),

5. Then Jesus has come again too! [202]

Note: It was common for the biblical writers to consider Jesus' first and second advents together, essentially as two aspects of the same event. Consider, for example, Daniel 9:24-27; 1 Corinthians 15, and Hebrews 9.

Will we return to a time on earth in which *nobody sins*? No. Does the *physical creation* need restoring? The answer again, in our view, is NO. The physical creation was pronounced *very good* by God himself (Genesis 1:31)! As suggested in previous discussions, what happened at the Fall was the emergence or manifestation of mankind's sin, and thus our separation from God (Isaiah 59:2). While it had ramifications about man's life afterward and how he related to his surroundings, it was not about the decline of the physical creation. Adam and Eve did not mess up God's earth; they messed up their relationship with God. The physical creation was not corrupted by the fall of Adam and Eve, and hence is not in need of restoration. In addition to other exegetical errors of futurists, we propose that *restorationism*—defined as a future return to an imagined pre-Fall utopian earthly world—is an error too. **Christianity, properly understood, explains history as a <u>linear progression</u> rather than as a <u>cycle</u> in eastern religions.**

The primary objection to the idea that the Fall was only a spiritual event is that Genesis 3 speaks of physical things such as the pain of childbirth, and the curse on the ground. But it should be noted that the text only states that the pain of childbirth would be *multiplied*, which clearly implies that such pain existed *before* the Fall. And regarding the cursing of the ground, we understand this to be a condemnation not unlike what is used in language even today. When someone "curses the ground someone else stands on," he or she is expressing great anger in the person, not in the ground. All mankind would inherit in some way the sinful nature of Adam and would suffer as a result of Adam's transgressions. But the curse was not upon creation itself which God had just declared as being very good.

Some people (skeptics) by the way, charge the Bible as being wrong because creation is not *perfect*. "See," they say, "God created an imperfect world. We see problems all around us. So God is not all powerful. In fact, He must be imperfect because He created an imperfect world." But the Bible never says that God created a "perfect" world. Nor does it say that He ever intended to do so. He created it by design as "good" or "very good"—not absolutely "perfect" in every way. (So goes another widespread misunderstanding about the Bible.) **But more importantly, who is man to define perfection, and why should God pay heed to such an opinion?**

As we argued from Scripture in Chapter 11, most Christians misunderstand what happened at the Fall of Adam and Eve. What changed at the Fall was not worldly things. Nor was physical death the result of the Fall. What happened at the Fall was mankind's spiritual separation from God. What was in need of restoration was our relationship to the Creator. What Adam and Eve forfeited at the Fall was life after death. [203]

When would this "restoration" of our relationship to God, and thus restitution, take place? We find the answer in the last chapter of Revelation, where we see that in context the end of the curse was imminent when John received the vision. Notice it was said that the events *must* (not "might" or "could") take place shortly:

And there **shall be no more curse**, but the throne of God and of the Lamb shall be in it, and his servants shall serve Him. They shall see his face, and his name shall be on their foreheads. There shall be no night there: They need no lamp nor light of the sun, for the Lord God gives them light. And they shall reign forever and ever. Then he said to me, "These words are faithful and true." And the Lord God of the holy prophets sent His angel to show his servants the things which **must shortly take place**. (*Revelation 22:3-6*)

For the amillennialist, the return of Christ occurs at the end of the millennium (a long, indefinite period of time that we are in now)—which culminates at the end of history. There is no literal earthly millennium (in the way that premillennialists believe), so the eternal state (heaven or hell) must, presumably, follow *immediately* at the end of time/end of the millennium. Amillennialists also are of the opinion that Christ's return is a necessary precursor to set the world straight prior to the eternal state. If Christ has already returned, their hope for this utopia is dashed—at least in their thinking. But let us explore some things with the amillennialist.

- Since your amillennialist view holds that the restoration happens at the end of time, which by reasonable inference ushers in the eternal state *immediately* (or in a very short period of time thereafter), why is this important to you? In other words, since the earthly utopian state only lasts a short time—or in fact is a heavenly occurrence—why does it matter? Isn't heaven what you are ultimately looking forward to anyway?

- How much of your expectation of restoration is based on assumption or wishful thinking, rather than Scripture?

- The Lutheran document accuses dispensationalists of offering "a dangerously false hope." [204] Can you see that any futurist view, as well, detracts from Christ's finished work?

- Is it biblical to insert a utopian period on earth between the end of history and the eternal state? (Isn't this the error of which you are accusing millennialists?)

- Have amillennialists misapplied Isaiah 65-66, as discussed in Chapter 8?

- Have amillennialists misapplied Romans 8? In the above quote from the Lutheran document, Romans 8:19-23 was cited. But the immediately preceding verse (which was conveniently left out in the document) clearly states the imminency of Paul's expectation: "For I reckon that the sufferings of the present time are not worthy to be compared with the glory **about to be** revealed in us." (Romans 8:18, *Young's Literal Translation*) Also note that *this very section* contains another imminency statement: "For we know that the whole creation groans and labors with birth pangs together **until now**." (*Romans 8:22*)

- Isn't the "creation" in Romans 8:20-22 (Greek *ktisis*) — which was to be set free from the bondage of decay unto freedom — a spiritual/covenantal term rather than a physical universe term? Isn't this confirmed by Paul's usage of the same word in 2 Corinthians 5:17 and Galatians 6:15 where Paul explains that **believers become a new covenant creature/creation** (*ktisis*) as the old, weak and beggarly elements pass away from their lives? Isn't the freedom in this passage referring to freedom from the *bondage* of sin that comes from the Law of Moses which Paul spoke of in the preceding and following chapters (Romans 7 and 9)? In other words, isn't the newness/restoration one *of relationship* with God rather than *of molecules*? Note: The goal of becoming children of God in Romans 8 precludes any part of the animal kingdom as being included in the promise, unless insects and rodents become children of God. This further confirms that the new creation is about the new covenant of today rather than a literal new universe.

- If you really-and-truly see a time *on earth* (before heaven) when no sin of any kind could possibly exist, what is left for heaven? If Jesus returned tonight in Jerusalem would *everyone* in the world wake up tomorrow without any sin, *including sins of omission*? Since we are sinful by *nature* (Psalm 51:5; Ephesians 2:3), would the *nature* of our carnal, fleshly, earthly bodies actually change overnight? While God could do anything, of course, can you even *imagine* an *earthly* world with not one single sin of omission? To explore this, can you envision a time when every living soul never fails to do every *possible* good thing? Would this mean that no one sleeps anymore, and just sits around doing nothing but thinking of ways to do just one more good deed (and nary even a bad thought ever enters the mind)? **Isn't the utopian state reserved for heaven?** [205]

- Isn't our ultimate hope really in heaven itself, rather than in some temporary earthly restoration?

- Doesn't Revelation 22:14-15 teach that sin (sexual immorality, murder, idolatry, etc.) still exists *after the Second Coming*? Don't these verses imply that the promise of "restoration" is for those inside the city sanctuary who receive the New Covenant tree of life, thus the New Jerusalem church (Revelation 21:9-27) — which was to soon to be ushered in with finality (Revelation 22:6-7)?

- How far should we take the restorationist's view? Will people once again, as before the Fall, live naked — as in a nudist colony?

- Is it necessary for Christ to return again in the future in order for us to get to heaven?

The idea that sin and evil still exist after Jesus' Parousia should really not be that difficult to accept. Most Protestant Christians embrace the doctrine of "imputed righteousness." Indeed, this is a signature doctrine of the Lutheran and Reformed traditions. The doctrine teaches that the righteousness of Christ is *imputed* to Christians through their faith. Even though Christians in actuality still sin, God overlooks our sin through a "legal fiction." In other words, it is an "alien" righteousness from God who *considers* us sinless because of Christ!

Thus imputed righteousness is the righteousness of Jesus *credited* to the Christian, making the Christian justified. So the restoration at the Parousia is merely the completion of imputed righteousness (Romans 4:23-34, *Young's Literal Translation*). Sin still exists after the AD 70 eschatological completion, but because of Christ's work the Christian has been, in a very real sense, freed from sin in finality.[206]

Now let's consider restoration from the perspective of postmillennialism. Amillennialists make one important point with which preterists agree. Amillennialists are highly skeptical of the postmillennialists' claim that mankind and society can progress into a utopian society by Christianizing the world. Certainly there is not much evidence from history to support this progression. The twentieth century proved again the depravity of mankind, as over 250 million people were *murdered* by their own governments. The worst and most extensive crimes against humanity have come from atheistic, communistic, animistic, and Islamic regimes. But even "Christian" cultures have been guilty of shameful crimes.[207]

We agree with the postmillennialists that it is the Christian duty to evangelize and to institute biblical values throughout the world — because our compassion demands it. No moral system is equal to Christianity. God is god *of all* or He is not God *at all*. Indeed, everyone on the planet is subject to the moral laws of the God of the Bible, even if they don't know it or don't want to believe it. But we think that the postmillennialists' hope of a utopian, or nearly perfect, society is a misplaced hope. We should remember that a critical distinctive of Christianity versus all other worldviews is the understanding that all men are *inherently sinful* (at least since the fall of Adam). While improvement is possible, anything near "perfection" is not possible given the *nature* of man. We are not equating Christian futurism to these other worldviews except on this one point—earthly utopianism is an ideal of such worldviews as Marxism and Islam, not biblical Christianity. "Heaven on earth" is dangerously close to mixing Christian hope with pagan ideas.

Partial preterist/postmillennialist Samuel M. Frost made this statement: "Salvation is at work 'daily' in our lives here on earth as we individually and collectively are conformed to his image." [208] David A. Green appropriately challenged Frost's utopianism facetiously: "So

the physical bodies of believers, over the past 2,000 years of generations, have been becoming more and more molecularly conformed to
the glorified physical body of Christ in heaven? So believers have an
incandescent glow today that they did not have 2,000 years ago? Are
we going to start walking through walls soon? It's 'a fair question.'"

There is another aspect of postmillennial teaching that we think is
in error. Postmillennialists believe, like premillennialists, that there will
be a time in which all believers (including Abraham and the other Old
Testament saints) will be resurrected and will live together *on earth*. (Yes.
That's what they believe. Abraham comes back to *earth*.) **Indeed, many
millennialists deny that heaven is the goal of the Christian**. Samuel M. Frost made this statement: "Notice this: he (Abraham himself)
would 'possess the land.' . . . This is heavenly derived land—heaven
on earth. . . . If Abraham does not stand again (resurrection) [on earth]
in the land God had given him as an everlasting possession, then God
has failed." [209]

This postmillennial error is precisely the same error that is made by
premillennialists. It is merely couched in different terminology. Such
a notion should be refuted. We will add some further context to our
refutation of millennialism in the next chapter.

But, what about the prophecy "the lion and lamb will lie down
together?" Doesn't this teach a utopian time on earth? This supposed
phrase in the Bible is ingrained in the minds of many as teaching restorationism—either in the millennium (premillennialists) or at the end
of the millennium (amillennialists).

Let us first point out that the phrase is not found in the Bible! The
closest we get to it is from Isaiah 11 and 65:

> The wolf also shall dwell with the lamb. The leopard shall lie
> down with the young goat. The calf and the young lion and the
> fatling together; and a little child shall lead them. The cow and
> the bear shall graze; their young ones shall lie down together;
> and the lion shall eat straw like the ox. (*Isaiah 11:6-7*)

> "The wolf and the lamb shall feed together. The lion shall
> eat straw like the ox, and dust shall be the serpent's food.
> They shall not hurt nor destroy in all my holy mountain," says
> the LORD. (*Isaiah 65:25*)

Contrary to common understanding, it is not the lion and lamb
together, but the wolf and the lamb—and neither pair lies down to-

gether. It is the leopard and the goat that do the lying down together. The details may be trifling. But it seems incredible that anyone would take these passages literally, though many do. What are these passages really about? Partial preterist Andrew Corbett explains:

> The Book of Isaiah employs metaphors. Metaphors are word pictures. The Promised Messiah is described in Isaiah as a "tender shoot" or a "root" (incidentally, both metaphors occur in Isaiah 11). These word pictures of the Christ paint Him as the *hope of Israel* and *One who would be born as a child and grow*. The particular metaphors in question: *the wolf* is frequently used in the Old Testament to speak of Israel's enemies. For example, Jeremiah speaks of Israel's enemies as *a lion, a wolf, and a leopard*. (Jeremiah 5:6) Similarly, Israel is frequently described as lambs or sheep. To speak of wolves and lambs lying down together, is to describe the effect of the New Covenant. That is, the largely ethnically-centered Old Covenant, would one day be replaced by the for-all-the-world-New-Covenant where Jew and (the previously hostile enemy) Gentiles are brought together under the same Covenant. (Ephesians 2:11-14) The context of Isaiah 11 is the ministry and achievement of the Messiah. The resultant New Covenant would make peace between formerly hostile enemies. There are some beautiful prophetic metaphors in Isaiah 11 which describe this. Such as verse 18: *The nursing child shall play over the hole of the cobra, and the weaned child shall put his hand on the adder's den*. This is not a picture of a Utopian Golden Era, referred to as The Millennium; rather it was a prophetic picture of the resultant peace from the spread of the New Covenant.[210]

So much for another widely held utopian misconception about the Bible.

Here are a couple of questions for further discussion with your pastor, church leaders, and friends:

- *Where in the Bible is the teaching of the lion and the lamb lying down together?*

- *Should we take Isaiah 11 and 65 literally?*

DUAL FULFILLMENT

As discussed previously, futurists often hold to an arbitrary interpretation of prophecy. Partial preterists, for example, hold to two Second Comings of Jesus. Does the New Testament really speak of two Second Comings? This would make a total of three comings—the first advent at the birth of Jesus, a second advent in judgment in AD 70, and a third advent at the end of time. If Jesus had meant to communicate dual fulfillment of his Parousia, surely He would have clearly communicated that.

Partial preterists may deny that their view has two Second Comings. They say that the judgment coming in AD 70 was a "metaphorical coming," not a literal coming. AD 70 was just one of numerous metaphorical comings of God, including those of Jehovah in the Old Testament. So, they argue, the AD 70 coming does not count. Very convenient.

Other futurists may say that any given New Testament prophetic passage is fulfilled in *one sense* in one time period, but fulfilled in another sense in a later time period. Partial preterist Joel McDurmon has described his method of interpreting Scripture as "one movement in God's symphony," and "Scripture is put together in an artistic way."

So partial preterists or other futurists may see, in various ways, not only two Parousias of Christ, but also two end times, two judgments and resurrections, two arrivals of the New Creations, and so forth—all separated by thousands of years. As David A. Green puts it, this approach is "yes-no-yes-no-yes-no." Such an elastic already-and-not-yet method of interpretation helps the futurist to avoid all serious exegesis of critical passages. With enough creativity, the futurist hypothesis can be stretched to achieve any desired result.

Most full preterists were once partial preterists. The partial position is often a stopping point for a while, as the student considers the issues in more depth. Having considered the possibilities, full preterists conclude that all dual fulfillment theories are based on a misconception of the last days. Futurists think the last days are at the end of time (or the end of the Christian era). The biblical writers, however, spoke neither of an end of time nor of an end to the Christian era! We have shown with clarity that the "last days" was a period that brought to a close the age of the Mosaic Law (the Old Covenant age). The last days were the approximately forty-year period that culminated in the Parousia in AD 70, just as Jesus promised.

The Bible speaks of only one Second Coming of Jesus. Elaborating on some previous ground, the primary Greek word to describe the Second Coming is *Parousia*. This noun is used twenty-four times in the New Testament including sixteen times in reference to the Second Coming of Jesus. <u>Fifteen of those sixteen times, it is translated with a definite article: *the,* or *his,* or *your*</u>. In the sixteenth usage (2 Peter 1:16) a definite article is implied. It is noted that The Parousia is found in the Olivet Discourse as well as in 1 Corinthians 15 (the resurrection) and 1 Thessalonians 4 (the rapture). So it seems clear enough that the New Testament writers, who all wrote in the same generation, spoke of only one Second Coming of Jesus—*The* **Parousia**.[211]

We have seen futurists use various arguments in an attempt to prove their case. For example, futurists may cite certain passages such as Matthew 2:15 in which Matthew says Jesus' parents took Jesus to Egypt for a time to avoid Herod's slaughter. According to Matthew this passage fulfilled Hosea 11:1 which speaks of God leading Israel out of Egypt at the Exodus. A similar example given is Matthew 2:17-18 in which Matthew ties the slaughter of children by Herod to Jeremiah 31:15 which speaks of Israel's mourning at the time of the Babylonian captivity.

But such defenses are extremely weak. These "types and shadows" fulfillment occurred with finality in the first century. We do not doubt Matthew, but rather the use of Matthew's citations to prove double fulfillment of *New Testament* prophecies.

To the extent that "types and shadows" of events are found in the Old Testament, there was no longer any reason for such shadows in the New Testament. The Old Testament foreshadowed Christ; everything pointed to Him. Christological fulfillments are not shadows of further christological fulfillments. With his First and Second Advents in the first century, *all things were fulfilled.*

There are other ways that futurists take specific prophecies and attempt to turn them into general ones. For example, in the Olivet Discourse Jesus prophesied wars and rumors of wars and false prophets before the end of the age. Futurists may admit that these things were fulfilled in the first century, but then *arbitrarily* say that they will happen again before the end of the world. If one uses these various hermeneutical techniques, he can twist Scripture to mean about anything. Jesus told us that the things He mentioned would happen in his generation. They did happen in his generation. That should end the debate.

Futurists, in many cases, simply refuse to believe what Jesus taught. Russell had strong thoughts about the hypothesis of double meaning in prophecy:

> The first objection to this hypothesis is that it has no foundation in the teaching of the Scriptures. There is not a scintilla of evidence that the apostles and primitive Christians had any suspicion of a twofold reference in the predictions of Jesus concerning the end. No hint is anywhere dropped that a primary and partial fulfillment of His sayings was to take place in that generation, but that the complete and exhaustive fulfillment was reserved for a future and far distant period. The very contrary is the fact.
>
> What can be more comprehensive and conclusive than our Lord's words, "Verily I say unto you, this generation shall not pass, till ALL these things be fulfilled"? What critical torture has been applied to these words to extort from them some other meaning than their obvious and natural one! How has *genea* [generation] been hunted through all its lineage and genealogy to discover that it may not mean the persons then living on the earth! But all such efforts are wholly futile.
>
> While the words remain in the text, their plain and obvious sense will prevail over all the glosses and perversions of ingenious criticism. The hypothesis of a twofold fulfillment receives no countenance from the Scriptures. We have only to read the language in which the apostles speak of the approaching consummation, to be convinced that they had one, and only one, great event in view, and that they thought and spoke of it as just at hand.[212]

Full preterist Michael Sullivan agrees. In a response to a book by partial preterist Keith A. Mathison (*When Shall These Things Be?*), Sullivan insists that in double fulfilling New Testament prophecies we set a dangerous precedent:

> Therefore, unless we want to end up adopting a liberal, post-modern approach to God's word and turn all of His promises into "yes

and no," Mathison's double-fulfillment theory must be firmly and finally rejected.[213]

THE CREEDS

Not all Christians recite the Apostles' Creed, Nicene Creed, or Athanasian Creed. For example, Baptists (who represent the largest Protestant group) usually do not use creeds in their worship services. However, Lutherans, Methodists, Presbyterians, Episcopalians, and Catholics do use the Apostles Creed and Nicene Creed often in their worship services. Various groups have slightly different versions of the creeds. But all three creeds state approximately that Jesus "will come again to judge the living and the dead."

A great deal of antagonism against full preterists is nothing but creed waving that is void of Scripture exegesis ("creedolatry" or "hyper-creedalism"). Futurists often take the position that they need not prove their arguments from Scripture, but merely assume the infallibility or necessary inerrancy of the creeds. Our position as full preterists is that the only necessarily inspired statement of faith is the Bible. The creeds are manmade documents, and while they are largely consistent with the Bible, they are not in themselves the Word of God.

The Apostles' Creed, by the way, was not written by the apostles. It was formulated and changed hundreds of years after the apostles. Its form today is from the eighth century AD. The Nicene Creed was also changed after its initial formulation at the Council of Nicea in the fourth century AD. If the creeds are infallible or necessarily inerrant, why were they changed? Why are there several different ones? How much credence should we put in men who knew that the Bible taught that the earth was the center of the universe?

The creeds were written by men. And we know that throughout the history of the church men have manifestly erred on even important theological issues. We also know how a few people at various times have been able to establish questionable doctrines within the church—doctrines that have become set in stone within various groups of Christians. This problem is universal—proved by the existence of thousands of Christian sects.

While the creeds are very helpful toward a general understanding of certain fundamental aspects of Christianity, especially the divinity of Christ, we should not simply *assume* that they conform perfectly to the Bible in all aspects. We are persuaded that they do differ from the Bible on the *timing* of the Second Coming.

Actually, many of us full preterists generally accept the Apostles' and Nicene creedal statements with the exception of the tense of a single verb. Instead of "will come," we believe that the accurate understanding of the Bible is simply "came." Even the Second Coming section of the creeds is correct from the perspective of the New Testament writers. The Second Coming was indeed future *to them*.[214]

We can track the various eschatological views (historicist, idealist, futurist, preterist) down through the ages; unlike other doctrinal issues we see no formal discussions of eschatology within the church. In the first few centuries there was tremendous debate on the issue of the Trinity. A case can be made that the church was too preoccupied with the Trinity to concern herself with eschatology. The creeds are concerned primarily with the nature of God. The statements made in the early creeds about eschatology simply quote Scripture regarding the coming of Christ. Since the language of the New Testament was future tense, they made their confessional language the same.

Over time, other issues came forward for debate. Incredibly, it wasn't until the sixteenth century that a serious debate arose on the *doctrine of justification* (how we are saved, that is how sinful man is made righteous before a holy God)—leading to the Protestant Reformation. Of course, this extremely important topic is being debated even today. Yet, still no real church-wide debate has occurred on eschatology. Preterists are at the forefront today of the call for a serious and open debate on the biblical "last things."

Actually, full preterists argue that we have more respect for the creeds than do many partial preterists, who are often the ones who are so reliant on the creeds. Full preterists accept the creedal statements about there being only one Parousia. Partial preterists see *two* Parousias of Christ in the New Testament, which is a doctrine that is alien to the creeds. As put by Kenneth J. Davies, "The partial preterist reads multiple comings of Christ into Scripture. The true preterist affirms only one, as do the Word of God, the Creeds, and the Reformed Confessions. The burden of proof lies with the partial preterist to demonstrate otherwise." [215]

Also of note is that absent from the creeds is any concept of an earthly kingdom of peace in which sin and its consequences have been overcome, or which the earthly rulers successfully enforce God's law. The premillennialists and postmillennialists come up empty with the creeds on this score, which is so important to their eschatology. So whose views are more faithful to the creeds?

Is it really possible to think that the church fathers who constructed the creeds were wrong about eschatology? The answer may simply be that either the creeds are wrong or the Bible is wrong. Partial preterist R. C. Sproul, Sr. honestly raised the question of whether the Bible may be in conflict with historical views on eschatology:

> . . . Skeptical criticism of the Bible has become almost universal in the world. And people have attacked the credibility of Jesus. Maybe some church fathers made a mistake. Maybe our favorite theologians have made mistakes. I can abide with that. I can't abide with Jesus being a false prophet, because if I am to understand that Jesus is a false prophet, my faith is in vain.[216]

There is a certain vocal community, noteworthy for its hostile attacks against full preterists, that insists that "orthodoxy" is not merely defined by the creeds, but defined by the creeds with *necessarily inerrant finality*. But the meaning of orthodoxy has changed throughout Christian history.[217] At times it has been defined as whatever the Roman Catholic Church taught. At other times it was defined as "adhering to an accepted or established doctrine." In the American Dictionary of the English Language (Noah Webster, 1828), orthodox was defined as "Sound in the Christian faith; believing the genuine doctrines taught in the Scriptures." Full preterists insist that we are completely orthodox by this definition. Charges of heresy have been liberally applied throughout history—some correctly, some not.

Orthodoxy has often been defined by whoever came first or whoever had the most ecclesiastical power. Indeed, it has been a moving target throughout church history, sometimes moving gradually, sometimes in giant leaps. Consider this quote:

> Your plea to be heard from Scripture is the one always made by heretics. . . . How can you assume that *you* are the *only one* to understand the sense of Scripture? Would you put your judgment above that of so many famous men and claim that you know more than they all? You have no right to call into question the most holy orthodox faith, instituted by Christ the perfect lawgiver, proclaimed throughout the world by the apostles, sealed by the red blood of martyrs, confirmed by the sacred councils, defined by the Church in which all our fathers believed until death and gave to us as an

inheritance, and which now we are forbidden by [Mother Church] and [her Creeds] to [debate] lest there be no end to debate.[218]

This quote is from Johann Eck, a defender of Roman Catholicism in condemnation of Martin Luther. David A. Green, editor of this book, replaced the words "pope" and "emperor" in the original quote with "Mother Church" and "her Creeds" to make a point. Ecclesiastical tyranny is just as evident today as then.

In summary, we are inclined to agree with the simple explanation of Daniel E. Harden, who stated: "The Church has never recovered from that early and fundamental error of first 'mildly elasticizing' the time of fulfillment, and then gradually 'indefinitely postponing' it [the Parousia] longer and longer, rather than reexamining and correcting their understanding of the nature of the resurrection. This is reflected in the early creeds." [219]

The creeds were changed after their initial formulation as their understanding improved. As our understanding continues to improve, we should consider again updating the creeds. Our call to update the creeds should find a sympathetic ear especially among Reformed Christians, who have historically seen their role as "reformed and continually reforming."

Only the Bible does not change. We believe that God does not lie or deceive, and ultimately we rely on the Holy Scriptures. We ask Reformed and Lutheran scholars especially: What happened to *Sola Scriptura*? We appeal to the famous testimony of Martin Luther at the Diet of Worms in 1521:

My conscience is held captive to the Word of God. Unless convinced by the testimony of Scripture and evident reason, here I stand. God help me.[220]

EISEGESIS

Traditions are an organic part of the church. But not every tradition is *automatically* biblical. Every part of Christianity has its own set of traditions that may differ with the traditions of other groups. Too often these hallowed traditions become so established in the minds of Christians that we unquestioningly assume that they are biblical. Christians hear certain doctrinal interpretations from the pulpit so often that they become ingrained in their thinking, regardless of whether the interpretations are grounded in the Bible.

We trust that the reader from now on will be able to see through the shallow explanations of eschatology that he or she hears from the doctors of the church or from apparently "informed" sources. Below is an example of someone on the Internet offering an explanation of a verse from Matthew 24. First consider the verse itself, then below it the comment in reference to the passage:

> Immediately after the tribulation of those days the sun will be darkened, and the moon will not give its light; the stars will fall from heaven, and the powers of the heavens will be shaken. (*Matthew 24:29*)

These are the most difficult words in the whole Olivet Discourse because they appear to link the Second Coming with the destruction of the Jewish state. Yet we know that this was not the meaning. Why? Because Jesus described the destruction of Jerusalem and the end of the world with the same set of symbols. And we obviously know that the end of the world has not come. Further, we know that Christ separated the two events by a most extensive period of time by Luke 21:24, "And they shall fall by the edge of the sword, and shall be led captive into all nations: and Jerusalem shall be trodden down of the Gentiles, until the times of the Gentiles be fulfilled." Most scholars agree.

When one first reads an explanation like this (or hears it from the pulpit!), one's first thought may be: "This person seems to know what he is talking about." Obviously the source must be correct because "most scholars agree." But on a moment's reflection, the king has no clothes. There is more than one slight-of-hand here, including an *assumption* about the end of the planet, and an *assumption* about the separation by thousands of years of fulfillment of prophecies. The proof text given by the expositor does not prove the point, which the diligent reader of this book up to this point will have no trouble recognizing. His conclusion results from *eisegesis*, which means reading a meaning **into the text**. The opposite, and correct method of biblical interpretation, is *exegesis*—which means gleaning meaning **from the text**.

The comments from this teacher are barely above gobbledygook (especially the last couple of sentences), and at best are influenced by ignorant assumptions about what Scripture teaches. This kind of biblical exposition is everywhere, especially in matters of eschatology. We pray that the reader will more easily recognize logical fallacies in such exposition and be able to think critically about what he hears or reads concerning these matters.

WHY NO WRITTEN RECORD OF THE PAROUSIA?

This is a significant question. If Jesus returned in AD 70, why didn't the early church record this event? First of all, when this question is asked, there is usually an assumption that the Second Coming would be a bodily physical coming. So, the question is something of an exercise in question begging. We have shown that the Second Coming was a non-physical coming. However, the question of why the early church did not speak more about the preterist perspective of the Parousia remains a valid question. We discussed this question briefly in Chapters 1 and 8, but here are some other considerations, mostly summarized from author Don K. Preston's writing:[221]

- There were really very few writers in the early church. Works of many of the early Christian writers have been lost. The limited number of available writers does not necessarily represent the views of the church. Preston quotes Charles Hodge: "Ten or twenty writers scattered over such a period cannot reasonably be assumed to speak the mind of the whole church." Thus there were so few writers and such a limited expression of eschatology among those few writers that we really do not know, based on documentation, what the "church" believed about eschatology in the decades after AD 70.

- The so-called Great Apostasy spoken of by Jesus and the apostles (Matthew 24:10-12; Luke 18:18; Acts 20:29-30; Romans 16:17-18; 2 Corinthians 11:13-15; 2 Peter 2:1; etc.) had a greater influence on the early Christian church than most people might suspect. Matthew 24:12 indicates that a *majority* (New American Standard Version) of Christians turned away from their faith. This apostasy was a result of false prophets, immorality, and persecution. So the faith became distorted and confused in the decades after AD 70.

- The Hellenization of the church had a great influence. In Romans 11 Paul explained that, contrary to what was being said at the time, God had not cut off the Jews, but the make-up of God's people was in transition. It could well be that because of the Gentile influence in the church, an understanding of Old Testament Hebraic apocalyptic language was lost.

- Silence does not prove anything.

- At least one very important early church father, Eusebius of Caesarea (c. AD 260/263-339/341) expressed clear preterist views in multiple places in his books. While his works lack a comprehensive systematic theology on eschatology, he did indicate a belief that the Second Coming (or at least *a* Second Coming per the Olivet Discourse) occurred in AD 70. As we mentioned in Chapter 1, Eusebius is an important witness because he is considered the Father of Church History. As a church historian, it is likely that Eusebius reflected the views of other early Christians for whom we have no written record. Among several citations from Eusebius that could be presented are these two:

> You have then in this prophecy of the Descent of the Lord among men from heaven, many other things foretold at the same time, the rejection of the Jews, the judgment on their impiety, the destruction of their royal city, the abolition of the worship practiced by them of old according to the Law of Moses; and on the other hand, promises of good for the nations, the knowledge of God, a new ideal of holiness, a new law and teaching coming forth from the land of the Jews. I leave you to see, how wonderful a fulfillment, how wonderful a completion; the prophecy has reached after the Coming of our Savior Jesus Christ.

> When, then, we see what was of old foretold for the nations fulfilled in our own day, and when the lamentation and wailing that was predicted for the Jews, and the burning of the Temple and its utter desolation, can also be seen even now to have occurred according to the prediction, surely we must also agree that the King who was prophesied, the Christ of God, has come, since the signs of His coming have been shown in each instance I have treated to have been clearly fulfilled.[222]

- Other writers in the early church expressed beliefs that certain events *associated* with the Second Coming were fulfilled by AD 70, such as the abomination of desolation, the great tribulation, the last days, the end of the age, the arrival of the kingdom, the arrival of the new heaven and new earth, the arrival of the New Jerusalem, the preaching of the gospel to the whole world, the general resurrection of the dead, the destruction of death, Daniel's 70th week, and the cessation of charismatic gifts. So, the *basics* of full preterism are found in many writings of the apostolic fathers.[223]

We would add some other considerations:

- Christians easily take on faith much that the Bible says happened in the past. For example, Christians never doubt that God created the universe out of nothing. Even though modern big bang science offers confirmation of the biblical account of creation, most Christians do not rely on science to believe in Genesis. They believe it because the Bible says it. Likewise, the Bible teaches that Jesus would come in his first-century generation to gather his own and to judge the living and the dead. The destruction of Jerusalem in AD 70 is *visible* evidence of the *invisible* events the Bible teaches would happen at the same time—resurrection, rapture, judgment, redemption, and the Parousia. Oh ye of little faith, do you not believe? As Jesus said, "Blessed are those who have not seen and yet have believed."

- How do you know that the Parousia was not confirmed or documented by those present? Just because we do not have documentation does not mean that documentation did not exist.

- The book of Revelation itself, to some degree, is a written testimony to the fulfillment of prophecy. We noted in Chapter 9 that John stated in Revelation that he was writing during the tribulation.

- Josephus, Tacitus, Eusebius, as well as the Jewish Talmud all record the fact that God's presence was perceived at the destruction of Jerusalem. They even record that angelic armies were seen in the clouds.[224]

- It should not be too surprising that the early church fathers may have misunderstood the nature of the Second Coming, just as the Jews misunderstood the nature of the First Coming. It was right there in front of them, but they still missed it!

- There are other doctrinal issues for which we have no written record. For example, today's raging debate between believer's baptism versus infant baptism is virtually absent from the ancient record. So, the absence of a coherent explanation of eschatology in the record is not unique.

- People ask, "Why isn't there more agreement among Christians about preterism?" Our response is: Are you kidding? While Christians are in broad agreement on central doctrines, they are, and historically have been, in disagreement over many things! A study of the theological views of the early church shows various beliefs that demonstrate gross misunderstandings of the faith. There was disagreement among the early church fathers on crucially important issues such as the nature of God as well as justification. For example, the doctrines of grace were a rarity among the writings of the early church fathers. Most of the early church fathers were, at least according to available writings, either semi-Pelagian (salvation by works plus grace) or even full Pelagian (salvation by works alone). There is precious little glimmer of any understanding that salvation (regeneration) is by grace through faith (belief) alone and not by any works or actions—as most modern Protestants understand justification. But even today, Christians, from sect to sect, are all over the map on justification. Other important topics on which Christians have misinterpreted (or disingenuously twisted) the Bible include slavery, abortion, homosexuality, evolution and other aspects of science such as geocentricity.[225]

Some other examples that reveal interesting beliefs of the early church fathers include: Origen believed in the pre-existence of souls and castrated himself due to a literal reading of Matthew 19:12. Tertullian succumbed to Montanism, a prophetic movement with Gnostic overtones that was declared a heresy. Demonization of Jews was commonplace in the early centuries of the church. Ignatius, writing around AD 100, made the same mistake as countless other Christians after AD 70, thinking that the time of the end was imminent. (He said, "The last times are come upon us.") Over-literalizing Scripture, Justin Martyr (AD 100-165) expected a literal temple to come down from heaven and set itself up in Jerusalem. These men were great contributors to the faith but were clearly wrong on some pretty major issues. Even today, there are wide-ranging and virulent disagreements among Christians on many, many issues.

- Expanding on the above, James B. Jordan wrote, "We have to remember that we only have a few Church Fathers to draw on. Often Christian scholars have strained mightily to build on evidence from these writings, writings of men clearly not familiar with the facts in other instances. Many of the Fathers were new converts to the faith who wrote apologetics, and who did not know much about Christianity (as can be seen when we compare them with the teachings of the New Testament). What we don't have are reams of sermons preached by pastors in local churches during the first two centuries, and that is the kind of material that would give us an accurate picture of the early church. Finally, though the Church Fathers are 'fathers' in a sense, and are of real value to us, they are also the 'Church Babies' in another sense. All this should be born in mind when it comes to their haphazard testimony. . . ." [226]

- Doctrinal issues can be misunderstood by a large majority, and such misinterpretations often get stuck in the church's psyche. Just consider the questionable views of Roman Catholicism including the veneration of an ever-virgin Mary, purgatory, infallibility of the Pope, transubstantiation, and so forth.

- Persecution would have made it very easy for the first Christians to hope for some sort of earthly relief. This would easily explain why they would have read this hope into the Bible. The human mind, being what it is, can turn desire into an illusion of truth. Take an unrelated issue—abortion. It is scientifically and theologically proven that an unborn child is a human being. Yet, incredibly, by force of will, combined with the force of cultural normalcy, even many professing Christians convince themselves that the child is only "a glob of tissue." They will take the life of a baby in the very place that should be the safest sanctuary—his or her mother's womb. Indeed, statistics show that the rate of abortion may be as high among professing Christians as it is in the population at large.

Ultimately, it does not matter what the early Christian writers said. What matters is what the Bible says.

AD HOMINEM ATTACKS

It is unfortunate that Christianity is so divided on so many issues. But here we are. Vicious attacks from one camp to another are nothing new in Christianity. If you read Martin Luther, for example, you will see some of the most stinging words possible against his detractors.

If the reader is not already aware of the verbal attacks against preterists, he soon will be. These attacks often sound like they are from cornered beasts. But we caution the reader to understand that such attacks are often *ad hominem* attacks. This means that the attacks are appealing to one's prejudices, emotions, or special interests rather than to one's intellect. In other words, an *ad hominem* attack is baseless name-calling.[227]

We have listened to debates and read the attacks against full preterists. The attacks often contain a great deal of anger, which is a sign of frustration in not having the facts on one's side. One should be aware that quite often the arguments against full preterism either misrepresent what we actually believe or are biblically shallow. For example, many of the challenges to full preterism conveniently leave out critical information, such as the time-texts. Be sure to check the arguments for the underlying facts. Test all things.

IS THAT ALL THERE IS?

Our reaction after discovering Covenant Eschatology was one of excited joy. The Bible became a complete book; many problematic passages became resolved. We could see the unity of Scripture that was previously obscured. We rejoiced that Jesus and his disciples were true prophets that we could proclaim without hesitation to the unbelieving world. And our salvation was revealed as complete.

But that is not the reaction of some people. They have this gnawing sense that something disappeared for them. If all is complete, where do we stand now? So let's address this feeling.

Proverbs 13:12 says, "Hope deferred makes the heart sick, but when the desire comes, it is a tree of life." Full preterist author Edward E. Stevens had this to say in light of this passage:

"Jesus promised to return in the first century. Because many of us think he hasn't returned yet, our hearts are indeed made very "sick." The Preterist view is a tree of life to those who hope to enjoy the blessings of Christ's Kingdom. We have that Kingdom now. It arrived in its fully established form when it was taken away from the unbelieving Jews of Jesus' generation and given to the Church. All of Jesus' parables about the nature and growth of that Kingdom apply now. Isaiah 9:7 says, "There will be no end to the increase of His government or of peace, on the throne of David and over his kingdom, to establish it and to uphold it with justice and righteousness from then on and forevermore." Daniel 2 talks about the little stone that becomes a huge mountain and fills the whole world. But I believe the best Biblical description of that on-going spread of the Kingdom's influence in the world is found in Revelation 21-22, where it says,

'The nations will WALK BY ITS LIGHT, and the kings of the earth will BRING THEIR GLORY INTO IT. In the daytime (for there will be no night there) its gates will never be closed; and they will BRING THE GLORY AND THE HONOR OF THE NATIONS INTO IT; and NOTHING UNCLEAN, AND NO ONE WHO PRACTICES ABOMI-NATION AND LYING, SHALL EVER COME INTO IT, but only those whose names are written in the Lamb's book of life. Then he showed me a river of the water of life, clear as crystal, coming from the throne of God and of the Lamb, in the middle of its street. On either side of the river was the tree of life, bearing twelve kinds of fruit, yielding its fruit every month; and the leaves of the tree were FOR THE HEALING OF THE NATIONS. (Rev. 21:24--22:2)'

Notice the words I have put in ALL CAPS above. These are things that indicate the world is still in existence after the New Jerusalem has come down out of heaven to dwell among men. Nations are still walking by its light and bringing their glory into it. The unclean, abominable and liars are still in existence, but are outside and unable to come into this city. The nations are still in existence and continually being healed by the leaves of the tree of life. This passage clearly describes the on-going Kingdom and its healing effects on the nations and cultures of this planet.

Ezekiel 47 talks about the little trickle of water that comes out of the new temple and eventually becomes a flooding river that baptizes all the nations. There is nothing said about that river of water ever diminishing back down to a trickle again. This is a very positive, optimistic and eternally long-term future for humanity. The futurists have nothing to compare with it.

Which gives God more glory? A finite number of people in heaven after the end of human life in the universe? Or a constantly growing number of saints coming into heaven throughout an eternity of human existence? The Kingdom will keep on spreading. Our children will grow up and become leaders in the next generation. They will raise godly children who will become leaders in the generations after that. They will continue taking the Gospel to every nation, saturating the whole world with Biblical principles and Christian culture, so that eventually Christian principles will "take every thought captive" in all the nations of the world the same way it did here in America. (2 Cor. 10:5) No culture can resist it forever. Christ will conquer every stronghold for His Kingdom, just like Ezekiel 47 envisioned. The Church will continue winning souls, multiplying disciples and filling the whole earth with the knowledge of God 'as the waters cover the sea.'" (Isa. 11:9) [228]

Another preterist author is Edward J. Hassertt. Ed's ministry is one to comfort the chronically ill. He himself suffers from chronic pain. But his view of biblical eschatology helps him experience joy:

Preterism is a theology that can bring answers for those who are sick, dying, struggling with faith, oppressed, addicted, and even living in sin. In fact preterism provides the only real answer to these problems since it is the only theology that addresses the whole of scripture, believing the word of God for what it actually says instead of for what men have claimed it has said in the past. . . . True faith is realizing the fulfilled hope we have to live today, in this moment, instead of some escape clause for the future. . . . When we read scripture through preterist eyes, verses we once glossed over and read without understanding spring to life. . . . Once we can realize all things have been fulfilled in Christ, a new joy opens up to us that reveals the vastness of the promise. . . . We find joy in finding new things, new power to live, new spiritual healing, and a new perspective that can only come when the blind man can finally see. . . . Only preterism provides the sound scriptural interpretation to open our eyes to all God has given us. Preterism removes our blindness to see the brightness of the Son and the blessedness of all that surrounds us. The truth in scripture summarized in preterism liberates us from the bondage of the past and postponement of our joy into the future. We are living in Gods Kingdom now with all the blessings He promised. . . .[229]

JESUS SAID THAT NO ONE KNOWS THE DAY OR THE HOUR

In Matthew 24:36, Jesus said: "But of that day and hour no one knows, not even the angels of heaven, but My Father only." This quote is from the Olivet Discourse and is in the context of when Jesus would return. It is surprising how often we hear this objection. The answer is so simple: Though Jesus did not know the day or the hour, He knew that his coming would occur in his generation.

PRETERISM DIMINISHES THE IMPORTANCE OF THE SACRAMENTS

Preterism may diminish the importance of the sacraments, namely communion, based on 1 Corinthians 11:26. But it does so by elevating the finished work of Christ! Yet this does not mean that the Lord's Supper cannot continue to be practiced as wonderful expressions of our faith in Christ's finished work, as these passages suggest: Luke 22:16 and Revelation 3:20.

I STILL BELIEVE IN A FUTURE SECOND COMING

This is a common reaction to the evidence. This objection simply denies the evidence—"Don't confuse me with the facts." We don't have much to say to those who see it and then dismiss it without providing reasons. Let us just suggest that this topic is important enough to avoid letting one's mind hit a mental cul-de-sac. What we ask is that those in this position at least do the following. Make a list of all the Second Coming passages that you think have been fulfilled. And make a second list of those you think are yet future—and why you think so. Sometimes, putting one's thoughts in writing helps to clarify it all.

We have tried to present the facts fairly. For those who may have other questions, there are various websites that offer answers to common objections to fulfilled prophecy. See Appendix E.

If you are a church leader, let us ask you a question. Are you willing to stand up for the truth even if it costs you your position?

Millennialism
Considered

I n this chapter we will review in more detail the theology of millennialism. *Millennium* is a derivation of a Latin word meaning a thousand.
In short, millennialism is the idea that we will have, in the future, a
literal 1,000-year period in which Christ will have returned in bodily
form to reign in person on earth in a political utopia. We will consider
the term millennialism as generally synonymous with premillennialism.
However, postmillennialism shares the idea of a utopian "millennial"
kingdom on earth, and thus can be considered a type of millennialism.

A synonym for millennialism is *chiliasm*, which is from the Greek
form of the word. A similar term that is sometimes seen is *millenari-
anism*, which is the idea of transformative 1,000-year cycles on earth.
This latter term is not necessarily a strictly Christian concept, but is
sometimes used more-or-less interchangeably with these other terms.
It is more correct to say that millennialism is a Christian form of mil-
lenarianism.

HISTORY

Various forms of millennialism have risen and fallen in popularity
throughout church history. It seems to have gained favor with some
early Christians. Many evangelical Christians today have been so steeped
in millennialism that they think it alone is normative and historic. A few
of the early church fathers such as Papias, Irenaeus, Justin Martyr, and

Tertullian seem to have held to some type of millennialist views. Justin Martyr, however, noted in his writings that even though he believed in millennialism, many of his contemporaries did not. It is known that other specific and important early church fathers such as Origen, Caius, Augustine, and Eusebius held views contrary to the millennialists.[230]

Author David Chilton, not being timid, made several rather bold accusations against millennialism. He stated that some early church fathers adopted premillennial literalism because, due to their heathen background, they were unfamiliar with biblical literary genres and imagery. He further made a claim that millennialism "seems to have been originated by the Ebionite arch-heretic Cerinthus, a 'false apostle' who was an opponent of both St. Paul and St. John." [231] On the other hand, there are other theories, including that millennialism had its roots in Jewish documents, that it was picked up by the apostolic father Papias and passed on to Irenaeus. From there the tradition was nurtured as a thread within segments of the church.[232]

There is a legitimate question as to whether the church fathers who are usually cited as being premillennial were premillennial at all, at least in the modern sense of the word. Research by Alan Patrick Boyd (in his master's thesis at Dallas Theological Seminary) concluded that premillennialists in the early church "were a rather limited number." He also discovered that no evidence supports the claim that several of the church fathers who are routinely claimed by dispensationalists as being fellow dispensationalists were even premillennial, much less dispensational. Thus, while dispensationalists will argue this point, no convincing evidence exists to prove that dispensational premillennialism, or anything like it, was ever taught in the church before the nineteenth century. Any evidence for such claims is sketchy at best.[233]

The issue seems to have been resolved by the fourth century as the church itself reportedly rejected millennialism at both the Ecumenical Council of Constantinople (AD 381) and the Council of Ephesus (AD 431). The Nicene Creed (AD 381) states that Christ's *kingdom shall have no end*, an obvious rejection of millennialism.[234]

The most prominent view throughout most of church history seems to have been amillennialism, but each of the various views, as discussed in Chapter 3—except dispensationalism—has been present in various forms since the beginning of post-apostolic church history. No single view has been able to consistently dominate. Postmillennialism, for example, was in the ascendancy in America from the Revolutionary War until the Civil War, in part because of the famous Puritan preacher Jonathan Edwards. John M. Brenner stated:

Postmillennial ideas of gradual progress toward a time of unparalleled peace and prosperity fit well with American pragmatism and can-do spirit, the American sense of destiny, and enlightenment optimism based on trust in science and technology. In addition, in the early nineteenth century Postmillennialists saw the success of revivals and mission efforts as signs of the approach of the millennium. They took note of the decline of the influence and power of the papacy and the threats of Islam. The Second Great Awakening (mid 1790s to c. 1840) spawned movements aimed at ridding society of various evils so that the millennium might be realized. They believed that "the golden age would see the culmination of current reform efforts to end slavery, oppression, and war." Social activism and political action were means by which Christians might bring about the realization of God's promises. The abolitionist movement, temperance movement, and women's movement flowed out of these postmillennial concerns.[235]

John Calvin (1509-1564) in his *Institutes of the Christian Religion* said that millennialism is a "fiction" that is "too childish either to need or to be worth a refutation." [236] Lutherans also formally rejected millennialism in *The Augsburg Confession (Article XVII)*, as did Martin Luther (1483-1546) himself. We believe that both Catholic and Protestant leadership had good reasons to soundly reject millennialism. However, it is also correct to say that, despite the strong views of highly influential theologians from Augustine to Calvin, speculations and false prophecies about the end times have been part of church history since the first century. These speculations are not always associated with millennialism, but often are.[237]

While such speculation has continued, the church had more or less suppressed the idea of a literal millennium until the Anglo-Irish preacher John Nelson Darby (1800-1882) arrived on the scene. Darby, whom we introduced in Chapter 11 as being associated with the modern rapture theory, developed an expanded version of millennialism which is now called dispensationalism, or dispensational premillennialism, or simply Darbyism.

Darby, an Irish Plymouth Brethren, traveled extensively to continental Europe, New Zealand, Canada, and the United States in an attempt to make converts to his ideas. His systems eventually caught hold in America, and today many American evangelicals hold to dispensationalism. Baptists, Pentecostals and other charismatics, as well as most Bible churches, are among those who usually believe in dispensationalism.

It may be noteworthy that it was during this same period in the early 1800s that a variety of other legalistic, sectarian, or cultic movements began in America—such as Seventh Day Adventism, Mormonism, and the Jehovah's Witnesses. It is interesting that Jehovah's Witnesses, having gotten their inspiration from Seventh Day Adventism, foisted itself on the world with a six volume set of books entitled *Millennial Dawn*.

Charles Haddon Spurgeon (1834-1892), a famous contemporary of Darby, published a criticism of Darby and his views, which was not limited to Darby's millennialism. Included in Spurgeon's criticism was that Darby and the Plymouth Brethren rejected the vicarious purpose of Christ's obedience, as well as imputed righteousness. Spurgeon viewed these matters of such importance and so central to the gospel that it led him to this statement about the rest of the beliefs of the Plymouth Brethren: "With the deadly heresies entertained and taught by the Plymouth Brethren, in relation to some of the most momentous of all the doctrines of the gospel, and to which I have adverted at some length, I feel assured that my readers will not be surprised at any other views, however unscriptural and pernicious they may be, which the Darbyites have embraced and zealously seek to propagate." [238]

Dispensationalism was given a few boosts after Darby. Cyrus I. Scofied published a study Bible in 1909 which supported dispensationalism. Then, U.S. evangelist and Bible teacher Lewis Sperry Chafer (1871–1952), who was influenced by Scofield, founded Dallas Theological Seminary in 1924. This seminary has become the flagship of dispensationalism in America. (Isn't it interesting how one man in history can ultimately have such an influence on the thinking of an entire body of believers? It must make one wonder about the validity of other cherished beliefs, especially given the myriad of irreconcilable opinions about various matters of theology within Christendom.)

In 1970 millennialist Hal Lindsey authored a book entitled *The Late Great Planet Earth*, which subsequently had some thirty printings. He seduced millions of gullible Christians into thinking that the end of the world was near. From 1995 to 2007 millennialists Tim LaHaye and Jerry B. Jenkins published the *Left Behind* series, which served to reconfirm to another generation of Bible-ignorant Christians that the rapture and the millennial kingdom were imminent. And of course, in 2011, another failed prediction of the end of the world by millennialist Harold Camping caught the attention of the media everywhere, again embarrassing Christianity. We never seem to have a dearth of false teachers.

The late 1800s and early 1900s was a period which saw liberalism and skepticism grow within the Christian church. Partly under the leadership of Dallas Theological Seminary, a strong reaction to liberalism erupted. The dual concepts of millennialism and conservatism became merged in the minds of many, and millennialism became the test for orthodoxy. Anyone who refused to take the book of Revelation literally, thus disagreeing with millennialism, became labeled a "liberal." This charge is still made today. This charge is preposterous, insulting, and damaging to the Christian cause.

DISPENSATIONAL PROPHECY

The term dispensationalism actually comes from the notion that there are distinct dispensations or time periods in history. Dispensationalists usually see seven such periods, but some see more or less than seven. For example, the patriarchal period, the Mosaic Law period, and the millennium appear in different systems. The exact breakdown is not crucial for us to understand. These dispensations are of less importance than the ideas that come along with the dispensational system.

Dispensationalism is a complicated system, which we think is just one factor that militates against it. We suspect that many Christians abiding in dispensational churches do not really grasp the whole system, but accept it as a given because of what these churches insist is correct. Members are content to let their leaders feed them news items that assure them that the end is near.

But to simplify, dispensationalism added this extra notion onto premillennialism: Israel and the church are separate and distinct entities today. They are so separate that Jews and Christians have separate paths to their eternal destinies. Jews are saved by works, Christians by faith.

Dispensationalists teach that Jesus offered the Jews a millennial kingdom on earth. But once it was rejected, Jesus withdrew the offer and died on the cross. (This should be a radical surprise to most Christians, especially since one cannot find biblical support for it.)

Most dispensationalists believe that the church age (in which we live now) is a prophetically unforeseen parenthetical period of thousands of years between the 69th and 70th weeks of Daniel's prophecy of seventy weeks (Daniel 9:24-27). The seventieth week is identified with a future seven-year tribulation period that precedes the millennium. God's program for Israel will be resumed at this time. While there are differences of opinion among dispensationalists, what follows below is a composite of their scheme as to how the future is supposed to work out.[239]

Christ will remove all born-again believers from the earth in the rapture. That is, the saints who are alive at that time will be "translated" into resurrection bodies and then be caught up to meet the Lord in the air (1 Thessalonians 4:13-18; 1 Corinthians 15:51-54), along with the "dead in Christ." The "dead in Christ" are defined as all the deceased saints who were saved after Pentecost (Acts 2). At the judgment seat of Christ, these believers will be rewarded for good works and faithful service during their time on earth or will lose rewards (but not eternal life) for lack of service and obedience (1 Corinthians 3:11-15; 2 Corinthians 5:10).

Meanwhile, back on earth, the Antichrist (the Beast) will come into power and will sign a covenant with Israel for seven years (Daniel 9:27). This seven-year period of time is the tribulation. During the tribulation, there will be terrible wars, famines, plagues, and natural disasters. God will be pouring out his wrath against sin, evil, and wickedness. The tribulation will include the appearance of the four horsemen of the Apocalypse, and the seven seal, trumpet, and bowl-judgments in the book of Revelation.

> The tribulation will be a holocaust in which some two-thirds of Jews will be killed. We parenthetically make a point here. Most dispensationalists state a very high regard for Israel and the Jews. But when they pray for "Jesus to come soon," the logical inference is that they are really asking for a soon holocaust of the Jews! This seems more than a bit anti-Semitic to us!

Anyway, those Jewish and Gentile Christians that are raptured will thus avoid the tribulation. While most dispensationalists are "pre-tribulationists," some are "post-tribulationists" or "mid-tribulationists" depending on when they think the rapture will occur relative to the seven-year tribulation.

The worst part of the tribulation begins about halfway through the seven years after the Antichrist has broken the peace covenant with Israel and makes war against her. The Antichrist will commit "the abomination of desolation" and set up an image of himself to be worshipped in the Jerusalem temple (Daniel 9:27; 2 Thessalonians 2:3-10), which will have been rebuilt. The second half of the tribulation is known as "the great tribulation" (Revelation 7:14) and "the time of Jacob's trouble" (Jeremiah 30:7).

At the end of the seven-year tribulation, the Antichrist will launch a final attack on Jerusalem, culminating in the battle of Armageddon. Jesus Christ will return, destroy the Antichrist and his armies, and cast them into the lake of fire (Revelation 19:11-21). Christ will then bind Satan in the abyss/pit for the millennium (Revelation 20:3).

Christ will then usher in the millennium, a literal 1,000-year period. Dispensationalists believe that the millennium is the *kingdom of God* of which the Bible speaks. This reign of Christ fulfills the promises, including the land promises, made to Israel in the Old Testament. (The land promises include Genesis 15:18-21; Genesis 28:13; Exodus 23:31; Deuteronomy 1:8.)

So Christ will set up a national kingdom on earth primarily for those Jews who have survived the tribulation. Depending on the version of dispensationalism, the vast majority of remaining Jews will have converted to Christianity (Romans 11:25-27). Those Jews who remain in unbelief will be put to death and not permitted to enter the millennium (Ezekiel 20:33-38).

There is, thankfully, provision for surviving Gentiles. All Gentiles who were not raptured and also survived the tribulation will be judged (Matthew 25:31-46); the sheep (saved) will enter the millennium and the goats (lost) will be cast into everlasting fire and condemnation. The saved Israelites, and probably the saved living Gentiles, will therefore enter the millennium in their natural, physical, unglorified bodies on earth. In any case, Christ will reign in this utopian earthly theocracy from his throne in Jerusalem for a literal 1,000 years.

Those who have entered the millennium in their natural bodies will marry and reproduce. Though they will live much longer than they would have prior to Christ's coming, at least some of them will die. This period is a time of unparalleled economic prosperity, political peace, and spiritual renewal. Worship in the millennium will center on a rebuilt temple in Jerusalem in which animal sacrifices will be offered. These sacrifices, however, may not be propitiatory, argue some dispensationalists, but rather "memorial offerings" in remembrance of Christ's death. Although dissimilarities exist, the millennial kingdom will see a virtual revival of much of the Levitical systems described in the Old Testament.

Meanwhile a massive heavenly Jerusalem, as described in Revelation 21:1-22:5, has descended to hover just above Palestine, where it will remain for the duration of the millennium. This New Jerusalem will be above the earth, in the air, shedding its light and glory thereon. Christ will resurrect the saved of all ages, except of course, for the "in Christ" saints who were resurrected or raptured seven years earlier and who presumably have been in heaven temporarily.

The heavenly Jerusalem will become the residence of believers who are not on earth, though there is some disagreement who will be on earth and who will be in the heavenly Jerusalem. In general, all resurrected saints (i.e., Old Testament saints, Christians raptured before the tribulation, and believers who came to faith during the tribulation but were put to death by the Antichrist) will live in the New Jerusalem. Some say that the earth will be populated only by the Jews who survived the tribulation period. And some believe that there is opportunity to go back and forth between earth and the heavenly city at least for certain residents. Resurrected saints will play some role in Christ's rule on the earth; their primary activity, however, will be in the New Heavenly Jerusalem.

Children will be born to those believers (both Jew and Gentile) who entered the earthly millennial kingdom in their natural bodies. Many will come to faith in Christ and be saved. Those who persist in unbelief will be restrained by the righteous rule and government of Christ. Depending on the interpreter, death will be rare except as a penal measure for overt sin.

The spirits of the wicked millennial residents who die will go to hell to await the final judgment. The millennial saints who die during the millennium apparently may be immediately resurrected and will enter the heavenly city as resurrected saints, or others say they have to wait till the end of the millennium to be resurrected. Because Christ is physically reigning and Satan is imprisoned in the abyss, evil is almost unknown during the millennial kingdom. The Jews continue to earn their eternal life by their works. (This relegation to slavery under the law is certainly another anti-Semitic aspect of dispensationalism.)

At the end of the millennium, Satan will be loosed from the abyss/pit and will gather all unbelievers in a final military revolt which Christ will quickly put down. The earthly millennial saints still living will be judged and translated into resurrected bodies of the eternal state. More resurrections occur—that of believers who died during the millennial kingdom (if they were not already resurrected immediately upon their death as indicated previously). Also the unsaved dead of all ages will be resurrected and condemned with Satan to the lake of fire for eternity (Revelation 20:7-10). The new heavens and the new earth will be formed, the heavenly city will descend to earth, and eternity will begin. There will be no more sin, sorrow, or death.

Even in eternity the Old Testament saints and the New Testament church are distinct and separate according to dispensationalists. At least according to one version of dispensationalism, the New Testament church is to spend eternity in heaven. But the Old Testament saints ("seed") will spend eternity on the new earth. (Yes, indeed—segregation of the saints in the eternal state.)

More recent dispensationalists have put the saints of all ages together on the new earth in eternity, but maintain their dichotomy throughout eternity by excluding Old Testament saints, tribulation saints, and millennial saints from the body and bride of Christ.

(Confused yet?)

The New Jerusalem heavenly city of Revelation 21 is a point of considerable interest. Like most other things in Revelation, it is interpreted literally by dispensationalists. This is a city prepared by God that is a fully functioning real city that has a length, width, and height of 12,000 furlongs/stadia—about 1,500 miles. Some interpreters see this as a cube; others see it as a pyramid. But in either case, it is enormous! It is almost as large as the moon, which is about 2,100 miles in diameter. It descends out of heaven to come to rest over the earth. It has literal foundation stones, but only a single street.

If the New Jerusalem was a literal city, it would cover the entire Middle East including all of Egypt, Turkey, Syria, Jordan, Israel, Saudi Arabia, and a huge section of the Mediterranean Sea as well as several parts of other neighboring countries—not to mention extending 1,200 miles *beyond* the International Space Station which is in a 220 mile low orbit. Not trying to be too facetious, this image immediately conjures up legitimate questions about gravitational mechanics. Would this enormous appendage wobble the earth?

Let us be perfectly frank, with due respect for our many brothers who believe all this, it is so bizarre that if it were not being taught in Christian churches it would certainly be considered cultic, or science fiction. But this craziness is where you can end up if you decide in advance to take everything in the Bible in a wooden literal fashion while completely misunderstanding Hebraic figures of speech, and ignoring the critical, but ubiquitous time-statements.

One of the main twentieth-century proponents of this New Jerusalem literalism was John Walvoord. This gentleman was president of Dallas Theological Seminary from 1952 to 1986. He was a leading spokesman of dispensationalism, and the author of over thirty books, including *The Revelation of Jesus Christ*, in which he discussed the literal New Jerusalem in detail.[240] Even very intelligent men have gotten caught up in millennial madness and its fantasies.

The reader should now be able to make a considered determination whether millennialism is a reasonable interpretation of the Bible or whether it is forced and fanciful. But let's dig a little deeper into the theology of dispensationalism. While the discussion below may seem like an unrelated detour, we will see that the errors of dispensational eschatology relate to other errors of the dispensational system. The discussion centers on *soteriology* (how we are saved, that is, how we are "justified" before God), which is an important topic to consider in *any* book about theology.

DISPENSATIONAL SOTERIOLOGY

We think dispensationalists make two critical errors. The first is to take the Bible in a wooden literal sense, in defiance of standard interpretive methodology and often in defiance of how the authors intended it. The second is to make a separation between ethnic Israel and the church. According to at least some dispensational systems, God has two different people groups for whom He has distinct promises, purposes, and destinies. This is a critical and profound error.

Various factors contribute to what we believe are these errors. An important contributing cause is that dispensationalists fail to see the continuity between the Old and New Testaments. They see in black and white that Old Testament Jews were saved by works and New Testament Christians are saved by grace through faith. But the Bible does not make the distinction as sharply as they make. Redemption through Jesus Christ is the unifying purpose of the Bible.

For example, Paul in Romans 4 argues forcefully that Abraham was justified by faith. Also we note that if the Old Testament saints were saved by works, heaven would not contain *any* of them. The Bible teaches that all men are sinners and fall short of the glory of God (Romans 3:23). Both Moses and David, two of God's greatest servants, were murderers. It is doubtful that such men earned their way to heaven!

Though there isn't consistency among them, many dispensationalists historically are what theologians call *antinomian*. In other words, they believe that works, law, and obedience have no necessary part at all in the salvation or life of Christians. But this is a shallow view. While the New Testament insists that we are saved by grace through faith apart from the law (Ephesians 2:8-9, Titus 3:4-7, etc.), it places great importance on obedience as an evidentiary part of a true saving faith.

Let us make a few key points about the debate between faith and works in salvation, which potentially could be a unifying list for biblical Christians (Protestants and Catholics alike):

- When the Bible says that we are not saved by "works" (Romans, Galatians, Ephesians, etc.) it is generally referring to works of the Mosaic Law, that is, the Old Testament civil and ceremonial law. The New Testament abrogated the ceremonial, dietary, and civil laws of the Old Testament (Acts 10:12-15; Romans 14:17; Colossians 2:11-16; 1 Timothy 4:1-5). The writer of Hebrews (Hebrews 10:1-4) stated that the Old Testament sacrificial system was never effective in forgiving sins (cf. Galatians 3:11). But this does not mean that obedience to God's *moral* commands is unimportant. Jesus, in fact, strengthened biblical commands for Christian living.

- When the Bible says that we are saved by believing in Jesus (John 3:16, etc.), it is implied in the original Greek language that to believe "in" (Greek word *eis*) Jesus means more than intellectual assent. It means to believe "into" Jesus. In other words, it means to accept what Jesus says so *fully and completely* that we will obey his commands, however imperfectly as we humans are able.

- An important passage is James 2:14-26, which says straightforwardly that we are not justified by faith alone. But we have some clues on how to understand this. James 2:14, as translated in the New International Version of the Bible says, "Can *such* faith [a faith without good deeds] save him?" The New King James Version says, "Can *that* faith save him?" This suggests that there is a saving faith and a false faith. James also used the phrase, "If someone *says* he has faith (but does not have works) . . . "

implying that just because people *say* they have faith does not mean that they really do have a sincere *saving* faith. James said that even the demons have what we might call "head knowledge" of God, but they do not have the type of faith that **trusts** in God. James went on to explain in this passage that faith without works is "dead." We conclude that James was telling us that a work-less faith does not save us, and that works demonstrate a true saving faith.

The Bible teaches that it is only by the grace and power of God that man can respond in faith and obedience (Psalm 16:2; John 15:5; Romans 1:16; 1 Corinthians 12:3-6; 15:10; Ephesians 1:3-12; 2:1-10; Philippians 1:6; 2:13; 1 Timothy 1:14; Hebrews 13:21). Yet, respond he must. A true saving faith will show itself by certain characteristics. Indeed, it could even be put a bit stronger. In order to reach heaven Christians must:

- persevere in believing the gospel (Matthew 10:22; Romans 11:17-24; 1 Corinthians 15:2; Colossians 1:21-23; Hebrews 3:6-14)

- love God and other believers (John 15:9-17; 1 Corinthians 13:2-3; Galatians 5:6)

- and live godly lives, however imperfectly (Matthew 7:16-22; 25:31-46; John 15:9-17; Romans 2:1-16; 3:31; 2 Thessalonians 1:8; Hebrews 3:13; 10:35-36; 12:14; 1 Peter 4:17-19; 1 John 2:2-6, 29; 3:3-10) [241]

Here's the point. Dispensationalists are guilty of teaching *easy believism*—or at least this is a rational conclusion from their theology. Easy believism is the view that persons are to be regarded as Christians who have made professions of faith, but whose lives are unchanged. Easy-believism is a potential problem throughout Christendom today, but it is *imbedded* in dispensational theology. This view is incompatible with biblical teaching. Both God and the believer are fully active in the believer's life, and active at the same time. God is sovereignly active and man is responsively active, even though the *ability and will to be so active is God-given.*

Crenshaw and Gunn, in their book on dispensationalism, state that some dispensationalists even teach that someone who *in the past* believed in Jesus, but no longer believes, may still go to heaven.[242] This too is certainly inconsistent with biblical teaching. Clearly, one must persevere in the faith to reach heaven.

The author of the book you are reading comes from Reformed and Lutheran backgrounds. But all traditions within the historic orthodox Christian faith teach that one must have a *living* faith in order to be saved—not a dead faith. This is true of Calvinists, Lutherans, Arminians, and Roman Catholics.[243]

At the center of the debate among the various groups is the nature of man's free will. Despite the certainty that various denominations claim to possess about this, we will never understand perfectly (on this side of heaven) how man's free will intersects with God's sovereignty. So Christians should show a measure of charity toward each other on this topic. However, we can affirm with certainty that the Bible teaches that we are **saved by God's grace through a living faith in Jesus Christ**.

Grover Dunn does a credible job summarizing the relationship between faith and works from the Reformed (and we believe biblical) perspective:

"Genuine saving faith is faith that progressively bears the fruit of holiness and good works (James 2:17; Ephesians 2:10; Hebrews 12:14). The saved then are, as a rule, those who do good before God (John 5:29; Romans 2:7; Ephesians 2:10) but the saved are not saved by means of or because of the good they do (Titus 3:5; Ephesians 2:8-9). . . . Every professed Christian has the God-given responsibility to work out his own salvation with fear and trembling (Philippians 2:12), but God works in His people's lives to enable them to will and to work according to His good pleasure (1 Corinthians 12:4-6; 15:10; Philippians 2:13; Hebrews 13:21). God unconditionally gives His chosen people the spiritual ability necessary to meet the conditions for receiving the blessings of the covenant. . . . Without faith, it is impossible to please God (Hebrews 11:6), and the natural, non-regenerate man is totally unable to please God (Romans 8:8; 1 Corinthians 2:14)." [244]

The Bible teaches that mankind has a sinful or "fleshly" nature which is universal and runs deep: Genesis 6:5, 8:21; 1 Kings 8:46; Job 14:1-4; 25:2-6; Psalm 14; 51:3-5; 53:1-3; 58:3-5; 143:1-2; Proverbs 14:12; Ecclesiastes 7:20; Isaiah 53:6; 55:8-9; 59:2; 64:6; Jeremiah 17:9; Daniel 9:1-11; Mark 7:20-23; Romans 3:9-20; 5:12-21; 7:13-25; 8:5-8; 14:23; Galatians 5:16-21; Ephesians 2:1-3; James 2:10-11; 1 John 1:8-10. The reader would benefit enormously by taking the time to look up these passages.

This is utterly crucial to understanding Christianity, and thus is germane to our discussion on eschatological promise. To miss the truth that all men are inherently sinful is to miss the distinction between Christianity and every other worldview or religion. Every other system teaches that man is basically good, or is at least perfectible through law and instruction. The gospel itself makes little sense if one does not grasp the sinful nature of mankind. Christianity is unique in its teaching that man is basically sinful, and thus critically in need of a Savior.[245]

Nobody is good enough to reach heaven by his or her works. So, both Old Testament and New Testament people are saved, that is they enter heaven, *by the same way*—by God's grace through a living faith. While the Old Testament saints did not know Jesus in the personal way that Christians do now (Christ having presented Himself on earth and made his eternal dwelling in us), their salvation rested on belief in God's covenant promises, including that of the promised Messiah.

We understand that the theological dichotomy between faith and works is tricky. There is a "tension" here. Theologians have long wrestled with this relationship. Over 240 times in the Bible we find people being proclaimed as *blameless, upright, righteous, guiltless*, or *above reproach*. See such passages as Psalm 119:1; Luke 1:6; Philippians 2:15; 1 Thessalonians 4:3-8; 1 Timothy 3:1-13; 5:3-8; 6:14; Titus 1:6; 1 John 3:4-10. How can this be if we are really depraved?

The concept of *blamelessness* is usually in the context of the avoidance of certain listed *major* sins—for example, sexual sin and lack of brotherly love. It is also found in the context of Christ's efficacious work making us *appear* blameless in God's eyes (Romans 3:22; 4:5-11, 22-24; 1 Corinthians 1:30; 2 Corinthians 5:21; Ephesians 1:4; Philippians 3:9; Colossians 1:22; 3:1-5; 1 John 1:5-9). This latter context is the concept of "imputed righteousness."

Elsewhere in the Bible, however, we find a broader understanding of sin that goes much deeper than the obvious "big" sins. In 1 Timothy 1:15 Paul, this giant of the faith, admitted that he was the "chief of sinners." In Romans 7:13-25 Paul discussed his own inability to shake his sinful proclivities. In Ephesians 2:3 he explained that men are *by nature* children of God's wrath. In Matthew 5:28 and Mark 7:15-23 Jesus taught that our sin runs deep; it is not the external things that defile a man but what is on the inside.

The truth is that down deep we all have tendencies to be conniving, spiteful, covetous, lying, lustful, and selfish creatures. It is the human condition. What the Bible teaches about our sinful condition is verified by observation. Just look in the mirror—or at your children, who need to be *taught* good manners and behavior. Our *thoughts* betray us before an omniscient God. Even our good deeds are often tainted by motivation of self-aggrandizement or self-worth rather than true selfless compassion. And when the constraints of biblical morality are removed, the evil tendencies in mankind easily flourish—for which there is no shortage of evidence.

So there are certain obvious and important big sins and bad lifestyle choices for which a person can be considered "blameless" if he resists them, but this is merely being blameless on one level. One can never overcome his sinful ("fleshly") *nature*. No one is without guilt; no one is good *enough*. No difference exists in the nature of Old Testament people and New Testament people as to our sinful nature.

The dichotomy established by dispensationalists between how Old Testament believers are saved and New Testament believers are saved is a false dichotomy. Their theology almost makes it appear that there are two different types of people and two different Gods—an Old Testament God and a New Testament God. But the Bible teaches that every sinful human who has ever lived is saved by the same God in the same way (Acts 15:8-11; Hebrews 11), even though the emphasis on grace over law came to its fullest fruition in the New Testament.

The New Testament church is not a side branch of Judaism. Redemptive history is not a fork in the road but a straight line. The Bible describes how believing Gentiles were *grafted in* as the Israel of God (Romans 11; Galatians 3-6; Ephesians 1-3; Hebrews 8-12). The Jew-Gentile church simply *became* the Israel of God. Those Jews who rejected Christ were *broken off* because of unbelief (Romans 11:11-24). The New Testament is about the finished work of Christ in the first century. The hope of Israel was and is Christ (Romans 9 and 15). The distinction that dispensationalists make between Israel and the church after AD 70 is a false distinction.

We must also comment on the land promises to Israel upon which millennialists put so much importance. These promises are instrumental to their belief that Israel will inherit a new earth in the millennium. But this is all based on an incomplete reading of the Bible. In the Old Testament (Genesis 15:18-21; Genesis 28:13; Exodus 23:31; Deuteronomy 1:8) God gave an "eternal" land promise to Israel. Israel received all of the land promised to Abraham in Joshua 21:43-45; 23:14-15. But continuity of the land covenant was clearly conditioned upon covenant obedience (Genesis 17:7-9; Deuteronomy 4:25-26; Deuteronomy chapter 28, Ezekiel 37:24-25). Israel failed the test and broke the covenant.

The land promise was one of *rest*, which is ultimately fulfilled in Christ—in the better, heavenly country—the New Jerusalem (Hebrews 4:8-9; 11:10, 14-16; 13:14). To make the ultimate meaning of the land promise literal—which not only premillennialists but postmillennialists do as well—is to carnalize the promises of God, to diminish his holiness, and to marginalize Christ's finished work.

Dispensationalists make a further error. They assume that God's election of fleshly Israel, as his people, was one of salvation. It is not. There is no reason to believe that Israel as a nation, or all Jews, will enter heaven. The election of Israel was one of service and example—not of salvation. Deuteronomy 28 (cf. Leviticus 26) makes it clear that Israel would be cursed for disobedience, and there is no doubt that neither the nation of Israel nor any of its people met God's standard of holiness and perfection. Quoting Eric Adams,

> For dispensationalists, religion plays no role in determining who is Jewish. An atheist Jew is still a Jew, and therefore, an heir of the promises. A Gentile convert to Judaism is not a Jew and therefore, is not an heir of the promises. The problem with this paradigm is that it does not fit the Scriptures. Even in the Old Testament, Israel was not a fixed entity based strictly upon blood [Esther 8:17]. Israel was always subject to grafting and pruning. From the beginning, unbelievers were pruned out of Israel and lost their inheritance. Ishmael, Saul, Absalom, and countless others were cut off from the promises because of unbelief.
>
> From the beginning, believing Gentiles were grafted into Israel and became heirs of the promises to Abraham. Rahab and Ruth are the preeminent examples.[246]

Many Jews today are not ethnic Jews. And no Jew can clearly trace his or her lineage since the genealogical records were destroyed with the temple in AD 70. This whole dispensational idea of salvation by blood is miserably flawed.[247]

By the way, we emphatically maintain that there is nothing about the year 1948 (when a new Israeli state was formed) that has any connection to Bible prophecy. Nothing in the Bible predicts a literal reconstitution of the biblical land promises, a rebuilt temple, reinstitution of temple sacrifices, and so forth. The modern nation of Israel is not even a religious state. If anything, it is *un*religious, as it tolerates persecution of Christians.

Christian America's political support of Israel should not be because of fulfillment of prophecy, but because it is a democracy in the midst of tyrannical states. Period. While we as Christians recognize the historic Jewish people as our spiritual forefathers, we honor modern Israel for its politics. The issue is political, not religious. Nothing in the Bible supports the dispensational craziness known as Christian Zionism, which seems to have arisen out of a mistaken sense that the destruction of Jerusalem in AD 70 was an injustice.[248]

The errors of dispensationalist teaching—indeed of all millennialists' teaching—are serious. First, they are not teaching the doctrine of justification correctly, potentially damning to hell those who listen to them. Second, they typically refuse to bring the gospel to the Jews because they think the Jews cannot be saved by the gospel—an extraordinary error! Third, they often tend to retreat from the culture because of their Jesus-is-coming-soon/the rapture-is-just-around-the-corner mentality. And fourth, since Jesus is not now ruling the world (and only will during the millennium), they assume that Satan is ruling the world now. To Quote Crenshaw, "How anyone could read the Bible and believe that Satan is the King of Kings and Lord of Lords is beyond me."[249]

Retreat and pessimism are hallmarks of millennialism. Millennialism is, at least implicitly, a false gospel, especially the dispensational form of millennialism that destroys the unity and coherency of Scripture. It is also dangerous to society, which is in desperate need of biblical truth. It is dangerous in both the spiritual sense and in the societal sense. Millennial theology is both impotent and threatening. Here is a summary list of some of the numerous problems we see with millennialism:

- It contradicts Scripture.

- It places the Christian hope on some speculative ideas about the future, rather than in Christ's atonement and finished work on the cross and final redemption in AD 70.

- At best, it is a distraction to Christian theology. At worst it is a serious error (Deuteronomy 18:20-22; Matthew 7:15-23). It is potentially a different gospel promising a misleading hope (2 Corinthians 11:1-4; Galatians 1:6).

- It is essentially the same error that the first-century Jews made concerning their expected Messiah, turning Him into a political figure in a materialistic earthly kingdom.

- It engenders a false concept of the kingdom of Christ. Premillennialists say that the kingdom of God is an earthly kingdom that begins only when Christ "comes again." But the Bible teaches that the kingdom of God is not, in fact, an earthly kingdom at all but a spiritual kingdom, and that it began with Christ's ministry in the first century (Daniel 2:44; Matthew 3:2; 4:17; 10:7; 12:24-29; 21:43; Mark 9:1; Luke 10:8; 11:20; 21:29-33; 22:30; John 3:5; 4:21-26; 6:15; 18:36; Colossians 1:13; Revelation 1:4-9). Millennialist belief diminishes Christ, his work, and his teachings.

- It leads people to look upon the Bible as an obscure and fanciful book.

- It confuses the important Christian distinctive that man is inherently sinful and incapable of utopian perfection.

- It relies too much on a single obscure passage of the Bible—Revelation 20, perhaps the most symbolic passage in the most symbolic book of the Bible.

- While it takes passages literally which were intended to be understood symbolically, it takes other passages that were clearly meant to be understood literally and gives them unintelligible meanings. For example, "soon" can mean its opposite "not soon, in the far away future." "Near" can mean "distant."

- The teaching that "Jesus is always coming soon" tends to make Christians forget their responsibilities on earth, functioning to justify social irresponsibility.

- Dispensationalism is logically anti-Semitic. While dispensationalists hold a warm view for Jews and Israel, when they pray for "Jesus to come soon" they are really praying for a Great Tribulation in which two-thirds of Israelis will be slaughtered in a holocaust, before the establishment of the utopian kingdom. Further, Jews, in their view, remain slaves to the law.

- Dispensationalists deny the clear biblical teaching that the gospel is for everybody, both Jew and Gentile (John 14:6; Romans 1:16; 2:28-29; 10:12; Galatians 3:28-29; 4:24-31; 6:15-16; Colossians 3:11; Hebrews 12:12-29; 1 Peter 2:5-10; Revelation 3:9).

- Dispensationalists also believe that the Jerusalem temple will be rebuilt, and animal sacrifices will be reinstituted. The dispensational interpretation of Ezekiel 40-48 notwithstanding, no Bible passage warrants such an idea; and worse, it implicitly suggests that Christ died in vain (Galatians 2:21).

- Millennialism is a breeding ground for false prophets.

As put by Don Preston, "Millennialism turns the shadow into the substance, the temporary into the permanent, the substance into the shadow, and the eternal into the temporary." [250]

Here is how this discussion ties to eschatology: Dispensationalists miss the covenantal thread that runs through the Bible. This covenantal theme unifies Scripture, not only for eschatology but also other aspects of theology, including soteriology. Though other futurists miss aspects of this, for dispensationalists the *error is comprehensive*.

Dispensationalists are not monolithic in their theology. Fortunately, many of them are moving away from some of their most egregious errors. But all futurist systems implicitly teach that our salvation is not complete until a yet-to-be fulfilled Second Coming. Preterism teaches that our salvation, and release from the bondage of sin, is indeed complete, as we discussed in Chapters 10 and 13.

We're not quite ready to let dispensationalists off the hook. We challenge dispensationalists further with the questions in Appendix C. If you have a dispensational pastor, or have dispensational friends, any of these questions can be employed to challenge and advance their theological understanding.[251]

Conclusion: Our Hope and Call for Renewal

OUR HOPE

Let's put eschatology in its proper place. It is important as it plays a greater, albeit different, role in the Bible than most Christians think. It is an integral part of Jesus' promises. It is part of the gospel because our salvation hope rests on the totality of God's promises. The gospel—the good news—is where we stand or fall as Christians. Let's understand what the gospel is. The *core* of the gospel is clearly defined in Scripture:

> **The gospel is the perfect life, substitutionary death, and resurrection of Jesus Christ, which is the power of God unto salvation for all who believe.**
> (*1 Corinthians 15:1-11; Romans 1:16; Ephesians 1:13-14; Colossians 1:22-23*)

In this lies the foundation of our hope. Everything else, however good and important, is secondary. The Bible teaches that our hope in heaven rests fundamentally on Christ's resurrection, but also on the *general resurrection*, which we believe are both facts of history (Daniel 12; Matthew 25:31-34; Acts 23:6; 24:15; Romans 6:5; 1 Corinthians 15; Philippians 3:8-11; 1 Peter 1:3; Revelation 20; etc.).

As solidified by the preterist view, believers may have confidence that when we die we will immediately begin eternity in heaven with Jesus. For the record, here are passages about heaven which the reader may want to take time to examine: Nehemiah 9:6; Job 19:26; Psalm 23:6;

33:13-14; 89:5; 103:4; Daniel 12:1-2; Matthew 5:8, 12; 6:9, 19-20; 8:11; 18:10; 22:30; Mark 12:25; 16:19; Luke 6:23; John 1:32; 3:13-16; 6:38; 11:24-26; 14:1-6; 17:24; Romans 8:11; 1 Corinthians 2:9; 13:12; 15:12-20, 35-54; 2 Corinthians 4:14-18; 5:1-10; 12:1-4; Ephesians 1:20; 4:10; Philippians 1:19-23; 3:10-14, 20-21; Colossians 1:5, 20; 3:2; 1 Thessalonians 4:14-16; 5:8-11; 2 Timothy 4:18; Titus 1:2; 3:7; Hebrews 8:1; 9:24; 11:13-16; 1 Peter 1:3-9; Revelation 2:10; 3:21; 11:12; 14:1-13; 19:1-9; 22:8-9.[252]

We are only given glimpses of what heaven will be like. It is described as *paradise* (2 Corinthians 12:2-3) where we will be like angels (Mark 12:25). It is described as a *place of rest* (Revelation 14:13). It is described as being a better existence than on earth in the flesh (Philippians 1:23). It is described as different from life on earth and the hope of the believer (1 Corinthians 15:19; Colossians 1:5; Titus 1:2).

> looking for the blessed **hope** and glorious <u>appearing</u> of our great God and Savior Jesus Christ, (*Titus 2:13*)

> Therefore gird up the loins of your mind, be sober, and rest your **hope** fully upon the grace that is to be brought to you at the <u>revelation</u> of Jesus Christ; (*1 Peter 1:13*)

> Beloved, now we are children of God; and it has not yet been revealed what we shall be, but we know that when He is <u>revealed</u>, we shall be like Him, for we shall see Him as He is. And everyone who has this **hope** in Him purifies himself, just as He is pure. (*1 John 3:2-3*)

But *our* hope for the future does not rest on yet another coming of Christ, but rather in Christ's completed first-century accomplishments! The view which expects a future return of Christ to save the world (again) steeply discounts, and wrongly makes contingent, what Christ has already done for us. Covenant eschatology solidifies our understanding of the gospel and unifies the message of Scripture. The preterist view reveals the immensity of Christ's victory. It puts an exclamation point on Jesus as a true prophet, and as our Savior, Lord, and King.

The basis for the Christian's hope has been fulfilled, just as the inspired writers expected. It has already been realized! Because we believe that the promises of his Second Coming have been fulfilled, we have even greater confidence that the promise of our own eternal life is a reality. As it says in Revelation 14:13: "Blessed are the dead who die in the Lord from now on."

Christ's death on the cross paid the penalty for our sins (Romans 8:1-4; 1 Corinthians 15:3; 2 Corinthians 5:17-21; Hebrews 9:15-22). His resurrection provides our hope for eternal life (1 Corinthians 15; 2 Timothy 1:10; etc.). His Parousia sealed our salvation (Luke 21:28; Romans 13:11-12; Hebrews 1:14; 9:26-28; 1 Peter 1:3-9). The old pre-Christ world of shadows and prophecies, the things which were "imperfect" and "in part" (Daniel 9:24; 1 Corinthians 13:8-12; etc.), were brought to completion. Unlike the futurist paradigm in which the Christian age is but a comma, Covenant Eschatology confirms Christ as completely triumphant—victorious even in the midst of sin.

Preterism is a mature eschatology. Our faith is that of an "adult" in the new covenant world (1 Corinthians 13:11). We put away our childish demand for a prophetic road map of the future and embrace fulfilled prophecy with full confidence and assurance. As put by David A. Green, "God's grown up people do not need prophetic predictions of future events in order to have eternal and divine purpose." [253] Russell had these encouraging words:

> The true interpretation of New Testament prophecy, instead of leaving us in darkness, encourages *hope*. It relieves the gloom which hung over a world which was believed to be destined to perish. . . . All sinister anticipation rests upon an erroneous interpretation of Scripture; and the fallacies cleared away, the prospect brightens with a *glorious hope*. We may trust the God of Love. He has not forsaken the earth, and He governs the world on a plan which He has not indeed disclosed to us, but which we may be well assured will finally evolve the highest good of the creature and the brightest glory of the Creator.[254]

Preterism is an optimistic eschatology. Christians do not need to fear a coming tribulation; it has already occurred. Preterists also believe that we need not wait in hades until the end of time to be reunited with our physical bodies and to be with our Lord in heaven; we go to heaven immediately upon physical death in our glorified bodies to be with God and the saints of all time. Hades was abolished in the Parousia, when the saints were resurrected from hades to heaven (Daniel 12:1-2, 13; Matthew 24:31; 25:32; John 5:28-29; 11:24; Acts 2:27, 31; 1 Corinthians 15:22-24; 1 Thessalonians 4:13-17; 1 Peter 3:18-19; 4:6; Revelation 20:1-15).

Scripture is validated as true and trustworthy as prophecy has been fulfilled just as Jesus and the New Testament writers predicted. Preterist eschatology is critically important in apologetics—using reason and evidence to defend the truth of Christianity—to demonstrate that Jesus is the way, the *truth*, and the life. Thus, preterist eschatology is crucial in the defense of the *gospel*! If Jesus and his disciples were false prophets, the Bible is unreliable, and the gospel is a sham.

Jesus taught that all Old Testament prophecy and all things specifically listed in the Olivet Discourse and in Revelation, including the Second Coming, would be fulfilled in his generation (Luke 21:22, 32; Revelation 1:1-3; 22:6-20; etc.) This time-restriction is reinforced by similar prophecies outside of the Olivet Discourse and Revelation. Christian scholars are in general agreement that this is exactly how all the New Testament writers, as guided by the inspiration of the Holy Spirit (John 16:13), understood Jesus' words. If they were wrong on something that is so central to the faith, how can we trust them to have conveyed other aspects of the faith accurately, such as the personal requirements for salvation?

No inspired New Testament writer ever corrected his Holy Spirit-guided understanding and expectations of fulfillment. Instead, the writers intensified their language as the "appointed time of the end" (Daniel 12:4) drew near—from Jesus' "this generation" (Matthew 16:27-28; Luke 21:22, 32), to Peter's "the end of all things is at hand" (1 Peter 4:7) and "for it is time for judgment to begin" (1 Peter 4:17), to John's "this/it is the last hour" (1 John 2:18).

Everything Jesus said would happen in his generation *did in fact happen* exactly **as** and **when** He said it would—within the lifetime of his contemporaries. And *everything* that each New Testament writer expected to happen, did indeed happen exactly **as** and **when** they expected it would—within their lifetime. Preterism disarms the skeptics' primary charge of Jesus' prophetic failures.

Partial fulfillment and/or double fulfillment are not satisfactory escape routes. *Partial* does not pass the test of a true prophet (Deuteronomy 18:18-22). Nowhere does the New Testament teach that there would be one fulfillment in Christ *soon*, and another fulfillment in Christ thousands of years *later*. Jesus and the apostles time-restricted their last-days/end-of-the-age predictions to occur within their generation. God is faithful (2 Peter 3:9) and does not lie (Numbers 23:19). Faithfulness means not only doing *what* was promised, but also doing it *when* it was promised.

First-century fulfillment expectations were the correct ones, and the things that were promised happened right on time—no gaps, no gimmicks, no double meanings, no interruptions, no postponements, no delays, no exegetical gymnastics, and no changing the meaning of commonly used and normally understood words. Such manipulative devices have only given skeptics a foothold to discredit Christ's deity and the inspiration of Scripture. What needs adjusting is our understanding of both the *time* and *nature* of fulfillment, and not manipulation of the time factor to conform to our popular, futuristic expectations.[255]

The word *hope* can be defined as "confident assurance." The Blue Letter Bible defines hope (Greek *elpis*, Strong's G1680) as "joyful and confident expectation of eternal salvation." The preterist view is that all eschatological promises have been fulfilled! With the knowledge that everything which secures our salvation has already been accomplished, how could we possibly possess greater confidence in our Christian hope?

The *kingdom of God* was a central teaching of our Lord Jesus Christ. It is a present, but greatly under-realized reality, and must again become a central teaching of his church. Christ reigns now everlastingly as King of Kings and Lord of Lords (Isaiah 9:7; Daniel 7:13-14; Matthew 3:2, 10:7; Mark 1:15; Luke 1:32-33; 10:9-11; 1 Corinthians 15:22-24; Revelation 11:15; 19:1, 16). As a result of Christ's Parousia we are no longer under law but under grace (Matthew 5:18).

We have been guilty of proclaiming a half-truth—a partially delivered faith to the world and to fellow Christians. We must repent and vigorously "contend for the faith that was once for all delivered to the saints" (Jude 1:3), giving "a reason for the *hope* that lies within" (1 Peter 3:15).[256]

Eternal life is not something just in the future. Christians possess eternal life at the moment of our God-given faith, when our trust is placed in Jesus (John 6:47; 11:25, 26; Romans 4:5). While we do not know exactly what heaven is like, we are comforted in knowing that the believer has salvation *now*. This knowledge sets us free not only to appreciate being part of God's eternal kingdom, but also to enjoy more fully our time on this magnificent planet. Our life here is not something to be seen as an ugly stop in God's plan for us.

Yes, there is no denying that life can be cruel at times. But the Bible teaches that *joy* is a fruit of the Spirit (Galatians 5:22-23). Whatever our carnal trials may be on this earth, God's promises in Jesus have been fulfilled. We transcend our problems in the appreciation that we are part of God's everlasting kingdom *now*. Our earthly circumstances may not change, but our attitude about them should change. "The peace that passes all understanding" is more than a religious slogan to end our church services. This is why we can sing the beautiful and instructive words of the hymn *Joyful, Joyful, We Adore Thee* (written by Henry van Dyke in 1907):

Joyful, joyful, we adore Thee, God of glory, Lord of love;
Hearts unfold like flowers before Thee, opening to the sun above.
Melt the clouds of sin and sadness; drive the dark of doubt away;
Giver of immortal gladness, fill us with the light of day!

All Thy works with joy surround Thee, earth and heaven reflect
     Thy rays,
Stars and angels sing around Thee, center of unbroken praise.
Field and forest, vale and mountain, flowery meadow, flashing sea,
Singing bird and flowing fountain call us to rejoice in Thee.

Thou art giving and forgiving, ever blessing, ever blessed,
Wellspring of the joy of living, ocean depth of happy rest!
Thou our Father, Christ our Brother, all who live in love are Thine;
Teach us how to love each other, lift us to the joy divine.

Mortals, join the happy chorus, which the morning stars began;
Father love is reigning o'er us, brother love binds man to man.
Ever singing, march we onward, victors in the midst of strife,
Joyful music leads us Sunward in the triumph song of life.

When we heard a young friend praying for Jesus to return, we pointed out to her what she was really asking for. With her prayer, she was asking for a worldwide tribulation and a burning of the planet. If her futurist eschatology were to come to pass "soon" as she prayed, she would have no more children, and no grandchildren or great grandchildren to join her in this life and in heaven. How discouraging an eschatology!

Covenant eschatology is the only worldview that gives ultimate meaning and purpose to our world right *now*. David A. Green contrasts the preterist view to that of the futurist view, which is a "temporary functional Gnosticism" in the sense that with futurism the material world, in contrast to the spiritual world, remains under the dominion of Satan until the end of history.[257]

We are not waiting for the end of a "gospel age" in which our world is replaced by a shiny new planet. Instead, we live here and now in the kingdom of God in Christ knowing *that all things work together for good to them who love God, to those who are called according to his purpose and predestined to be conformed to the image of Christ* (Romans 8:28-29). This gives us the mandate and the courage to preach the gospel of Christ, and its mind-renewing and society-transforming message, and to do so into the "world without end" (Ephesians 3:21; Hebrews 13:20; Revelation 14:6).

Covenant eschatology is the only eschatological view that is faithful to Scripture, answers the hard questions about Bible prophecy, unifies the Bible, answers the skeptics' objections about Christ as a true prophet, and is truly optimistic. Tina Rae Collins offers some lovely thoughts about fulfilled prophecy:

> Because of God's love for me all I want to do is share this good news of fulfilled prophecy with others and enjoy God every single day of my life. *I* do not matter any longer. I want to give my body as a living sacrifice for the God who gave His only Son just so I could live with Him forever. What an awesome God He is! Praise Him forever! Am I the only proponent of fulfilled eschatology that feels this way? Absolutely not! I think we all (those of us new to this belief) are experiencing an incredible change. I have heard story after story and they are all the same. And the joy we are exhibiting all boils down to love. Love has burst forth in my heart and I sense it all around me like a warm blanket. It is like I suddenly stepped into a pool of love and it is washing over me. My understanding is opened up and the Scriptures have become more alive. I am finally able to take God's word for what it says without trying to force it to say what I think it means. My heart is open to whatever God has in store for me for the rest of my life because my trust in Him has become much greater.[258]

In summary, here's why we have **Christian Hope through Fulfilled Prophecy**:

- *Christ's work in securing our salvation is complete.*
- We know that Jesus and the biblical writers were proven to be true prophets, so we can count on their teaching about salvation being true.

- The New Covenant Age being established with finality at the Parousia assures us that the gospel—salvation by grace through faith because of Christ's finished work, rather than by our own effort—is in effect.

- We know that death will never befall us. We have eternal life now.

- We know that we do not have to suffer either a Great Tribulation on earth or an undetermined time in the grave after biological death to be with the Lord forever in heaven.

- Jesus crushed Satan at the Parousia and reigns now as King of Kings and Lord of Lords.

- Jesus has returned as promised and is among us now to guide and comfort us.

- We have greater confidence that we need not sorrow like men who have no hope.

CALL FOR RENEWAL

Take off your shoes. If you haven't had your toes stepped on yet, they probably will be now.

The church's problem with eschatology is a symptom of a greater problem. It is time for us Christians to be honest with ourselves. The visible Christian church is frankly a mess. It is doctrinally separated into divisive sects, and our practices have diverged significantly from primitive Christianity. The message this gives the world is that the true God is irrelevant, confused, or even debased. This is not to say that individual American churches are not proclaiming the gospel, at least in part. But are they proclaiming the full counsel of God (Acts 20:27)? Some serious introspection may be in order.

Each sect places itself apart, or even above the others, thinking that it uniquely possesses the truth. But we can't all be correct in our many contradictory opinions. We all seek comfort and constancy in our theology as we struggle in our daily lives. But we make here a serious challenge: We think that Christians are complacent. Indeed, members of every group seem to *fear* the thought of seriously examining their own doctrines and practices. Peer pressure too often outweighs critical scholarship.

Christians often deal with passages of the Bible that are challenging to them with either *trepidation* or even *anger*. Walls are erected. Each group assumes that their leaders must have theology right. They fail to do as Paul instructs us in 1 Thessalonians 5:21, to test everything—which would sharpen the Christian faith.

We often simply choose to ignore challenges to our preconceived notions about what the Bible actually teaches. We have built doctrines by picking and choosing the passages that fit our ideas and ignoring those that challenge us. This has led to a shallow, lazy, distorted, and divisive Christianity. It is high time to open our minds to reasonable challenges to our thinking.

Fortunately, with the Internet, the days of Christians being able to duck doctrinal challenges are over. We should not fear challenges, but rather welcome them. One can learn more about his own position by studying the challenges to it.

Let's survey the Christian landscape. The cults are gaining ground. Mainline denominations are losing members like never before. Liberal Christians have arbitrarily thrown out anything in Scripture they don't like. Even conservatives, in spite of giving lip service to inerrancy, often dismiss many passages that don't fit their paradigm. But our doctrinal divisiveness is only the half of it; we have gotten off the mark in our practice. In an article entitled, "Quitting Church: Why the Faithful are Fleeing," Ingrid Schlueter exposes the state of the American church:

> The choices [of churches] a friend of mine faces in her area are these: an apostate mainline church with a lesbian pastor, a go-go evangelical circus church featuring everything but a trapeze apparatus in the ceiling, (the pastor has a ring in his nose), a stone dead Reformed church comprised of the 24 original founders in various stages of spiritual desiccation, a German Lutheran ethnic club along the lines of the Reformed church, a oneness Pentecostal church that gets so wild the police are occasionally called for noise ordinance violations, an IFB (independent, fundamental Baptist) church where the women are required to have their hair below their shoulders and where they market their own church-sewn culottes, and a Roman Catholic outpost named after someone called St. Veronica. . . . Churches that two decades ago were preaching the Word, evangelizing and making an impact for Christ in the community are now featuring Elvis impersonators, car shows and the like. These are the churches that bought into the Purpose-Driven mentality that the church must change to be like the culture. This

thinking has wrought unbelievable carnage that leaves many Bible-believing Christians standing on the outside with few options for a church left. What is really needed is another Reformation.[259]

Non-Christians can see right through our bickering and through the fakers, pseudo-intellectuals, hypocrites, and false prophets. The modern church is an embarrassment to biblical Christianity, and is too often a stumbling block to seekers. These things must change, and perhaps are beginning to change. We sense that young people especially, at least those that have not left the church for good and still give a whit, are fed up with questionable doctrines and practices in the church. We could suggest a list of such things that would include slaying-in-the-spirit, transubstantiation, left-behind rapturism, TV televangelist fakery, and on and on.

Depending on your vantage point, you either don't care or you are thinking that all this is true about the other groups out there, but not about yours. We submit that every group has blind spots. We need to humble ourselves before God and ask Him to reveal truth. The author includes himself in this humility and asks the reader's forgiveness for errors we may have made. We will gladly correct any such errors, and we solicit your input.

Who has a heart hardened by biases and preconceptions, Lord? Is it I? Show me the blind spot in my own eye, Lord! Give me the fortitude to deal with error that I might hold. Give me a passion for biblical truth. May I not be satisfied with the status quo. And give me the courage to speak up, even among my peers.

Our thesis is that these problems result from an often shallow and distorted view of Scripture! We want to challenge our Christian brothers and sisters into re-examination. Let us say here that we affirm our belief in the inerrancy of Scripture. Our studies over the years have led us to conclude that we can proclaim the validity of the Bible with confidence. We think that the toughest challenges to the Bible can be met. It is time to overcome our timidity about the Bible cast upon us from the "higher critics" — from outside and even from inside the church.[260]

In addition to the Roman Catholic church, which has its own set of issues, broadly speaking, there are two major groupings of Protestant churches in America — (1) the denominational/institutional church and (2) the non-denominational Bible/community church movement. As regards the first group, nearly all of the "mainstream" denominational churches have been steadily losing adherents for a half century or more for a number of reasons, which include creeping culturalization and liberalization associated with arbitrary denial of historic biblical truths. Even denominations which have retained a strong official commitment to historic Christian beliefs have experienced an incursion of skepticism, and many of their local churches continue to pursue worship and outreach strategies designed more to accommodate the gospel to the culture than to speak truth to the culture.

At the root of these troubling trends are serial failures. Among them are: a failure to respond to skeptics and to communicate the many solid reasons why the Bible is true and trustworthy, failure to impart a biblical worldview to its members, failure to hold people accountable for their faith (easy believism), malaise from institutionalization and bureaucracy, ecclesiastical tyranny, reliance on tradition rather than on a strong biblical foundation—and more. Viewpoints that diverge from biblical truth, including *liberalism, antinomianism,* and *legalism,* are rampant within the church. **These are failures of the institutional church, not of God, his truth, his power, or his love.**

On the other hand, the non-denominational church movement has experienced growth in recent decades. But while this movement continues to grow rapidly in the third world, we perceive that it is slowing and is probably capped in the U. S. This is likely due to several factors, including the erosion of the credibility of certain highly visible preachers and authors (especially in the neo-pentecostal movement), the dubious gospel of prosperity, fundamentalism (the hyper-literalization of clearly symbolical biblical texts), and especially the pervasive influence of *millennialism*—in particular *dispensational premillennialism.*

Though not limited to millennialists, the evangelical millennialist camp has been the principal breeding ground for "false prophets." Failed predictions are a continuing embarrassment to Christianity. Yes, some Christians throughout Christian history have wrongly predicted that various eschatological events would happen in their day, even the imminent destruction of the planet or the ushering in of Utopia. But this does not excuse the continuation of these distractions.

While "end times" prophecy has become a hallmark of modern American evangelicalism, its sister error, "restorationism," is present in non-evangelical or non-millennialist churches—liberal and conservative churches alike. So, whether it is the millennialists' expectation of the millennial kingdom, or the amillennialists' hope for restoration, all such utopian futurist ideas are teaching a misplaced hope.

We have made our case that inadequate biblical warrant can be found for a utopian rule of Christ on earth. This is essentially the same error that the first-century Jews made concerning the advent of the Messiah. While we are repeating our charge, it is worth repeating: We see millennialism as at best a prominent distraction and at worst a serious error (Deuteronomy 18:20-22; Matthew 7:15-23). It can be seen potentially as a different gospel promising a false hope (2 Corinthians 11:1-4; Galatians 1:6). Our hope is not in a coming political kingdom, but heaven itself.

A related problem is the sense which many people have, especially our Christian youth, that the church is irrelevant. Some 70% of young people leave the church; most never return. While people leave the church for many reasons—desire for autonomy, hypocrisy in the church, etc.—perhaps the biggest reason, according to studies, is that people do not believe Christianity to be true. *Doubt* is a persistent reason given for their exit. The church has utterly failed to present a defense of the truth of the Bible. And when such facts are pointed out to pastors, there is an unending list of excuses to ignore the problem.[261]

Speaking especially to pastors, apologetics should be higher on your agenda than your seminary probably taught you it should be! The best exposition of the gospel in the New Testament is 1 Corinthians 15:1-11. In this passage, Paul gives an apologetic *along with the gospel*. If you are routinely presenting the gospel without an apologetic, you are not presenting the gospel biblically! Parents, as well, have been guilty of not giving the many valid *reasons* for the biblical faith to their children. Christianity is not based on a blind or unreasonable faith ("fideism")— but faith *in evidence*.[262]

We need to better delineate to skeptics why Christianity is not only **true**, but also why it is **relevant**. No other religion or worldview makes life as meaningful and abundant NOW. The atheist is living a lie, as he attempts to explain how we can come *from* nowhere, then go *to* nowhere after we die—but life is somehow filled with meaning in between. Meaning in the Christian life, and its hope offered for our destiny, are unique.

Another charge made against Christians by outsiders is that we are hypocrites. There is validity to this charge. While the statistics waver on this, the Protestant Christians, at least, suffer too many abortions and failed marriages. There is obviously something terribly wrong here. So another critical area for the church to address is discipleship. A person whose life is not transformed by the gospel is probably not a true Christian. Pastors, we need to hear the pulpits roaring for righteousness—not as a message *of* salvation, but a message of *working out* our salvation (Philippians 12:2), so that the flock can be examples of the power of Christianity.

And what about evangelism? One study suggested that only about 2% of Christians *ever* share their faith! This is astounding. How much confidence do Christians really have in their beliefs? Apparently, not much. They lack the conviction (or the training) to tell their unbelieving friends about the majesty and power of the Christian faith.

In all of this, survey after survey has revealed widespread ignorance among professing Christians about *truly important* Christian doctrines — the nature of God, the nature of man, how sinful man is reconciled to a holy God, why the Bible is true and trustworthy, and how Christianity compares to other religions. All of these factors have contributed to our anemic church. These things are unacceptable and must be reversed in order for the church to be credible and healthy.

We believe that it is time for a new Reformation and revival. It is time for a renewed dynamic church based on principles that meet the biblical test for unity while rejecting the errant theology that has been damaging both the Protestant and the Catholic Church. As reformers in previous eras have addressed issues plaguing the church, we do so again today, while reasserting our commitment to biblical truth.

The New Testament has strong and consistent demands for unity among Christians and warnings against sectarianism, which is a *sin* (Luke 9:49-50; John 17:20-23; Romans 15:5-6; 1 Corinthians 1:10-31; Ephesians 4:1-16). In matters of doctrine, we implore Christians to re-think our divisions. While Christians will never agree on every detail, perhaps we have divided wrongly.

Our position on eschatology is that full preterism is the best biblical fit. While we find no evidence that any statements by Jesus or any biblical writer are referring to events that would happen past the first century, we acknowledge that differences of opinion will continue to exist about certain specific passages.

Here's where we stand more specifically on this matter. The various futurist views on eschatology are so different as to be incompatible. They cannot all be true. However, none of these beliefs are necessarily damnable. One can potentially be a true Christian and hold to any of these. We believe that amillennialists, postmillennialists, partial preterists, and full preterists can *debate* without *dividing* over our views.

On the other hand, we believe—as stated by the Catholic Church as well as the Protestant Reformers—that millennialism is a more serious error within futurism. We reject it and call on Christians everywhere to join us. Again, our greatest concerns with millennialism are that it detracts from the gospel and does not give Christ the Lordship He is due. Even so, no eschatological position should be a reason to exclude fellowship to anyone. In time, the church will come to a biblical consensus on eschatology. In the meantime, charity is in order.

Some futurists, as well as some full preterists, believe that preterism is damaging to classical Christianity. We do not think so. Evangelical preterism, properly understood, does not do violence to Christianity. It enhances it. It completes it.

While some will see our views themselves as divisive, we view them as uniting. We are reaching out across denominational lines. Out of the ashes of the dissolving mainline denominations, we see the emergence of a unifying conservative movement. This movement is one that continues to move away from sectarianism toward a new conservative biblical church concept that unites Christians on a short list of affirmations. The following list can serve as a framework for discussion in your own church:

YOU WILL KNOW THEM BY THEIR FRUITS:

TWELVE TESTS OF A HEALTHY, WELL-BALANCED AND VIGOROUS BIBLICAL CHURCH

1. It has a high view of Scripture and is unafraid to boldly proclaim the Bible as the inspired Word of God—from Genesis to Revelation (*2 Timothy 3:16-17; Hebrews 4:12; 2 Peter 3:16;* etc.). Members have a biblical worldview, that is, they see all of life (including art, music, science, government, history, and philosophy) through the lens of their faith. They are enthusiastic about learning more about what the Bible teaches (rather than merely what someone tells them it says).

2. It affirms the Trinity—one God (Deuteronomy 32:39; Isaiah 43:10; 44:6, 8; 45:5; John 1:1; 1 Corinthians 8:4, 6) in three

coexistent eternal persons: Father, Son, and Holy Spirit (Matthew 28:19; 2 Corinthians 13:14; etc.) [263]

3. Its members understand and can clearly communicate the gospel (Romans 1:16-17; 1 Corinthians 15:1-11) to others, as well as the distinction between *law* and *gospel* (John 1:17; Romans 3:20; Ephesians 2:8-10).

4. It teaches that we are saved by grace through a living faith in Jesus Christ (Acts 4:12; Romans 10:8-13; Ephesians 2:8-10)—but that *easy believism* is not a Christian doctrine (James 2:14-26; 1 John 2:2-6; etc.). Members repent of their sins individually as well as corporately, and are *accountable* for their faith (Matthew 4:17; 7:16-22; John 15:9-17; Acts 17:30; 26:20; Romans 2:1-16; 12:1-21; Galatians 5:16-26; Hebrews 3:13; etc.).

5. The members grasp the unique Christian concept about the nature of mankind—that we are at our core **sinful** (Genesis 6:5; Psalm 51:3-5; Jeremiah 17:9; Mark 7:20-23; Romans 3:9-20; Ephesians 2:1-3; 1 John 1:8; etc.)—not that we are as bad as we could be but that every aspect of our lives is touched by sin. Further, they can explain to others how our sinful nature is why we are in **critical need of a savior**.

6. The church teaches its members to be ready to give the *reasons* why Christianity is true and why its claims of exclusivity are valid (Acts 1:3; 17:17; 1 Corinthians 15:1-11; 1 Peter 3:15; 1 John 5:12; Jude 3; etc.). The members can easily communicate evidence about (1) why God exists, (2) why the Bible is true and trustworthy, and (3) why Jesus really-and-truly rose from the dead.[264]

7. The members *regularly* share their faith with others and demonstrate love to all (Matthew 5:43-45; Mark 16:15; John 13:34-35; 1 Corinthians 13:2-3; Galatians 5:6; Hebrews 12:14).

8. The church understands its obligation to *engage and transform the culture*, rather than letting culture transform the church (Proverbs 21:22; 29:16; Matthew 5:13-16; 6:10; 28:18; 1 Corinthians 10:26; 2 Corinthians 10:4-5; Ephesians 5:11; etc.). Churches have programs to help the needy in their commu-

nity. At least occasionally there are sermons on scientific, social, and political issues that present the case for biblical truth for society including pro-life and traditional family values (Isaiah 5:20-21), while at the same time offering a message of forgiveness for those who need healing.

9. Its hymnology is worshipful and singable—and not a rock-and-roll concert. Songs and hymns are Christ-centered rather than "me-centered."

10. Given that eschatology represents more than one-fourth of the New Testament, its leaders do not read Bible prophecy through the lens of the daily newspaper, but through the lens of Jesus—how He intended it be understood and how the disciples understood it. Thus, they respect the over 100 New Testament passages proclaiming the imminence of the prophesied "last things" events.

11. The church sees itself as Christians first—rather than members of a particular sect or denomination first (Romans 15:5-6; 1 Corinthians 1:10-13; Ephesians 4:1-16).

12. The church rejects aberrant doctrines such *millennialism, fideism, nominalism, antinomianism, universalism, liberalism, and legalism.*[265]

The first five items on the list above, among others, are "First Things" doctrines of the church. Eschatology concerns matters of "Last Things." Christians, especially preterists, have a tendency to want to limit their fellowship to those with common views on eschatology. This is an error. The gospel and the other First Things doctrines are more important than any particular view of eschatology, and should be the basis for fellowship.

Absent from our list of affirmations are a variety of doctrines that have historically divided the church. We lift up God rather than ourselves and our differences. While there are certainly debatable and serious differences on many matters, we consider within the "circle of orthodoxy" those holding to the four primary views on justification: Calvinists, Lutherans, Arminians, and Catholics. Theologians from all four groups will shudder at the thought, but we call on Christians in each group to be more charitable toward each other. (While we do not view Calvinists, Lutherans, Arminians, and Catholics as equally correct, we acknowledge all to be within the circle of orthodoxy, defined as broadly as we can.) [266]

In unity on these matters, the conservative vibrant church will have a less divisive presence and a stronger voice in society. We will be able to communicate the gospel and biblical truth more effectively to the world. We will be a force for positive change in the lives of individuals throughout society.

This book will not be the last word on this subject either for the reader or the author. There is yet much to consider and we shall all continue our studies. I invite you, the reader, to offer your thoughts. Readers may email the author with your thoughts on eschatology or for a more detailed version of my church concept. My email address is faithfacts@msn.com. Please put "book" in the subject line. I hope that this is a book you will want to give copies of to your Christian friends. If you tell me you have bought at least three copies, I will send you a ball cap with "preterism" on it (as long as they last). I will also send you a cap if you recommend the book to at least 50 friends by email or Facebook, with a link to the book's listing at Amazon.com. Just let me know. God bless.

—Charles Meek

Addendum and Invitation:

Readers are invited to see my articles on various aspects of theology at my websites:

www.FaithFacts.org

www.ProphecyQuestions.com

Also see my Facebook sites:

FaithFacts.org

Evangelical Preterism

Be sure to "like" us and share them with your friends!

Charles Meek

APPENDICES

Appendix A

Preterism 101

Here is a list of preterist passages compiled by David A. Green.[267] This compilation puts an exclamation point to the importance of the imminency passages in the New Testament:

1. The kingdom of heaven is at hand. (Matthew 3:2)

2. Who warned you to flee from the wrath about to come? (Matthew 3:7)

3. The axe is already laid at the root of the trees. (Matthew 3:10)

4. His winnowing fork is in His hand. (Matthew 3:12)

5. The kingdom of heaven is at hand. (Matthew 4:17)

6. The kingdom of heaven is at hand. (Matthew 10:7)

7. You shall not finish going through the cities of Israel, until the Son of Man comes. (Matthew 10:23)

8. the age about to come (Matthew 12:32)

9. The Son of Man is about to come in the glory of His Father with His angels; and will then recompense every man according to his deeds. (Matthew 16:27)

10. There are some of those who are standing here who shall not taste death until they see the Son of Man coming in His kingdom. (Matthew 16:28; cf. Mark 9:1; Luke 9:27)

11. "When the owner of the vineyard comes, what will he do to those vine-growers?" They said to Him, "He will bring those wretches to a wretched end, and will rent out the vineyard to other vine-growers, who will pay him the proceeds at the proper seasons." . . . "Therefore I say to you, the kingdom of God will be taken away

from you, and be given to a nation producing the fruit of it.". . .
When the chief priests and the Pharisees heard His parables, they
understood that He was speaking about them. (Matthew. 21:40-
41, 43, 45)

12. This generation will not pass away until all these things take place.
(Matthew 24:34)

13. From now on, you [Caiaphas, the chief priests, the scribes, the elders, the whole Sanhedrin] shall be seeing the Son of Man sitting
at the right hand of Power, and coming on the clouds of heaven.
(Matthew 26:64; Mark 14:62; Luke 22:69)

14. The kingdom of God is at hand. (Mark 1:15)

15. What will the owner of the vineyard do? He will come and destroy
the vine-growers, and will give the vineyard to others. . . . They
[the chief priests, scribes and elders] understood that He spoke the
parable against them. (Mark 12:9, 12)

16. This generation will not pass away until all these things take place.
(Mark 13:30)

17. Who warned you to flee from the wrath about to come? (Luke
3:7)

18. The axe is already laid at the root of the trees. (Luke 3:9)

19. His winnowing fork is in His hand. (Luke 3:17)

20. The kingdom of God has come near to you. (Luke 10:9)

21. The kingdom of God has come near. (Luke 10:11)

22. What, therefore, will the owner of the vineyard do to them?
He will come and destroy these vine-growers and will give
the vineyard to others. . . . The scribes and the chief priests. . . .
understood that He spoke this parable against them. (Luke 20:15-
16, 19)

23. These are days of vengeance, in order that all things which are
written may be fulfilled. (Luke 21:22)

24. This generation will not pass away until all things take place. (Luke
21:32)

25. Daughters of Jerusalem, stop weeping for Me, but weep for yourselves and for your children. For behold, the days are coming when they will say, "Blessed are the barren, and the wombs that never bore, and the breasts that never nursed.' Then they will begin to say to the mountains, 'Fall on us,' and to the hills, 'Cover us'" (Luke 23:28-30; compare Revelation 6:14-17)

26. We were hoping that He was the One who is about to redeem Israel. (Luke 24:21)

27. I will come to you. . . . In that Day you shall know that I am in my Father, and you in Me, and I in you. . . . Lord, what then has happened that You are about to disclose Yourself to us, and not to the world? (John 14:18, 20, 22)

28. If I want him to remain until I come, what is that to you? (John 21:22)

29. This is what was spoken of through the prophet Joel: "And it shall be in the last days. . . ." (Acts 2:16-17)

30. He has fixed a day in which He is about to judge the world in righteousness. (Acts 17:31)

31. There is about to be a resurrection of both the righteous and the wicked. (Acts 24:15)

32. As he was discussing righteousness, self-control and the judgment about to come. (Acts 24:25)

33. Not for [Abraham's] sake only was it written, that [faith] was reckoned to him [as righteousness], but for our sake also, to whom it is about to be reckoned. (Romans 4:23-24)

34. If you are living according to the flesh, you are about to die. (Romans 8:13)

35. I consider that the sufferings of this present time are not worthy to be compared with the glory that is about to be revealed to us. (Romans 8:18)

36. It is already the hour for you to awaken from sleep; for now salvation is nearer to us than when we believed. The night is almost gone, and the day is at hand. (Romans 13:11-12)

37. The God of peace will soon crush Satan under your feet. (Romans 16:20)

38. The time has been shortened. (1 Corinthians 7:29)

39. The form of this world is passing away. (1 Corinthians 7:31)

40. Now these things . . . were written for our instruction, upon whom the end of the ages has come. (1 Corinthians 10:11)

41. We shall not all fall sleep, but we shall all be changed, in a moment, in the twinkling of an eye, at the last trumpet; for the trumpet will sound, and the dead will be raised imperishable, and we shall be changed. (1 Corinthians 15:51-52)

42. Maranatha! [The Lord comes!] (1 Corinthians 16:22)

43. not only in this age, but also in the one about to come (Ephesians 1:21)

44. The Lord is near. (Philippians 4:5)

45. The gospel . . . was proclaimed in all creation under heaven. (Colossians 1:23; compare Matthew 24:14; Romans 10:18, 16:26; Colossians 1:5-6; 2 Timothy 4:17; Revelation 14:6-7; cf. 1 Clement 5, 7)

46. things which are a shadow of what is about to come (Colossians 2:16-17)

47. We who are alive, and remain until the coming of the Lord. . . . We who are alive and remain shall be caught up together with them in the clouds. . . . You, brethren, are not in darkness, that the Day should overtake you like a thief. . . . (1 Thessalonians 4:15, 17; 5:4)

48. May your spirit and soul and body be preserved complete, without blame at the coming of our Lord Jesus Christ. (1 Thessalonians 5:23)

49. It is only just for God to repay with affliction those who afflict you, and to give relief to you who are afflicted and to us as well when the Lord Jesus shall be revealed from heaven with His mighty angels in flaming fire. (2 Thessalonians 1:6-7)

50. Godliness . . . holds promise for the present life and that which is about to come. (I Timothy 4:8)

51. I charge you . . . that you keep the commandment without stain or reproach until the appearing of our Lord Jesus Christ. (1 Timothy 6:14)

52. storing up for themselves the treasure of a good foundation for that which is about to come, so that they may take hold of that which is life indeed (1 Timothy 6:19)

53. In the last days difficult times will come. For men will be lovers of self . . . Avoid these men. For of these are those who enter into households and captivate weak women . . . These also oppose the truth . . . But they will not make further progress; for their folly will be obvious to all. (2 Timothy 3:1-2, 5-6, 8-9)

54. I solemnly charge you in the presence of God and of Christ Jesus, who is about to judge the living and the dead. (2 Timothy 4:1)

55. God, after He spoke long ago to the fathers in the prophets in many portions and in many ways, in these last days has spoken to us in His Son. (Hebrews 1:1-2)

56. Are they not all ministering spirits, sent out to render service for the sake of those who are about to inherit salvation? (Hebrews 1:14)

57. He did not subject to angels the world about to come. (Hebrews 2:5)

58. and have tasted . . . the powers of the age about to come (Hebrews 6:5)

59. For ground that drinks the rain which often falls upon it and brings forth vegetation useful to those for whose sake it is also tilled, receives a blessing from God; but if it yields thorns and thistles, it is worthless and near a curse, and its end is for burning. (Hebrews 6:7-8)

60. When He said, "A new covenant," He has made the first obsolete. But whatever is becoming obsolete and growing old is ready to disappear. (Hebrews 8:13)

61. The Holy Spirit is signifying this, that the way of the [heavenly] Holy Places has not yet been revealed, while the outer tabernacle is still standing, which is a symbol for the present time. Accordingly both gifts and sacrifices are offered which cannot make the worshiper perfect in conscience, since they relate only to food and drink and various washings, regulations for the body imposed until a time of reformation. (Hebrews 9:8-10)

62. But when Christ appeared as a high priest of the good things about to come. (Hebrews 9:11)

63. Now once at the consummation of the ages He has been manifested to put away sin. (Hebrews 9:26)

64. For the Law, since it has only a shadow of the good things about to come. (Hebrews 10:1)

65. as you see the Day drawing near (Hebrews 10:25)

66. the fury of a fire which is about to consume the adversaries (Hebrews 10:27)

67. For yet in a very little while, He who is coming will come, and will not delay. (Hebrews 10:37)

68. For here we do not have a lasting city, but we are seeking the one that is about to come. (Hebrews 13:14)

69. Speak and so act, as those who are about to be judged by the law of liberty. (James 2:12)

70. Come now, you rich, weep and howl for your miseries which are coming upon you. . . . It is in the last days that you have stored up your treasure! (James 5:1, 3)

71. Be patient, therefore, brethren, until the coming of the Lord. (James 5:7)

72. You too be patient; strengthen your hearts, for the coming of the Lord is at hand. (James 5:8)

73. salvation ready to be revealed in the last time (1 Peter 1:5)

74. He . . . has appeared in these last times for the sake of you. (1 Peter 1:20)

75. They shall give account to Him who is ready to judge the living and the dead. (1 Peter 4:5)

76. The end of all things is at hand; therefore, be of sound judgment and sober spirit for the purpose of prayer. (1 Peter 4:7)

77. For it is time for judgment to begin with the household of God. (1 Peter 4:17)

78. as your fellow elder and witness of the sufferings of Christ, and a partaker also of the glory that is about to be revealed (1 Peter 5:1)

79. We have the prophetic word . . . which you do well to pay attention as to a lamp shining in a dark place, until the Day dawns and the morning star arises in your hearts. (2 Peter 1:19)

80. Their judgment from long ago is not idle, and their destruction is not asleep. (2 Peter 2:3)

81. In the last days mockers will come. . . . For this they willingly are ignorant of . . . . (2 Peter 3:3, 5)

82. But the day of the Lord will come like a thief, in which the heavens will pass away with a roar and the elements will be destroyed with intense heat, and the earth and its works will be burned up. Since all these things are to be destroyed in this way, what sort of people ought you to be in holy conduct and godliness, looking for and hastening the coming of the day of God. (2 Peter 3:10-12)

83. The darkness is passing away, and the true light is already shining. (1 John 2:8)

84. The world is passing away, and its desires. (1 John 2:17)

85. It is the last hour. (1 John 2:18)

86. Even now many antichrists have arisen; from this we know that it is the last hour. (1 John 2:18; compare Matthew 24:23-34)

87. This is that of the antichrist, of which you have heard that it is coming, and now it is already in the world. (1 John 4:3; compare 2 Thessalonians 2:7)

88. For certain persons have crept in unnoticed, those who were long beforehand marked out for this condemnation. . . . About these also Enoch . . . prophesied, saying, "Behold, the Lord came with many thousands of His holy ones, to execute judgment upon all, and to convict all the ungodly. . . ." (Jude 1:4, 14-15)

89. But you, beloved, ought to remember the words that were spoken beforehand by the apostles of our Lord Jesus Christ, that they were saying to you, "In the last time there shall be mockers, following after their own ungodly lusts." These are the ones who cause divisions. . . . (Jude 1:17-19)

90. to show to His bond-servants, the things which must shortly take place (Revelation 1:1)

91. The time is near. (Revelation 1:3)

92. Nevertheless what you have, hold fast until I come. (Revelation 2:25)

93. I also will keep you from the hour of testing which is about to come upon the whole world. (Revelation 3:10)

94. I am coming quickly. (Revelation 3:11)

95. And she gave birth to a son, a male child, who is about to rule all the nations with a rod of iron. (Revelation 12:5)

96. And in her [the Great City Babylon] was found the blood of prophets and of saints and of all who have been slain on the earth. (Revelation 18:24; compare Matthew 23:35-36; Luke 11:50-51)

97. to show to His bond-servants the things which must shortly take place (Revelation 22:6)

98. Behold, I am coming quickly. (Revelation 22:7)

99. Do not seal up the words of the prophecy of this book, for the time is near. (Revelation 22:10; compare Daniel 8:26; 12:4)

100. Behold, I am coming quickly. (Revelation 22:12)

101. Yes, I am coming quickly. (Revelation 22:20)

Note: These verses are a merger of different versions of the Bible, primarily The New American Standard Version and secondarily Young's Literal Translation. In some of the above passages you will see the term "about to," which does not appear in most translations. The Greek word translated as "about to" is *mello* (Strong's G3195). Futurists sometimes object to the translation "about to," and most Bible versions translate *mello* as "will/going to, is to, etc." However, Young's Literal Translation of the Bible usually translates *mello* as "about to." Interlinear Bibles also generally translate *mello* as "about to," including Paul McReynold's *Word Study Greek-English New Testament* which translates *mello* as "about to" in all 109 places it occurs.

According to the online *Blue Letter Bible* lexicon the usage of the word *mello* is "to be about, to be on the point of doing or suffering something, or to intend, have in mind, think to." This translation is confirmed by these other sources: *Vine's Theological Dictionary, Thayer's Greek/English Lexicon, The Analytical Greek Lexicon, Bauer-Arndt-Gingrich, Second Edition*, and *Strong's Exhaustive Concordance*. So while there are different potential translations, "about to" is a good and reasonable rendering as such passages are consistent with the numerous other imminency passages.

Question for your pastor, church leaders, and friends:
Do any passages in the Bible support the preterist view?

Appendix B

Charts

A TALE OF TWO AGES

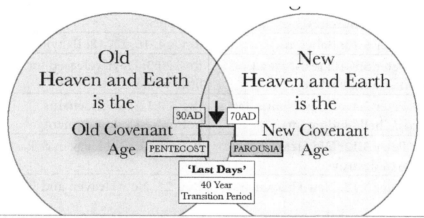

The Bible divides time into two worlds or ages: "this age" and "the age to come."
They correspond to Old and New Covenant ages.
The New Testament was written during the "Last Days" of the Old Covenant age
or what *THEY* call "this age." The **Last Days of that Old Covenant age** *were* the
40-year Transition Period that ended in the destruction of the Temple and the
Old Covenant World of law & sacrifice.

Millenium

Peter	Revelation
1 Peter 1:1: church in Asia	Rev. 1:4: church in Asia
1 Peter 2:9: made a priesthood	Rev. 1:6; 20:6: kingdom of priests
1 Peter 4:5: ready to judge living and the dead	Rev. 11, and 20: soon judge the living and the dead
1 Peter 1:20: foundation of the world	Rev. 13:8: foundation of the world
1 Peter 4:17: judging the family of God (churches)	Rev. 4: warnings about judging churches
1 Peter 5:13: Babylon	Rev. 14, 16, 17, 18: Babylon
1 Peter 5:8-10: resist Devil, suffer a little while	Rev. 20:3: Devil released for a little while
2 Peter 2:4: angels, chains, tartaros/ "hell," judgment	Rev. 20:1-3: angel, chains, bottomless pit, judgment
2 Peter 3:12: Old Heaven & Earth destroyed	Rev. 20:11: Old Heaven & Earth flee
2 Peter 3:13: New Heaven and Earth	Rev. 21: New Heaven and Earth
2 Peter 3:8: one day a 1000 years, 1000 years a day	Rev. 20:2: a 1000 years
2 Peter 3:10: the Day will come like a thief in night	Rev. 3:3; 16:15: Jesus will come like a thief in night

John and Peter wrote to their audiences in apcalyptic language about eschatological events that would happen soon - to *THEM*. The close of the age-changing eschaton was upon them! The Day, the Coming of Jesus, the Judgment and the New World were on the brink of arrival. With reference to the "1000 years" mentioned by Peter and John, both use the term figuratively and qualitatively, *not literally and not quantitatively,* to describe the Transition Period through which they were living, when the Old Covenant world was giving way to the New Covenant world of life and righteousness in Christ.

THE SAME RESURRECTION EVENTS

Matthew 24, 1 Thessalonians 4, 1 Corinthians 15

	Event	Matthew 24	1 Thessalonians	1 Corinthians 15
1	Christ Comes - Parousia	Matt. 24:27, 30	1 Thess. 4:16	1 Cor. 15:23
2	From Heaven	Matt. 24:30	1 Thess. 4:16	1 Cor. 15:23
3	With a Shout / Power	Matt. 24:30	1 Thess. 4:16	1 Cor. 15:52
4	With Angels	Matt. 24:31	1 Thess. 4:16	
5	With Trumpet of God	Matt. 24:31	1 Thess. 4:16	1 Cor. 15:52
6	Believers Gathered with Christ	Matt. 24:31	1 Thess. 4:17	1 Cor. 15:51, 52
7	In Clouds	Matt. 24:30; 25:6	1 Thess. 4:17	
8	Time Unknown	Matt. 24:36	1 Thess. 5:1-2	
9	Christ Comes as a Thief	Matt. 24:43	1 Thess. 5:2, 4	1 Cor. 15:51
10	Believers Unaware of Impending Judgment	Matt. 24:37-39	1 Thess. 3	
11	Judgment Comes Like Birth Pains	Matt. 24:8	1 Thess. 3	
12	Believers to Watch	Matt. 24:42	1 Thess. 4, 6	
13	Warning against Drunkenness	Matt. 24:49	1 Thess. 7	1 Cor. 15:58
14	The Day	Matt. 24:36	1 Thess. 5:2, 8	

Resurrection

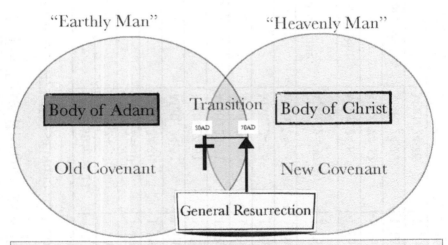

The New Testament was written during the "Last Days" of the *Old Covenant world*. Those "Last Days" were the 40-year transition period. This is why all the eschatological passages in the New testament were addressed to their first century audience and imminent.

Appendix C
Questions for Dispensationalists

This appendix is addressed specifically to dispensationalists. But there is much here that may be enlightening to others, especially concerning the covenantal theme that unifies the Bible. Any serious student of the Bible might enjoy thinking about these questions and looking up the passages cited.

A. Hasn't the focus of premillennialists on end-time theories contributed to a lot of false prophecies? [268]

B. Questions about Israel and God's Covenantal Plan of Salvation:

1. Could the dispensational distinctive of the separation between Israel and the church be incorrect? On the Jewish Day of Pentecost in Acts 2, if you asked Peter and the other disciples if they were part of "Israel" or the "church" (Acts 2:47), what would they say? Wouldn't they say they were both? Don't Romans 11; Galatians 3-6; Ephesians 1-3, and Hebrews 8 show that the Gentiles were grafted in, and the Jews and Gentiles together are the Israel of God, rather than the Jews maintaining a separate line of salvation? Doesn't Galatians 3:14 further identify the nature of the blessing that would come to all nations, including Israel, through Christ? Don't Galatians 3:6-8 and Galatians 3:29 tell us that all believers, whether Jew or Gentile, are the spiritual descendants of Abraham?

2. If God has two different plans for Jews and Gentiles, why does Paul say there is no longer a distinction (Romans 10:12; Galatians 3:28-29; Colossians 3:11)?

3.   Isn't gospel salvation for everyone who believes—both Jew and Gentile (Romans 1:16)? Wasn't Abraham justified by faith (Romans 4)? Didn't Paul teach that God preached the gospel to Abraham (Galatians 3:8)?

4.   If the salvation of the Jews is salvation by race instead of salvation by grace, why does John 1:12-13 (written by a Jew) say that salvation is not by blood?

5.   God's covenant promise has never changed, even though man's knowledge and understanding of his promise has progressed throughout the ages. Wasn't the object of Abraham's faith the covenant promise which God began to reveal in the Seed-Redeemer promise of Genesis 3:15? (Compare Luke 24:25-27; Acts 26:22-23; 28:23-24; Romans 1:1-3; 1 Corinthians 10:2-4; 2 Timothy 3:14-17; 1 Peter 1:3-12; 2 Peter 3:16.) Hasn't the one object of saving faith always been the Messianic promise and the gospel of Christ?

6.   If law is not important to New Testament believers (antinomianism), why do we find more than a hundred passages in the New Testament about the importance of law and obedience for believers, both Jew and Gentile (Matthew 5:17-19; 6:15; John 5:29; 15:1-10; Acts 5:32, Romans 2:1-16; 8:13; Galatians 5:6; 6:7-9; Philippians 2:12-18; Hebrews 8:10; James 2:8-26; 1 John 1:6-7; 2:15-17; etc.)?

7.   While civil and ceremonial laws of the Old Testament have been repealed (Acts 10:12-15; Romans 14:17; Colossians 2:11-16), isn't there a *moral* law that applies to Old and New Testament believers (Romans 13:8-10; 15:4; 1 Corinthians 10:11; 2 Timothy 3:16-17; James 2:8-13; 4:11-12)? Isn't positing two conflicting systems of morality implying two gods, thus incipient idolatry?

8.   Don't the following passages further confirm that the New Israel (New Jerusalem) does not mean a literal restored nation of Israel?: Matthew 21:43; Romans 2:28-29; 9:6; 10:12; Galatians 6:15-16; Philippians 3:3; Colossians 3:11; Hebrews 8:8, 13; 12:18-29; 1 Peter 2:9-10; Revelation 21:2. In 1 Peter 2:9-10 isn't Peter applying Old Testament terms for Israel to the church, asserting the continuity between Old Testament Israel and the

New Testament church—representing the Jew-Gentile church as the fulfillment of Old Testament Israel?

9. Isn't it reasonable to believe that the use of the number 12,000 for the New Jerusalem (Revelation 21) is symbolic of the full number of the people of God of all ages? (The number twelve is associated with the twelve tribes of Israel and the twelve apostles, and therefore symbolic of the covenant people of both ages.)

10. Aren't all God's people citizens of the heavenly Jerusalem (Galatians 4:25-26; Hebrews 11:10, 16; 12:22-29; Revelation 21:2)? Doesn't Revelation specifically tell us that the New Jerusalem is the bride, thus the bride of Christ—that is, the church?

11. Are there any references in the Bible to the temple being built a third time? If the Jewish temple will be rebuilt in the future, why does Scripture say God does not dwell in temples made with human hands (Acts 17:24)? Why do you hope for a new temple when the Bible teaches that we no longer need a temple because Christ brings the presence of God to his people (Revelation 21:22)?

12. Don't the New Testament texts comparing Israel to a fig tree (Matthew 21:19-21; Mark 11:13-23; Luke 13:6-9; Revelation 6:13-17) point to Jerusalem's destruction rather than to its restoration?

13. Weren't the Jews permanently rejected as God's covenant nation (Matthew 8:8-13; 21:33-46; 22:1-14; 23:31-39; John 8:37-47; Romans 9:30-10:4; Romans 11:7)?

14. Isn't the "Israel of God" made up of those individuals, either Jew or Gentile, who believe (Matthew 3:9; Romans 2:28-29; Galatians 3:28-29; 4:21-31; 6:11-16; Hebrews 8:13; 12:12-24; 1 Peter 2:5-10; Revelation 3:9)?

15. Isn't the church called Israel (Romans 9:6; 24-29; Ephesians 2:11ff; Galatians 6:16)?

16. Isn't it true that the genealogical records of the Jews were destroyed with the destruction of temple in AD 70, making any future claim of Hebrew lineage impossible to prove?

17. Doesn't God have *one* flock composed of Jews and Gentiles (John 10:16; Ephesians 2:11ff)? Doesn't God have *one* house with Christ as its head (Hebrews 3:2-6)?

18. Aren't the New Testament saints perfected together with the Old Testament saints in the one body of Christ (Hebrews 11:39-40)? Aren't all saved men made alive in Christ (1 Corinthians 15:22)?

19. When the Jews rejected Jesus, weren't their branches broken off and the Gentiles "grafted in" (Romans 9:6-8; 11:11-24), along with the remnant of Jews (Romans 11:5)?

20. Since the Gentiles are heirs to the promise along with the Jews (Romans 15:8-12; Ephesians 2:11ff), isn't the conclusion inescapable that the church is the continuation of God's Israel with this difference: Jew and Gentile are on equal footing in the new Israel? Hasn't Christ now made both Jew and Gentile together into *one new man,* having *reconciled them both in one body to God?*

21. Doesn't the New Testament explain that, while the physical temple was about to be destroyed, it was being replaced by the church, with Christ as the cornerstone and Christians as the living stones (Ephesians 2:19-22; 1 Peter 2:4-9)?

22. Doesn't the distinctive of the separation between Israel and the church inevitably teach that there are two paths to salvation—law for Jews and grace for everyone else? Didn't C. I. Scofield himself say: "As a dispensation, grace begins with the death and resurrection of Christ. . . . The point of testing is no longer legal obedience as the condition of salvation, but acceptance or rejection of Christ. . . . " (*Scofield Reference Bible,* page 1115)? Doesn't the labeling of the current dispensation as the *Age of Grace* at the very least confuse the issue of justification? Aren't both law and grace (gospel) present in both the Old Testament and New Testaments? Isn't the notion that God saved Old Testament Jews by law, but now saves New Testament Christians by

grace unbiblical (Romans 4, 5)? Doesn't Paul in Galatians 3 clearly state that no man is justified by the law, and does he not quote the Old Testament to prove it? On the other hand, doesn't the New Testament contain many statements about obeying the law (Matthew 5:19; 7:16-20; 13:36-43; 25:31-46; Romans 2:13; 3:31; James 2:8-26)?

23. When Jesus said in John 14:6 that no man comes to the Father but through Him, didn't Jesus mean what He said? "No man" would include Jew or Gentile, would it not?

24. Does any passage in the New Testament explicitly support the idea that the land promises made to Israel are yet to be fulfilled?

25. If the land promises to Israel are forever and unconditional, why did God say they were conditional in Deuteronomy 4 and 28? And doesn't Hebrews 6:11-20 tell us that the promises to Abraham were fulfilled? Isn't God's unchanging promise to bless the world through the seed of Abraham (Genesis 12:3) fulfilled in the gospel (Galatians 3:6-9)? [269]

26. Do you believe that two-thirds of Israelis will be slaughtered in a Holocaust II (John Walvoord's book *Israel in Prophecy*)? If so, how can you call yourself pro-Israel? When you pray for Jesus to come soon or for the imminent rapture, aren't you asking for a near term slaughter of the Jews? Isn't this teaching based almost entirely on one verse—Zechariah 13:8? But doesn't the New Testament place the previous verse (13:7) squarely in the time of Christ? Isn't it true that there is no prediction in the book of Revelation about the annihilation of two-thirds of all Jews living in Israel?

27. Why do you support the modern nation of Israel, which tolerates persecution of Christianity?

28. If we are in the New Covenant era, which Scripture says is forever, why would God go back to the temple system of the Old Covenant which Paul called bondage (Galatians 4)?

29. If God is going to re-institute animal sacrifices in a future millennium, does that mean Christ died in vain (Galatians 2:21)? Why would you expect Ezekiel's temple and sacri-

fices to be a literal reinstitution since Christ's blood has annulled all animal sacrifices (Hebrews 9 and 10)?

30.   Weren't all Old Testament prophecies about a rebuilt temple fulfilled in the rebuilding of the temple under Zerubbabel (Haggai 2:21-23), or in the rebuilt temple in first century under Herod, or in the building up of the Jew-Gentile church in the first century (Acts 15:16)?

Summary: The Jews as God's covenant nation were rejected. The "Israel of God" was given to those individuals, either Jew or Gentile, who believe. When the Jews rejected Jesus, they were "broken off," and the Gentiles were "grafted in" along with the believing remnant of the Jews. The Bible explains that while the physical temple was about to be destroyed, it was being replaced by the church with Christ as the cornerstone and Christians as the living stones. There is no compelling scriptural support for the dispensationalist views about a yet-future Israel/temple or a renewal and salvation for the Jews by a separate path.

C. QUESTIONS ABOUT HERMENEUTICS (BIBLICAL INTERPRETIVE METHOD):

1.   As dispensationalists, you say that you interpret the Bible literally, but do you do so appropriately and consistently? For example, when Isaiah (55:12) described the mountains and the hills breaking into song and the trees clapping their hands, is this to be taken literally? When Isaiah (13:9-13) described God's shaking the earth from its place and making the stars not show their light (predicting doom on Babylon), wasn't this intended to be taken seriously but non-literally? Or, when God said that He would make the sun go down at noon (Amos 8:8-9), was this literal or rather a metaphorical statement about his coming judgment on the northern kingdom of Israel (2 Kings 17:3-6)? When Jesus said that He was the "vine," does that mean He is a plant?

2.   You say that you interpret the Bible literally, but do the land promises to Israel being "forever" mean forever literally? You really think that "forever" means only 1,000 years don't you—which is not exactly forever? How can the kingdom be a literal thousand years when Isaiah, Daniel, and Luke

said it would have no end (Isaiah 9:6-7; Daniel 2:44-45, 7:14; Luke 1:32-33)?

3. If you think, using your "literal" hermeneutic, that the seed associated with the Abrahamic covenant means the physical Jews, doesn't this directly contradict what Paul said in Galatians 3:7, 29 — that the Christian is the seed of Abraham and heir to the promise?

4. When Colossians 1:23 states, "This is the gospel you heard and that has been proclaimed [present perfect tense] to *'every living creature under heaven'"* — do you interpret this literally? Had the gospel been declared to the American Indians? (No, of course not. This passage, and many others that could be given, refers to the preaching of the gospel in the first century to all ethnicities of men across the known world.)

5. Doesn't the Bible throughout use figures of speech such as symbolism, allegory, parable, hyperbole, and so forth to make a point — which are not intended to be interpreted literally?

6. If the Bible is to be interpreted 100% literally, why are terms like "at hand," "quickly," "shortly," etc., not read literally?

7. If "soon/shortly" means "2,000 years or longer," does that mean it was going to take Timothy 2,000 years to be sent to the Philippians (or to us) by Paul (Philippians 2:19)?

8. If the Bible is to be interpreted 100% literally, why do some dispensationalists say the seven churches in Asia (Revelation 1-3) are "church ages" and not "literal" churches?

9. If you think that 2 Timothy 2:15, which in the King James Version says "rightly *dividing* the word of truth," means to separate the Bible into dispensations, how do you deal with other versions of the Bible (ESV, ASV, etc.) that say "rightly *handling* the word of truth"?

Gary DeMar, author of the book *Last Days Madness*, says this about interpretation of words: "If the Bible can be interpreted so 'soon' can mean 'late,' and 'near' can mean 'distant,' and 'shortly' can mean 'delayed,' and vice versa, then the Bible can mean anything and nothing. Does God have two methods of measurement? When God says 'love,' are we to read 'hate'? Can we trust a God whose words can mean their opposite?"

D. QUESTIONS ABOUT THE RAPTURE AND THE TRIBULATION:

1. Do we find anywhere in the New Testament a trace of evidence for a secret, invisible, rapture of the church?

2. If Jesus is going to rapture the church out of the world, why did Jesus pray for the exact opposite thing to happen (that the church would *not* be taken out of the world) in John 17:15?

3. Does any verse in the Bible clearly teach a "seven-year tribulation"?

4. Don't the horrors endured by the Jews described by Josephus, culminating in the Jewish-Roman War of AD 66-70, qualify as the Great Tribulation—given that more than a million Jews were killed, their nation was dissolved, their temple was destroyed, and along with it their whole covenantal world order and the centerpiece of their religion— the centuries old system of animal sacrifices for sin?

5. If the Great Tribulation (Daniel 12:1; Matthew 24:21) is *global*, why did Jesus tell those living in Judea to flee to the mountains to avoid the tribulation (Matthew 24:16, Luke 21:20-22)? In other words, how could the Great Tribulation be a global event if people could escape it by fleeing to the mountains? If the Great Tribulation is global, why did God tell Daniel that it would come upon the Jews (Daniel 12:1)? If the Great Tribulation was to be global, why did Jesus and Peter compare it to the wrath that came upon Sodom and Gomorrah, which was clearly local (Luke 17:25-32; 2 Peter 2:4-9)?

6. If the Great Tribulation is future, why did Jesus say it would fall upon his generation (Matthew 12:38-45; 16:1-4; 23:35-39)?

7. Doesn't Daniel tell us that the *time of trouble/distress* (12:1), the *resurrection* (12:2), the *time of the end* (12:9), and the *abomination of desolation* (12:11)—would all occur when the *power of the holy people had finally been broken* (12:7) and the *burnt offering taken away* (12:11)? Can there be *any* doubt that this was AD 70?

8. If the rapture in 1 Thessalonians 4 is still an event to come in the future, why did Paul expect that the prophesied events in 1 and 2 Thessalonians would occur while some of his contemporaries were still living? (Go back and re-read these passages with this idea in mind: 1 Thessalonians 1:6-10; 2:13-16; 4:17; 5:4; 5:8-9; 2 Thessalonians 1:7.)

Dispensationalists cannot find even a single verse in the New Testament that explicitly supports any of the following necessary dispensationalists distinctives: The church will be raptured prior to a seven-year tribulation period; the land promises made to Israel are yet to be fulfilled; the Antichrist will make a covenant with the Jews and then break it; a seven-year tribulation period; Jesus will sit on David's throne in Jerusalem during the millennium; the temple will be rebuilt during the millennium; animal sacrifices and circumcision will be reinstituted during the millennium.

E. Questions about the Kingdom of God:

1. How can Jesus' kingdom be physical/earthly when Jesus rejected a physical kingdom in John 18:36?

2. How could Jesus' kingdom have not yet come, when John the Baptist, Jesus Christ, and the apostles all declared that the kingdom of God was "about to come" (Matthew 3:2; 4:17; 10:7; Acts 28:31)?

3. Why would Jesus' kingdom be set up in earthly Jerusalem, if

Paul equated earthly Jerusalem to bondage (Galatians 4:21-31)?

4. Since Jesus declared that the kingdom had come when He cast out demons, didn't He usher in the kingdom during his time on earth (Matthew 12:28; Luke 10:9; Luke 11:20)?

5. How can Jesus' kingdom be seen by everyone when Jesus Himself said it would *not come with observation* (Luke 17:20)?

6. Is it a conflict to long for an earthly kingdom of peace and joy while expecting God to destroy the planet?

7. How can the "millennial" kingdom of God be of the Jews when Jesus himself said that He took the kingdom away from them and gave it to the Jew-Gentile church, which produces the fruits thereof (Matthew 8:12; 21:43)? If Jesus took the kingdom from the Jews and gave it to the church, why is there no scripture to show another transfer back to the Jews?

8. How can Jesus' earthly kingdom be set up in earthly Jerusalem, when Jesus himself said the hour was coming when worshipping God would *not* be in Jerusalem (John 4:21)?

9. Doesn't the Bible make it clear that Jesus began his reign with his resurrection (Acts 2:29-36; Revelation 1:5)?

10. Has the failure to recognize that we are living in the kingdom of heaven today contributed to the malaise of the church? Has the expectation of the soon tribulation also contributed to a lack of energy in the church and its witness to the world?

11. If the kingdom is limited to a thousand years, why does Jesus say that his kingdom will have no end (Luke 1:33)?

12. Does the idea of a future millennial reign of Jesus on earth sound too much like Jehovah's Witness theology? (The Jehovah's Witnesses got their start with a book series entitled *Millennial Dawn*.)

J. Stuart Russell said, "The *coming*, the *judgment*, the *kingdom*, are all coincident and contemporaneous, and not only so, but also *nigh at hand*. . . . So long as the Theocratic nation existed, and the temple, with its priesthood and sacrifices and ritual, remained, and the Mosaic law continued, or seemed to continue, in force, the distinction between Jew and Gentile could not be obliterated. But the barrier was effectually broken down when law, temple, city, and nation were swept away together, and the Theocracy was visibly brought to a final consummation. That event was, so to speak, the formal and public declaration that God was no longer God of the Jews only, but that He was now the common Father of all men. . . . " [270]

F. MORE QUESTIONS FOR DISPENSATIONALISTS:

1. Does any single verse of the Bible explicitly teach that the Antichrist will make a covenant with the Jews and then break it?

2. Does a single verse explicitly teach that Jesus will reign on earth for a literal thousand years?

3. Does the Bible speak of a literal thousand-year reign of the saints outside of Revelation 20—a chapter that is perhaps the most symbolic section of the most symbolic and complex book in the Bible? Is it likely that something so dramatically significant would not appear elsewhere in the Bible? Why are we not told in clear passages of the gospels or epistles of a thousand-year reign of Christ?

4. Isn't the number 1,000 used symbolically in other places in the Bible (Deuteronomy 7:9, Psalm 50:10)?

5. In a literal millennium, are premillennialists relying on faith in total bureaucracy for the world? Doesn't this view put too much faith in man's ability to live sinlessly?

For more questions, see the endnote.[271]

If you are in a dispensational church, you might want to give your pastor a copy of the book **Dispensationalism: Today, Yesterday, and Tomorrow** *by Curtis I. Crenshaw and Grover E. Gunn, III—and ask him to read it and give you a written response.*

APPENDIX D
The Soul

Christians generally hold to the idea that body and soul are separate entities which can survive independently. Of course, *body* and *soul* are concepts of the Bible, but their distinct separation and destiny, in the way that most people understand, is in question. Is the soul really an *immortal entity* that survives the death of the body? There is reason for doubt that this idea is actually supported by the Bible.[272]

In the Old Testament the Hebrew word for soul is *nephesh* (also spelled *nehphesh*). In the New Testament, the Greek word for soul is *psyche* (sometimes spelled *psukee, psuchay,* or *psuche*). You can look up these words, if you want to take the time, in the online *Blue Letter Bible* lexicon at www.blueletterbible.org. Then, go to "Search" in the upper left hand corner. Next, click on "Strong's Search." Then, for *nephesh* type in the Strong's Number which is H5315 and check "Hebrew." For *psyche,* use Strong's Number G5590 and check "Greek." Or, you can go to these URL's:

nephesh:

> *(http://www.blueletterbible.org/lang/lexicon/lexicon.
> cfm?Strongs=H5315&t=KJV)*

psyche:

> (http://www.blueletterbible.org/lang/lexicon/lexicon.
> cfm?Strongs=G5590&t=KJV)

Many people argue that the idea of the soul being separate from the body originated from Greek thought, and Christians have borrowed from Greek philosophy and adopted the concept in error. Check the endnotes for some articles on this.[273]

What does the Bible actually teach? Of particular interest, about one-third of the uses of soul (*nephesh*) in the Old Testament are associated with the **death of the soul**. For examples, see Joshua 10:28; Judges 16:16; Job 7:15; Psalm 33:19; 35:17; 78:50; Isaiah 53:12; Ezekiel 13:19; 18:4, 20, 27. (Note: Nephesh is often translated as something other than "soul" in English. Since you will not always see the word "soul" in these passages, you may have to use an interlinear Bible such as the *Blue Letter Bible* that shows the Hebrew in order to see that the word nephesh/soul is actually in these passages.) In fact, the word *nephesh* appears over 750 times in the Old Testament and is subject to death over 200 times.

Many people, by the way, think that only humans have a soul. But in Genesis we see that **animals also have a soul**. In several places (for example, Genesis 1:21, 24, 30) we see *nephesh* applied to animals and is usually translated as "living creatures" or as "life."

Similarly, in the New Testament there are numerous passages in which soul (*psyche*) means *life* and can die, be killed, or perish! See Matthew 10:28; 26:38; Acts 3:23; James 5:20, and Revelation 16:3. *Psyche* (or a derivation) appears over 100 times in the New Testament and is **subject to death** approximately 30 times. The word "immortal" never appears in the Bible together with "soul." The analysis of this can become confusing because there are a wide variety of uses for the Hebrew and Greek words. But the preponderance of the evidence indicates that *soul* is not really an entity that lives apart from the body. Rather *soul* is a term that means *life* or the *essence of life*. Thus the soul is more about what one *is* rather that what one *has*.

So, the standard view that an immortal soul is an entity that lives *separately* or *independently* from the body—is problematic. We discussed at length in the book what happens at biological death. This brief discussion of the soul does not interfere with our conclusions in any way. We ultimately enter heaven in our new glorified bodies, which is the ultimate hope of the believer.

Some people actually believe that we have *three* components: body, soul, and spirit. Is *this* biblical? There are a couple of places in the Bible where we see the terms body, soul, and spirit used together, for example 1 Thessalonians 5:23, which reads "Now may the God of peace himself sanctify you completely, and may your whole spirit and soul and body be kept blameless at the coming of the Lord Jesus Christ."

But this does not really prove that we are three-part persons. Here is how the *Reformation Study Bible* puts it in the annotations:

> Three words are used to emphasize the wholeness of the perfection. "Spirit" and "soul" are used as virtual synonyms in the Bible for the spiritual component of a person. When

the terms appear together (as here and in Hebrews 4:12) it is difficult to find any significant difference in meaning. Compare the fourfold representation of "heart," "soul," "mind," and "strength" in Mark 12:30.[274]

Appendix E

Bibliography and Resources

Bondar, Alan. *Reading the Bible through New Covenant Eyes*. Baltimore, MD: Publish America, 2010.

Bray, John L. *Matthew 24 Fulfilled*. Powder Springs, Georgia: American Vision, 1996.

Chilton, David. *Paradise Restored: An Eschatology of Dominion*. Tyler, Texas: Dominion Press, 2000.

Chilton, David. *The Days of Vengeance: An Exposition of the Book of Revelation*. Tyler, Texas: Dominion Press, 1987.

Collins, Tina Rae. *The Gathering in the Last Days*. New York: M. F. Sohn Publications, 2012.

Crenshaw, Curtis I. and Gunn, Grover E. III, *Dispensationalism Today, Yesterday, and Tomorrow*. Memphis, TN: Footstool Publications, 1985, reprinted in 1989.

Dawson, Samuel G. *Essays on Eschatology: An Introductory Overview of the Study of Last Things*. Amarillo, Texas: SGD Press, 2009.

Day, Michael, editor. *Fulfilled Covenant Bible*. Tucson, AZ: Wheatmark, Inc., 2012.

DeMar, Gary. *End Times Fiction: A Biblical Consideration of the Left Behind Theology*. Nashville, TN: Thomas Nelson Publishers, 2001.

DeMar, Gary. *Is Jesus Coming Soon?* Powder Springs, Georgia: American Vision, 2006.

DeMar, Gary. *Last Days Madness: Obsession of the Modern Church*, fourth revised edition. Powder Springs, Georgia: American Vision, 1999.

DeMar, Gary and Gumerlock, Francis X. *The Early Church and the End of the World*. Powder Springs, Georgia: American Vision, 2006.

Denton, T. Everett. *Hebrews: From Flawed to Flawless Fulfilled*, 2012.

Fenemore, Michael A. and Simmons, Kurt M. *The Twilight of Postmillennialism; Fatal Errors in the Teachings of Keith A. Mathison, Kenneth L. Gentry, Jr. etc.* Preterism.info Publishing, 2010.

Frost, Samuel M. *Misplaced Hope: The Origins of First and Second Century Eschatology* (Colorado Springs, CO: Bimillennial Press, 2002.

Frost, Samuel; Green, David; Hassertt, Edward; Sullivan, Michael. *House Divided: Bridging the Gap in Reformed Eschatology, A Response to When Shall These Things Be?* Romana, CA: Vision Publishing, 2009.

Fudge, Edward William. *The Fire That Consumes.* Houston, TX: Providential Press, 1982.

Gentry, Kenneth L., Jr. *Before Jerusalem Fell: Dating the Book of Revelation.* Powder Springs, Georgia: American Vision, 1998.

Gregg, Steve. *Revelation, Four Views: A Parallel Commentary.* Nashville, Tennessee: Thomas Nelson Publishers, 1997.

Gumerlock, Francis X. *The Day and the Hour: Christianity's Perennial Fascination with Predicting the End of the World.* Powder Springs, Georgia: American Vision, 2000.

Harden, Daniel E. *Overcoming Sproul's Resurrection Obstacles.* Bradford, PA: IPA Publishers, 1999.

Hill, Glenn L. *Christianity's Great Dilemma: Is Jesus Coming Again or Is He Not?* Lexington, KY: Moonbeam Publications, 2010.

Hoekema, Anthony A. *The Meaning of the Millennium.* Downers Grove, IL: Intervarsity Press, 1977.

King, Max R., *The Cross and the Parousia of Christ.* Warren, OH: Writing and Research Ministry, Parkman Road Church of Christ, 1987.

Martin, Brian L. *Behind the Veil of Moses: Piecing Together the Mystery of the Second Coming.* Xulon Press, 2009.

Martin, Timothy P. and Vaughn, Jeffrey L., PhD. *Beyond Creation Science: New Covenant Creation from Genesis to Revelation.* Whitehall, MT: Apocalyptic Vision Press, 2207.

McKenzie, Duncan, PhD. *The Antichrist and the Second Coming: A Preterist Examination.* Xulon Press, 2009.

Noe, John. *Shattering the Left Behind Delusion.* Bradford, PA: International Preterist Association, 2000.

Ogden, Arthur M. *The Avenging of the Apostles and Prophets.* Pinson, Alabama: Ogden Publications, 2006, Third Edition.

Otto, Randall E. *Coming in the Clouds: An Evangelical Case for the Invisibility of Christ at His Second Coming.* University Press of America, 1994.

Preston, Don K., D. Div. *The Elements Shall Melt with Fervent Heat: A Study of 2 Peter 3.* Ardmore, Oklahoma: JaDon Productions LLC, 2006.

Preston, Don K. *The Last Days Identified.* Ardmore, Oklahoma: JaDon Productions LLC, 2004.

Preston, Don K., D. Div. *We Shall Meet Him in The Air: The Wedding of the King of Kings.* Ardmore, Oklahoma: JaDon Management Inc., 2010.

Preston, Don K., D. Div. *Who Is This Babylon?* Ardmore, Oklahoma: JaDon Management, Inc., 2006.

Ratzinger, Joseph. *Eschatology: Death and Eternal Life, Second Edition.* Washington, DC: The Catholic University of America Press, 1988, originally published in German in 1977.

Robinson, John A. T. *Redating the New Testament.* Philadelphia, Pennsylvania: The Westminster Press, 1976.

Russell, J. Stuart. *The Parousia: The New Testament Doctrine of Christ's Second Coming.* Bradford, Pennsylvania: International Preterist Association, 2003, originally published in 1878.

Sproul, R. C., editor. *The Reformation Study Bible.* Lake Mary, Florida: Ligonier Ministries, 2005.

Sproul, R. C. *The Last Days according to Jesus.* Grand Rapids, Michigan: Baker Books, 1998.

Stevens, Edward E. *Questions about the Afterlife.* Bradford, PA: International Preterist Association, 1999.

Stevens, Edward E. *First Century Events in Chronological Order: from the Birth of Christ to the Destruction of Jerusalem in AD 70 (A Pre-publication Manuscript).* : International Preterist Association, 2009.

Terry, Milton S. *Biblical Apocalyptics: A Study of the Most Notable Revelations of God and of Christ in the Canonical Scriptures*, 1898.

Terry, Milton S. *Biblical Hermeneutics: A Treatise on the Interpretation of the Old and New Testaments.* Grand Rapids, Michigan: Academie Books, a division of Zondervan Publishing House, 1984, originally published in 1898.

Vanderwaal, Cornelius. *Hal Lindsey and Biblical Prophecy.* St. Catharines, Ontario, Canada: Paideia Press, 1978.

Vincent, Joseph M. II. *The Millennium: Past, Present, or Future? A Biblical Defense for the 40 Year Transition Period.* Ardmore, OK: JaDon Publishing, 2012.

Virkler, Henry A. *Hermeneutics: Principles and Processes of Biblical Interpretation.* Grand Rapids, MI: Baker Books, 1981.

Wilkinson, Douglas. *Making Sense of the Millennium* (Kindle Edition, 2013).

Wilkinson, Douglas. *Preterist Time Statements* (Kindle Edition, 2014).

Wright, N. T. *Paul: In Fresh Perspective.* Great Britain: First Fortress Press, 2005.

Young, Robert. *Young's Literal Translation.* Ada, MI: Baker Publishing Group, 1986, originally published in 1862.

Online Bibles:

http://www.biblegateway.com

http://www.biblestudytools.com

http://www.blueletterbible.org

http://www.studylight.org

Preterist websites are exploding in number. Some websites as of 2014 are listed below. Many, though not all, are from a full preterist perspective; others are from a partial preterist perspective. *We are not endorsing any of these in particular.* Some are much better than others, and some may be teaching things with which we strongly disagree. The list will be outdated as soon as the book is published, but we offer it here to give the reader an opportunity to see differing views and to do independent research. They are in no particular order. The list may also be viewed online, and occasionally updated, at:

www.prophecyquestions.wordpress.com (search for "preterist websites")

Preterist Questions and Answers:

http://preteristcosmos.com/questionsandanswers.html (David A. Green)

http://www.preterist.org/preteristQA.asp (Edward E. Stevens)

http://livingthequestion.org/resources (Riley O'Brien Powell)

http://ecclesia.org/truth/preterist-questions.html (Richard Anthony)

http://apostolicpreterist.com/Preterist_Q___A.html (Virgil Vaduva quoted)

http://www.preteristvision.org/questions.html

Here are places to go for preterist books and other resources:
http://www.preterist.org/preteristbookstore.asp
http://americanvision.com
http://www.bibleprophecy.com/banners-view/bpstore

These sites are hubs for preterist websites, books, sermons, Facebook pages, and networking:

http://www.thefulfilledconnection.com (Allyn Morton)
http://asiteforthelord.com/id20.html (Tony Denton)

Misc. Preterist Websites:

http://www.faithfacts.org (the apologetics site of the author, Charles S. Meek)

http://www.allthingsfulfilled.com (William Bell)

http://www.lastdays-eschatology.net (William Bell)

http://americanvision.org (Gary DeMar)

http://www.asiteforthelord.com (Tony Everett Denton)

http://www.bereanbiblechurch.org/home.php (Berean Bible Church, David Curtis)

http://beyondtheendtimes.com/index.html (Ken Davies)

http://www.bibleprophecy.com (Don K. Preston)

http://www.eschatology.org (Don K. Preston)

http://donkpreston.com (Don K. Preston)

http://fulfilledradio.com (Don Preston)

http://www.biblepreterist.com (Michael Alan Nichols)

http://www.biblicalpreteristarchive.com

http://bibleprophecyfulfilled.com (Gary Parrish, Michael Day, Terry Kashian, David Warren)

http://www.biblicalfulfillment.org (Jessie Mills)

http://www.bluepointbiblechurch.org/peace (Blue Point Bible Church)

http://www.charlescoty.com/Theology.html (Charles Coty)

http://www.charlescoty.blogspot.com (Charles Coty)

http://lastdayspast.com(Charles Coty)

http://congregationofchrist.org (Spring and Case Church of Christ)

http://deathisdefeated.ning.com (John Scargy)

http://www.drkellynelsonbirks.com (Kelly Birks)

http://www.equip.org (Hank Hanegraaff)

http://eschatology.com (Ward Fenley)

http://www.eschatology101.com (Jim Wade)

http://www.fulfilledcg.com (Brian Martin)

http://fulfilled-eschatology.blogspot.com (Tim Liwanag)

http://fullpreterism.com (Mike Sullivan with various contributors David Green, Ed Hassertt, Don Preston, William Bell)

http://www.kennethgentry.com (Kenneth Gentry)

http://kloposmasm.com/ (Adam Maarschalk)

http://lightshine70.wordpress.com (Frank Speer)

http://www.ligionier.org (R. C. Sproul)

http://lynnish.tripod.com/index.html (Lynn Schuldt)

http://moonmeanderings.wordpress.com (Tina Rae Collins)

http://newcovenanteyes.com (New Covenant Eyes Church, Alan Bondar) http://www.newcreationministries.tv (Ward Fenley, Brian Maxwell, Shannon Shogren)

http://www.ncfgeorgetown.com/#/Home (New Covenant Fellowship Church)

http://ontimejournal.com (Thomas K. Burk)

http://planetpreterist.com (Virgil Vaduva)

http://premillpreterism.ning.com (Douglas Wilkinson)

http://www.preterism.info (Michael Fenemore)

http://preterismmatters.webs.com

http://preterism.ning.com (Michael Bennett)

http://preterism-preterist-taffy.blogspot.in (Taffy Boyo)

http://preterist.org (Edward E. Stevens, International Preterist Association)

http://www.buzzsprout.com/11633 (Edward E. Stevens)

http://www.preteristarchive.com (Todd Dennis)

http://www.preteristcentral.com (Kurt Simmons)

http://www.prophecyrefi.org (John Noe)

http://www.raptureless.com (Jonathan Welton)

http://restorationgj.com (Timothy King)

http://revelationrevolution.org (Daniel Morais)

http://www.treeoflifeministries.info (Mike Sullivan)

http://www.wix.com/edwhynotme/fandd#! (Ed Hassertt)

http://reasonbyfaith.wix.com/rbfm (Ed Hassertt)

http://www.thenarrowpath.com (Steve Gregg)

http://www.theos.org/forum/index.php (Steve Gregg)

http://theparousiaofchrist.blogspot.com (Terry Cropper)

http://www.truthaccordingtoscripture.com/index.php (Mesa Biblical Church)

http://truthinliving.net/category/eschatology (Robert Pike)

http://worldwithoutend.info/wwewp (John Paul Crandell)

http://www.worldwithoutend.info (Victory Baptist Church, Philippines)

APPENDIX F

ENDNOTES

The endnotes may be viewed online at http://prophecyquestions. wordpress.com/. There, search for "Endnotes."

1. http://uk.reuters.com/article/2012/12/13/us-usa-weather-religion-idUKBRE8BC1CX20121213

2. The war is sometimes referred to as the First Jewish Roman War or The Great Revolt. See http://en.wikipedia.org/wiki/First_Jewish%E2%80%93Roman_War.

3. Flavius Josephus, *The Wars of the Jews, Book 6 (6.9.3)*. Available online at http://www.ccel.org/j/josephus/works/JOSEPHUS.HTM. The number of dead is far more even than the US Civil War, which is estimated to be between 600,000 and 750,000.

4. Flavius Josephus, *The Wars of the Jews, Book 6 (6.3.4)*. Available online at http://www.ccel.org/j/josephus/works/JOSEPHUS.HTM.

5. Flavius Josephus, *The Wars of the Jews, Book 5 (5.10.5)* and *Book 6 (6.9.4)*. Available online at http://www.ccel.org/j/josephus/works/JOSEPHUS.HTM.

6. See these websites:

*   http://en.wikipedia.org/wiki/First_Jewish%E2%80%93Roman_Wa

*   http://en.wikipedia.org/wiki/Jewish%E2%80%93Roman_wars

*   http://en.wikipedia.org/wiki/Siege_of_Masada

*   http://www.eyewitnesstohistory.com/jewishtemple.htm.

7. http://www.preteristcosmos.com/question5.html#note95.

8. Many scholars place the year of Jesus' death on the cross at AD 33. So the intervening time till the destruction of the temple would have been 37 years.

9. Edward E. Stevens, *Introduction to the New Testament Canon*, for the *Fulfilled Covenant Bible*, Michael Day, editor, April 2011. This work was still in progress and yet unpublished as of mid 2012. Here is the entire article: http://www.bibleprophecyfulfilled.com/bible/Intro_to_ NT_Stevens.pdf. We highly recommend this article to our readers. Stevens is the founder of the International Preterist Association, website http://preterist.org.

10. *The Reformation Study Bible*, published in 2005, has contributions from over fifty esteemed scholars; General Editor R. C. Sproul, Sr. In the introduction to the book of Luke, this source says (page 1451), "Luke and Acts may have been written about A.D. 63. Acts ends with Paul still under house arrest in Rome, and it is reasonable to think that if Luke knew of Paul's release or death he would have mentioned it. Luke notes that the prophecy of Agabus was fulfilled (Acts 11:28); he would surely have done the same with Jesus' prophecy of the destruction of Jerusalem (Luke 21:20) if he was writing after A.D. 70. Acts mentions nothing that must be dated after A.D. 62 and shows no knowledge of Paul's letters. All these factors argue for an early date." In the introduction to the book of Matthew, *The Reformation Study Bible* (page 1359) states, "Further, there is some evidence in the context of the book that Matthew was written before the destruction of Jerusalem in A.D. 70. The Gospel warns against the Sadducees, a group that rapidly declined from prominence after A.D. 70 and ultimately ceased to exist. The language used to describe the destruction of Jerusalem in ch. 24 reflects Old Testament prophecies of the divine judgment that Jesus foresaw as connected with the coming of His kingdom. There is no need to explain the content of ch. 24 as the author's memory of a historical event." Scholars generally agree that Mark was written before Matthew and Luke. *The Reformation Study Bible* was published by Ligonier Ministries, 400 Technology Park, Lake Mary, FL 32746.

11. Here is a partial list of authors who argue for dating the New Testament prior to AD 70:

- David Chilton, *Paradise Restored: An Eschatology of Dominion* (Tyler, Texas: Dominion Press, 2000).

- Gary DeMar, *Last Days Madness: Obsession of the Modern Church* (Powder Springs, Georgia: American Vision, 1999), Fourth revised edition. Available from their website www.americanvision.org. DeMar is considered a partial preterist.

- Kenneth L. Gentry, Jr., *Before Jerusalem Fell: Dating the Book of Revelation* (Powder Springs, Georgia: American Vision, 1998). Gentry is considered a partial preterist/postmillennialist.

- Arthur M. Ogden, *The Avenging of the Apostles and Prophets.* (Pinson, Alabama: Ogden Publications, 2006), Third Edition. Excellent argumentation for the early pre-70 date of the book of Revelation. Available from their website: www.aogden.com.

- John A. T. Robinson, *Redating the New Testament* (Philadelphia, Pennsylvania: The Westminster Press, 1976). (Robinson is considered a liberal scholar who was convinced that the entire New Testament was written prior to AD 70.)

- J. Stuart Russell, *The Parousia: The New Testament Doctrine of Christ's Second Coming* (Bradford, Pennsylvania: International Preterist Association, 2003), originally published in 1878.

- Milton S. Terry, *Biblical Hermeneutics: A Treatise on the Interpretation of the Old and New Testaments* (Grand Rapids, Michigan: Academie Books, a division of Zondervan Publishing House, 1984), originally published in 1898. Available in a free online version at http://www.preteristarchive.com/Books/1883_terry_biblical-hermeneutics.html.

- Cornelius Vanderwaal, *Hal Lindsey and Biblical Prophecy* (St. Catharines, Ontario, Canada: Paideia Press, 1978).

12. *The Reformation Study Bible* says, "Revelation was written during a time of persecution, probably near the end of the reign of the Roman Emperor Nero (A.D. 54-68) or during the reign of Domitian (A.D. 81-96). Most scholars favor a date about A.D. 95." As a preview to Chapter 9, these websites list numerous advocates for a pre-AD 70 authorship of Revelation:

- http://livingthequestion.org/revelation/,
- http://www.preteristarchive.com/BibleStudies/ApocalypseCommentaries/Dating/Early/index.html.

13. C. S. Lewis, *The World's Last Night: And Other Essays* (New York, NY: Harcourt, Brace and Company, 1960), pages 97-98. Available online at http://www.archive.org/details/worldslastnighta012859mbp.

14. Quote by Michael A. Fenemore and Kurt M. Simmons in *The Twilight of Postmillennialism; Fatal Errors in the Teachings of Keith A. Mathison, Kenneth L. Gentry, Jr. etc.*(Preterism.info Publishing, 2010), page 57. See http://www.preterism.info/jews-reject-futurism.htm.

15. http://en.wikipedia.org/wiki/List_of_prophecies_of_Joseph_Smith.

16. Stevens is the founder of the International Preterist Association, website http://preterist.org.

17. J. I. Packer, *Fundamentalism and the Word of God*, (Grand Rapids, MI: William B. Eerdmans Publishing Co., 1958), pages 69-70.

18. Francis X. Gumerlock, *The Day and the Hour: Christianity's Perennial Fascination with Predicting the End of the World* (Powder Springs, Georgia: American Vision, 2000), page 2. One can also find various lists of historic false prophets on the Internet, such as these websites:

- http://en.wikipedia.org/wiki/Unfulfilled_Christian_religious_predictions
- http://www.abhota.info/index.htm
- http://www.ministryserver.com/rwsr/Part01_Introduction.htm
- http://americanvision.org/4545/before-harold-camping-there-was-chuck-smith/
- http://publisherscorner.nordskogpublishing.com/2009/01/is-it-time-for-doomsday-or-for-building.html
- http://politicaloutcast.com/2012/12/bible-scholar-predicts-end-of-world-and-immobilizes-millions/.
- The interested reader can search for more such sites in the Internet.

19. Cited by Don K. Preston, *The Last Days Identified* (Ardmore, OK: JaDon Productions LLC, 2004), page 79. See also this article by Daniel Walther entitled "RESEARCH: Martin Luther and the End of the World": http://www.ministrymagazine.org/archive/1951/December/martin-luther-and-the-end-of-the-world.

20. From "American Lutheran Views on Eschatology and How They Related to the American Protestants" by John M. Brenner.

21. The reader can find numerous lists of failed predictions on the Internet. Sources include:

- Kenneth Dahl, http://www.facebook.com/notes/letting-god-escape/50-things-i-did-not-learn-in-church-about-the-end-times-by-ken-dahl/301690093241071, also Dahl's book *All These Things* http://kennethdahl.com/allthesethings.pdf.

- Gary DeMar, *Last Days Madness: Obsession of the Modern Church* (Powder Springs, Georgia: American Vision, 1999), Fourth revised edition, chapter 1.

- http://www.bible.ca/pre-date-setters.htm.

- http://en.wikipedia.org/wiki/List_of_dates_predicted_for_apocalyptic_events.

22. See:

- Gary DeMar and Francis X. Gumerlock, *The Early Church and the End of the World* (Powder Springs, Georgia: American Vision, 2006), pages 27-38.

- Gary DeMar, *Is Jesus Coming Soon?* (Powder Springs, Georgia: American Vision, 2006).

- See also Samuel M. Frost, *Misplaced Hope: The Origins of First and Second Century Eschatology* (Colorado Springs, CO: Bimillennial Press, 2002).

- Online sources for many of the preterist quotes from the early church fathers include:
    - http://revivalculture.wordpress.com/evidence-of-preterism-in-church-history/
    - http://www.preteristarchive.com/ChurchHistory/index.html, http://www.preteristarchive.com/Preterism/index.html
    - http://free-in-truth.blogspot.com/2007/03/back-to-future-preterist-perspective.html?m=1
    - http://beyondtheendtimes.com/writing/articles/guest_articles/demar_bib_min_hist_pret.html

23.   See Francis X. Gumerlock, *The Day and the Hour: A Chronicle of Christianity's Perennial Fascination with Predicting the End of the World* (Powder Springs, Georgia: American Vision, 2000). Most of what the early Church Fathers wrote remain untranslated—some 218 Latin and 166 Greek volumes.

24.   Eusebius, *Ecclesiastical History* (*Church History*), Book lll, chapters 28, 39. Available online here: http://ncbible.info/MoodRes/History/EusebiusChurchHistory.pdf. See also http://en.wikipedia.org/wiki/Eusebius_of_Caesarea, and http://en.wikipedia.org/wiki/Papias_of_Hierapolis.

25.   Eusebius, *Ecclesiastical History* (*Church History*). Noteworthy are Book lll, chapters 7, 8, and 39 (against Papias and Irenaeus). Available online here: http://www.newadvent.org/fathers

- Eusebius, *The Proof of the Gospel* (*Demonstratio Evangelica*) trans. W. J. Ferrar, 2 vols. in 1 (Grand Rapids, MI: Baker Books, 1981). Some noteworthy passages about the Lord's coming in AD 70 include: Book VI, Chapter 13, paragraphs 13-18; Book VI, Chapter 18, paragraphs 26 and 27; Book VIII, Introduction first paragraph; Book VIII, Chapter 4, paragraphs 144, 146, 147; Book X, Chapter 7, paragraph 214. Available online at these sites: http://www.tertullian.org/fathers, http://www.intratext.com/X/ENG0882.HTM.

- Eusebius, *Theophania*. Noteworthy sections include: Book III, paragraph 4; Book IV, paragraphs 16-22, 28-29, 34-36; Book V, paragraph 17. You can see the work online at these links, as well as a summary by Samuel Lee: http://www.tertullian.org/fathers, http://www.preteristarchive.com/ChurchHistory/0310_eusebius_theophania.html#147, http://www.preteristarchive.com/Books/1843_lee_dissertations-eusebius.html

- See also: http://www.preteristarchive.com/StudyArchive/e/eusebius.html.

- See also Gary DeMar and Francis X. Gumerlock, *The Early Church and the End of the World* (Powder Springs, Georgia: American Vision, 2006), Chapter 2 and pages 74-75. The authors point out that in addition to Eusebius' view that Matthew 24 was fulfilled in AD 70, Eusebius also placed crucial passages from Zechariah as having been fulfilled prior to the destruction of Jerusalem in AD 70.

- See also Don K. Preston, *We Shall Meet Him in The Air: The Wedding of the King of Kings* (Ardmore, Oklahoma: JaDon Management Inc., 2010), pages 292-294.

26. *The Reformation Study Bible* (Lake Mary, Florida: Ligonier Ministries, 2005), page 1185.

27. Henry A. Virkler, *Hermeneutics: Principles and Processes of Biblical Interpretation* (Grand Rapids, MI: Baker Books, 1981), page 16.

28. Christians take different approaches to the Bible. (1) It is *authoritative*. This view holds that, while there may be errors in the Bible, it is accurate enough to be a basis for Christianity. In this view, the Bible "contains" the word of God but is not in its entirety the word of God. (2) It is the *inspired word of God* in its entirety. This is a higher standard based on self-identification within the Bible itself, including: the term "thus says the Lord" used over 400 times in the Old Testament, the term "God said" used 42 times in the Old Testament and 4 times in the New Testament, the term "God spoke" used 9 times in the Old Testament and 3 times in the New Testament, the term "the Spirit of the Lord Spoke" used 3 times in the Old Testament, also specific passages such as Psalm 119:99, 160; Matthew 15:6; Mark 7:13; John 10:35; Acts 3:18; Romans 15:4; 1 Corinthians 7:12; 1 Timothy 3:15-16; 2 Peter 1:20-21; 2 Peter 3:14-16. (3) It is *inerrant* (without any error in the original manuscripts). This is an inference from the previous position, as well as a result of critical textual analysis. (4) It is *infallible*, that is it could not possibly err—this being the highest standard. See the Chicago Statement on Biblical Inerrancy: http://www.bible-researcher.com/chicago1.html. See also http://www.faithfacts.org/search-for-truth/questions-of-christians/is-the-bible-really-gods-word.

29. http://en.wikipedia.org/wiki/Antichrist_(historicism). The Westminster Confession formerly had a statement in it about the Pope being the antichrist, but that was removed. There is at least one denomination that we are aware of that still says the Pope is the antichrist in its official statements: the Wisconsin Evangelical Lutheran Church.

30.   We are not suggesting that the Bible contradicts science. It does not. Sometimes Christians assume that the Bible is speaking of scientific things when it is really speaking of theological things.

31.   J. Stuart Russell, *The Parousia: The New Testament Doctrine of Christ's Second Coming* (Bradford, Pennsylvania: International Preterist Association, 2003), originally published in 1878, page 328-329.

32.   http://www.blueletterbible.org/lang/lexicon/lexicon.cfm?Strongs=G2889&t=KJV.

33.   See http://en.wikipedia.org/wiki/Epistle_of_Barnabas and also specifically verse 16:5 of the Epistle of Barnabas: http://www.earlychristianwritings.com/text/barnabas-lightfoot.html.

34.   J. Stuart Russell, *The Parousia: The New Testament Doctrine of Christ's Second Coming* (Bradford, Pennsylvania: International Preterist Association, 2003, originally published in 1878), page 198.

35.   Don K. Preston, from an article "The Passing of the Elements: 2 Peter 3:10": http://www.preteristarchive.com/Hyper/0000_preston_elements.html.

36.   David Green, Michael Sullivan, Edward Hassertt, Samuel Frost, *House Divided: Bridging the Gap in Reformed Eschatology, A Response to When Shall These Things Be?* (Romana, CA: Vision Publishing, 2009), page 165.

37.   See Joseph M. Vincent II, *The Millennium: Past, Present, or Future? A Biblical Defense for the 40 Year Transition Period* (Ardmore, OK: JaDon Publishing, 2012), pages 63-80. Jubilees is considered canonical by the Ethiopian Orthodox Church, as well as Jews in Ethiopia (http://en.wikipedia.org/wiki/Book_Of_Jubilees).

38.   Daniel 2:28; 7:26; 8:17; 8:19; 9:26-27; 10:14; 11:27; 11:40; 12:4; 12:9; 12:13. Not all of these refer to the same end. There are various periods of time prophesied in Daniel. Some are clearly about pre-Messianic worldly kingdom dynasties and are often identified as such in the text, for example Daniel 8:20 and 8:21. So the "time of the end" in these instances refers to the end of those dynasties. However, some are clearly Messianic references, such as those identified with the term "Son of Man" (Daniel 7:13 and 8:17), which Jesus applied to himself. Daniel 7:9-27 clearly ties to the Second Coming predictions made by Jesus in

the Olivet Discourse (Matthew 24/25; Mark 13; Luke 21) in which Jesus promises to return in *judgment* on *clouds* in his generation. In terms of confirming full preterism, Daniel 12 is the most important first century AD eschatological reference in the book of Daniel.

39.   The NASV translates Daniel 12:4 as the "end of time." But this is a mistranslation. Other translations such as NKJV, ASV, and NIV correctly translate it "time of the end."

40.   The removal of the daily sacrifice could refer to a time shortly before the destruction, when the zealots brought an end to the priesthood and sacrifices. Or it could potentially refer to a time even earlier around AD 66 when the Jews stopped making sacrifices to Caesar.

41.   While this can be a bit confusing, the taking away of the burnt offering is also mentioned in Daniel 8:11 and 11:31. These mentions probably refer to the first such cessation of the burnt offering in the mid-2nd century BC, when King Antiochus IV Epiphanes (ruler of the Seleucid Kingdom from 175-164 BC) forbade ceremonies and the worship of God in the Jerusalem temple and in the cities of Judah. In around 168 (or perhaps 167) BC Antiochus entered the Most Holy Place and plundered the silver and gold vessels. He erected an altar to the Olympian Zeus on the altar of God in the temple court and sacrificed pigs there. The books of 1 and 2 Maccabees (books in the Roman Catholic Bible but not in the Protestant Bible) mention the *abomination of desolation* in reference to these actions of Antiochus. There are some confirming indications within Daniel that at least the 8:11-14 mention of the abomination of desolation/cessation of the burnt offering refers to the Antiochus abomination. First, the context is the pre-Messianic visions. Secondly, verse 8:14 indicates that the temple would be restored. The temple was indeed cleansed and rededicated under the leadership of Judas Maccabeus in 164 BC. Other instances of the burnt offering cessation and the abomination of desolation (Daniel 9:27 and 12:11) are portrayed differently by Daniel than the Antiochus situation. At the end of the AD 66-70 abomination period, instead of being cleansed, the temple would be destroyed (Daniel 9:26) and the Jewish nation would be shattered (Daniel 12:7-11).

42.   Citations for these quotes are from Flavius Josephus, *Jewish Wars*, trans. H. St. J. Thackeray (Cambridge, MA: Harvard University Press, 1976), 5:401-403, 417-420. Also, *Josephus, The Essential Works*, ed. Paul L. Maier (Grand Rapids, MI: Kregel Academic & Professional, 1988;

Revised edition, May 17, 1995), page 358. We derived this information from Tina Rae Collins, *The Gathering in the Last Days* (New York: M. F. Sohn Publications, 2012), page 66.

43.   The Apocrypha is a group of ancient writings that are not considered canonical, but have appeared in some versions of the Bible throughout history. Most modern Protestant Bibles omit them.

44.   See Flavius Josephus, *The Wars of the Jews, Book 4, Chapter 5, Paragraph 1 (4.5.1)*. Available online at http://www.ccel.org/j/josephus/ works/JOSEPHUS.HTM. See also these links: http://www.preteristarchive.com/JewishWars/timeline_factional.html and http://www. preterist.org/preteristQA.asp#question17.

45.   Michael A. Fenemore and Kurt M. Simmons, *The Twilight of Postmillennialism; Fatal Errors in the Teachings of Keith A. Mathison, Kenneth L. Gentry, Jr. etc.*(Preterism.info Publishing, 2010), pages 13-17, 88.

46.   Three and a half years, on a 360 day calendar, is 1260 days. On a 365 day calendar three and a half years is 1278 days. According to one source who has worked on these numbers, the Jewish month was either 29 or 30 days. Corrections were made from time to time to keep the calendar in line with the seasons. According to this source, the Jews added an "intercalary" thirteenth month to their calendar (sort of a leap-month) every third year or so. This adjustment could account for the difference between 1290 days and 1260 days. But a strong conclusion with absolute precision remains elusive.

47.   Flavius Josephus, *The Wars of the Jews, Book 6 (6.1.1)*. Available online at http://www.ccel.org/j/josephus/works/JOSEPHUS.HTM.

48.   Flavius Josephus, *The Wars of the Jews, Book 7 (7.1.1)*. Available online at http://www.ccel.org/j/josephus/works/JOSEPHUS.HTM.

49.   If the reader is concerned that the destruction of Jerusalem in AD 70 was limited in scope compared to the Great Flood which you assume was worldwide, there is a book that might be of interest: *Beyond Creation Science* by Timothy P. Martin & Jeffrey L. Vaughn, PhD. This book makes a strong case that the Great Flood was *not*, as many Christians think, worldwide. Rather it was regional. They give many valid biblical arguments; for example, the Bible tells us that the Nephilim were present on the earth before the flood as well as after the flood, so not everyone outside of Noah's family was killed in the flood. If their

arguments are valid, Jesus' comparing the destruction of Jerusalem and the destruction of the Great Flood makes even more sense than previously thought.

50. http://preterism.ning.com/profiles/blogs/the-abomination-of-desolation.

51. J. Stuart Russell, *The Parousia: The New Testament Doctrine of Christ's Second Coming* (Bradford, Pennsylvania: International Preterist Association, 2003, originally published in 1878), page 45. Available from the International Preterist Association at their website: www.preterist.org.

52. David Chilton, *The Days of Vengeance: An Exposition of the Book of Revelation* (Tyler, Texas: Dominion Press, 1987).

53. J. Stuart Russell, *The Parousia: The New Testament Doctrine of Christ's Second Coming* (Bradford, Pennsylvania: International Preterist Association, 2003, originally published in 1878), pages 64, 65, and 546.

54. For the uses of these words in the New Testament see: http://www.blueletterbible.org/. See also this article: http://www.verumserum.com/the-return-of-christ/eschatological-word-studies#toc-three-greek-words-for-the-return.

55. Hebrews 9:28 in most translations states that Christ "will appear a second time." The phrase "will appear" is the Greek verb *optanomai*. In John 14:3 Jesus says He "will come again." Here the phrase "will come" is the Greek verb *erchomai*. See also Luke 9:11-27.

56. Gary DeMar, *Last Days Madness: Obsession of the Modern Church* (Powder Springs, Georgia: American Vision, 1999), Fourth revised edition, page 160.

57. J. Stuart Russell, *The Parousia: The New Testament Doctrine of Christ's Second Coming* (Bradford, Pennsylvania: International Preterist Association, 2003, originally published in 1878), Appendix to Part II, pages 350-354.

58. Found at various sources on the Internet.

59. Some people might focus on Matthew 23:39, where Jesus says: "You will not see Me again, until you say, 'Blessed is He who comes in the name of the Lord." Their objection is that this seems to be a visible coming of Jesus which they believe has not yet occurred. But this state-

ment is in the immediate context of Jesus' lament over Jerusalem, and in the "this generation" time frame of verse 36. Coming "in the name of the Lord" could be an affirmation of his divinity and thus consistent with Matthew 24. It seems best to understand this as "see Me in the judgment that I will bring." Thus, the Jews would see the effects of the judgment, not Jesus visibly. See also Chapter 12 for a discussion of the visibility of Jesus' return.

60. http://www.verumserum.com/the-return-of-christ/eschatological-word-studies#toc-three-greek-words-for-the-return.

61. J. Stuart Russell, *The Parousia: The New Testament Doctrine of Christ's Second Coming* (Bradford, Pennsylvania: International Preterist Association, 2003, originally published in 1878), page 69.

62. For an interesting discussion of how some partial preterists see two separate Second Comings of Jesus in the Oliver Discourse, see this article by Daniel E. Harden entitled "When Is a Heretic Not a Heretic?": http://www.preterist.org/articles/heretic.asp.

63. http://www.worldwithoutend.info/start/articles/ed_stevens_03-matt24.htm. Stevens is the founder of the International Preterist Association, website http://preterist.org.

64. We note that Jesus spoke Hebrew and/or Aramaic. But the New Testament was written in Greek. The region at the time was multicultural and multilingual. So Jesus perhaps may have known Greek, or even Latin. See http://www.hebrew4christians.com/Articles/Jesus_Hebrew/jesus_hebrew.html.

65. Gary DeMar, *Last Days Madness: Obsession of the Modern Church* (Powder Springs, Georgia: American Vision), Fourth revised edition 1999, . DeMar is a partial preterist postmillennialist rather than a full preterist. See also these additional books: (1) Kenneth Dahl's book *All These Things*: http://kennethdahl.com/allthesethings.pdf. (2) Samuel G. Dawson, *Essays on Eschatology: An Introductory Overview of the Study of Last Things* (Amarillo, Texas: SGD Press, 2009), pages 47-64.

66. http://www.eschatology.org

67. J. Stuart Russell, *The Parousia: The New Testament Doctrine of Christ's Second Coming* (Bradford, Pennsylvania: International Preterist

Association, 2003, originally published in 1878). This quote is a summary of Russell's comments on pages 56 and 57.

68. John L. Bray, *Matthew 24 Fulfilled* (Powder Springs, Georgia: American Vision, 1996), page 85.

69. Joseph Ratzinger, *Eschatology, Death and Eternal Life, Second Edition* (Washington, DC: The Catholic University of America Press, 1988, originally published in German in 1977), page 39.

70. Ibid, page 46.

71. We will see the word *mello* numerous times in our study. While some would deny the imminency connotation of this Greek word, author Joseph Vincent analyzes how the word is used in non-eschatological passages and shows that the word normally means "near in time." See Joseph M. Vincent II, *The Millennium: Past, Present, or Future? A Biblical Defense for the 40 Year Transition Period* (Ardmore, OK: JaDon Publishing, 2012), pages 95-99.

72. The Parousia of Christ may have *begun* at Pentecost per Matthew 26:64, but the *consummation* (i.e., his coming with his angels in the glory of his Father and rewarding every man according to his works) happened in AD 70.

73. http://www.youtube.com/watch?v=u7lGKIGFpNM&feature=relmfu. According to Preston there are three exceptions. See the next endnote for the full quote.

74. http://www.preteristarchive.com/Hyper/0000_preston_critical-text.html.

75. Milton S. Terry, *Biblical Apocalyptics: A Study of the Most Notable Revelations of God and of Christ in the Canonical Scriptures*, originally published in 1898, page 222. Terry was also the author of a classic work on hermeneutics entitled *Biblical Hermeneutics: A Treatise on the Interpretation of the Old and New Testaments*. See also: http://www.verumserum. com/the-return-of-christ.

76. Taken from the foreword by Gary DeMar in *The Day and the Hour* by Francis X. Gumerlock. These authors cite as the source for the quote: Gerald B. Stanton, "The Doctrine of Imminency: Is It Biblical?" in Thomas Ice and Timothy Demy, eds., *When the Trumpet Sounds* (Eugene, OR: Harvest House, 1997), page 222.

77.   Brian L. Martin, *Behind the Veil of Moses: Piecing Together the Mystery of the Second Coming* (Xulon Press, 2009), page 163.

78.   Scholars disagree about how long after the giving of the prophecy that its fulfillment took place. For example, some say 200 years, others say 142 years. Alan Bondar cites Walvoord's *Bible Knowledge Commentary* (page 1060) as saying that Babylon was destroyed within 15 years after the prophecy. See Alan Bondar, *Reading the Bible through New Covenant Eyes* (Baltimore, MD: Publish America, 2010), pages 193, 331.

79.   Some people challenge preterists by pointing out that certain Old Testament texts that were to be fulfilled "soon" didn't happen until hundreds of years later. Certain of these texts are Isaiah 51:5; Ezekiel 7:7; 30:3; Jeremiah 48:16; Joel 1:15; 2:1; 3:14; Obadiah 1:15; Zephaniah 1:7, 14. Alan Bondar cites non-preterist authors who have each of these passages being fulfilled within a generation of the actual prophecy. He cites (1) Homer Hailey, *Commentary on the Minor Prophets* (Grand Rapids, MI: Baker Publishing, 1973), and (2) John F. Walvoord and Roy B. Zuck, *Bible Knowledge Commentary* (Wheaton, IL: Victor Books, 1985). See Alan Bondar, *Reading the Bible through New Covenant Eyes* (Baltimore, MD: Publish America, 2010), pages 193, 331.

80.   http://revelationrevolution.org/isaiah-65-a-preterist-commentary

81.   http://www.andrewcorbett.net/articles/new-heavens.html.

82.   http://www.preteristarchive.com/Hyper/0000_preston_no-death.html

83.   See this article by Duncan McKenzie: http://planetpreterist.com/news-5109.html.

84.   Flavius Josephus, *The Wars of the Jews, Book 6 (6.5.3)*. Available online at http://www.ccel.org/j/josephus/works/JOSEPHUS.HTM.

85.   In addition to Josephus, Tacitus, Eusebius, and the Jewish Talmud mentioned this phenomenon. See: Josephus *Wars* (6.5.3.296 to 300), Tacitus *Histories* (Book 5), Eusebius *Ecclesiastical History* (Book 3, Chapter 8, Sections 1-6), Sepher Yosippon *A Mediaeval History of Ancient Israel* (Chapter 87, "Burning of the Temple"). See also Edward E. Stevens http://www.preterist.org/preteristQA.asp#question7.

86. Flavius Josephus, *Antiquities of the Jews, Book 3* (3.6.4, and 3.7.7). Available online at http://www.ccel.org/j/josephus/works/JOSEPHUS. HTM. See also http://ontimejournal.com/new-heaven-and-new-earth

87. http://en.wikipedia.org/wiki/Persecution_of_Christians_in_the_ Roman_Empire.

88. J. Stuart Russell, *The Parousia: The New Testament Doctrine of Christ's Second Coming* (Bradford, Pennsylvania: International Preterist Association, 2003, originally published in 1878), page 366.

89. For details, see Don K. Preston, D. Div., *Who Is This Babylon* (Ardmore, Oklahoma: JaDon Management, Inc., 2006), pages 2-3.

90. See http://livingthequestion.org/revelation/ (lists 62 scholars who support a pre-AD 70 date for Revelation). This book contains lists of authors who argue for a pre-AD 70 date for Revelation: Kenneth L. Gentry, Jr., *Before Jerusalem Fell: Dating the Book of Revelation* (Powder Springs, Georgia: American Vision, 1998), chapter 4. Among numerous other books that address this and which argue for a pre-AD 70 date include: (1) Don K. Preston, D. Div., *Who Is This Babylon* (Ardmore, Oklahoma: JaDon Management, Inc., 2006), page 249-250. (2) Gary DeMar and Francis X. Gumerlock, *The Early Church and the End of the World* (Powder Springs, Georgia: American Vision, 2006), pages 167-177.

Articles about the dating of Revelation:

- http://www.preteristarchive.com/BibleStudies/ApocalypseC-ommentaries/Dating/Early/index.html,

- http://www.preteristarchive.com/Hyper/0000_preston_revela-tion-date.html,

- http://biblicaleschatology.org/2009/01/05/research-insights-into-the-date-of-revelation-part-iv/

- http://api.ning.com/files/y43g75DEG9wIQpsxrkrl0esZAFk3z-5ZolOQDVar16vGVjLGJH*5cNs6BTLNpt8uwyFxmmpgK-PNQZNQSmV5JydE9GtOhybO7c/DidJohnLiveBeyond70.pdf

We also note commentary by Edward E. Stevens from *Introduction to the New Testament Canon, for the Fulfilled Covenant Bible project*, April 2011. It is a particularly interesting and helpful article. In it Stevens lists the probable dates that each New Testament book was written: http://www.bibleprophecyfulfilled.com/bible/Intro_to_NT_Stevens.pdf. Stevens wrote that the apostle John died during the Neronic persecution, about the same time as Peter and Paul (ca. AD 64-65). Eusebius (AD 263-339) cites two men before him that said that John lived until the reign of the Roman emperor Trajan (AD 98-117)—Irenaeus and Clement of Alexandria. But Eusebius also said that there were doubts as to John's authorship of Revelation, so the accuracy of such statements is doubtful. In any case, assuming that John wrote Revelation as is commonly held, even if he did live past AD 70, that does not mean that Revelation was written after AD 70.

We also refer the reader to: Edward E. Stevens, *First Century Events in Chronological Order: from the Birth of Christ to the Destruction of Jerusalem in AD 70, A Pre-publication Manuscript* (International Preterist Association, 2009), pages 19-21. See also: Edward E. Stevens, "Did John Live Beyond AD 70?" — http://api.ning.com/files/y43g75DEG9wIQpsxrkrl0esZAF-k3z5ZolOQDVar16vGVjLGJH*5cNs6BTLNpt8uwyFxmmpgKPNQZN-QSmV5JydE9GtOhybO7c/DidJohnLiveBeyond70.pdf

91. R. C. Sproul, *The Last Days according to Jesus* (Grand Rapids, Michigan: Baker Books, 1998), page 141.

92. There are other possibilities concerning the Irenaeus quote, which purports to tie the writing of the book of Revelation to the reign of Domitian (AD 81-96). One possibility is that the family name of Nero was Domitius, so Irenaeus could have been referring to Nero. Another is that Domitian was the son of Vespasian (and brother of Titus). Vespasian was elected Emperor in December 69. But he was not in Rome at the time. It took Vespasian six months to make his way back to Rome from Jerusalem and Egypt, where he was securing foodstuff for his soldiers. During this half year, Domitian assumed the role temporarily as Caesar. So, if Irenaeus was indeed saying that John was writing Revelation during the reign of Domitian, he may have been referring to this period!

93. R. C. Sproul, *The Last Days according to Jesus* (Grand Rapids, Michigan: Baker Books, 1998), page 147. See also: "When Was the Book of Revelation Written" by Wolfgang Schneider: http://www.biblecenter.de/bibel/studien/e-std310.php

94. Frederic Myers, *Catholic Thoughts on the Bible and Theology* (London: Dalby, Isbister & Co, 1879), The Fourth Book, chapter 35, page 327.

Available online at http://www.archive.org/stream/catholicthoughtson-bible00myer#page/n3/mode/2up.

95.   http://livingthequestion.org/revelation/.

96.   http://www.truthaccordingtoscripture.com/documents/eschatology/beast.php.

97.   http://blog.adw.org/2012/11/why-the-modern-view-of-the-book-of-revelation-may-be-flawed/.

98.   http://newjerusalemcommunity.blogspot.com/2012/10/behold-he-cometh-with-clouds-and-every.html

99.   http://en.wikipedia.org/wiki/The_Beast_(Revelation).

100.   Don K. Preston, D. Div., *Who Is This Babylon* (Ardmore, Oklahoma: JaDon Management, Inc., 2006), pages 52f. This is an excellent book for those desiring to get deeper into this topic.

101.   Gary DeMar, *End Times Fiction: A Biblical Consideration of the Left Behind Theology* (Nashville, TN: Thomas Nelson Publishers, 2001), pages 126-127.

102.   Gary DeMar, *Last Days Madness: Obsession of the Modern Church* (Powder Springs, Georgia: American Vision, Fourth Revised Edition 1999).

103.   R. C. Sproul, *The Last Days according to Jesus* (Grand Rapids, Michigan: Baker Books, 1998).

104.   See endnote 21 at this source: http://www.freedominchrist.net/BIBLICAL%20STUDIES/New%20Testament/Revelation/Chapter%20
2--Identity%20of%20the%20Beast%20of%20Revelation.htm.

105.   For a description of Nero, see Kenneth Dahl's book *All These Things*: http://kennethdahl.com/allthesethings.pdf, page 43.

106.   There is quite a bit of discussion about this on the Internet, which the reader could check if so inclined.

107.   http://www.truthaccordingtoscripture.com/documents/eschatology/beast.php.

108.   Gary DeMar, *End Times Fiction: a Biblical Consideration of the Left Behind Theology* (Nashville, TN: Thomas Nelson Publishers), page 143.

109.   There are other preterist views of who the beast was. Edward E. Stevens has written about certain clues in Revelation that suggest that the beast was Jewish, therefore was not Nero. See *Fulfilled!* Magazine, Spring 2012, pages 10-12: http://www.fulfilledcg.com/Site/Magazine/magazine_previous_issues.htm.

110.   Steve Gregg, *Revelation, Four Views: A Parallel Commentary.* (Nashville, Tennessee: Thomas Nelson Publishers, 1997), pages 466-468.

111.   Anthony A. Hoekema, *The Meaning of the Millennium* (Downers Grove, IL: Intervarsity Press, 1977), page 161. Cited from Joseph M. Vincent II, *The Millennium: Past, Present, or Future? A Biblical Defense for the 40 Year Transition Period* (Ardmore, OK: JaDon Publishing, 2012), page 103. It should be noted that Hoekema was not a preterist.

112.   A helpful book is *Revelation: Four Views, a Parallel Commentary,* by Steve Gregg (Nashville, TN: Thomas Nelson Publishers, 1997.)

113.   ibid.

114.   Very helpful resources are Don Preston's book *Who Is This Babylon* and his multi-part YouTube series (http://www.youtube.com/watch?v=cnzgVRo-eqA&feature=related).

115.   Joseph M. Vincent II, *The Millennium: Past, Present, or Future? A Biblical Defense for the 40 Year Transition Period* (Ardmore, OK: JaDon Publishing, 2012), page 98.

116.   While some scholars place AD 30 as the year of Jesus' crucifixion and ascension, others including the respected Lutheran historian Dr. Paul L. Maier, professor of Ancient History at Western Michigan University, places the date of the crucifixion as April 3, AD 33. See http://www.mtio.com/articles/aissar30.htm. While this would make the millennium 37 years, the student of Scripture can scarcely miss the parallel of 40 years to other uses of 40 in the Bible, especially the 40 year wandering of the Exodus.

117.   See David A. Green http://www.preterist.org/articles/ezekiel_38_39.asp.

118.   J. Stuart Russell, *The Parousia: The New Testament Doctrine of Christ's Second Coming* (Bradford, Pennsylvania: International Preterist Association, 2003, originally published in 1878), page 525.

119.   It could also be that John 3 refers to national rebirth/restoration of Israel, as explained in this article by Derrick Olliff: http://beatenbrains.blogspot.com.au/2006/08/eschatology-of-being-born-again.html.

120.   It is conceivable that this first resurrection also included a physical resurrection of already martyred saints from the dead. If this is the case, one might conclude that the time span between the first and second resurrections was a period considerably shorter than 40 years. This would be consistent with Revelation 6:9-11 ("rest a little longer"). The student should not get hung up on this detail. The key to understanding Revelation 20 is verses 11-15 which was the general resurrection and judgment that happened coincident with the Second Coming.

121.   Preterists offer somewhat different interpretations of *who* was resurrected and *when* per Revelation 20. Some preterists think that the first resurrection was the resurrection of the just, while the second resurrection was the resurrection of the unjust. Other preterists believe that the first resurrection refers to the resurrection from hades. And so forth.

122.   Satan in these texts may be symbolic for apostate Israel.

123.   One can get around this argument of the premillennial preterists by pointing out that the text does not say the beheaded were resurrected AFTER they were beheaded. It merely says "they lived and reigned with Christ a thousand years." Thus, they "lived" before they were beheaded.

124.   James Stuart Russel held to a version of this view. Modern author Duncan McKenzie is the major present writer in support of this view. There are variations in the details from different writers. Russell held that verses 5-10 are still future. McKenzie thinks that only verses 7-10 are still future. See Duncan McKenzie's articles:

- http://planetpreterist.com/news-5017.html,

- http://planetpreterist.com/news-5174.html,

- Also see his book *The Antichrist and the Second Coming, A Preterist Examination* (Xulon Press, 2012).

- Preterist Milton Terry, a contemporary of Russell, held that verses 11-15 were still future (Milton S. Terry, *Biblical Apocalyptics*, 1898: http://www.preteristarchive.com/Books/1898_terry_apocalyptics.html).

Most preterists take issue with McKenzie, Russell, and Terry's conclusion in this matter. Don Preston has a section in his book that argues against the views of McKenzie : Don K. Preston, D. Div., *Who Is This Babylon* (Ardmore, Oklahoma: JaDon Management, Inc., 2006), pages 281-321.

125.   See articles by Kurt M. Simmons: http://www.preteristcentral.com/Studies%20in%20the%20Millennia.html. Also see Simmons' book *The Consummation of the Ages*. And see the book by Douglass Wilkinson, *Making Sense of the Millennium* (Kindle Edition).

126.   See article by Ed Stevens, "A 40-Year Millennium": http://planetpreterist.com/content/40-year-millennium. Stevens is the founder of the International Preterist Association, website http://preterist.org.

127.   For a detailed discussion of this, see David Chilton, *The Days of Vengeance: An Exposition of the Book of Revelation* (Tyler, Texas: Dominion Press, 1987), chapter 21.

128.   http://www.preterism.info/why-still-death.htm. Fenemore has also co-authored a book with Kurt M. Simmons: *The Twilight of Postmillennialism: Fatal Errors in the Teaching of Keith A. Mathison, Kenneth L. Gentry, Jr. et. al.*

129.   http://planetpreterist.com/news-5109.html. The bride of Christ (Revelation 21:2, 9-10) is elsewhere in the Bible described as the church (Matthew 9:15; John 3:29; 2 Corinthians 11:2; Ephesians 5:22-23, etc.).

130.   http://www.preterist.org/articles/answering_mathison.asp.

131.   David Chilton, *The Days of Vengeance: An Exposition of the Book of Revelation* (Tyler, Texas: Dominion Press, 1987), page 494, 502.

132.   J. Stuart Russell, *The Parousia*, pages 228-229. The concepts of *salvation* and *redemption* are linked in the New Testament to the point of being essentially equivalent. See such passages as Colossians 1:14 and Hebrews 9:15.

133. The reader can also consider such passages as Isaiah 27:9-12 and 59:17-21, as well as Romans 11:25-27.

134. Isaiah 28:11 and Joel 2:28-29 are further evidence, according to some, that speaking in tongues was a sign of God's oncoming judgment. So, when God did judge the nation of Israel in AD 70, the gift of tongues was no longer to serve a purpose. Those who object to the interpretation that tongues ceased in AD 70 argue that in the same passage Paul says that "knowledge" will also cease. How can knowledge cease? One interpretation is that this means knowledge from the writings of the apostles; that is, the canon of Scripture would be complete by AD 70. This lends credence to the Reformation tenet that Scripture alone is sufficient for all matters of faith and life. Or perhaps a better understanding of the cessation of knowledge is that with the fulfillment of prophecy in the first century, the matters of the Old Testament that were vague for Jews became clear in their completion. For some additional discussion of the gift of tongues, see these links:

- http://www.preteristarchive.com/PartialPreterism/ma_speak. html,

- http://www.treeoflifeministries.info/index.php?view=article&catid=35%3Apreterist-eschatology-all-prophecy-fulfilled-by-ad-70&id=149%3Amike-sullivan&option=com_content&Itemid=75,

- http://so4j.com/faq.php#speaking_in_tongues, and

- http://www.preteristcosmos.com/gift.htm.

135. By one count, "kingdom" is found 122 times in the New Testament. Millennialists sometimes separate the two terms "kingdom of God" and "kingdom of heaven" in order to attempt to find a spiritual kingdom and an earthly kingdom. But this is incorrect. According to Joseph Ratzinger (*Eschatology*, page 26), Matthew used the term Kingdom of Heaven instead of Kingdom of God out of respect for Jewish tradition, which did not mention the name of God out of reverence. See also http://www.gotquestions.org/kingdom-heaven-God.html.

136. J. Stuart Russell, *The Parousia: The New Testament Doctrine of Christ's Second Coming* (Bradford, Pennsylvania: International Preterist Association, 2003, originally published in 1878), page 344.

137. Brian L. Martin, *Behind the Veil of Moses: Piecing Together the Mystery of the Second Coming* (Xulon Press, 2009), page 135.

138. Partial preterist/postmillennialist Gary DeMar said, emphasizing his postmillennialism: "The only signs that are yet to be fulfilled are the discipleship of the nations and Jesus putting all His enemies under His feet." See DeMar, Gary, *End Times Fiction: A Biblical Consideration of the Left Behind Theology* (Thomas Nelson Publishers, 2001), page 214.

139. Joseph Ratzinger, *Eschatology, Death and Eternal Life, Second Edition* (Washington, DC: The Catholic University of America Press, 1988, originally published in German in 1977), pages 101, 103.

140. See Samuel G. Dawson, *Essays on Eschatology: An Introductory Overview of the Study of Last Things* (Amarillo, Texas: SGD Press, 2009), Section lll.

141. Annihilationism seems to be gaining adherents in the church as some well respected scholars are proponents of this view. An Internet site that has some good articles on this view is the "Death and Immortality" section of http://www.truthaccordingtoscripture.com/index.php.

142. Scholars who hold to annihilationism believe either that hell means instant destruction to the damned, or that the damned may reside in hell for a period of time before their ultimate destruction. Here is a link to a lecture on the subject by a well-known proponent Edward Fudge: http://vimeo.com/30967402. Fudge is a major proponent of annihilationism and has written books on the subject, notably *The Fire that Consumes: A Biblical and Historical Study of the Doctrine of Final Punishment*. The reader can also check out Samuel G. Dawson, *Essays on Eschatology: An Introductory Overview of the Study of Last Things* (Amarillo, Texas: SGD Press, 2009), Section lll. Here is another link for study: http://robertwr.com/. For a defense of eternal conscious punishment, see *Hell on Trial* by Robert A. Peterson.

143. Actually, it does seem doubtful that most Christians, who claim to hold to eternal conscious punishment, really do believe in it. If they really believed in it, they would be much for active in their evangelism effort. One study suggested that only 2% of Christians ever share their faith! If they really thought the non-believers around them were destined to burn in hell forever, they would be constantly evangelizing!

144.   Paul in 1 Corinthians 7 confirms that those married should remain married.

145.   Source: www.reformedonline.com

146.   The Greek word is *mello* (Strong's G3195). Futurists sometimes object to the translation "about to." Indeed, most Bible versions translate *mello* as "will" and thus do not have the imminency connotation. However, the online *Blue Letter Bible* lexicon states that the biblical usage of the word is "to be about, to be on the point of doing or suffering something, or to intend, have in mind, think to." So while there are different potential translations, the context determines that "about to" is a good and reasonable rendering such that this passage and others like it are consistent with the numerous other imminency passages. The imminency connotation is clear in Young's Literal Translation which one can access online at such sites as Bible Gateway. This translation is confirmed by these other sources: *Vine's Theological Dictionary, Thayer's Greek/English Lexicon, The Analytical Greek Lexicon, Bauer-Arndt-Gingrich, Second Edition,* and *Strong's Exhaustive Concordance.* The following is an article by Parker Voll about this word: *Fulfilled!* Magazine, Spring 2012, http://www.fulfilledcg.com/Site/Magazine/magazine_previous_issues. htm, pages 12, 13, 18.

147.   Don K. Preston D. Div., *We Shall Meet Him in the Air: The Wedding of the King of Kings* (Ardmore, Oklahoma: JaDon Management Inc., 2010), page 174. For clarification, Preston does believe that the general resurrection occurred in AD 70, but does not believe it was the "physically dead being raised out of the dirt."

148.   http://beatenbrains.blogspot.com.au/2006/08/eschatology-of-being-born-again.html.

149.   Those who expect a fleshly physical body in the resurrection cite Job 19:25-26. According to Kurt Simmons, "This is the *only* verse in the Bible that makes reference to the flesh in apparent connection with the resurrection. However, the Hebrew of this verse is so obscure and ambiguous that scholars cannot decide *how* it is to be translated." See Kurt M. Simmons, "The Resurrection of the Flesh."

150.   For supplementary material on resurrection, see the author's articles at http://prophecyquestions.wordpress.com/2013/02/02/articles-by-charles-meek

151.   Interestingly, Adam was not even the first person to die in the Bible. Abel holds that distinction. The primary objection to the idea that the Fall was only a spiritual event is that Genesis 3 speaks of physical things, such as the pain of childbirth, and also that the ground itself was cursed. But it should be pointed out that the text only states that the pain of childbirth would be *multiplied*, which clearly implies that such pain existed before the Fall.

152.   Samuel G. Dawson, *Essays on Eschatology: An Introductory Overview of the Study of Last Things* (Amarillo, Texas: SGD Press, 2009), page 157.

153.   http://www.preterist.org/articles/answering_mathison.asp.

154.   These young earth creationists also teach that even though predator animals like lions had teeth specifically made for killing and eating meat, they only ate vegetable matter at first. For information about the old earth viewpoint, go to www.reasons.org and search for "Animal Death before the Fall." There you should find an article by Lee Irons, as well as other interesting material.

155.   Samuel G. Dawson, *Essays on Eschatology: An Introductory Overview of the Study of Last Things* (Amarillo, Texas: SGD Press, 2009), page 159-160.

156.   From the PretCosmos Yahoo chatroom, comment on February 28, 2012.

157.   Joseph Ratzinger, *Eschatology, Death and Eternal Life, Second Edition* (Washington, DC: The Catholic University of America Press, 1988, originally published in German in 1977), page 169.

158.   A charge that is sometimes made against preterists is that we are guilty of the "hymenaen heresy," which has sometimes been described as believing that the resurrection occurred before AD 70. Preterists do not believe that. See http://www.preteristarchive.com/Hyper/1999_birks_response-sandlin.html.

159.   Max R. King, *The Cross and the Parousia of Christ* (Warren, OH: Writing and Research Ministry, 1987). For refutations of the CBV see these articles by Edward E. Stevens: "Refuting Resurrection Errors (July 28, 2013)" and "Fruit of the Collective Body Tree (August 25, 2013)" at http://preterist.org.

160. Douglas Wilkinson summarizes some of the research on the meaning of "pneuma" in his book *Making Sense of the Millennium* published in 2013.

Also see articles by Jerel Kratt (and others) at http://prophecyquestions.wordpress.com/2013/02/02/articles-by-charles-meek

161. Ed Stevens points out the inconsistency of partial preterists such as Kenneth Gentry in this article: http://planetpreterist.com/content/40-year-millennium. Stevens is the founder of the International Preterist Association, website http://preterist.org.

162. Some preterists believe that this change was a literal rapture. Ask for articles on this subject at www.preterist.org.

163. "See articles by Charles Meek "The Personhood View of the Resurrection" and "Salvation after AD 70" here: http://prophecyquestions.wordpress.com/2013/02/02/articles-by-charles-meek/

164. Tina Rae Collins, *The Gathering in the Last Days* (New York: M. F. Sohn Publications, 2012), page 156.

165. Most scholars say that the writer of Hebrews was probably Paul. Both Paul (1 Corinthians 10:11) and the writer of Hebrews (Hebrews: 9:26) use the same term, "the end of the ages," to describe the changes they were witnessing in the first century.

166. Edward E. Stevens, *Questions about the Afterlife*, pages 43 and 45, and *Refuting Resurrection Errors*, page 3..

167. A couple of Old Testament passages that relate to this covenantal promise aspect of the resurrection discussion are Isaiah 25:8 and Hosea 13:14.

168. Michael A. Fenemore and Kurt M. Simmons, *The Twilight of Post-millennialism; Fatal Errors in the Teachings of Keith A. Mathison, Kenneth L. Gentry, Jr. etc.*(Preterism.info Publishing, 2010), page 22.

169. The reader is invited to examine the author's website where there are several helpful articles about resurrection: http://prophecyquestions.wordpress.com/2013/02/02/articles-by-charles-meek

170. For those desiring a detailed examination of all passages that relate to physical versus spiritual resurrection, we recommend the discussion by Kurt Simmons: Michael A. Fenemore and Kurt M. Simmons, *The Twilight of Postmillennialism; Fatal Errors in the Teachings of Keith A. Mathison, Kenneth L. Gentry, Jr. etc.*(Preterism.info Publishing, 2010), pages 93-113. See also Kurt Simmons' website www.preteristcentral. com.

171. For example, Matthew Henry's commentary on this passage says, "They shall be raised up from the dead, and awakened out of their sleep, for God will bring them with him, v 14. They then are with God. . . . when God comes he will bring them with him. The doctrine of the resurrection and the second coming of Christ is a great antidote against the fear of death and inordinate sorrow for the death of our Christian friends. . . . v.17. At, or immediately before, this rapture into the clouds, those who are alive will undergo a mighty change, which will be equivalent to dying. . . ." Morgan Edwards (1731-1801) may have been the first to teach the modern rapture doctrine. Some say that there were a couple of Catholic priests who also taught the secret rapture doctrine: Francisco Ribera (1537-1591) and Emmanuel Lacunza (1731-1801). They also were apparently the first to teach a "gap" between the 69th and 70th weeks of Daniel's vision. It seems that they came up with the idea in order to deflect reformation fervor that claimed that the Pope was the antichrist and the Catholic Church the beast of Revelation. This idea pushed the antichrist and the beast into the future so it did not seem so likely that it was the sixteenth-century pope/church. Dispensationalist Thomas Ice has written about other sources that seem to support a pre-Darby rapture view: http://www.raptureready.com/ featured/ice/YetAnotherPreDarbyRaptureStatement.html and http:// www.raptureme.com/tt3.html.

172. *Fulfilled!* Magazine, Fall 2008, http://www.fulfilledcg.com/Site/ Magazine/magazine_previous_issues.htm.

173. David Green, Michael Sullivan, Edward Hassertt, Samuel Frost, *House Divided: Bridging the Gap in Reformed Eschatology, A Response to When Shall These Things Be?* (Romana, CA: Vision Publishing, 2009), page 106.

174. N. T. Wright, *Paul: In Fresh Perspective* (Great Britain: First Fortress Press, 2005), pages 55-56.

175. Don K. Preston D. Div., *We Shall Meet Him in The Air: The Wedding of the King of Kings* (Ardmore, Oklahoma: JaDon Management Inc., 2010), page 145.

176. J. Stuart Russell, *The Parousia: The New Testament Doctrine of Christ's Second Coming* (Bradford, Pennsylvania: International Preterist Association, 2003, originally published in 1878), page 169.

177. Glenn L. Hill, *Christianity's Great Dilemma: Is Jesus Coming Again or Is He Not?* (Lexington, KY: Moonbeam Publications, 2010), page 172.

178. For many more parallels between 1 Thessalonians 4 and other passages throughout the Bible, see Don K. Preston D. Div., *We Shall Meet Him in The Air: The Wedding of the King of Kings* (Ardmore, Oklahoma: JaDon Management Inc., 2010).

179. Samuel M. Frost has changed his views over time. He was a full preterist for some nine years and wrote from that perspective. However, as of early 2012 he was writing as a partial preterist. The citations of his views were gleaned from various writings and reports. He is an active writer and participant on Internet forums.

180. Kenneth L. Gentry, Jr., *Perilous Time: A Study in Eschatological Evil* (Texarkana, AR: Covenant Media Press, 1999), page 100. Here is a quote from Gentry's book: "Though he [Paul] speaks of the Second Advent just a few verses before ([in 2 Thess.] 1:10), he is not dealing with that event here [in 2 Thess. 2:1-2]. Of course, similarities exist between the Day of the Lord upon Jerusalem in AD 70 and the universal Day of the Lord at the Second Advent. The one is a temporal betokening of the other, being a distant adumbration of it. The Second Advent provides a final hope for the eternal resolution to their suffering; the A.D. 70 Day of the Lord affords an approaching temporal resolution (cf. Rev. 6:10). Orthodox scholars from each of the millennial schools agree that Christ brings these two events into close connection in the Olivet Discourse. Indeed, Christ's disciples almost certainly confuse the two (Matt. 24:3). The same connection seems to exist here as well." Of this position Duncan McKenzie commented, "Gentry is forced into this far-fetched position because 2 Thessalonians 1:7-10 is talking about the judgment (which Gentry says is still future) while 2:1 is talking about the AD 70 gathering of God's people (cf. Matt. 24:29-34), which Gentry correctly believes is AD 70."

181. To be more precise, the word in 2 Thessalonians 1:10 is *elthe*, a derivative of *erchomai*.

182. Don K. Preston D. Div., *We Shall Meet Him in The Air: The Wedding of the King of Kings* (Ardmore, Oklahoma: JaDon Management Inc., 2010), page 345.

183. For further analysis of Dr. Gentry's writings see Don K. Preston, D. Div. *The Elements Shall Melt with Fervent Heat: A Study of 2 Peter 3* (Ardmore, OK: JaDon Productions LLC, 2006), pages 223-224. Also, Don K. Preston D. Div., *We Shall Meet Him in The Air: The Wedding of the King of Kings* (Ardmore, Oklahoma: JaDon Management Inc., 2010), page 337f. In these works, Preston details other inconsistencies in Dr. Gentry's writings.

184. "The" precedes (modifies) *parousia* in these instances: 1 Thessalonians 3:13; 4:15; 5:23; 2 Thessalonians 2:1. "His" precedes (modifies) *parousia* in these instances: 1 Thessalonians 2:19; 2 Thessalonians 2:8. "Whose" precedes (modifies) *parousia* in this instance: 2 Thessalonians 2:19. *Erchomai* is used in 1 Thessalonians 5:2 and 2 Thessalonians 1:10.

185. Examples of this can be found in Michael Sullivan's writings in *House Divided*. David Green, Michael Sullivan, Edward Hassertt, Samuel Frost, *House Divided: Bridging the Gap in Reformed Eschatology, A Response to When Shall These Things Be?* (Romana, CA: Vision Publishing, 2009).

186. Samuel M. Frost, *Why I Left Full Preterism* (Powder Springs, GA: American Vision Press), pages 78-80.

187. There are at least two books that are helpful in demonstrating that the writings of notable Reformed opponents of full preterism (namely Kenneth L. Gentry, Jr., Keith A. Mathison, R. C. Sproul, Jr., Charles E. Hill, Richard L. Pratt, Jr., Simon J. Kistemaker, Douglas Wilson, Robert Strimple, and others) are at key points inconsistent, arbitrary, and even contrary to the creeds. We believe that these books leave the arguments of these men in shambles: (1) David Green, Michael Sullivan, Edward Hassertt, Samuel Frost, *House Divided: Bridging the Gap in Reformed Eschatology, A Response to When Shall These Things Be?* (Romana, CA: Vision Publishing, 2009). (2) Michael A. Fenemore and Kurt M. Simmons, *The Twilight of Postmillennialism; Fatal Errors in the Teachings of Keith A. Mathison, Kenneth L. Gentry, Jr. etc.*(Preterism.

info Publishing, 2010). Also see these articles: (1) *Response to Gentry's Analysis of the Full Preterist* View (Edward E. Stevens, editor) online at http://www.preterist.org/articles-old/gentry/response_index.htm. (2) "The Arbitrary Principle of Hyper-Creedalism" (by David A. Green), online at http://preteristcosmos.com/arbitrary-gentry.html.

188. Edward E. Stevens, *Expectations Demand a First Century Rapture.* Available at the International Preterist Association, http://www.preterist.org/preteristbookstore.asp.

189. Daniel E. Harden, *Gathered Into the Kingdom.*

190. http://en.wikipedia.org/wiki/Ascension_of_Jesus_in_Christian_art.

191. Source: http://www.charlescoty.com/user/In%20Like%20Manner%20-%20Acts%201.11%20-%20Joseph%20Vincent.pdf

192. From http://www.quodlibet.net/articles/otto-sproul.shtml. Randall E. Otto has also written a book entitled *Coming in the Clouds: An Evangelical Case for the Invisibility of Christ at His Second Coming* (University Press of America, 1994).

193. Milton S. Terry, *Biblical Apocalyptics*, 1898, note 34. Note: We have cleaned up the language of this quote a bit to put it in modern English, and added the bold emphasis. The entire book is available here: http://www.preteristarchive.com/Books/1898_terry_apocalyptics.html.

194. From this source: http://www.truthaccordingtoscripture.com.

195. *The Reformation Study Bible,* (Lake Mary, Florida: Ligonier Ministries, 2005), page 1741.

196. http://www.gotquestions.org/twelve-tribes-Israel.html.

197. Edward E. Stevens in the foreword to: J. Stuart Russell, *The Parousia: The New Testament Doctrine of Christ's Second Coming,* (Bradford, Pennsylvania: International Preterist Association, 2003), originally published in 1878, page xii. Stevens is the founder of the International Preterist Association, website http://preterist.org.

198. http://www.preteristcentral.com/The%20Resurrection%20of%20the%20Flesh.html.

199. "The 'End Times' A Study on Eschatology and Millennialism," A Report of the Commission on Theology and Church Relations of The Lutheran Church—Missouri Synod, September 1989. This 65 page document, which is from a major conservative denomination, does an excellent job of explaining the various eschatological positions. The interested reader can find the document online via a Google search.

200. Ibid, page 19.

201. Ibid, page 33.

202. Glenn L. Hill, *Christianity's Great Dilemma: Is Jesus Coming Again or Is He Not?* (Lexington, KY: Moonbeam Publications, 2010), page 131.

203. For an alternative view supporting physical death at the Fall, see Ed Stevens, "What Kind of Death?" Mr. Stevens can be contacted at www.preterist.org.

204. "The 'End Times' A Study on Eschatology and Millennialism," A Report of the Commission on Theology and Church Relations of The Lutheran Church—Missouri Synod, September 1989, p. 45.

205. We do not see the physical body as evil, like the Gnostics. We only see human beings as the Bible describes us, and as observations confirm—sinful.

206. http://en.wikipedia.org/wiki/Imputed_righteousness.

207. http://en.wikipedia.org/wiki/Democide. Dinesh D'Souza in his book *What's So Great about Christianity* shows that crimes supposedly committed by Christians, such as the Spanish Inquisition and the Salem Witch trials, were much smaller than generally supposed. Any such crimes committed by professing Christians were committed *contrary* to the principles of Christianity, while similar crimes committed by atheistic/communistic regimes can be shown to be *consistent* with their Darwinian model.

208. Samuel M. Frost, *Why I Left Full Preterism* (Powder Springs, GA: American Vision Press, 2012), page 62.

209. Ibid, page 47.

210. http://www.andrewcorbett.net/articles/lion-lamb/index. See also http://ontimejournal.com/every-knee-bow-every-tongue-confess. html.

211.   Here is where we find *Parousia* associated with Jesus: Matthew 24:3, 27, 37, 39; 1 Corinthians 15:23; 1 Thessalonians 2:19; 3:13; 4:15; 5:23; 2 Thessalonians 2:1, 8; James 5:7, 8; 2 Peter 1:16; 3:4; 1 John 2:28. http://www.blueletterbible.org/lang/lexicon/lexicon.cfm?Strongs=G3952&t=KJV. See also this article: http://www.verumserum.com/the-return-of-christ/eschatological-word-studies#toc-three-greek-words-for-the-return.

212.   J. Stuart Russell, *The Parousia: The New Testament Doctrine of Christ's Second Coming* (Bradford, Pennsylvania: International Preterist Association, 2003, originally published in 1878), page 545.

213.   David Green, Michael Sullivan, Edward Hassertt, Samuel Frost, *House Divided: Bridging the Gap in Reformed Eschatology, A Response to When Shall These Things Be?* (Romana, CA: Vision Publishing, 2009), page 87.

214.   Some full preterists also question the statement in the Nicene Creed that says, "I look for the resurrection of the dead." While every full preterist agrees that those believers who have not yet died will be resurrected in the future, this statement implies that the *general resurrection* is yet future. Full preterists believe that the general resurrection happened in AD 70.

215.   http://beyondtheendtimes.com/writing/articles/k_davies/k_davies_responses/fals_wit_math.html.

216.   Spoken at the Covenant Eschatology Symposium in Florida 1993: http://preterist.org, http://www.preteristarchive.com/StudyArchive/s/sproul-rc_sr.html

217.   See:

- http://www.preterist.org/articles/what_about_creeds.asp,
- http://planetpreterist.com/content/resurrected-body-jesus-christ-edited-walt-hibbard,
- http://preterist.org/articles-old/what_if_the_creeds_are_wrong.htm
- http://beyondtheendtimes.com/writing/articles/k_davies/k_davies_responses/fals_wit_math.html.

218.   David Green, Michael Sullivan, Edward Hassertt, Samuel Frost, *House Divided: Bridging the Gap in Reformed Eschatology, A Response to When Shall These Things Be?* (Romana, CA: Vision Publishing, 2009), page

13. This source in turn quoted Roland H. Bainton, Here I Stand: A Life of Martin Luther (Peabody, MA: Hendrickson Publishers, 2009), 185.

219. Daniel E. Harden, *Overcoming Sproul's Resurrection Obstacles* (Bradford, PA: IPA Publishers, 1999), page 21. The error of elasticizing the time statements can be traced to three sources in the mid-second century: Justin Martyr, Shepherd of Hermas, and 2nd Clement. See Edward E. Stevens, *Questions about the Afterlife* (Bradford, PA: International Preterist Association, 1999), page 13.

220. This famous statement by Luther appears in various slightly different formulations. See: http://www.luther.de/en/worms.html and http://www.imdb.com/title/tt0309820/quotes and http://www.bible-researcher.com/luther03.html. Also see Edward E. Stevens' article, "What If the Creeds Are Wrong?": http://www.preterist.org/articles-old/what_if_the_creeds_are_wrong.htm.

221. Don K. Preston, *We Shall Meet Him in The Air: The Wedding of the King of Kings* (Ardmore, Oklahoma: JaDon Management Inc., 2010), pages 274ff.

222. First quote from: *Proof of the Gospel*, Book VI, Chapter 13, paragraph 18. Second quote from: *Proof of the Gospel*, Book VIII, Chapter 4, paragraph 147). Eusebius' works are laborious. He may have been lumping Jesus' first and second advents together to affirm fulfillment, in particular, of the events of the Olivet Discourse. Eusebius did affirm the Nicene Creed, but was apparently concerned primarily with the Divinity of Christ aspect of the Creed rather than the Parousia. (See http://www.earlychurchtexts.com/public/eusebius_letter_to_his_church_about_nicaea.htm). Eusebius apparently thought that Revelation was written after AD 70, but his witness is on Revelation is not credible because he even doubted that the apostle John wrote the book. But we can confidently conclude that his numerous statements throughout his writings about a first century fulfillment of prophesied events confirm his preterist orientation. The reader is also referred back to Chapter 1, endnote number 25 for more places in Eusebius' writings that confirm his preterist views.

223. Don K. Preston, *We Shall Meet Him in The Air: The Wedding of the King of Kings* (Ardmore, Oklahoma: JaDon Management Inc., 2010), pages 286-295. See also these various references: (1) Gary DeMar and Francis X. Gumerlock, *The Early Church and the End of the World* (Powder Springs, Georgia: American Vision, 2006). (2) Samuel M. Frost, *Mis-*

placed Hope: The Origins of First and Second Century Eschatology (Colorado Springs, CO: Bimillennial Press, 2006), page 151. (3) Living the Question website article "Historic Preterist Quotes": http://livingthequestion.org/historic-quotes/. The Bible teaches that speaking in tongues would cease when "completion" came (1 Corinthians 13:8-10).

224.   See Edward E. Stevens http://www.preterist.org/preteristQA. asp#question7. Josephus *Wars* (6.5.3.296 to 300), Tacitus *Histories* (Book 5:13), Eusebius *Ecclesiastical History* (Book 3 Chapter 8 Sections 1-6), Sepher Yosippon *A Mediaeval History of Ancient Israel* (Chapter 87, "Burning of the Temple").

225.   See Covenant Theological Seminary online course "Ancient and Medieval Church History" at this link: http://www.worldwide-classroom.com/. Another source is David Green, Michael Sullivan, Edward Hassertt, Samuel Frost, *House Divided: Bridging the Gap in Reformed Eschatology, A Response to When Shall These Things Be?* (Romana, CA: Vision Publishing, 2009), pages 45-47. See also this article by Riley O'Brien Powell: http://livingthequestion.org/church-error/.

226.   James B. Jordan, *Biblical Chronology*, "Problems with New Testament History, "Vol. 5, No. 1, Jan. 1993, p. 1. Quoted by Edward E. Stevens in this article "What if the Creeds Are Wrong": http://preterist. org/articles-old/what_if_the_creeds_are_wrong.htm.

227.   The question of how to define heresy is an interesting one. Samuel M. Frost, when he was a full preterist, had some thoughts on this: "What then is a heretic? In my understanding, a heretic is one who seeks to destroy the fabric of the church by infiltration. The *modus operandi* is destruction. . . . Joseph Smith was a heretic by proclaiming the Mormons to be the one and only truly restored church. . . . Heretics, by and large, use either false prophecy, or some extra revelation. They deny the central tenets of the Christian faith, the nature of God, the divinity of Christ, or make man into a god of some sort. . . . Preterists hardly have the desire to subvert, manipulate, or destroy the church. Rather, seeking God's word above all else, fulfilled prophecy thrives in that community with the purpose of strengthening the body through correcting what it sees as misapprehensions from our forefathers. . . . " Samuel M. Frost, *Misplaced Hope: The Origins of First and Second Century Eschatology* (Colorado Springs, CO: Bimillennial Press, 2006), page 48.

228. http://www.preterist.org/articles/article08-21-01.asp. Stevens is the founder of the International Preterist Association, website http://preterist.org.

229. http://www.wix.com/edwhynotme/fandd#!articles.

230. Gary DeMar stated that Justin Martyr and Papias were the only two early church fathers who could be classified as premillennial during the earliest decades of the 2nd century. See Gary DeMar (and Francis X. Gumerlock), *The Early Church and the End of the Word* (Powder Springs, GA: American Vision, 2006), Chapter 4. DeMar also points out that while Papias (died c. AD 155) is often a favorite church father of premillennialists, the claims that Papias got his views from the apostles is a shaky claim. Papias probably got his information second or third hand. Eusebius was highly critical of Papias' premillennial views (Ecclesiastical History, Book III, Chapter 39: http://www.newadvent.org/fathers/250103.htm). DeMar also argues that the sources for Justin Martyr's premillennialism are questionable. Gumerlock, in the same book (page 99), quotes Augustine as giving alternate interpretations for the Second Coming, including that it could refer to a coming of "Christ to the Church" in a continuous sense, or to a bodily return to earth at the end of history. Gumerlock quotes others throughout church history that saw the Second Coming as non-bodily.

231. David Chilton, *The Days of Vengeance: An Exposition of the Book of Revelation,* (Tyler, Texas: Dominion Press, 1987), page 494.

232. See the writings of Samuel M. Frost.

233. Alan Patrick Boyd, "A Dispensational Premillennial Analysis of the Eschatology of the Post-Apostolic Fathers (until the Death of Justin Martyr)," Th. M. thesis, Dallas Theological Seminary, 1977. Curtis I. Crenshaw and Grover E. Gunn III, *Dispensationalism Today, Yesterday, and Tomorrow,* (Memphis, TN: Footstool Publications, 1985), reprinted in 1989, page 114. See also Joseph M. Vincent II, *The Millennium: Past, Present, or Future? A Biblical Defense for the 40 Year Transition Period* (Ardmore, OK: JaDon Publishing, 2012), Chapter 1. See also See Gary DeMar (and Francis X. Gumerlock), *The Early Church and the End of the Word* (Powder Springs, GA: American Vision, 2006), Chapter 4.

234. There seems to be some doubt or debate about exactly what was agreed upon at these ancient councils, especially at the Council of Ephesus. Apparently the reports of condemnations of millennialism at these councils are from secondary sources. But it does seem clear that Augustine thought

that millennialism was a superstition, and his thoughts were accepted as authoritative. This seems to be confirmed by the Nicene Creed. The Italian abbot Joachim of Fiore (c. 1130-1202) revived chiliasm for a time.

235. From "American Lutheran Views on Eschatology and How They Related to the American Protestants" by John M. Brenner.

236. John Calvin, *Institutes of the Christian Religion* (3.25.5).

237. See Francis X. Gumerlock, *The Day and the Hour: Christianity's Perennial Fascination with Predicting the End of the World* (Powder Springs, Georgia: American Vision, 2000). One can also find various lists of historic false prophets on the Internet, such as these websites:

- http://www.abhota.info/index.htm
- http://www.ministryserver.com/rwsr/Part01_Introduction.htm
- http://americanvision.org/4545/before-harold-camping-there-was-chuck-smith/
- http://publisherscorner.nordskogpublishing.com/2009/01/is-it-time-for-doomsday-or-for-building.html.
  The interested reader can search for more such sites in the Internet.

238. http://en.wikipedia.org/wiki/John_Nelson_Darby.

239. We are especially indebted to the authors of this book: Curtis I. Crenshaw and Grover E. Gunn III, *Dispensationalism Today, Yesterday, and Tomorrow*, (Memphis, TN: Footstool Publications, 1985, reprinted 1989). We draw from chapters 5, 8, 14, and 16. This book is considered by some to be authoritative concerning dispensationalism. Both were pastors in Presbyterian churches at the time of the writing of their book. Crenshaw is a graduate of Dallas Theological Seminary. Both authors were dispensationalists for more than 30 years. Neither author is a preterist, but presumably were amillennialists at the time of the writing of the book. We also used a summary from an online source www. gotquestions.org, as well as other sources. Another very helpful book is by Gary DeMar, *End Times Fiction: a Biblical Consideration of the Left Behind Theology* (Nashville, TN: Thomas Nelson Publishers).

240. John F. Walvoord, *The Revelation of Jesus Christ* (Chicago: Moody Press, 1966).

241. We credit this book for help with this outline: Robert A. Peterson and Michael D. Williams, *Why I Am Not an Arminian* (Downers

Grove, Il: Intervarsity Press, 2004). We also recommend the this book for the opposing view: Jerry L. Walls and Joseph R. Dongell, *Why I Am Not a Calvinist* (Downers Grove, Il: Intervarsity Press, 2004).

242.   Curtis I. Crenshaw and Grover E. Gunn III, *Dispensationalism Today, Yesterday, and Tomorrow*, (Memphis, TN: Footstool Publications, 1985, reprinted 1989).

243.   The term "Reformed" is often understood as a synonym for Calvinist. Calvinists are most often found in Presbyterian churches but also increasingly in some Baptist and some Bible churches. Calvinists emphasize God's election. Lutherans hold to similar beliefs, emphasizing salvation by grace through the work of the Holy Spirit. But Lutherans believe, unlike Calvinists, that salvation is potentially for all who believe (not just those predestined to believe), and they also believe that man can turn away from faith (rather than "once saved always saved"). Arminians in the modern church are represented by Methodists and some Baptists/Bible churches, and teach salvation by grace but emphasize man's free will to accept God's gift of grace. Catholics believe that we are saved by grace *infused* with works and sacrament. Semi-Pelagians take a further step towards works righteousness, believing that we are saved by grace plus works, and may be found in various sects including some Churches of Christ. Full-Pelagians believe that we are saved by our good works only. Both semi-Pelagians and full-Pelagians are considered *legalists*, and we consider legalism outside the circle of orthodoxy on matters of justification. At best, semi-Pelagians are on the edge of the circle of orthodoxy, depending on how they understand grace. (It is contradictory and not adequately biblical to say we are saved by grace, *but* here is a list of things that one has to do to be saved. . . .)

244.   Curtis I. Crenshaw and Grover E. Gunn III, *Dispensationalism Today, Yesterday, and Tomorrow*, (Memphis, TN: Footstool Publications, 1985), reprinted 1989, pages 404-405.

245.   There is much confusion on the doctrine of man's sinful nature. Theologians make a distinction between "total depravity" and "utter depravity." Utter depravity would mean that man can do no good whatsoever. Christianity does not teach utter depravity, but rather teaches that man is *totally* depraved, which means that every aspect of his life is touched by sin. Orthodox Christianity does not teach that man can do no good at all in any sense.

246. http://dispensationalist.blogspot.com/2012/05/what-about-esther-817.html.

247. The Ashkenazi Jews may not be descended from Abraham.

248. See the book by Don K. Preston, *Israel 1948: Countdown to No Where*.

249. Curtis I. Crenshaw and Grover E. Gunn III, *Dispensationalism Today, Yesterday, and Tomorrow* (Memphis, TN: Footstool Publications, 1985), reprinted 1989, page 106.

250. Don K. Preston, D. Div., *Who Is This Babylon* (Ardmore, Oklahoma: JaDon Management, Inc., 2006), page 326.

251. There is apparently a movement within the dispensational camp to modernize and correct its theology at key points, as explained in this article by Kenneth L. Gentry entitled "Recent Developments in the Eschatological Debate": http://www.reformationonline.com/debate.htm.

252. Here is an excellent article By David Curtis about our hope: http://preteristvoice.org/Fun12.html, and an article about contemplating heaven: http://www.conversiondiary.com/2013/07/how-to-think-about-the-afterlife-hint-you-cant-because-you-live-in-flatland.html.

253. David Green is editor of The Preterist Cosmos: http://www.preteristcosmos.com.

254. J. Stuart Russell, *The Parousia: The New Testament Doctrine of Christ's Second Coming*, (Bradford, Pennsylvania: International Preterist Association, 2003, originally published in 1878), pages 551-552.

255. Wording in this section is from this source: http://www.prophecyrefi.org/release_95-theses.htm.

256. We are grateful to John Noe for some of the wording of this section. We found his article on the Internet: http://planetpreterist.com/content/only-defense-major-case-against-christ-christianity-and-bible.

257. David Green is editor of The Preterist Cosmos as well as editor of this book. See http://www.preteristcosmos.com.

258. Tina Rae Collins, *The Gathering in the Last* Days (New York: M. F. Sohn Publications, 2012), page 157.

259. http://www.truthaccordingtoscripture.com/documents/ church-practice/quitting-church.php. This site has several thought-provoking articles about ecclesiology: http://www.truthaccordingtoscripture.com/index.php.

260. See the Chicago Statement on Biblical Inerrancy: http://www.theopedia.com/Chicago_Statement_on_Biblical_Inerrancy.

261. See these articles about the shocking decline of Christianity in America:

- http://endoftheamericandream.com/archives/how-will-the-shocking-decline-of-christianity-in-america-affect-the-future-of-this-nation,

- http://www.barna.org/teens-next-gen-articles/528-six-reasons-young-christians-leave-church,

- http://marc5solas.wordpress.com/2013/02/08/top-10-reasons-our-kids-leave-church/,

- http://www.gotquestions.org/falling-away.html.

262. Paul does not always give an apologetic with the gospel. Paul's model teaches us to be discerning about who our audience is and to mold our message accordingly (1 Corinthians 9:16-23). We favor evidentiary classical apologetics over presuppositional apologetics. Sproul and Gerstner adequately discredited presuppositional apologetics, a fad in some Reformed circles. See R. C. Sproul, John Gerstner, and Arthur Lindsley, *Classical Apologetics: A Rational Defense of the Christian Faith and a Critique of Presuppositional Apologetics*, (Grand Rapids, Michigan: Zondervan Publishing House, 1984). See a website of the author for helpful apologetic material: www.faithfacts.org.

263. See http://www.faithfacts.org/bible-101/christian-cram-course#trinity.

264. See http://www.faithfacts.org/search-for-truth.

265. *Nominalism* is dead, inactive Christianity. *Antinomianism* is the idea that moral law does not apply to the Christian's salvation or life. Together, nominalism and antinomianism combine to produce easy believism. *Fideism* is the unbiblical view that faith and reason are incompatible. That is, Christianity is true because we believe it, rather than we believe it because

it is objectively true. The Christian faith is unique among religions, as it is based on evidence, and thus is not blind faith. See www.faithfacts.org.

266.   For definitions of these terms, see the endnote above earlier in this chapter. We specifically reject semi-Pelagianism and full-Pelagianism.

267.   Used with permission. Source: David Green, http://www.preteristcosmos.com/preterism101.html.

268.   See Francis X. Gumerlock, *The Day and the Hour: Christianity's Perennial Fascination with Predicting the End of the World*, (Powder Springs, Georgia: American Vision, 2000). One can also find various lists of historic false prophets on the Internet, such as these websites:

- http://www.abhota.info/index.htm,

- http://www.ministryserver.com/rwsr/Part01_Introduction.htm,

- http://americanvision.org/4545/before-harold-camping-there-was-chuck-smith/,

- http://publisherscorner.nordskogpublishing.com/2009/01/is-it-time-for-doomsday-or-for-building.html. The interested reader can search for more such sites in the Internet.

269.   See http://www.treeoflifeministries.info/index.php?option=com_content&view=article&id=198%3Amike-sullivan&catid=35%3Apreterist-eschatology-all-prophecy-fulfilled-by-ad-70&Itemid=77.

270.   J. Stuart Russell, *The Parousia: The New Testament Doctrine of Christ's Second Coming*, (Bradford, Pennsylvania: International Preterist Association, 2003, originally published in 1878), pages 344, 346.

271.   See also: http://www.biblicalpreteristarchive.com/statements/70-Qs.htm. (Many of our questions came from this source.)

272.   The passages that are often given to prove that the soul survives the body include: Luke 16:22-26; 23:43; Philippians 1:21-23; 2 Corinthians 5:8; Revelation 6:9-11; 20:4, 14; 21:8. But even John Ratzinger (Pope Benedict XVI) said this: "The immortality of the soul must be firmly rejected as an idea which goes against the grain of biblical thought." (Joseph Ratzinger, *Eschatology, Death and Eternal Life, Second Edition* (Washington, DC: The Catholic University of America Press, 1988, originally published in German in 1977), page 74.) Ratzinger also stated

concerning the duality of soul and body, ". . . the work of Thomas and the Council of Vienne, has conceived this duality in such a way that it is not dualistic but rather brings to light the worth and unity of the human being as a whole." (Ibid, page 159)

273. Here's a smattering of articles we found on the Internet:

- http://en.wikipedia.org/wiki/Soul_in_the_Bible,
- http://www.ucg.org/death/what-does-bible-say-about-immortal-soul/,
- http://www.truthaccordingtoscripture.com/documents/death/is-the-soul-immortal.php,
- http://www.truthaccordingtoscripture.com/documents/death/life-in-christ/chapter8.php

274. *The Reformation Study Bible* (Lake Mary, Florida: Ligonier Ministries, 2005), page 1743.

Appendix G

Index of Scriptures

Below is an abbreviated list of books of the Bible with page numbers. If you desire a more accurate and complete list, and If you have purchased this book, I will send you a free PDF copy of the book on request. With that, you can be more precise with the search function available with PDF. Email me at faithfacts@msn.com.

Appendix H

Index of Subjects

Below is an abbreviated list of books of the Bible with page numbers. If you desire a more accurate and complete list, and If you have purchased this book, I will send you a free PDF copy of the book on request. With that, you can be more precise with the search function available with PDF. Email me at faith-facts@msn.com.

The reader is referred to the Table of Contents *for such subjects as Ascension, Different Views (amillennialism, premillennialism, postmillennialism, preterism), Day of the Lord, Great Tribulation, Judgment, Kingdom of Heaven, Last Day(s), Millennialism, Rapture, Restoration, Resurrection, New Heaven and New Earth, Olivet Discourse, Revelation, and Second Coming.*

Made in the USA
Coppell, TX
03 September 2024

36746759R00233